PARTY IDEOLOGIES IN AMERICA, 1828–1996

This book challenges traditional notions of American party politics and political culture. Usually, American politics is looked on as relatively consensual and nonideological, but John Gerring argues that American party history and, by extension, American political history at large have been irreducibly ideological. He contends that the major parties have articulated views that were, and are, coherent, differentiated, and stable.

The argument rests on evidence provided by election rhetoric – speeches, party platforms, and other campaign tracts disseminated by party leaders during presidential campaigns. Using these texts, Professor Gerring traces the values, beliefs, and issue-positions that have defined party life from the 1830s to the 1990s. *Party Ideologies in America, 1828–1996* thus presents a historical synthesis of mainstream party politics from the birth of competitive parties to the present day.

John Gerring is Assistant Professor of Political Science at Boston University. He has published in *Political Research Quarterly, Polity,* and *Studies in American Political Development.*

PARTY IDEOLOGIES IN AMERICA, 1828–1996

JOHN GERRING

CAMBRIDGE
UNIVERSITY PRESS

CAMBRIDGE UNIVERSITY PRESS
Cambridge, New York, Melbourne, Madrid, Cape Town,
Singapore, São Paulo, Delhi, Mexico City

Cambridge University Press
The Edinburgh Building, Cambridge CB2 8RU, UK

Published in the United States of America by Cambridge University Press, New York

www.cambridge.org
Information on this title: www.cambridge.org/9780521592628

© John Gerring 1998

Chapter 3 appeared in revised form as "Party Ideology in America: The National-Republican
Chapter (1928–1924)," in *Studies in American Political Development* II:I
(Spring 1997); chapter 5 appeared in revised form as "A Chapter in the History of
American Party Ideology: The Nineteenth-Century Democratic Party, 1828–1892,"
Polity 26:4 (Summer 1994)

First published 1998
First paperback edition 2001
Reprinted 2001
Transferred to digital printing 2004

A catalogue record for this publication is available from the British Library

Library of Congress Cataloguing in Publication Data
Gerring, John, 1962–
Party ideologies in America, 1828–1996 / John Gerring.
p. cm.
Includes bibliographical references and index.
ISBN 0-521-59262-3 (hb)
1. Political parties – United States – History.   I. Title.
JK2261.G47   1998   97-46088
CIP

ISBN 978-0-521-59262-8 Hardback
ISBN 978-0-521-78590-7 Paperback

FOR MY MOTHER AND FATHER

Life is to an organism, [what] principles are to a party.
James Bryce, *The American Commonwealth*

It is unthinkable that these organizations [political parties] can be understood without examination of the objectives of the participants in the enterprises: What do people want to accomplish?
E. E. Schattschneider, "United States:
The Functional Approach to Party Government"

Contents

Figures and Tables

Acknowledgments

One of the slightly uncomfortable things about writing a book is that one finds oneself continually asking for help and seldom in a position to reciprocate. A regular rhythm asserts itself in which calls for assistance, if answered, are followed by more calls for assistance (as in, "Now that you've finished with that chapter, here's another"). Naturally, the generous souls of the academic world are most exploited in this iterated game. It is thus enormously gratifying when one has an opportunity, at long last, to thank those who have so generously contributed their time to one's cause.

For comments and suggestions on various portions of the manuscript, I thank Jeff Berry, Bob Bullock, Taylor Dark, Richard Ellis, Lawrence Gerring, Jim Glaser, Marissa Golden, Andrew Gould, Judy Gruber, Serge Halimi, David Hart, Philip Klinkner, Dan Kryder, Aline Kuntz, Brian Loynd, Jason Macdonald, Cathie Martin, David Mayhew, Eileen McDonagh, Jerry Mileur, William Muir, Chris Muste, Duane Oldfield, Karen Orren, Beth Reingold, Howard Reiter, Daniel Rodgers, Jim Schmidt, Mark Silverstein, Arun Swamy, Judith Swanson, Craig Thomas, David Waldner, John White, and Aaron Wildavsky. Sid Milkis gave the manuscript an extraordinarily detailed reading at a most propitious moment. Michael Rogin and Jim Gregory read innumerable drafts, giving comments and much-needed encouragement all along the way.

I am indebted to Gordon Adams, who rescued me from daily computer crises; to Christine Rossell, who assumed this task when I arrived in Boston; to interlibrary loan workers at the University of California – Berkeley and Boston University, who retrieved more books and manuscripts from libraries around the country than I, or they, would care to recall; to Liesbet Heyse, Sabrina Underwood, and Dawn Skorczewski, who assisted in preparing the manuscript; and to my editor, Alex Holzman; my production coordinator, Mary Byers; and my copy editor,

Tammy Zambo, who together gracefully shepherded the manuscript through the publication process.

I also extend my appreciation to the faculty at Boston University, who made my transition from graduate school to teaching, and from West Coast to East, a happy one. I feel blessed to be a member of the most congenial, most supportive political science department in the world (empirical data to follow).

Finally, I want to acknowledge Larry Ceplair and Martin Jay, who cultivated my passion for the study of political history at two important points in my life.

To all these generous and exploited souls, I will aways be grateful.

PART I

Introduction: The Existence of Party Ideology

1

Arguments

Are the major American parties ideological? That is, do they carry messages that are internally coherent, externally differentiated (from one another), and stable (through time)? Most observers would say no, perhaps with the qualification that they once were.

The decline-of-ideology jeremiad, one finds, has quite a long history. In the 1830s, Tocqueville complained, "The political parties that I style great are those which cling to principles rather than to their consequences; to general and not to special cases; to ideas and not to men." America, he concluded shortly after the demise of the Federalist party, "has had great parties, but has them no longer."[1] In 1879, Woodrow Wilson, then an undergraduate at Princeton, went even further: "Eight words contain the sum of the present degradation of our political parties: No leaders, no principles; no principles, no parties."[2] A decade later, James Bryce charged that "Neither party has anything definite to say on [the] issues; neither party has any principles, any distinctive tenets. Both have traditions. Both claim to have tendencies. Both have certainly war cries, organizations, interests enlisted in their support. But those interests are in the main the interests of getting or keeping the patronage of the government. Tenets and policies, points of political doctrine and points of political practice, have all but vanished."[3]

After the turn of the century, under the stimulus of the Progressive vision and of crusading party leaders like William Jennings Bryan, Teddy Roosevelt, Woodrow Wilson, and Franklin Roosevelt, party politics was more likely to be portrayed as conflictual.[4] By mid-century, however, the failure of socialism and the softening of the New Deal's agenda seemed

---

1. "[A]nd if her happiness is thereby considerably increased," continued Tocqueville (1835/1960: 182), "her morality has suffered."
2. Wilson (1879/1965: 48).   3. Bryce (1891, 2: 20).
4. See Beard (1929), Binkley (1943/1945), Croly (1909), and Schlesinger (1945).

to confirm the older, nonideological view. "The fierceness of the political struggles has often been misleading," Richard Hofstadter wrote in 1948, "for the range of vision embraced by the primary contestants in the major parties has always been bounded by the horizons of property and enterprise. However much at odds on specific issues, the major political traditions have shared a belief in the rights of property, the philosophy of economic individualism, the value of competition; they have accepted the economic virtues of capitalist culture as necessary qualities of man."[5] Louis Hartz, whose *Liberal Tradition in America* became one of the few enduring classics of American political science, came to similar conclusions. The parties, thought Hartz, could not mobilize the electorate with ideological appeals, because electors were strapped securely in the cultural straitjacket of liberalism.[6] Of course, none of these writers portrayed American party politics as utterly bereft of orienting goals and ideas. Hartz himself presumed not the absence of partisan conflict but rather the *containment* of that conflict within the confines of the liberal tradition. Even so, there was more than a grain of truth to the consensus label attached to Hofstadter, Hartz, and other scholars of the postwar generation.

For many writers within the fields of political science and history, the Hartzian synthesis of American politics still holds. To be sure, the idea of an ideological consensus in American politics has come under sustained assault by the current generation. However, this assault has usually focused on conflict at the margins of American politics or at rare moments of crisis. When looking at politics at the center and during periods of normal politics, writers bemoan the *absence* of ideologically rooted conflict. In this respect Hartz has proven to be as popular with leftists, who decry this state of affairs, as with centrists, who applaud it.[7] From both perspectives, American party politics appears to be an internecine quarrel embedded in a shared political culture. Thus, it seems fair to say that *most* work on the American parties continues to echo the analyses set forth by Tocqueville, Wilson, Bryce, and others writing a century ago.[8]

5. Hofstadter (1948: xxxvii).
6. See Hartz (1955). By "liberalism," of course, Hartz was referring to the general political culture of the United States – not the ideology of the modern Democratic party. This will also be my usage of this key term.
7. If Hartz may be regarded as America's Hegel, then it is appropriate that there be left-Hartzians (e.g., Walter Dean Burnham), as well as right-Hartzians (e.g., John Diggins).
8. It would be impossible to account comprehensively for all references to the "nonprogrammatic," "consensual," or "nonideological" nature of American party politics. The following compendium is intended simply to demonstrate the strength and persistence

At the same time, recent academic work seems to be moving toward a greater appreciation of ideology within the American parties. Work in the realignment genre, for example, supposes that American politics has been riven by fundamental conflict during critical election periods (though *not*, it should be noted, during periods of normal politics).[9] Studies of party activists generally show high levels of ideological cohesion among this select group of citizens.[10] Studies of campaign promises and public policy performance indicate that American party ideology is more than mere rhetoric.[11] Studies by historians have illuminated the ideological quality of party behavior in various eras of American political history.[12] Spatial models of party behavior have begun to portray political parties – including the American parties – in a more ideological light.[13] Finally, studies focused on other (nonideological) aspects of party life have begun to dispute the notion that parties are in steep decline,

of this view, which extends in some incipient form from the early nineteenth century to the present day. The list, in rough chronological order, runs as follows: Tocqueville (1835/1960; 1840/1945), Wilson (1879/1965; 1885/1956), Bryce (1891, 2), Ford (1898/1967: 325–26), Merriam (1922: 201–46), Holcombe (1924: 122, 384), Sait (1927), Herring (1940/1965: 131–33, 192, 288–89, 427–28), Schattschneider (1942: 92), Hofstadter (1948; 1968a), Duverger (1951/1959: 418), Boorstin (1953), Hartz (1955), Ranney and Kendall (1956: 423, 533), Downs (1957: 25), Rossiter (1960: 11), Beer (1965: 49), Dahl (1966), Foner (1970: 8; 1984: 59), Ladd (1970: 30, 158), Lowi (1975), Skocpol (1980), Burnham (1981), Eldersveld (1982), Wilentz (1982: 53), Hanson (1985: 15), Diggins (1984), Epstein (1986: 266), Silbey (1991: 75).

9. "The differences between the parties," writes the founding father of realignment theory, "vary from stage to stage in the conversion of controversy into new Consensus" (Key 1955; quoted in Sundquist 1983: 326). Thus, if conflict occasionally bursts forth, the normal pattern of American party politics is to suppress such conflict behind the veneer of an all-encompassing political culture. See also Brady (1988) and Burnham (1981). For further discussion of realignment theory, see chapter 8.

10. See, e.g., Baer and Bositis (1988), Bruce, Clark, and Kessel (1991), Kirkpatrick (1976), McClosky (1964), McClosky et al. (1960), Miller and Jennings (1986), and Smith (1989).

11. See Blais, Blake, and Dion (1996), Budge and Hofferbert (1990), Budge, Robertson, and Hearl (1987), Cameron (1984), Castles (1982), Epstein and O'Halloran (1996), Fishel (1985), Ginsberg (1976), Hibbs (1977), Keman (1984), King (1981), Klingemann et al. (1994), Krukones (1984), Monroe (1983), Pomper (1967, 1980), Royed (1996), and Tufte (1978). The do-parties-matter question is discussed at greater length in chapter 2.

12. See, e.g., Ashworth (1983/1987), Baker (1983), Foner (1970), Kelley (1977), and Kleppner (1970). On party ideology through American history, see Reichley (1992).

13. See Aldrich (1995), Alesina and Rosenthal (1995), Budge (1994), Chappell and Keech (1986), Enelow and Hinich (1990), Hinich and Munger (1994), Ingberman and Villani (1993), Morton (1993), Rabinowitz et al. (1991), and Wittman (1973; 1983). For commentary on this literature, see the Appendix.

rendering more plausible the notion that party ideology matters in American public life in the latter twentieth century.[14]

Work on these various topics raises important questions about the traditional view of American party ideology. To put it baldly, the premise of nonideological parties no longer seems to fit the facts as we know them. Indeed, contemporary work by political scientists and historians points toward a new understanding of ideology's involvement in American party politics.

This book presents a historical synthesis of American party ideology from the birth of party politics to the present day. The evidence consists of presidential election rhetoric – speeches, party platforms, and other campaign tracts disseminated by party leaders during presidential campaigns. With these texts I trace the values, beliefs, and issue-positions that have defined party life from the 1830s to the 1990s. In line with revisionist interpretations, I argue that the major American parties have articulated views that were (and are) coherent, differentiated, and stable. American party history and, by extension, American political history at large have been irreducibly ideological.[15]

This is a broad argument, to be sure, and it requires some qualification. First, it pertains primarily to the *presidential* parties – those aggregations of local, state, and national party elites, as well as attentive members of the public, who select (or endorse) a party's national platform and presidential nominee.[16] Second, the study is limited to a consideration of each party's *public* ideology – the words and actions by which leaders represented their party before the general electorate. Private communications, motivations, and interests play a minor role in the

14. On parties in Congress, see Cox and McCubbins (1991; 1993), Davidson (1992), Kiewiet and McCubbins (1991), Krehbiel (1993), Levitt and Snyder (1995), and Rohde (1991). On the party in the electorate, see Keith et al. (1992). On party organization, see Herrnson (1988), Kayden and Mahe (1985), Reichley (1992), and Sabato (1988). Aldrich (1995: ch 8) offers a sensible interpretation of the evidence, pro and con.

15. Authors working on ideology customarily expend a good deal of effort trying to define what this elusive concept means. My position (see Gerring 1997) is that the definitional core of the concept consists of three intertwined attributes – *coherence, differentiation*, and *stability*. These are the only definitional traits generally agreed upon by writers in the social sciences. One might note that this core definition of ideology takes no cognizance of whether a party's views on political matters are distorting, dogmatic, repressive, self-interested, or reflective of a particular social class or social order. Such matters, I would argue, are better left for empirical investigation.

16. This focus has the virtue of catching the parties in their most national guise. It does not, however, aim to represent the views of everyone sporting the party label. On the concept of a "presidential party," see Burns (1963), Kessel (1984), Schattschneider (1942: ch 6), and Sundquist (1980).

narrative (except, of course, insofar as such speculation might be warranted by leaders' public pronouncements).[17] Finally, because foreign policy has rarely played a significant role in American electoral politics, I focus primarily on *domestic* policies, including those policies, like immigration and trade, which responded primarily to domestic cues.[18]

With these caveats in mind, a formidable case can be made for the proposition that ideology has mattered in American political history. In this introduction I briefly summarize the historical arguments of the book, focusing first on conflicts between each party's views and issue-positions, then on changes in each party's ideology, and finally on underlying continuities throughout the 1828–1996 period.

Conflict in Party Ideology

In some sense, it must be granted that the exceptionalist view of American party life is correct. American party ideology *is* different from European varieties, relying less on party labels (Liberal, Labour, and Conservative in the British case), party constitutions (e.g., the infamous Clause IV in the Labour party's constitution), and readily identifiable philosophies (liberalism, Toryism, radicalism, socialism, communism, et al.), and more on the consensual symbols of the national political culture. Because of the fragmented constitutional structure of American politics, politicians have been forced to campaign as leaders of the nation rather than as party leaders. The presidential candidate is the closest American analogue to the prime ministerial candidate in parliamentary systems; however, he (or potentially she) is discouraged from emphasizing his party affiliation while appealing for votes among the general public. Within a parliamentary system, by contrast, the function of the prime ministerial candidate is to bring his or her *party* to power. This fosters a different style of presentation, one more directly rooted in party

17. The advantage of this focus is that the subject matter is manifest; it does not require us to interpret hidden meanings or to speculate on the inner motivations of party members. Of course, one might object that the real story, and hence the true principles of a party, lies behind the scenes.

18. Foreign policy issues have entered debate at infrequent intervals (generally under conditions of open or imminent military conflict) after which politics has resumed its normal pace and usual domestic preoccupations. In general, there have been strong partisan and ideological components to such debates. However, party views on foreign policy have not corresponded neatly with the historical development of party views on domestic policy matters; which is to say, foreign policy ideologies have changed at different times and (often) for different reasons than domestic policy ideologies. Therefore, foreign policy provides a somewhat misleading guide to the public political identities of the American parties, and is best analyzed separately.

history – emphasizing, for example, party founders (Gladstone, Disraeli, Hardie) rather than nation founders, party symbols and philosophies rather than national symbols and philosophies, and so forth. There are, to be sure, some grounds for the Hartzian lament.

Yet the broad symbols of America that both parties appropriate – liberty, freedom, democracy, equal opportunity, and so forth – often mean fundamentally different things to spokespersons of different parties. Take, for example, the fabled work ethic.[19] While modern Republicans harp on the idleness of poor people, immigrants, and government bureaucrats, Democrats are wont to point out the idleness of the rich. "Equal opportunity," similarly, is usually treated as an accomplished fact within Whig-Republican rhetoric, but as a promise unfulfilled within Democratic rhetoric.

A classic example of the way in which consensual symbols could be employed for radically different programmatic purposes can be found in Bryan's "Cross of Gold" speech at the 1896 Chicago convention. "When you come before us and tell us that we are about to disturb your business interests," cried Bryan, turning to the Gold delegates,

> we reply that you have disturbed our business interests by your course. We say to you that you have made the definition of a business man too limited in its application. The man who is employed for wages is as much a business man as his employer; . . . the miners who go down a thousand feet into the earth, or climb two thousand feet upon the cliffs, and bring forth from their hiding places the precious metals to be poured into the channels of trade are as much business men as the few financial magnates who, in a back room, corner the money of the world. We come to speak for the broader class of business men.[20]

One might interpret this as a bow to Hartzian liberalism, since Bryan is constrained to appeal not to the rights of the working class but rather to the rights of the business class. Yet this apparently all-embracing symbol was employed in subversive ways.[21] There could be no confusing the speeches of William Jennings Bryan with those issued by his opponent in that election, William McKinley.

Moreover, just because American ideologies were often hidden from view did not make them any less real (not, at least, for party elites). Consider, for example, the following passage from an address by Lincoln

19. Rodgers (1974) offers a fine intellectual history of this concept in late-nineteenth- and early-twentieth-century America.
20. Bryan, speech, 7/8/1896 (Bryan 1896: 200).
21. Actually, labor was a much more common rhetorical symbol at the turn of the century than business was (see chapters 3 and 6).

early in 1860 – one of only two major public addresses he gave in that climactic year:

> If slavery is right, all words, acts, laws, and constitutions against it, are themselves wrong, and should be silenced, and swept away. If it is right, we cannot justly object to its nationality – its universality; if it is wrong, they cannot justly insist upon its extension – its enlargement. All they ask, we could readily grant, if we thought slavery right; all we ask, they could as readily grant, if they thought it wrong. Their thinking it right, and our thinking it wrong, is the precise fact upon which depends the whole controversy. Thinking it right, as they do, they are not to blame for desiring its full recognition, as being right; but, thinking it wrong, as we do, can we yield to them? Can we cast our votes with their view, and against our own? In view of our moral, social, and political responsibilities, can we do this? . . . [C]an we, while our votes will prevent it, allow it to spread into the National Territories, and to overrun us here in these Free States? If our sense of duty forbids this, then let us stand by our duty, fearlessly and effectively. Let us be diverted by none of those sophistical contrivances wherewith we are so industriously plied and belabored – contrivances such as groping for some middle ground between the right and the wrong, vain as the search for a man who should be neither a living man nor dead man – such as a policy of "don't care" on a question about which all true men do care – such as Union appeals beseeching true Union men to yield to Disunionists, reversing the divine rule, and calling, not the sinners, but the righteous to repentance – such as invocations to Washington, imploring men to unsay what Washington said, and undo what Washington did. Neither let us be slandered from our duty by false accusations against us, nor frightened from it by menaces of destruction to the Government nor of dungeons to ourselves. LET US HAVE FAITH THAT RIGHT MAKES MIGHT, AND IN THAT FAITH, LET US, TO THE END, DARE TO DO OUR DUTY AS WE UNDERSTAND IT.[22]

To what does the Republican presidential hopeful appeal on the eve of the Civil War? Not to images of party but rather to values Lincoln assumes all Americans share, or at least ought to share – to Washington, the Union, the Constitution, divine rule, and the imperatives of duty. This much of the narrative seems to vindicate Hartz. Yet, on the other side of the coin, it may be observed that Lincoln manipulates these consensual symbols in partisan directions, moving his audience to an appreciation of the rightness of his party's cause and the moral turpitude of his opponents. He systematically undermines any pretense that the subject of slavery can be avoided or the status quo endured. Moderation is derided as a "sophistical contrivance"; in questions of right and wrong

---

22. Lincoln, speech, 2/27/1860 (Lincoln 1989b: 129–30); emphasis in original.

there can be no middle ground. The audience is given no option but to enlist wholeheartedly in the cause of Republicanism or Democracy. Lincoln's policy position might be considered moderate; he calls not for the repeal of slavery where it existed but rather for the prevention of its further spread (into the territories). Yet, once again, in the context of the political situation of 1860, this meant a militant rejection of the position of the Democratic party, one that Lincoln and other Republican leaders knew might lead to civil war.

This was a canny strategy for the Republican party in the late 1850s and, indeed, was partly responsible for that party's success on an issue that somehow escaped the northern Whigs. It was not that the party's position on slavery was so different from that of their forerunners (a point I belabor in chapter 3). However, the Republicans had taken the bold move of writing off the South so as to concentrate their ammunition on the North, where slavery had few defenders. The task of party leaders was to make slavery the preeminent issue of the campaign. Doing so, they figured that a majority of the voting public in the non-Southern states would end up on the side of freedom (and "free labor") and against the conspiracy of the Slave Power.

Here we have a good example of the propagation of ideology in the American party system, where value and policy differences imply conspiracies against the public (Democrats were following the same strategy in the South), where ideologies come disguised in all-embracing "national" appeals, and where both parties invoke biblical imagery. This does not mean that the force of partisan ideas has been any less powerful, any less consistent, or any less conflictual in the American polity than elsewhere. Indeed, Lincoln goes to some lengths to emphasize the vast gulf between his position and his opponents', framing the issue of slavery in dichotomous terms that were calculated to move voters away from the center and into one of the two partisan encampments.

One may reasonably object, of course, that an election immediately preceding a civil war sheds little light on electoral politics during periods of "normalcy" (a Harding neologism). A broader consideration of this complex period of American history would seem to be in order. What follows, therefore, is a review of Whig-Republican and Democratic perspectives during the nineteenth century, a synthesis of matters explored in chapters 3 and 5.

Despite the tumultuous times, American party debate from 1828 to 1892 was surprisingly repetitive. On economic matters, Whig-Republican policy could be summarized as mercantilist, Democratic policy as laissez-faire. Democrats looked with suspicion on the industrial revolution; Whig-Republicans were its champions. Democrats criticized the tyrannies of the marketplace, while Whig-Republicans criticized the tyrannies of slave labor. Whig-Republicans regarded the freedom of the individual laborer as the basis of community prosperity; Democrats were less optimistic and less attached to market-based definitions of human relationships. Though neither party was fond of taxes, Whig-Republicans saw the need for raising sufficient revenue to keep government strong; Democrats insisted that taxes were an instrument of federal tyranny. Whereas Whig-Republican economic policies favored industry, Democratic policies were slanted toward agriculture.

The perennial tariff dispute amply illustrates the peculiar mix of moral, economic, and political arguments that animated nineteenth-century political debate. Whig-Republicans were high-tariff men, viewing Protection as necessary to foster manufacturing enterprises, protect the relatively high salaries of American workingmen, and maintain the treasury. Democrats favored Tariff Reform, on the grounds that tariffs punished consumers and farmers, stifled free competition, encouraged monopolies, fostered a corrupt relationship between government and business, and allowed the central government to grow in a way that would not otherwise be supported by its vigilant citizens (because the tariff constituted a hidden tax).

On cultural matters, Democrats stood proudly for white supremacy, whereas the Whigs – and, more forthrightly, the Republicans – registered their distaste for slavery. Democrats favored increased immigration from Europe; Whig-Republicans were cool toward the entry of non–English speakers and non–Protestants. Democrats, partly by virtue of their Catholic constituents, were secularists, opposing the reformist bent of the Whig-Republicans on matters such as sumptuary laws,[23] temperance legislation, and public schools. Republicans (though not Whigs) were more likely than Democrats to drape themselves and their political arguments in the garb of Americanism. Whig-Republicans were, generally speaking, reformers, and Democrats stand patters. Democrats defended the rights and liberties of the individual against the expansive tendencies of the federal state. Whig-Republicans defended the prerogatives of government and the necessity of national union against the "sectional," and perhaps even treasonous, tendencies of the Democratic party. It was Liberty versus Power, over and over again. Democrats, whose antistatist messages were woven tightly around the civic republican themes of the Revolutionary era, sought to preserve the fragile republic from its would-be usurpers. Whig-Republicans advocated the preservation of a tradi-

---

23. Sumptuary laws were laws regulating personal behavior on moral or religious grounds.

tional social order within a rapidly evolving economic order. They were champions of economic progress as well as conservators of American culture.

Both parties, in a sense, were traditional. But for Whig-Republicans, the defense of tradition and the maintenance of social order demanded energetic intervention by government (by nineteenth-century standards) in the affairs of men and women. Democrats viewed the principle of democracy through Jeffersonian eyes. "Eternal vigilance is the price of liberty," party orators reiterated like a mantra. It was a minoritarian view of government: popular rule meant the right, indeed the duty, of popular majorities to veto the actions of political elites when they infringed on their personal liberties. Whereas Democrats extolled the virtues of the general public, Whig-Republicans looked to institutions, and in particular to government, to moderate the passions of the multitude. To put the case bluntly, Democrats worried about too much government; Whig-Republicans worried about too much democracy. The bête noire of Democracy was tyranny, the bête noire of Whig-Republicanism, anarchy.

Such were the terms of debate in the nineteenth century. Not all matters divided clearly and consistently along partisan lines during this period. But the party label was a good predictor of the positions a presidential candidate might take on most issues of domestic policy. What, then, can be said about the *style* of debate?

Although social and economic policies have been prominent in American party rhetoric, such policies have rarely been presented as simple matters of economic welfare. Without avoiding the prosperity issue, party leaders have always been careful to indicate that their views do not represent a "materialistic" point of view. Principles, not appeals to self-interest, have dominated American campaign rhetoric. When making the full-dinner-pail argument, orators carefully qualified this economistic line with an emphasis on spiritual goods. "Economic advancement is not an end in itself," cautioned Hoover in 1928. "Successful democracy rests wholly upon the moral and spiritual quality of its people. Our growth in spiritual achievements must keep pace with our growth in physical accomplishments."[24] "All things flow from doing what is right," insisted Bob Dole many years later. "The triumph of this nation lies not in its material wealth but in courage, sacrifice, and honor."[25]

To American orators of the nineteenth century, Protection and Free Trade represented more than simple expedience; they were, to quote Grover Cleveland, shibboleths. Monetary and currency questions were

24. Hoover, acceptance speech, 8/11/1928 (Singer 1976: 8).
25. Dole, acceptance address, 8/15/1996 (*New York Times* 8/16/1996).

cast as ethical matters, matters upon which the survival of a virtuous republic rested. Debates over government involvement in the economy in
the twentieth century reflect the same virulent moralism. Free enterprise
presented itself as an ethical system, a system ensuring the freedom of the
individual and the survival of democracy, not simply a growth-machine.

Thus, over the course of American party history one finds economic
and governmental issues burning in party leaders' hearts with the same
intensity as issues of "cultural" import (temperance, immigration, slavery, abortion, and the like) – and structured in similarly Manichaean
forms (free labor versus slave labor, free enterprise versus communism,
and so forth). Perhaps such issues were dogmatically approached because political matters were themselves matters of cultural definition.
Lacking a specific ethnic identity, a long historical tradition, and a clear
geographic location (since borders have been in flux through most of
American history), Americans seem to have turned to politics as a mode
of self-definition.

This may explain something about the peculiar urgency invested in
economic and governmental questions in American political life. Although both major parties swore loyalty to the Constitution,[26] they often
had radically different interpretations of this sacred document. In this
sense, the election of 1860 was typical, not atypical, of American electoral discourse. Indeed, few issues in American history have *not* been
framed in constitutional terms. Where else in the Anglo-European world
can one find such recurring disagreement over matters of sovereignty as
that which pits advocates of states' rights (in modern parlance, "local
communities") against advocates of national supremacy – advocates of
moral order against advocates of individual liberty? Some might point
to this as evidence of the Hartzian notion that the parties agreed on
fundamentals; but it might equally be considered an example of partisan
fundamentalism. Are struggles between Protestants and Catholics, one
might ask, any less ideological for having roots in a single text?[27]

Changes in Party Ideology

If the major parties have argued with each other throughout American
history, it is equally clear that the nature of that argument has changed

---

26. The northern wing of the Democratic party, the largest Democratic contingent in the
    election of 1860, continued to support the Union throughout the Civil War.
27. Religious analogies suggest themselves not only because American political rhetoric
    was imbued with religious symbolism but also because the style of argumentation
    seems to lean heavily on Old and New Testament forms. See, e.g., Bellah (1967),
    Levinson (1988).

considerably from the 1830s to the 1990s. How can one make sense of these fundamental transformations in party ideology?

If asked to describe the ideology of the major parties in America, most observers would identify the Republicans as conservative and the Democrats as liberal. Although there is nothing incorrect in this typology, there is surely much that is misleading. Are Republicans of today to be placed in the company of Republicans in other historical periods, and of the Whigs and of the Federalists, and, for that matter, of conservatives abroad (e.g., Macaulay, Coleridge, Bagehot, Oakeshott, Burke, Disraeli, Churchill)? Each of these temporal and geographic frames suggests a different definition of conservatism and hence of the modern Republican party. The problem with conservatism, as with liberalism, is that the labels apply to too many things. The analysis of American party ideologies rightly begins, therefore, with the identification of concepts that can be more clearly delineated in time and space.

Defining those concepts is made more difficult in the American case because of the unusual longevity of the parties. Compared with the major American parties, Schattschneider notes, "nine tenths of the governments of the world have had a volatile and turbulent existence."[28] When, precisely, did the Democratic party achieve its current programmatic orientation? Was this point reached with the accession of Thomas Jefferson, Andrew Jackson, William Jennings Bryan, Woodrow Wilson, or Franklin Roosevelt? Each of these points of origin leaves us with a different understanding of what the Democratic party of today espouses.[29] Only by examining the evolution of party rhetoric over the course of many decades can we hope to tease the present out of the past.[30]

Given the shortcomings of standard terminology (liberalism, conservatism) and the presentist perspective of most work on the American parties, it seems reasonable to propose a modest reconceptualization of American party ideology along historical lines. Following, therefore, is a synoptic view of American party history from the 1830s to the 1990s, as viewed through the lens of presidential election rhetoric. (To present

---

28. Schattschneider (1942: 2).
29. Beard (1929), Binkley (1943/1945), and Kelley (1977) emphasize the role of Jefferson; Schlesinger (1945) emphasizes Jackson; Sarasohn (1989) champions Bryan; and Beer (1965), Milkis (1992), Rotunda (1968), and Sundquist (1983) highlight FDR. A similar quandary arises, of course, when considering the ideological origins of the Republican party. Indeed, it is virtually impossible to speak about the parties of today without invoking – at least implicitly – some version of each party's history.
30. "A conception of the party system must take into account its dimension of time," writes V. O. Key (1942/1958: 243). "It may even be more useful to think of the party system as an historical process than as patterned institutional behavior."

these arguments in a reasonably concise form, I am obliged to portray this vast subject with rather broad strokes; readers should be aware that considerable amplification occurs in subsequent chapters.)

In contrast to most studies of the Whig and early Republican parties, I place these two organizations within a single ideological epoch, stretching from 1828 to 1924.[31] *National* Republicans were state builders and economic nationalists who believed that a strong federal government was necessary not only to preserve the union but also to achieve prosperity and preserve the fabric of American society. They were moral reformers with a Yankee-Protestant tinge, adhering to the perfectibility of human nature and the utility of government guidance to that end. Suspicious of the leveling tendencies of their partisan opponents, National Republicans looked to political institutions like the Senate and the Supreme Court to moderate and direct the force of public opinion. Uniting all these values were a defensive nationalism and an underlying search for order in civil and political affairs.

In the 1920s, the Republican party cast out the spirit of Edmund Burke in favor of Herbert Spencer, remaking itself in a *Neoliberal* image (see table 1). Whereas in the previous century the party had worked to contain the passions of the individual, largely through the actions of an interventionist state, now Republicans reversed this polarity: the individual was to be set free from the machinations of the state. Through Neoliberal eyes, all political measures flowed from the central assumption that government was dangerous and needed to be contained. In economic policy the party adopted the general philosophy of laissez-faire or, more practically, "as little government as possible." On the hustings, the party exchanged dignity and restraint for an openly plebiscitarian style. Whig-Republican history thus divides neatly into two major ideological epochs – National (1828–1924) and Neoliberal (1928–1992).

The ideological history of the Democratic party is somewhat more complex (see table 2). From Jackson to Cleveland (1828 to 1892), the party reiterated the views of its purported founder, Thomas Jefferson. Economic policy supported property rights and opposed federal intervention in the marketplace. Political norms revolved around limited government, libertarianism, minority rights, civic virtue, and an adherence to tradition (to counter the inevitable corruptions of power). Equal rights were to be extended to all white men, but not to inferior races. This I shall refer to as the *Jeffersonian* epoch.

In 1896, the Democrats transformed themselves into a party of *Pop-*

---

31. To avoid terminological confusion, I shall use "Whig-Republican" whenever referring to the combined histories of these two parties.

Table 1. *Ideological epochs of the Whig-Republican party (persisting themes: social order, economic growth, patriotism)*

NATIONALISM (1828–1924)

Central dichotomy: order versus anarchy
Themes: Protestantism, moral reform, mercantilism, free labor, social harmony, statism
Presidential nominees:

1828 John Adams	1880 James A. Garfield
1832 Henry Clay	1884 James G. Blaine
1836 William H. Harrison	1888 Benjamin Harrison
1840 William H. Harrison	1892 Benjamin Harrison
1844 Henry Clay	1896 William McKinley
1848 Zachary Taylor	1900 William McKinley
1852 Winfield Scott	1904 Theodore Roosevelt
1856 John C. Fremont	1908 William H. Taft
1860 Abraham Lincoln	1912 William H. Taft
1864 Abraham Lincoln	1916 Charles Evans Hughes
1868 Ulysses S. Grant	1920 Warren G. Harding
1872 Ulysses S. Grant	1924 Calvin Coolidge
1876 Rutherford B. Hayes	

NEOLIBERALISM (1928–1992)

Central dichotomy: the state versus the individual
Themes: antistatism, free market capitalism, right-wing populism, individualism
Presidential nominees:

1928 Herbert Hoover	1964 Barry Goldwater
1932 Herbert Hoover	1968 Richard Nixon
1936 Alfred M. Landon	1972 Richard Nixon
1940 Wendell Willkie	1976 Gerald Ford
1944 Thomas E. Dewey	1980 Ronald Reagan
1948 Thomas E. Dewey	1984 Ronald Reagan
1952 Dwight Eisenhower	1988 George Bush
1956 Dwight Eisenhower	1992 George Bush
1960 Richard Nixon	

Table 2. *Ideological epochs of the Democratic party*
(persisting theme: equality)

JEFFERSONIANISM (1828–1892)

Central dichotomy: liberty versus tyranny
Themes: white supremacy, antistatism, civic republicanism
Presidential nominees:

1828 Andrew Jackson	1864 George McClellan
1832 Andrew Jackson	1868 Horatio Seymour
1836 Martin Van Buren	1872 Horace Greeley
1840 Martin Van Buren	1876 Samuel Tilden
1844 James K. Polk	1880 Winfield S. Hancock
1848 Lewis Cass	1884 Grover Cleveland
1852 Franklin Pierce	1888 Grover Cleveland
1856 James Buchanan	1892 Grover Cleveland
1860 Stephen A. Douglas	

POPULISM (1896–1948)

Central dichtomy: the people versus the interests
Themes: egalitarianism, majoritarianism, Christian humanism
Presidential nominees:

1896 William J. Bryan	1924 John W. Davis
1900 William J. Bryan	1928 Alfred E. Smith
1904 Alton B. Parker	1932 Franklin D. Roosevelt
1908 William J. Bryan	1936 Franklin D. Roosevelt
1912 Woodrow Wilson	1940 Franklin D. Roosevelt
1916 Woodrow Wilson	1944 Franklin D. Roosevelt
1920 James M. Cox	1948 Harry S. Truman

UNIVERSALISM (1952–1992)

Central dichotomy: inclusion versus exclusion
Themes: civil rights, social welfare, redistribution, inclusion
Presidential nominees:

1952 Adlai E. Stevenson	1976 Jimmy Carter
1956 Adlai E. Stevenson	1980 Jimmy Carter
1960 John F. Kennedy	1984 Walter Mondale
1964 Lyndon B. Johnson	1988 Michael Dukakis
1968 Hubert H. Humphrey	1992 Bill Clinton
1972 George S. McGovern	

ulism. Although not exactly statists, twentieth-century Democrats backed increasing government intervention in and regulation of the marketplace, the redistribution of wealth through government transfers, loose monetary policies, and demand-led economic growth. They were suspicious of monopolies and of big business in general. Their political philosophy could be encapsulated in the ideal of majority rule and in the populist narrative in which the people fought for their rights against an unholy elite.

By the 1950s, however, the party discarded its abrasive, class-tinged ethos in favor of a *Universalist* perspective – the extension of rights to all aggrieved claimants and a general rhetoric of inclusion. Bryan, the evangelical crusader of the Populist era, was traded in for the moderate, ecumenical Lyndon Johnson. Party leaders now praised capitalism without qualification. Arguments for progressive social policies relied on empathy, social responsibility, and impassioned appeals for aid, rather than attacks on privilege and power. Postwar Democrats also reached beyond economic issues to address a wide range of "postmaterialist" concerns.

Thus, throughout the long histories of their parties, Democratic and Whig-Republican leaders viewed a whole range of heterogeneous policies from within their partisan redoubts. Each ideological formation was structured around a central conceptual dichotomy, a single organizing principle within which a panoply of values, beliefs, attitudes, and issue-positions made sense to partisans. For the National Republicans, this was the opposition of anarchy and order; for Neoliberal Republicans the functioning antinomy became the state and the individual. Democratic ideology evolved through three conceptual prisms: virtue versus corruption (Jeffersonian), the people versus the interests (Populist), and, finally, inclusion versus exclusion (Universalist). The simple and compelling logic of these central dichotomies oriented, justified, and gave meaning to each party's programmatic agenda. In the following chapters I try to show how the different views propagated by party spokespersons were implicated in a single ideological plot, a plot strung together and sustained by the core values that party members held most dear.[32]

---

32. This periodization of American party history differs considerably from standard views of the subject. Most work on the American parties, for example, assumes that these organizations have changed their views concurrently during periods of critical realignment (the 1830s, 1850s, 1890s, 1930s) – or perhaps even more frequently. In any case, party change is understood as a systemwide phenomenon. In this reading, one has a Jacksonian era, a Civil War era, a Gilded Age, and so forth, each with distinct party-system characteristics. I argue, however, that American ideological history is best conceptualized not as a series of party systems or historical eras but rather as a

Continuities in Party Ideology

To be sure, ideological transformations within each party did not occur suddenly and in toto from one election to the next. Rather, such changes tended to occur over a period of several elections, building on that party's established traditions. In most cases, it was not possible for leaders to make a clean break with the past – or rather, one might say it was in their interest to do so as subtly as possible, emphasizing continuities rather than discontinuities. What, then, were these ongoing traditions?[33]

The underlying unity of Whig-Republican ideology from Whiggism to Reaganism can be found in three interrelated values – *prosperity, social order,* and *patriotism.* From the early nineteenth century to the early twentieth, the question of prosperity was situated from within the optic of mercantilism. By the end of the 1920s, however, state intervention came to be viewed as impeding, rather than furthering, economic progress. Similarly, during the National epoch, Whig-Republican leaders believed the firm and conscientious arm of government to be necessary to preserve the social order. By the end of the 1920s, however, the party's perspectives on the maintenance of order had been virtually reversed: centralized government was now viewed as destructive of a natural social order inhering in civil society. A parallel shift can be seen in the final element of the Whig-Republican trinity. For almost a century, Whigs and Republicans equated state and nation. The U.S. government stood for the American country; the flag and the glorious capital were indistinguishable. After the Progressive era, however, Republicans began to distinguish between love of country and love of government; the former was still blessed, the latter more often cursed.

On the most basic level, the Democratic party's programmatic attachments from Jackson to Clinton may be seen as varying attempts to realize the ideal of *equality.* In the nineteenth century, this ideal was restricted to white men. Its achievement was assumed to flow from the free movement of men, goods, and services. In this context, the struggle for equality entailed a defense of the established order. Political equality was something that could be lost (the fate of most republics) but not

set of five ideological epochs – two Whig-Republican and three Democratic. In this view, ideological change has been staggered, affecting one party at a time. The major parties revolved around each other and were vitally affected by each other, but they did not respond in tandem to historical events. The parties' histories, therefore, must be understood as the product of *independent* trajectories.

33. The following arguments parallel some of the conclusions reached by Reichley (1992).

improved upon. The main threat to this happy state was felt to lie in the federal government, the only entity powerful enough to threaten the liberties of the people or to privilege permanently one group above another. By the end of the century, most party members were convinced that social and political equality was threatened by the growth of corporate power and by the undue political influence wielded by economic elites. Government was perceived as an ally for greater equality, and democracy as an exercise in majority rule rather than minority rights. In the postwar era, the party's vision of equality expanded from this "class" focus to include a host of new claimants and new demands.

Thus, it might be said that through all periods of American history one party has adhered to the interests of business and the advance of a capitalist economy, whereas the other has often been more critical of this advance. One has been more concerned with preserving social order and liberty, the other has emphasized equality. While one has trumpeted the glories of the nation, the other has done so more hesitantly. These core values, although interpreted differently in different periods, grant an element of continuity to party conflict in America. If most things changed, a few basic things remained the same.

The Plan of the Book

This chapter has presented the overarching argument of the book – that the presidential wings of the American parties are ideologically driven – and has described general patterns of conflict, change, and continuity in these ideologies over the past century and a half. A great deal of historical and analytic ground has been covered in the space of several pages. This ground will be re-covered, slowly and carefully, in succeeding chapters. What follows is a map of the book's progress through this terrain.

The ideology argument is likely to strike many readers as implausible, given general assumptions about how politics works in the United States. The porous organization of the American parties, coupled with the strength of the political culture within which they operate, would seem to militate against the formation of strong party ideologies. In chapter 2 I reexamine these assumptions from three angles – the party campaign (Are campaigns ideological?), the party in government (Do party ideologies matter to the formation of public policy?), and American parties in cross-national perspective (Are the American parties less ideological than their European brethren?). My argument, broadly stated, is that although parties and politics are different in the United States, they are not so different as is commonly presumed; nor should these differences be seen as precluding the existence of party ideology.

The following chapters proceed to a detailed presentation of the evidence gathered in this study. I begin with the Whig-Republicans. Chapter 3 looks at the National epoch (1828–1924) and chapter 4 at the Neoliberal epoch (1928–1992). Chapters 5, 6, and 7 focus on the Democrats in their Jeffersonian (1828–1892), Populist (1896–1948), and Universalist (1952–1992) incarnations. (A brief epilogue examines the most recent presidential race in light of each party's ideological history.)

The concluding chapter explores questions of derivation and causation. What might account for the content of American party ideology? What mechanisms, pressures, or concerns drive the formation and periodic reformation of ideology within these party organizations? Four common explanatory frameworks are observed – classical, socioeconomic, ethnocultural, and realignment-oriented. I argue, however, that no single mechanism or framework provides a satisfactory account of the changing content of American party ideologies over the past century and a half. Party ideological change resists generalizable causal analysis.

The book thus divides the subject of party ideology into four general questions. Why might we expect to find strong ideologies in the American parties (chapter 2)? What is the content of these ideologies (chapters 3 through 7)? And, finally, what explains their transformation through time (chapter 8)?

Strictly speaking, this is a book about party ideology in America. Speaking somewhat less strictly, this might be considered a book about the culture of high politics from the early years of the republic to the waning decades of the twentieth century. What did politicians say when courting the public? Which issues and symbols dominated campaign politics at presidential levels, and which were avoided? How did this discourse change over the course of American history?

Any study of party ideologies is also, inadvertently, a study of what politics is about. Since political parties are one of the chief disseminators of political culture, partisan rhetoric provides a window into the values and attitudes that have guided American politics – at least, politics at the top of the political pyramid. It is my hope, therefore, that this book will prove useful to those interested in American political history, political culture, and political rhetoric, as well as to those who are curious about the role of ideology in American party life.

2

Rethinking the Role of Ideology in American Party Life

In looking at the role of ideology in American party life, it is helpful to disaggregate the concept of party into three components: (a) the party in the electorate (party voters), (b) the party organization (party campaign activities, activists, and leaders), and (c) the party in government (the party's role as policy maker). I am not concerned with the first component. Indeed, I am prepared to believe that party ideology is less meaningful as a cue for voters in the United States than elsewhere. On this level, the standard nonideological view of party politics in America may be correct.[1]

This book is concerned primarily with the second component of partyness, the party as campaign or organization and, more schematically, with the third component of partyness, the party as policy maker. Before proceeding to the evidence, however, it is important to overcome certain objections to the general argument (that American parties are ideological). These objections rest not so much in an empirical debate as in a set of analytic assumptions about American politics. The parties are assumed to be innocent of ideology because it is difficult to envision how coherent and differentiated ideologies could endure in such a fragmented political structure. This chapter begins, therefore, with a review and reconsideration of various features of the American political landscape that might affect the ability of the parties to present themselves in an ideological fashion before the electorate.

Evidently, a party's campaign may be highly ideological without bringing any specific policy consequences in its train. The party may lack the desire, or simply the means, to implement its ideology once elected

---

1. See, e.g., Granberg and Holmberg (1988), Huber (1989), Inglehart and Klingemann (1976), Listhaug et al. (1994), Niemi and Westholm (1984), and Sani and Sartori (1983). But see also Converse (1990: 380), who argues that French voters – although more likely to be able to locate themselves on a left/right scale – should not be considered more ideological than American voters.

to office. This, it should be noted, is a particular concern within the fragmented governmental apparatus established by the U.S. Constitution which, it is commonly thought, imposes obstacles to ideologically based legislating. We wish to know, therefore, not only whether campaigns are ideological but also whether these campaigns have important policy consequences – whether party ideology "matters." This brings us to a consideration of the third facet of party, the party in government.

The chapter ends with a review of cross-national comparisons as they pertain to the question of party ideology in America. Although American party ideologies were (and are) different in content from those in other democratic nations, I argue that they have not been, on the whole, less coherent, differentiated, or enduring. The argument of this chapter is thus twofold: the American parties are more ideological than is usually conceived, and parties abroad, in many cases, are *less* so.

The Party as Campaign or Organization

Eight structural features appear to prohibit, or at least inhibit, the development of ideology within the American parties: (1) diversity of opinion within the parties, (2) interest-based (rather than value-based) political behavior, (3) diffuse party membership, (4) the centrist dynamic of two-party politics, (5) the absence of responsible party government, (6) the prevalence of patronage within the parties, (7) the absence of a viable socialist party, and (8) the consensual nature of American political culture. I shall argue that none of these features constitutes a strong a priori objection to the thesis of this book. Indeed, rather than denigrating the role of ideology, a reconsideration of the political landscape may strengthen the case for ideology as a factor in American political life.

Intra-party Strife

The American parties are catch-all parties, and probably more demographically heterogeneous than most. Not surprisingly, writers have dwelled at length on factional disputes within the American parties – between northern and southern factions in the Whig party, between eastern and western factions in the Gilded Age Democratic party, between stalwart and progressive factions in the Republican party, and so forth.[2]

2. For period-specific treatments, see Burner (1967/1968), Key (1949), G. Mayer (1973), W. Mayer (1996), Rae (1989; 1994), and Schlesinger (1973). For more comprehensive treatments, see Goldman (1990) and Roback and James (1978).

"Both parties," comments Everett Carll Ladd, "contained disparate groups, and interests were never neatly polarized. . . . Presumably any political party has some internal ideological disagreements, but the big American parties . . . have contained the *entire* spectrum of substantial ideological argument."[3] Parties with such strong internal divisions, it is commonly assumed, must violate the precept of coherence, and therefore fail to qualify as fully ideological.

Yet, when viewed in a broad, cross-national context, factionalism does *not* appear to be a salient characteristic of the American party system. Howard Reiter's work on factionalism within national party conventions, for example, suggests that only two periods – the antebellum era (within the Whig party) and the postwar era (within both parties) – saw the formation of enduring factional alignments. At other times, factions seem to have been relatively weak and undefined within the presidential parties.[4] State politics, of course, has sometimes been highly factional, particularly in those states dominated by a single party, and factions have also been prominent in Congress.[5] However, within the presidential wings of the parties, factionalism has not been particularly debilitating. Certainly, there is no American analogue to the faction-ridden parties of Japan, Italy, and France.[6]

Even in Britain, the paradigm case of centralized parties and tight parliamentary discipline, factionalism often seems to have prevailed. Surely there are few examples of ideological schizophrenia so heinous as that provided by the Liberal party. From the mid-nineteenth century to

3. Ladd (1970: 30–31). On the "coalitional" view of American parties, see Eldersveld (1964), Key (1942/1958), Ladd and Hadley (1975), Petrocik (1981), and Sorauf and Beck (1988).
4. See Reiter (1996a). One might, of course, interpret this lack of factional strife as an indication of an absence of ideological commitment among party members. But an ideological approach to politics need not result in intraparty division; indeed, it might be thought to produce intraparty *cohesion*. (If disagreements within a party occur over relatively pragmatic matters such as who will be chosen as the party's nominee, rather than over fundamentals, this may be an indication that party members agree with one another on fundamentals and are willing to work toward compromise.)
5. On factionalism in the South, see Key (1949). On factionalism in Congress, see Bensel (1984) and Patterson (1967).
6. Of course, not all parties in these three polities are faction-ridden. Communist parties are rarely factionally divided, and small parties are less likely than large parties to exhibit enduring intraparty cleavages, for obvious reasons. However, writers commonly identify major parties within these three polities as exceptionally prone to factionalism. On the Liberal Democrats in Japan, see Curtis (1988: ch. 3). On the Christian Democrats and Socialists in Italy, see Hine (1993: 129–44). On the Socialists in France, see Bell and Criddle (1984) and Cole (1989). Belloni and Beller (1978) and Hine (1982) offer overviews of factional strife across many countries.

the latter twentieth, members of this party managed to disagree on virtually every issue of importance they faced – the extension of the franchise, the granting of independence to Ireland, electoral alliances with the other parties, the expansion of social welfare legislation, and trade union legislation, to name just a few. At times it seemed that free trade was the *only* issue on which Liberals could consistently agree. A strong dose of the party's ideological confusion heading into the First World War is demonstrated by the number of different labels affixed to factions within the party, which included moderate, pure liberal, pure radical, advanced socialistic or semisocialistic, radical and social, advanced radical, convinced collectivist, economist, imperialist, and individualist.[7] George Dangerfield assessed the Liberals of the early twentieth century as "an irrational mixture of whig aristocrats, industrialists, dissenters, reformers, trade unionists, quacks and Mr Lloyd George."[8] A more sober report put it this way:

> The Liberal Party, like any Radical party at any time, was a mixture of factions. Potential reformers who wished to see their ideas actually implemented or who were personally ambitious had been left with no real alternative but to sail into power on the Liberal side. . . . The term liberal, then as now, was vague enough to allow unlimited latitude and respectable enough to attract support from all levels of society. High Churchmen and Nonconformists, fiery Radicals and cautious reformers, Imperialists and little Englanders, staid suburbians and the apostles of anarchy, were able to pull together in the same boat without too many questions asked about individual destinations.[9]

Almost as much intraparty strife could be found within the Conservative party, which oscillated back and forth between Disraelian (statism, protectionism, social welfare) and Thatcherian (antistatism, Free Trade, laissez-faire) persuasions through most of the twentieth century. One historian identifies three ideological currents competing with one another for primacy within the party; another finds four.[10] An indication of the general fluidity of the British party system in the early twentieth century can be found in Winston Churchill's storied career. In the words of one writer, Churchill was "first a Tory, then a Liberal, then a Coalition Liberal, then a Constitutionalist, and finally a Tory again."[11] According to Francis Pym, the Conservative party has survived "by combining a strong motive for unity with a firm refusal to let ideology

7. See Hosking and King (1977: 142).   8. Dangerfield (1936: 15).
9. Rowland (1968: 31–32), quoted in Hosking and King (1977: 143).
10. See Charmley (1996: ch 1) and Norton and Aughey (1981: 68).
11. Harris (1966: 155).

threaten it."[12] This is the party, one might recall, for whom the term *creative opportunism* was coined.[13]

In 1909, A. Lawrence Lowell, an American political scientist, noted the phenomenal number of Liberal and Conservative party leaders who changed "either their party, or their principles, in the course of their career. Except for Lord John Russell, Mr. Disraeli, Lord Salisbury and Mr. Balfour," Lowell concluded, "it may be said that almost all the most famous ministers from 1832 to the end of the century did one or the other."[14] To be sure, this sort of ideological instability became much less pronounced after World War II, when the party system solidified into two main camps. However, although the modern Conservative and Labour parties have managed to stanch the flow of defectors, they have not been able to overcome the centrifugal force of intraparty debates.

Even the stolid Labour party has been accused of backing and filling on major questions of the day. Labour leaders have suffered continual bickering between "Conference" (the party's national convention) and the parliamentary Labour party, between trade unions and unaffiliated members, and between working-class members and the party's largely Oxbridge-trained elite. In the early twentieth century, key battles took place over such basic matters as socialism, syndicalism, public ownership, electoral alliances with the Liberals, public welfare programs, the entry of Britain into the First and Second World Wars, women's suffrage, the admission of communists into the party, and support for the 1926 general strike.[15]

Ideological cohesion and consistency, it seems, are rather elusive traits, even in a Westminster system of government. The Liberals, the

12. Pym (1985: 192), quoted in Barnes (1994: 315).
13. See Glickman (1961). Samuel Beer's estimation was that "the term ideological can be applied to the Conservatives in only the most tenuous sense. An array of diverse and contradictory perspectives inhibits simple theoretical formulations and purposes" (quoted in Cyr 1978: 298). On intraparty strife, see also Barnes (1994), Christoph (1967: 94–95), and Lowe (1986).
14. Lowell (1909, 2: 98) continues: "Sir Robert Peel twice carried measures of the highest political moment against the convictions he had earlier held. Lord Palmerston was long a Conservative minister, and still longer a Liberal one. Lord Stanley and Sir James Graham both changed sides, the latter with kaleidoscopic rapidity. Mr. Gladstone from a high Tory minister became the most famous of the Liberal premiers. Lord Hartington and Mr. Chamberlain both passed from leading positions in Liberal cabinets to powerful influence in Conservative ones."
15. In the 1950s and 1960s, the party divided over socialism, German rearmament, nationalization, and disarmament. On factionalism within the Labour party, see Christoph (1967: 94), Drucker (1979), Janosik (1976), Miliband (1961), Minkin (1978), Norton (1975), Pelling (1968), Seyd (1987), and Shaw (1988).

Tories, and the Labourites have not always been parties of principle – or rather, they have been parties of many principles.[16] Indeed, the general picture one obtains from a perusal of the literature on British party politics is of an embarrassing lack of rectitude. Acknowledgment of this point might lead to a more tolerant view of the occasional lapses and indiscretions committed by members of the American parties.

Interests

The interest-based approach to the American parties has a long lineage in political science. According to this view, party coalitions, although relatively stable, were based on calculations of self-interest rather than on core values and beliefs. "The parties by which the Union is menaced do not rest on principles," thought Tocqueville, "but upon material interests. . . . Thus, upon a recent occasion the North contended for the system of commercial prohibition, and the South took up arms in favor of free trade, simply because the North is a manufacturing and the South an agricultural community; and the restrictive system that was profitable to the one was prejudicial to the other."[17] Interest-based perspectives – from Madison and Tocqueville in the nineteenth century to Beard and Truman in the twentieth – share a common suspicion that each party is coalitional, brokering agreements with its fractious constituencies on an issue-by-issue basis rather than on the basis of a general ideology.[18]

The interest-based model of political behavior, however, sidesteps important questions of causal priority. Indisputably, voters had concrete interests, and parties responded to those interests wherever possible; but

16. For a general treatment of factionalism in British parties, see Rose (1967) and Brady and Bullock (1985: 155–56).
17. Tocqueville (1835/1960: 184–85).
18. Madison's famed *Federalist* no. 10, which inspired Progressives like Charles Beard, remains a staple of high school and college textbooks. "From the protection of different and unequal faculties of acquiring property, the possession of different degrees and kinds of property immediately results," wrote Madison, "and from the influence of these on the sentiments and views of the respective proprietors, ensures a division of the society into different interests and parties" (Hamilton et al. 1961: 78). Evidently, one need not be a Progressive or a Marxist to take an interest-based view of political behavior. The predominant view of American political life is that interests matter but that these interests have been highly disaggregated; hence the peculiarly American concept of an "interest group." Local or sectoral interests, rather than broad socioeconomic classes, are commonly said to form the building blocks of American party activity. See Beard (1929), Bentley (1908/1967), Downs (1957), Herring (1940), Key (1942/1958), Mayhew (1974), Schattschneider (1942), Truman (1951), and Turner (1932).

how were those interests constructed? Which, in other words, came first – the interest or the ideology? Most issues that reached the forefront of political debate in presidential elections did not appear as specific policy propositions (from which individual self-interests could be calculated). They emerged, instead, through a dense ideological fog. The infamous tariff debate, for example, was framed for voters as a contest of "Tariff Reform" versus "Protection," not as a set of specific rates and schedules. The economic repercussions of "internal improvements" were almost as direct as those of the tariff; yet nineteenth-century voters must have had a difficult time ascertaining what they were. Whereas Democrats argued that infrastructural development would advantage eastern merchants and manufacturers, Whig-Republicans argued that southern and western states were most in need of harbors, roads, and railroads. Moreover, Whig-Republicans claimed, markets for commodities would develop in the cities of the Northeast if interstate commerce were encouraged such that the growth of that region would benefit agricultural sections as well. Moving from the particular (e.g., specific tariff schedules or public works projects) to the general (economic policy at large), and from short time-horizons to longer ones, it was no longer so clear where the interests of constituents lay.

The classic example, perhaps, of the inseparability of ideology and interest was the debate over slavery. Rarely does one find a reasoned discussion of the economics of slave versus free-labor methods of production, and even if such a debate had occurred, the results, one imagines, would have been highly equivocal. (How, for example, could one judge the economic impact of abolition on the South – or, more to the point, on an individual Southerner?) The more abstract the level of analysis, the more difficult it was to avoid inflecting economic issues with ideological terms. Here, instrumental calculations merged with general, and highly partisan, economic philosophies; for in calculating one's self-interest, one had to assume some overall model of how the economic world was put together. Then, as now, the force of ideology was enhanced by the lack of a neutral body of economic law stipulating who would win and lose if a particular policy option were adopted.[19]

Thus were self-interests converted into ideologies, and rational voters into partisans. Ideology, in other words, was constitutive of interest, and vice versa. "It is futile," writes Schattschneider, "to try to determine whether men are stimulated politically by interests or by ideas, for people have ideas about interests."[20] Why did most members of the working

---

19. See Roemer (1994).
20. Schattschneider (1942: 37). An excellent literature review and evaluation of the "interests versus ideology" debate can be found in Kingdon (1993), who makes a similar

class identify with the Republican party during the first three decades of the twentieth century, when that party was distinctly unenthusiastic about the organization of labor unions, redistributive social policies, and restrictive regulations on business? Why did business leaders define their interests as antagonistic to government? Naturally, one can construct explanations for such counterintuitive patterns of behavior.[21] The point is, as the examples of tariffs, internal improvements, and slavery attest, a purely interest-based model of politics does not take one very far in explaining the American parties.

Diffuse Membership

Most work on the American parties takes a society-centered view of these organizations. For writers in the Progressive tradition, the relevant voting groups are economic; for ethnocultural historians, they are ethnic and religious; and for other realignment theorists, voting cues change with each passing era. In each case, analysts have tended to look at the parties as institutions whose primary function is representative. Gaining insight into a party's ideology thus involves a search into the opinion profiles of its constituent groups.[22] Because these constituent groups were quite heterogeneous, writers have usually concluded that the parties themselves were polyglot formations.

At the same time, research on party elites – usually focused on activists or delegates to the national conventions – generally finds these partisans to be quite ideological. They demonstrate impressive levels of political knowledge and consistent views on matters of public policy, and they arrange those views around a few core principles. By any definition, these participants in American party life would appear to merit the term *ideologue*.[23] To be sure, the American parties are uniquely diffuse in membership and organizational structure, so that party elites do

---

set of observations with respect to American politics at large. See also Mansbridge (1990) and Bauer, Pool, and Dexter (1963/1972).

21. On the working class and its political involvements, see Foner (1984), Hattam (1993), Heffer and Rovet (1988), Karabel (1979), Katznelson (1981), Laslett and Lipset (1974), Leon (1971), Lipset (1977; 1992), Mink (1986), Orren (1991), and Shafer (1992). On the political views of American businessmen and -women, see Martin (1995) and Vogel (1978).
22. For further discussion of theories of American party ideology, see chapter 8.
23. The great scholarly debate over the ideological proclivities of the mass public – initiated more than three decades ago by Campbell et al. (1960) and Converse (1964) – continues unabated. Yet, whatever may be the resolution of this debate, it seems inescapable that party leaders are more ideological than their followers. See, e.g., Baer and Bositis (1988), Bruce, Clark, and Kessel (1991), Kirkpatrick (1976), McClosky (1964), McClosky et al. (1960), Miller and Jennings (1986), and Smith (1989).

not enjoy the same perquisites and power enjoyed by party elites in other party systems. Yet it is not clear that an open and decentralized system of candidate selection results in a less ideological style of party behavior. Indeed, some have argued that the party reforms of the 1970s, which vastly increased levels of participation in candidate selection and dethroned whatever remained of state and local party machines, led to a radicalization of the parties in subsequent decades.[24] Without entering into this lengthy debate, let us simply observe that it is the *kind* of elector and the *process* of selection, not the sheer number of electors, that are critical in determining a party's ideological profile.[25]

Whatever the effect of the much-discussed party reforms, it would appear that leaders of core constituency groups in the latter twentieth century still have many means at their disposal to keep party leaders on the path of true belief. They may withhold financial support as well as logistical support. They may become a political embarrassment to the candidate by openly parading their disaffection before the general public.[26] They may, finally, defect. (The formation of third parties by disgruntled party activists has been a surprisingly frequent event in the annals of American political history and a constant worry to major party leaders.[27]) Thus, to the extent that a party's members may be considered

24. See Jackson et al. (1978), Kirkpatrick (1976), Polsby (1983), Roback (1975), Shafer (1983), Soule and McGrath (1975), and Sullivan et al. (1974). But see also Stone and Abramowitz (1983).

25. For a review of candidate selection practices around the democratic world, see Gallagher and Marsh (1988).

26. A party visibly at war with itself cuts a poor figure among the undecided voters it is seeking to convert. Democratic campaigns in 1896, 1924, 1948, 1968, and 1972 and Republican campaigns in 1912 and 1992 were probably hurt by the open defection of traditional party supporters during party conventions in those years. Mayer (1996) claims that the Democrats' chances in presidential elections in the postreform era have been undercut by party divisiveness during primary campaigns.

27. Third-party challenges of some force have faced the major parties in every decade of the twentieth century and were even more credible in the nineteenth century (Rosenstone et al. 1984). As Gerald Pomper (1992: 47) points out, the Free-Soilers (1848), "Dixiecrats" (1948), Peace and Freedom party (1970s), Anderson Independents (1980), and many other minor parties may be more accurately classed as attempts to influence the policy programs of the major parties rather than genuine efforts to build permanent new parties (see also Key 1942/1964: 280). In a highly competitive electoral environment, a few votes in the right places may mean the difference between winning and losing for one of the major parties. Even if minor parties have rarely possessed this wherewithal, scattered evidence suggests that the leaders of the major parties *thought* they might and acted accordingly. Franklin Roosevelt, for example, seems to have moved left prior to the 1936 election in part to counter an expected challenge from Huey Long (Brinkley 1983: 80–81; Williams 1981: 836–37), just as Clinton seems to have reaffirmed his support for affirmative action in 1992 to discourage a potential challenge from Jesse Jackson.

keepers of its ideological flame, there are strong indications that they performed this function within the American parties – despite the diffuse membership and decentralized structures of these parties.[28]

In short, one must qualify the "instrumental" view of party propaganda. Whether one focuses on those at the apex of the presidential parties or on those further down within the leadership structure one cannot help but appreciate the depth of commitment that the Whig, Republican, and Democratic labels have called forth among their principal followers. Thus, arguments that base their conclusions on the opinions and behavior of the parties in the electorate may be, in a crucial sense, beside the point. It may not matter, that is, whether the American voter is less ideologically inclined than voters in other countries if the leaders of the major parties are as ideologically inclined as most of the available evidence suggests. Ideology, in this country at least, may be preeminently an elite-level phenomenon. If so, the logical site for an investigation into party ideology is the leadership stratum, not the rank and file.

Two-party Politics

The fourth argument against ideology concerns the two-party monopoly in American political life. Bipolar competition forces parties to aggregate a majority (or at least a plurality) within the general electorate and hence to pay greatest attention to swing voters in the center. Thus, even though their most loyal constituents might be ideologically inclined, party leaders may be obliged by the dynamics of a party system to ignore such differences of opinion in calculating electoral appeals. Many would argue, therefore, that two-party competition creates the conditions for broad, catchall parties with weakly differentiated ideologies.[29]

Judging the "ideologicalness" of party systems turns out to be a rather complicated matter, however. Ideological polarization hinges upon which parties one chooses to count within a multiparty system. If one includes extreme parties within these party systems, then the moderating effects of two-partyism are virtually axiomatic. A larger party system translates into a wider ideological spread and hence greater differentiation between the extremes.[30] After the 1994 elections in Germany, for example, five parties gained seats in the Bundestag; they were – from

---

28. For discussions of the effects of party activists in moving parties away from the center, see Baer and Bositis (1988), Bruce, Clark, and Kessel (1991), Gold (1989), Kirkpatrick (1976), McClosky et al. (1960), McClosky (1964), Miller and Jennings (1986), Monroe (1983), Page (1978), Polsby (1983), Rae (1989), Weed (1994), and Wilson (1962).
29. See, e.g., Downs (1957) and Hermens (1941).
30. See Bartolini and Mair (1990: 202).

left to right – the Greens, the PDS (the reformed communist party of East Germany), the SPD (Social Democrats), the FDP (the Liberals), and the CDU-CSU (Christian Democrat-Christian Social Union alliance). In addition, the Republikaner, a small, far-right party, gained 1.9 percent of the vote, failing, however, to clear the 5 percent threshold that would have qualified it for seats in the Bundestag. Evidently, considerably more policy distance separates the Greens from the Republikaner than separates Democrats from Republicans. By one measure, therefore, the German party system appears a good deal more ideological than any two-party system possibly could.

However, the three minor parties on the extremes – the Greens, the PDS, and the Republikaner – compiled a total of only 14.7 percent of the votes cast in that election. To judge ideology in a party system by the distance separating parties on either extreme of a multiparty system when these parties are small and seldom exert much influence within parliament may grossly misrepresent the distance separating most of the voters (or leaders). Arguably, the more appropriate reference point for the American parties is to be found among *major* parties abroad – parties, let us say, aggregating at least one-fifth of the popular vote. In Germany, this would include the major party on the right, the CDU-CSU, and the major party on the left, the SPD. In this context, the American parties no longer appear so unusual, for these parties are moderate, centrist, and highly inclusive.[31]

Notice, as well, that "spreading" effects in a multiparty system – discussed earlier – are mitigated to some extent by "crowding" effects. For example, in between the extremes defined by the Greens and the Republikaner, one finds four or five parties separated by very little ideological space.[32] Is the average German able to differentiate between the policies pursued by the FDP and the CDU-CSU? The task, one imagines, is considerably more complicated than the task facing an elector within a two-party system. The more parties there are within a party system (all other things being equal), the more difficult it becomes to differentiate between parties adjacent to one another on the ideological spectrum. Greater differentiation vis-à-vis distant parties occurs at the cost of lesser differentiation vis-à-vis neighboring parties.[33] Thus, from a

31. German election statistics are drawn from Derbyshire and Derbyshire (1996: 490–91).
32. Whether one counts four or five depends upon whether the CDU and CSU are counted separately or as a single party.
33. It should be clear that the term *differentiation*, introduced in chapter 1, is used synonymously with the terms polarization, distance, and issue-conflict. Each connotes the degree of difference, or separation, between two or more parties.

purely formal, definitional perspective it is not at all clear whether polities like Denmark and the Netherlands, where dozens of parties vie with one another for the voter's attention, are more or less ideological than the staid examples provided by Britain and America.

It should also be noted that two-party systems have sometimes been looked upon as an *incentive* to ideological behavior. For S. E. Finer, the bane of British politics is to be found in its "adversarial" style, a style rooted in an electoral system that produces winners and losers, but nothing in between. Proportional systems, Finer argues, moderate party conflict by ensuring that each party will receive a consistent level of support in the electorate and a commensurate number of seats in the legislature, and that no single party will monopolize political power after the election. When power is shared and electoral support consistent (landslides are rare in proportional systems), parties generally have greater incentive to cooperate, inside and outside parliament. Where power is indivisible, however, a zero-sum struggle ensues in which each side is interested primarily in embarrassing its opponent rather than in reaching consensus.[34] Arguably, negative campaigning is more persistent in two-party systems, where one can readily define oneself in oppositional terms, than in multiparty systems, where a negative campaign would have to smear a number of opponents with the same brush (or different brushes – an even more difficult feat).

The oppositional dynamic of two-party systems is further enhanced in the American case by the presidency, an office that, unlike a legislature – which leaves room for opposition parties in committee work, floor debate, and floor votes – has no inclusionary features at all. (A party either controls the White House or does not; there is no middle ground.) Scholars are virtually unanimous in declaring parliamentary regimes more stable than presidential regimes, largely because of their greater capacity to compensate losing parties.[35] Indeed, some writers have speculated that the American Civil War was facilitated by the oppositional format of a winner-take-all electoral system.[36] Although the United States survived this challenge to its constitutional authority and territorial integrity, the Civil War remains one of the bloodiest internal conflicts in the history of Western nation-states – a reminder that two-party

---

34. See Bogdanor (1981), Finer (1975), and Steinmo (1993).
35. See Jones (1995), Linz and Valenzuela (1994), and Lijphart (1992). Of course, the winner-take-all aspect of the American electoral system is mitigated somewhat by the fragmented nature of the American parties (discussed later in this chapter). One might also argue, with Lijphart (1984), that presidential systems are more consensual than Westminster systems, since each branch is obliged to share power with the other.
36. See Lazare (1996: 43–44).

politics may not be, as scholars used to think, a recipe for moderate, nonideological politics.

The Absence of Party Government

It is commonly supposed that ideologies are encouraged by a system of party government. On the one hand, when a single party assumes sole responsibility for governance, parties within that system are thought to be more likely to articulate clear and consistent stands on matters of public policy – to have "programmatic" orientations. In a system of weak parties and fragmented sovereignty, on the other hand, political leaders are thought to have fewer incentives to present an integrated, policy-specific plan when trolling for votes among the general electorate. Here, the British Westminster model of centralized parties and single-party rule serves as the negative reference point, the model for everything America appears to lack.[37]

In issuing their influential call for British-style party government in the United States, E. E. Schattschneider and his colleagues argued that strong parties would lead to a more *responsible* style of rhetoric and position-taking, however, not a more ideological one. "[C]larification of party policy in itself will not cause the parties to differ more fundamentally or more sharply than they have in the past," the authors speculated. "The contrary is much more likely to be the case. The clarification of party policy may be expected to produce a more reasonable discussion of public affairs, more closely related to the political performance of the parties in their actions rather than their words."[38] The logic of this argument leads one to the conclusion that although strong parties and unitary government might enhance the connection between promise and performance (a matter taken up later in this chapter), this connection probably would have negligible effects on the ideological qualities of the campaigns. Indeed, it might even *moderate* the parties' positions.

The same point can be found, a century ago, in Bagehot's famous work on the English Constitution. "Of all modes of enforcing moderation on a party," Bagehot wrote,

> the best is to contrive that the members of that party shall be intrinsically moderate, careful, and almost shrinking men; and the next best to contrive that the leaders of the party, who have protested most in its behalf, shall

---

37. For an intellectual history of the theory of responsible party government, see Ranney (1962). For discussion of this ideal as it pertains to contemporary American politics, see White and Mileur (1992).
38. American Political Science Association (1950: 20).

be placed in the closest contact with the actual world. Our English system contains both contrivances; it makes party government permanent and possible in the sole way in which it can be so, by making it mild. . . . Constituency government is the precise opposite of Parliamentary government. It is the government of immoderate persons far from the scene of action, instead of the government of moderate persons close to the scene of action; it is the judgment of persons judging in the last resort and without a penalty, in lieu of persons judging in fear of a dissolution, and ever conscious that they are subject to an appeal.[39]

Historical evidence from the history of British parties also leads one to doubt the familiar equation of weak parties with nonideological styles. In an early and influential study of the House of Commons, Hugh Berrington observes that the development of party discipline in the late nineteenth century was accompanied not by a polarization of party leaderships but instead by a moderation of party backbenchers now forced to share in the responsibilities of governance. Prior to this point, MPs – technically members of the governing party – were "untroubled by administrative needs, or the pressure of harsh political fact." Consequently, these backbenchers "could still declaim the slogans they had voiced in opposition." Members on the extremes – particularly within the Liberal party, which housed a large and restive Radical contingent – were allowed to trumpet their views without fear of retribution by party leaders or by constituents (who were often egging them on). "It was the party leaders," concludes Berrington, "perhaps more so than the backbenchers, who were the cornerstone of 'moderation' in the nineteenth-century House." The rise of party government thus corresponded with a rise in moderate, leader-controlled conflict within the Commons and a concomitant decline in the extremism of the nineteenth-century "independent."[40] Whatever benefits responsible party government might bring to the United States, a more ideological style of campaigning is not likely to be among them.

Patronage

Ironically, one of the factors behind the strength of party organization in the nineteenth century – the extensive patronage appointments available to party leaders – has also been accused of rendering those parties nonideological. James Scott writes:

> "Patronage," "spoils," "bribery," and "corruption" are inevitably associated with the urban machine as it evolved in the United States. . . . The machine party is . . . best characterized not only by the degree of its electoral

39. Bagehot (1867/1963: 160–61).   40. Berrington (1967–68: 362, 373).

control but also by the distinctive resources that knitted it together. Ties based on charisma, coercion, or ideology were often minor chords of machine orchestration; the "boss" might be viewed as a hero by some, he might use hired toughs or the police now and again to discourage opposition, and a populist ideology might accompany his appeals. For the machine party, however, such bonds were definitely subsidiary to the concrete particularistic rewards that represented its staple means of political coordination and distinguished it as a form.[41]

Scott, in common with many writers, counterposes patronage parties to ideological parties – the former offering supporters a set of incentives that are primarily material in nature and the latter relying more on purposive incentives.[42]

However, traditional wisdom regarding the irreconcilability of ideology and patronage does not jibe very well with traditional wisdom about Anglo-European democracies. Those countries with the most patronage – for example, Iceland, Israel, Italy, Greece, India, and France (during the Third and Fourth Republics) – are seemingly among the most ideological. By the same token, some of the most consensual party systems – postwar Germany, and most of Scandinavia – seem to have been relatively free of patronage concerns. There are, of course, countries where patronage practices are rampant and party ideology relatively weak (e.g., Canada and Ireland), but the relationship between these two political phenomena seems inconsistent at best.[43]

A number of reasons may be surmised to explain why patronage does not always suppress ideological concerns within a party. First, patronage is more likely to affect policy making than electioneering. The latter is likely to remain an ideological activity for the basic reason that party leaders cannot buy enough votes among the general public under conditions of extended suffrage to swing an election; they simply do not have enough jobs and perquisites to go around. As Aristotle observed, the many are less corruptible than the few.[44] Second, patronage networks offer a way to build party organization. If we assume that party activists

---

41. Scott (1972: 108).
42. Wilson (1973/1995: 6) affirms: "To the extent a party member is motivated by material rewards, he will be indifferent to, or at least not make his party work contingent on, the policy positions of either the party or its candidates." See also Neumann (1956: 400). On the influence of patronage within the American parties, see also Epstein (1986: 137), Lowi (1985: ch 2), Shefter (1994), and various works on nineteenth-century party history cited throughout this book.
43. For discussion of all these cases, see Heidenheimer et al. (1989) and Kristinsson (1996).
44. The classic treatment of this point is Namier (1965).

– even those receiving compensation for their participation – are driven by purposive as well as material goals, then it may be concluded that a patronage party has an extensive constituency of ideologues whom it must in some way satisfy.

The Absence of Socialism

The question what to make of the absence of socialism in America has bedeviled scholars ever since this absence became conspicuous in the early twentieth century.[45] There are really two questions that must be addressed: the first concerns the Democratic party's relationship to European socialism (Is it different?), and the second concerns what we are to conclude from this comparison (Is there less ideological polarization in the United States than in polities with large socialist parties?). I shall argue yes to the first question and no to the second.

Some writers, many of them socialists themselves, have argued that the failure of socialism has had only a marginal impact on political life in America. Viewing its appeal to labor constituencies and its embrace of the welfare state, these writers have described the New Deal Democratic party as the functional equivalent of social democracy abroad.[46] This argument is difficult to sustain, however, if one relies on party platforms and speeches for evidence of party ideology. There simply was no American counterpart to the rhetoric pounded out by parties that were avowedly, and for a time unapologetically, socialist. Even the British Labour party – a moderate party, by all accounts – was situated considerably to the left of the American Democratic party. In 1931, for example, Labour's manifesto read: "The capitalist system has broken down. . . . Socialism provides the only solution for the evils resulting from unregulated competition and the domination of vested interests. It presses for the extension of publicly-owned industries and services operated solely in the interests of the people. It works for the substitution of coordinated planning for the anarchy of individualistic enterprise."[47]

Perhaps the most obvious policy separating European leftists from American Democrats through most of the twentieth century was the former's repeated call for the nationalization of basic industries. Bryan, upon his return from Europe in 1906, proposed nationalizing the rail-

---

45. For evaluations of the classic debate about American exceptionalism – from which the question of American party conflict takes many of its cues – see sources listed in footnote 21 of this chapter.
46. See, e.g., Greenstone (1977), Harrington (1972), Lipset (1977), Mowry (1968), Shannon (1968), and Vaudagna (1987).
47. "Call to Action," reprinted in the *Times* (London) (10/10/1931).

roads but was quickly forced to recant by the intense public outcry registered in (orchestrated by?) the country's newspapers. Al Smith's call for public utilities in 1928 was a mere shadow of European arguments for public-sector capitalism. (Public utilities, for example, were to be operated by semiautonomous boards of directors, not regular state bureaucracies.) Only in 1995, after decades of internal agony, did Labour finally remove the clause in its constitution calling for the "common ownership of the means of production, distribution and exchange."[48]

So, does the Democratic party share the same basic outlook and policies of left parties abroad? Clearly not.[49] What, then, are we to make of socialism's absence? Without a viable socialist party, the American party system appears to many writers bereft of meaningful conflict – two bourgeois parties wandering distractedly through a field of liberal values. The absence of socialism and the general weakness of class conflict in America thus becomes perhaps the strongest piece of evidence in the "nonideology" argument.[50]

There are problems with this line of reasoning, however. To begin

---

48. *New York Times* (3/14/1995 and 4/30/1995). The removal of Clause IV was part of an ongoing deradicalization process within the Labour party, a process that mirrored developments in socialist parties across the democratic world. Yet the Labour party's point of arrival in the 1990s is still considerably to the left of the American Democratic party.

49. This, indeed, is the majority view, one shared by Engels, Sombart, Hartz, and most commentators. See Laslett and Lipset (1974) for a summary of these positions.

50. Some of this confusion stems from varying understandings of what it means to be an "ideological" party. Thus, Wilson (1973/1995: 102) writes: "An ideological party need not . . . be Marxian . . . , but in American history most parties professing a systematic world view and a radical critique of existing institutions have in fact been Marxian." One might respond that "radical critiques of existing institutions" have in fact emanated from the major American parties at various points in American history – from both parties during the nineteenth century and from the Democrats during their Populist phase. If the Republican party's opposition to slavery and the Democratic party's opposition to the Union are not "radical" enough – as some might still maintain – then one must, I think, also brand *most* parties in democratic party systems as nonideological. Setting such a high definitional threshold for what constitutes ideology may be considered a purely "semantic" argument. However, if we banish ideology from the discussion of mainstream party politics, what shall we use to account for the values, beliefs, and issue-positions taken by those parties? Clearly, there is an affective-cognitive dimension to party behavior, and "belief system" functions awkwardly to convey that meaning. The sub-rosa argument in Wilson's discussion is perhaps the more important one (I intuit): only parties that reject *capitalism* are to be considered fully "ideological." This understanding of ideology, although common (and usually unstated), is even less helpful in understanding evaluative dimensions of party politics because, once again, we are unable to talk about such dimensions except for the fairly narrow case of Marxian parties.

with, the mere presence of a party with socialist ideals says nothing about the degree of ideological differentiation within that system. Sweden, with one of the world's most successful socialist parties, has often been noted for its pragmatic, consensual political style (see the following discussion). Evidently, the question of conflict rests on the positions of the major parties *relative to each other.*

I would argue that although the Democratic party has been to the right of its ideological cousins in the Anglo-European world, the Republican party has been to the right of *its* ideological cousins on most redistributive questions since the 1920s. True, themes of antistatism, individualism, and capitalism could be found in party rhetoric on both sides of the Atlantic. Yet, with the possible exception of campaigns led by Winston Churchill and Margaret Thatcher, the Tories were never as vitriolic or as convinced in their neoliberalism as were their American counterparts. In 1929, the Conservative manifesto boasted, "During our tenure of office we have carried through a great programme of social welfare."[51] In 1974, the party advocated "a Government that is strong in order to protect the weak."[52] Such sentiments rarely passed Republican lips. Tories were visceral opponents of "socialism" (the term they preferred for the stance of their Labour opponents). But so were Republicans, and they had no socialist opponents – yet another sign, perhaps, that being conservative in the United States signified a more extreme ideological commitment than it did elsewhere in the Anglo-European world.[53]

Thus, although the absence of socialism has clearly mattered, it has not mattered in the way Hartz and others imagined. Briefly and schematically put, party conflict on redistributive matters in the United States has taken place further to the right on the ideological spectrum but with at least as much space separating the major parties as in most other party systems. The absence of socialism – which *did* make American party ideology exceptional by the end of the 1920s – did not mean the

---

51. Craig (1975: 76).   52. Craig (1975: 377).

53. The proof, one might argue, is to be found in public policy outcomes. The government of Britain, where public-sector spending is considerably higher than in the United States (relative to each country's GNP), has been dominated by the Conservative party for (roughly) sixty of the last one hundred years. During that same period, Republicans controlled the presidency for sixty years, the House of Representatives for thirty-six years, and the Senate for forty-two years. In other words, Britain has developed a more redistributive welfare state *with* a more successful conservative party. Of course, many factors other than political parties influence a country's level of public-sector spending (Cameron 1978; Hicks and Swank 1992; Rose 1980; Roubini and Sachs 1989). Even so, it is difficult to explain this contrast without concluding that the Tories have been more moderate than the Republicans on social policy matters.

absence of ideological conflict. The major American parties have found a great deal to debate in their centuries-long existence, even if the expropriation of capital by the state has been scrupulously excluded from that debate.

Political Culture

Finally, there are those who argue that American partisan cultures are weak because the national political culture is so strong. Louis Hartz's *Liberal Tradition in America*, still perhaps the most influential book on American politics – nearly half a century after its original publication – argues that American politics has been constrained by the recurring thought-patterns of the American democrat. Born equal (i.e., classless), Americans have remained egalitarian without developing any fondness for the state. Children of Locke, Americans have remained passionate, yet wholly unconscious, Lockeans. Although acknowledging the virulence, and the more-than-occasional violence, of political conflict in American political life, Hartz argues that such conflict has been contained within the parameters of an all-embracing liberal tradition. There is a liberalism of the left ("petit-bourgeois") and a liberalism of the right ("big, propertied"), but no socialism and no Tory conservatism. Conflict, yes; ideology, no.[54]

But how coherent is the culture of politics in the United States? Rogers Smith, in a recent treatment of the subject, argues that American politics is grounded not just in liberal values but also in civic republicanism and Americanism. Smith thus proposes a pluralistic political culture composed of three very independent paradigms.[55] The situation may be more complicated still. A glance at the enormous literature pertaining to American political culture reveals that this culture has been described as tolerant and xenophobic, multicultural and racist, pragmatic and idealistic, self-interested and moralistic, individualistic and communitarian, progressive and traditional, majoritarian and minoritarian, nondenominational and deeply religious, nationalistic and universalistic, egalitarian and libertarian. One writer has gone so far as to declare that contradiction is the essence of American political culture.[56]

---

54. Hartz (1955: 14–15).   55. See Smith (1993).
56. See Kammen (1972/1980). The diversity and internal contradictions of American political structure have also been stressed by Ellis (1992), Huntington (1981), McClosky and Zaller (1984: 7), and Steinmo (1994: 110–11). It is interesting to note that other political cultures seem to suffer from internal hemorrhaging as well. Warwick (1990: 135) finds that English political culture has been described as "judicious admixtures of modernity and tradition, dignity and efficiency, pragmatism and principle, deference and participation, individualism and collectivism."

Whatever defines the values of American politics, this set of cultural markers seems a good deal more elusive today than it did to the 1950s generation of scholars and social critics. If such a revision (toward general murkiness) is in order, then it seems reasonable to suppose that American political culture has been a looser constraint on the development of party ideologies than was hitherto supposed. Arguably, there has been even more room for ideological improvisation in the New World than in countries with a single religious and ethnic identity and a longer historical tradition. In any case, it seems much too simple to imagine that the strength of a political culture varies directly with the strength of partisan cultures. Ideologies necessarily build upon a country's history and upon a widely shared understanding of that history. The Labour, Liberal, and Conservative parties are preeminently British, just as the Democratic and Whig-Republican parties are American. It is hard to see how it could be otherwise in a democracy, since all but the most antisystem parties will find it in their interest to identify themselves as bearers of that country's political tradition.[57]

The case of Sweden is illustrative. If judged by aggregate levels of taxing and spending, Sweden is undoubtedly one of the most redistributive regimes in the world. Because this paradise of equality was created by the Social Democratic party and the closely allied labor movement, party ideology has often been considered the key to Swedish politics. How, indeed, could one explain this extraordinary outcome without recourse to the ideas that animated this party – the democratic world's most successful socialist party?[58]

Yet the success of the Social Democrats in controlling the course of public policy and in establishing the terms of political debate might also be looked upon as an example of political *consensus* within Sweden. This party, by all accounts, enjoyed hegemonic status from the 1930s to the 1970s (and perhaps beyond). Hegemony, of course, presupposes a high level of agreement on fundamentals. It has often been noted that parties on the "right" (one uses the term with some hesitation in the context of Swedish politics) offered only weak dissent to policies that would have been anathema to most liberal and conservative parties elsewhere. What, then, did this cultural consensus consist of?

As summarized by Asard and Bennett, modern Swedish political culture revolves around the notion of the *folkhem*, the people's home. This, the writers claim, is "the great metaphor of twentieth-century Swedish politics."[59] The metaphor itself apparently stems from the writings of

---

57. For a discussion of the interaction of consensual and partisan elements of British political culture, see Beer (1969).
58. See, e.g., Korpi (1983) and Lewin (1988).   59. Asard and Bennett (1997: 91).

various liberals and conservatives at the turn of the century, at which point it carried distinctly conservative – and nationalistic – overtones. In the 1920s, as Social Democratic (SAP) leaders looked to shed their Marxist vocabulary and to enhance their electoral appeal, the concept of the *folkhem* seemed to offer the party a way to establish links with Swedish history and culture without shedding its commitment to social equality. The classic statement on the matter was issued in 1928 in a speech by Per Albin Hansson:

> The basis of the home is togetherness and common feeling. The good home does not consider anyone as privileged or unappreciated; it knows no special favourites and no stepchildren. There no one looks down upon anyone else, there no one tries to gain advantage at another's expense, and the stronger do not suppress and plunder the weaker. In the good home equality, consideration, co-operation, and helpfulness prevail. Applied to the great people's and citizens' home this would mean the breaking down of all the social and economic barriers that now divide citizens into the privileged and the unfortunate, into rulers and subjects, into rich and poor, the glutted and the destitute, the plunderers and the plundered.[60]

As Asard and Bennett note, "The language of the Social Democrats established itself as the political rhetoric of the land, contributing to the SAP's long reign of power and replacing the former liberal rhetoric in the process."[61] In short, if one looks at the ideological (rhetorical and programmatic) field before and after the 1920s, one discovers a *narrowing* of vision. In the postwar period, Klingemann and associates note that "Swedish partisan differences, for all their apparent drama, do not seem to run deep." Indeed, "deep divisions would hardly be expected in a country with virtually no minorities, one religion, and a generally wealthy populace."[62]

Thus, the world's most socialistic democracy may also be one of the world's most consensual democracies. This does not mean, of course, that ideology is of no account in Sweden; it means, however, that ideology is not as differentiated (between parties) as the "European" model supposes. In the Swedish case, as in the American, the line between party ideology and political culture is not always easy to discern.

The Party in Government

Having discussed the probable role of ideology within campaigns, I turn now to the role of ideology in *governance*. Does political rhetoric – the

---

60. Quoted in Asard and Bennett (1997: 93).   61. Asard and Bennett (1997: 95).
62. Klingemann et al. (1994: 261). See also Anton (1969), Elder, Thomas, and Arter (1982), Heclo and Madsen (1987), Lijphart (1977: 111), Tilton (1992), and Tingsten (1941/1973).

ideology of the campaign – direct the behavior of partisans once they are elected to public office, or is it, as many lay observers assume, merely "rhetoric"?

Upon his nomination for the vice presidency in 1832, Martin Van Buren – the chief architect of the fledgling Democratic party – was asked by constituents to clarify his opinions vis-à-vis the pressing issues of the day. He responded:

> The right of those you represent, to be informed of my opinions upon these interesting subjects, as derived from the position in which the favor of my fellow citizens has placed me, is undoubted, and in cheerfully complying with their request, I have only to regret, that the inconvenience of the situation in which it finds me, consequent upon the hurry and confusion attending the further prosecution of my journey, and the importance, to the fulfillment of the objects of your constituents, of as little delay as possible in the transmission of the communication, preclude anything like an elaborate discussion of the subjects under consideration, if indeed such a course would, under more favorable circumstances, be desirable to you.[63]

Plenty of anecdotal evidence may be gathered for the "mere rhetoric" perspective on party ideology.[64] (It is worth noting that Van Buren did go on to address the major questions of the day – internal improvements, states' rights, tariffs, and so forth.)

There is, in any case, a more serious objection to the notion that ideology matters in American political life. The problem, many writers would claim, is not that American politicians are cagey or insincere but, rather, that they lack the necessary political power to fulfill their promises. The Democrats and Republicans qualify as two of the weakest and most fragmented political party organizations in the democratic world. Party membership is diffuse, national party organization ephemeral, splits between the different wings (presidential, congressional, state, local) persistent, and legislative cohesion weak. Party *ideology* may exist, but where, one might reasonably ask, is the party? In the absence of strong parties such as are common in parliamentary democracies, it has been difficult for many writers to conceive of ideology as an important influence on public policy.

Yet a substantial body of contemporary work has matched each party's promise with its subsequent performance and has found the con-

---

63. Van Buren, open letter, 10/4/1832, Owasco, Cayuga County, NY (*New York Evening Post* 10/18/1832).
64. "In making his appeal to the voters," writes Peter Odegard (1930: 159–60), "the candidate relies largely on vague generalities and sheer 'bunk.' He promises everything. When his opponent asks embarrassing questions, he either does not reply at all or changes the subject."

nection to be quite intimate. In operationalizing the concept of party ideology, scholars have generally relied on party platforms and campaign speeches – the same set of indicators used in this study – which are then correlated with legislative outcomes (or fiscal outcomes) in succeeding years.[65] Jeff Fishel, for example, finds that five recent presidents have "submitted legislation or signed executive orders that are broadly consistent with about two-thirds of their campaign pledges," and Michael Krukones's study of presidential campaigns and administrations from 1912 to 1980 reaches similar conclusions.[66] By and large, presidents mean what they say on the campaign trail. Studies of party ideology based on voting behavior in Congress and in state legislatures during the nineteenth century also show clear differences between the parties, differences that corresponded to broader ideological rifts.[67] Comparative studies of the promise-performance question reiterate the picture drawn by studies focused solely on the United States. Indeed, the most systematic study to date concludes that the promise-performance connection in the United States is slightly *stronger* than the mean among the ten Anglo-European countries under investigation.[68]

One could stop here. However, to make these claims is to set forth a set of empirical facts with very little theoretical support. Party ideology seems to matter, but parties evidently do not. Indeed, one of the principal reasons that ideology has not been taken seriously in the study of American politics is that those ideologies do not seem to have at their disposal vehicles sturdy enough to take them where they wish to go. No quantity of empirical studies is likely to overturn this view of things unless a plausible explanation can be offered for why ideology might matter in the fragmented context of American politics. Here, as elsewhere, theory is necessary before evidence can become fully persuasive. The remainder of this section is therefore devoted to rethinking the question of how, and why, party ideology might have an effect on the American policy-making process.[69]

65. For work on party platforms, see Budge and Hofferbert (1990), Ginsberg (1976), Monroe (1983), and Pomper (1967, 1980). For work focused specifically on tariff positions taken by the American parties in the late nineteenth and early twentieth century, see Epstein and O'Halloran (1996).
66. See Fishel (1985: 38) and Krukones (1984).
67. See Alexander (1967), Ershkowitz and Shade (1971), Gerring (forthcoming), and Silbey (1967a).
68. See Klingemann et al. (1994: 54). See also Blais, Blake, and Dion (1996), Budge, Robertson, and Hearl (1987), Cameron (1984), Castles (1982), Hibbs (1977), Keman (1984), King (1981), Royed (1996), and Tufte (1978).
69. A number of the points I will make pertaining to party cohesion scores are discussed in Loynd (1997). I am grateful to the author for sharing his research.

One caveat is in order before I begin. Most of the following arguments pertain to the state of policy making in the latter twentieth century. As organizational entities, nineteenth-century parties were considerably stronger – and policy making more party-centered – than is currently the case. Thus, we do not need to strain for an explanation for why ideology mattered in the "party period" of American history. The postwar era, however, presents a formidable challenge.

Explaining the Promise-Performance Connection

Let us begin with the observation that parties are weak in the American legislature. In Britain, the perennial exemplar of party government, an "in" party governs, and an "out" party opposes. After the franchise was extended and cabinet government established, parties in the House of Commons developed extraordinarily high levels of voting cohesion. In the postwar period, an average of 89 percent of all (whipped) votes in the Commons saw all Conservative members lined up against all Labour members – maximal cohesion and maximal conflict, in other words. In the remaining votes, dissent was likely to concern only a few wayward MPs. Consequently, an average of 93 percent of all bills introduced by the governing party were enacted.[70]

Things were quite otherwise within the American Congress. Party cohesion, although slightly higher in recent years, remains lower than virtually anywhere else in the democratic world. Committees, although more responsive to party caucuses today than in the past, are still highly independent of party leadership. Since committees control the flow of legislation to the floor, this is a fact of no small importance. In the Senate, a wide array of tactics may be used by recalcitrant members to stave off or alter unwanted legislation. In both houses, members are thought to respond primarily to local, rather than national, demands. In sum, the U.S. Congress would seem to be one of the most fragmented legislatures in the Anglo-American world.[71]

70. See Rose (1986). Although there has been some loss of party strength in the last several decades, Rose notes that this strength is still far above that found in the U.S. Congress. For party voting in the Commons during the nineteenth century, see Berrington (1967–68) and Cox (1987). For further data on party strength in European parliaments, see Peters (1997: 79).

71. The only significant exception to this two-century pattern occurred during the Reed-Cannon interregnum at the turn of the century; yet, even at this high point of party government, Henry Jones Ford would write in his classic text on party politics, "Congress represents locality; the President represents the nation" (1898/1967; xv). Epstein, in his magisterial study of the parties (1986; 85), concludes, "The presidential party

Yet appearances can be deceiving. Apparently erratic voting patterns within the U.S. Congress probably exaggerate the disarray within the party caucuses, just as cohesive voting patterns within parliamentary systems exaggerate the unity of these parties. Cox and McCubbins argue that if one counts only those votes on which each party's leadership takes a clear stand – exempting, that is, "free" votes in the Congress, just as such votes are ignored in calculating party cohesion scores for European parliaments – party cohesion in the House of Representatives reaches more respectable levels.[72]

A more important objection to the standard view of Congress concerns what happens *off* the floor. In the United States, as abroad, most of the important decisions are made long before a bill reaches a floor vote. It is at the exploratory stages – while in committee or before a commission – that legislation is hammered into shape or discarded. Do parties play an important role in policy disputes at the committee level? Recent work on congressional policy making has argued persuasively that the committee process of hearings, deliberations, and markup is a *partisan* process in which committees respond to cues from each party's leadership and caucus.[73] Of course, committees in other legislatures around the world are also likely to be dominated by the majority party (or parties). However, most descriptions of the policy-making process in multiparty systems emphasize the consensual dynamics of this process. Indeed, behind-the-scenes policy making in European democracies may be, on the whole, *less* partisan than in the United States.[74]

None of these patterns are reflected in votes on final passage. The salient characteristic of cross-party compromise in European democracies is the way that such compromises are shielded from public view. Committee deliberations are generally held behind closed doors, and official votes (within the committee) are rare. A revealing episode in Swedish party politics is related by a former Conservative party chairman,

---

is a more coherent *national* phenomenon than is any other kind of American party. Congressional parties are national too, but each is so diverse, given the considerable independence of its members in relating to their separate constituencies, that it unites only for limited purposes." See also Mayhew (1974) and Arnold (1990). For a good review of this literature, see Cox and McCubbins (1993: 1–14). For longitudinal studies of party cohesion, see Hurley and Wilson (1989) on the Senate, and Clubb and Traugott (1977) on the House. On the importance of party cohesion, see Corrado (1996) and Wattenberg (1991).

72. See Cox and McCubbins (1991).
73. See Cox and McCubbins (1993) and Kiewiet and McCubbins (1991).
74. See Hine (1982; 1993) on Italy; Anton (1969), Heclo and Madsen (1987), and Steinmo (1993) on Sweden; Arter (1984) on Nordic parliaments generally; Hughes (1962) on Switzerland; and Katzenstein (1987) on Germany.

who recalls a conversation he had in 1984, while leading the opposition, with the Minister of Finance: "When I said that there are some things which we agree on, he [the Minister] said that 'we agree on quite a lot, but we are not allowed to show that.' "[75]

In the American Congress, by contrast, the sausage-production machine is in full view. Compromise, where it occurs, occurs in front of the public, for committee hearings are open and well attended by interest-group representatives and the media, and roll call votes are common. Durr, Gilmour, and Wolbrecht note:

> Not only does Congress produce a great deal of controversy, it does so in an exceptionally open and public way. Virtually all deliberations of Congress are open to the public and many of them to television cameras. When its members disagree, they do so as visibly as they can, seeking publicity for themselves and to discredit their rivals and opponents. As proposals are shaped in Congress, every disagreement is magnified and broadcast, so that when the bargaining and amending are done, the finished product appears not as a coherent whole but as a patchwork of compromises.[76]

In short, the operation of the American legislature – both on and off the floor – accentuates the disarray of the legislative parties. In most parliamentary systems, dissension within party caucuses is handled discreetly; compromises are reached so as to maintain party unity on the final vote. Squabbling is done in private, and calm serenity obtains in public. These systems are able to accommodate a great deal of cross-party compromising without bringing the notion of "standing for something" into question, for parties will show up on different sides of the aisle to shout at each other – or at least to vote against each other – in parliament. In the final tally, members of a party stand shoulder to shoulder.[77]

Third, voting cohesion, at best, is an intermediate variable between

---

75. Quoted in Asard and Bennett (1997: 215).
76. Durr, Gilmour, and Wolbrecht (1997: 182).
77. Bert Rockman (1997: 46) notes: "Resistance in parliamentary systems tends to come early and to be decisive at that stage and less decisive when a matter moves to public debate. In the United States, resistance tends to accumulate and, therefore, to develop later in the process and to become more decisive as matters move to public debate." Thus, the observer of a parliamentary system gains the impression of party ideology at work, while being spared the realities of logrolling, favor trading, and party dissension. In the United States, of course, low levels of party cohesion give the general public the impression that parties are weak and ineffectual. For the media, the attraction of the dissident – "Fighting Bob" LaFollette facing down the Republican stalwarts, or "Cosmic Bob" Kerrey making up his mind on the president's budget – has been irresistible. The same incentives are in operation elsewhere, of course, but in most parliamentary systems there are few dissidents to pillory (or deify). (On Kerrey's endless budget deliberations, see *New York Times* 8/7/1993: 1.)

party ideology and public policy. A party that votes together may be implementing party policy as stated in the platform, or it may be kowtowing to current public demand. Indeed, political systems with high levels of accountability are likely to encourage Downsian (median-voter) patterns of policy making, since both the constituents and the governing party are well aware of whom to praise or blame at the end of the party's term in office.

Fourth, weak party cohesion within the U.S. Congress does not necessarily countermand the influence of party ideology in determining vote *outcomes*. It is to be remembered that on many votes – particularly those of great policy significance – House and Senate party leaders have votes "in reserve." This means that a number of members of the winning side will have communicated to their leaders that if their vote is absolutely needed to ensure victory, it can be counted on. Such a tactic allows leaders a way to win floor votes without compromising the reelection prospects of their members (whose constituents, let us say, disapprove of the party line).[78] In short, congressional leaders with few carrots and sticks at their disposal (relative to their counterparts in parliamentary democracies) still find ways – devious ways, to be sure – to achieve party governance.

Fifth, the fragmented nature of the two houses of Congress, particularly of the Senate, may have no effect on each party's ideological center of gravity, since those on the left of a party's caucus are presumably balanced by those on the right. For every Olympia Snowe, one generally finds a Jesse Helms. In other words, a more centralized system of party nominations – as obtains, for example, in Britain – might yield a slightly more homogeneous set of legislators on either side of the aisle; it would *not* necessarily yield a differently situated set of party ideologies. Indeed, a median-legislator theory of policy making within each party's caucus yields identical results in strong-party and weak-party regimes.

This brings us to a fundamental fact about two-party systems. Each side is likely to remain relatively stable, despite shifts of adherents (voters or legislators) from side to side, because of the fact that dissidents have only one route of exit – the other side. Most adherents, in other words, are effectively captives of the party they inhabit. Only those near the center of the ideological spectrum can contemplate apostasy. But a movement of centrists from one side to the other is unlikely to change the basic ideological configuration of the party system; though the spectrum may move

---

78. See King and Zeckhauser (1997). This strategy seemed to be much in evidence on the Democratic side in votes on term-limit amendments in 1997.

slightly to the left or right, the distance separating the parties is likely to remain constant, and each party's core values will remain intact.

In a multiparty system, by contrast, all but the most extreme partisans will find *several* routes of escape. These routes are more ideologically acceptable, since the neighboring parties within a multiparty system occupy positions that are relatively close together (the "crowding" phenomenon noted earlier). In Germany, for example, the trip from the liberal camp (the FDP) to the conservative camp (CDU-CSU) is not nearly so far as the trip from Democracy to Republicanism in the United States. Under this set of circumstances, party leadership, party organization, and voting cohesion within the legislature are absolutely essential to preserving a sense of identity among the participants. In other words, voting cohesion *matters* in a multiparty system in ways that it does not within two-party systems, for the simple reason that in two-party systems defectors are more easily tolerated. A war fought on a single front requires a lower threshold of organization than a war with multiple fronts.[79]

Two-partyism has yet another, more obvious effect on the viability of party ideology in the legislative process. With the purest two-party monopoly of any democracy in the world (excluding microstates),[80] the American party platform operates as a "contract" or "mandate" to an extent unimaginable within multiparty systems. Where coalition government is the rule, a party's platform is *necessarily* compromised on the way to becoming public law. Indeed, such compromises may reach across the government/opposition divide, fragmenting policy-making power and further weakening the connection between promise and performance. Multiple coalition partners, argues George Tsebelis, mean that each partner has an effective veto over changes in policy, leading to a situation in which the most likely policy outcome is a reiteration, or slight alteration, of the status quo.[81] Empirical work by Huber and Powell shows that policy makers in two-party systems are more likely to deviate from median-voter demands than are policy makers within multiparty systems, indicating once again that partisanship matters quite a lot in the American case.[82]

---

79. Following Hirschman (1970), one might say that two-party systems tend to register intraparty dissent through *voice* (because, for many, there are no attractive exit options), and multiparty systems through *exit*. Party leaders in both party systems are, of course, equally concerned with vote getting; the point is, losing votes has fewer ideological consequences in a two-party system. (I am indebted to Howard Reiter for reminding me of this.)

80. See Lijphart (1984).   81. See Tsebelis (1995).

82. See Huber and Powell (1994).

This line of argument becomes stronger still if one considers the factors impinging upon policy makers from *outside* the political system. Although the matter is difficult to operationalize, it is generally recognized that the degree of policy-making sovereignty enjoyed by a nation-state – the ability to conduct its own affairs on its own terms – will affect the ability of policy makers to deliver on their campaign promises.[83] Small countries with a high degree of trade dependence, especially if hampered by transnational confederations (such as the European Union), are much less able to set the terms of their fiscal, monetary, and security policies.[84] Policy making in a small state is a largely reactive affair, and this reactiveness means that party ideology is likely to be sacrificed to the practical realities imposed by world markets and world politics. A megastate like the United States, with the world's largest economy, regional hegemony through most of its history, and few "entangling alliances" that it cannot control, is not as susceptible to external pressures. It might be added that the objective features of American hegemony (economic, territorial, and military) have been reinforced by features of American political culture emphasizing the uniqueness of America, the dangers of foreign involvements, and the need to preserve American independence. The twin doctrines of "isolationism" and "exceptionalism" encourage American policy makers to place domestic needs ahead of foreign exigencies.

Conclusion

As a general formulation, the strength of party ideology in the policy-making process of a given country may be thought of as the product of factors internal and external to the policy process. The endogenous factors revolve around the extent to which a given polity exemplifies the paradigm of party government, or majoritarian democracy. The central issue here is *centralization of power*, and the most important institutional features of centralization, I submit, are (1) the number of effective parties in the party system, (2) the internal cohesiveness (organizational strength) of those parties, and (3) the unity or disunity of the legislative and executive branches of government.[85] The exogenous variable in this

---

83. One possible way of operationalizing this variable would be to look at relative levels of trade dependency (see, e.g., Cameron 1978).
84. See Katzenstein (1985). To be sure, the United States is less autonomous than it was several decades ago, as is noted by Rose (1991). However, it still enjoys more room for policy maneuvering than any other democracy in the world.
85. Federalism, I would argue, affects policy making at the *implementation* stage more than at the legislative stage. Since promise-performance studies usually operationalize

equation concerns the degree to which a country enjoys policy-making sovereignty.

If this formulation is, in the main, an accurate appraisal of the factors leading to a strong promise-performance connection, it may be concluded that the United States occupies an *intermediate* position on this scale. The weakness of party organization and the fragmentation of government are mitigated by the small number of parties, their surreptitious control of policy-making channels, and the high degree of sovereignty enjoyed by the American state. It seems safe to assume, along these lines, that party ideology would matter even more under circumstances imposed by a Westminster system of government.[86] Even so, the goal of party government is much closer to a reality than people generally suppose.[87] It should be no surprise, therefore, that party programs, as articulated in party platforms and election speeches, serve as strong predictors of what will be accomplished by the party chosen to lead.

International Comparisons

Any argument in which the unit of analysis is a country rests – at least implicitly – on cross-national comparisons. This is certainly the case for arguments about party ideology in America. Here, as we have seen, the contrast is usually "Europe," the home of communism, socialism, Christian democracy, monarchism, and fascism – the home, that is, of properly "ideological" parties.

It should be noted at the outset that if *non*-European democracies are brought into the picture, the United States appears much closer to the norm in this regard. (Coherent, differentiated, and enduring ideologies are not generally considered to be a hallmark of party life in other Anglo-American polities, in Latin America, in East Asia, or in Africa.) In turning to the European cases, two preliminary concessions are in order. First, there was probably less ideological space separating major parties in the United States than in Germany during the Weimar Republic, Italy during most periods, and France until recently. Second, party politics

policy making at the legislative stage, federalism can be construed a subordinate factor. For discussion of these and other factors, see Lijphart (1984).

86. This is the general finding of Royed (1996). Since presidential success on roll call votes in Congress is primarily the product of the partisan composition of the legislature (Bond and Fleisher 1990; Edwards 1989), one would expect presidential party ideology to have greater effect under circumstances of unified party control – a situation approximating the circumstance of "party government" in a Westminster system.

87. See Cox and McCubbins (1993: 277) and Klingemann et al. (1994: 154).

was exceptionally highly charged during the interwar years in most European polities – to an extent not attained in the United States since perhaps the Civil War.

Yet these three cases, and the interwar period more generally, have received more than their due. Indeed, the immense quantity of academic and popular-culture work devoted to Germany, Italy, and France, and to the fascist and communist movements of these countries, has overwhelmed our knowledge of other countries and other time periods in modern European history. It seems to have been forgotten, for example, that not all countries succumbed to antidemocratic temptations or to extreme ideologies. Arguably, were it not for the intrusion of Nazism, most European polities would have enjoyed a continuous democratic political history from World War I to the present, and most would have been dominated by parties of the modern left or right.

Regrettably, there has been little cross-national research of an empirical nature into these matters, What we know about party ideology is derived mostly from country-specific studies, like the present work. A few intrepid writers, however, have attempted to quantify party-ideological distance across party systems. Needless to say, these studies deserve our close attention.

The work of John Thomas begins with the hypothesis that party conflict in Western democracies has been declining over the past several decades (commonly referred to as the end-of-ideology thesis). An extensive coding of primary and secondary materials on political parties in Australia, Austria, France, Great Britain, Italy, Japan, New Zealand, Sweden, the United States, and West Germany leads Thomas to conclude that issue-differences among parties in most polities have declined – but only slightly – since the interwar period. More interesting for our purposes is the finding that this decline is not at all noticeable in the United States, where party differences have remained at moderate levels throughout the twentieth century. Data from Thomas's study indicate that issue-conflict in the United States was significantly lower than the mean among these countries during the years 1910–1919, slightly lower in the 1950s and 1960s, and slightly *higher* in the 1970s. With the exception of the epoch of World War I, when European polities were for a moment sharply polarized, this research seems to show issue-conflict to be at roughly comparable levels on both sides of the Atlantic.[88]

---

88. See Thomas (1979). Issues observed include nationalization of industry, government roles in economic planning, the distribution of wealth, the provision of social welfare, the secularization of society, the extension of the franchise, the electoral system, party

Klingemann and associates, on the basis of an enormous cross-national coding of party platforms in the postwar period, offer an even stronger argument for *non*exceptionalism, which I shall quote at some length:

> The analyses presented here suggest not only that the Democrats and Republicans are reasonably cohesive internally, when compared with political parties in other systems, but also that their platforms are quite clearly differentiated from each other in an ideologically consistent fashion. . . . The U.S. parties, contrary to the "Tweedledum and Tweedledee" thesis, have maintained enduring ideological differences. . . . A comparison . . . with the British ideal of the critics or with the presumably more sharply delineated German parties shows no less difference or distinctiveness in the United States than elsewhere. In fact, U.S. Democrats appear to have been more ideologically consistent, if not downright stubborn, than the leftist parties in most other countries.[89]

The American party system has puzzled observers because, in one way or another, it does not seem to conform to established Anglo-European models. There is indeed much to be said for the exceptionalist thesis. The nonclass basis of politics, the two-party monopoly, the structure of the American parties, the absence of party government, the absence of socialism, and the character of the political culture all seem quite different from parallel phenomena in other Western democracies. None of these features, however – nor others that are clearly not unique to the United States – should be interpreted as *anti*-ideological. In short, there

---

government, and governmental centralization. It should be noted that this study is not free of methodological difficulties. Thomas's reliance on secondary literature, for example, raises the possibility that the study reflects standard wisdom but does not provide an independent test of that standard wisdom.

89. Klingemann et al (1994: 138–40). Naturally, the literature is not unanimous in declaring American parties ideological. A study conducted by Castles and Mair (1984) shows less issue-space separating the American parties than parties in other Anglo-European party systems. However, several methodological objections can be made to this conclusion (which, it should be noted, the authors themselves do not state explicitly). First, the study depends upon evaluations by area specialists. Although knowledgeable on a single country or region, area specialists may not be in the best position to judge how one party system compares with others. They may, in other words, simply reiterate standard wisdom. Second, distance space is judged by classifying parties across a left/right spectrum divided into ultraleft, moderate left, center, moderate right, and ultraright categories. Here, the difficulty is that the meaning of these terms is country-specific: what is "ultraleft" in one setting may be "left" in another. Other studies based on expert assessments are subject to similar difficulties. See, e.g., de Swaan (1973), Dodd (1976), Huber and Inglehart (1995), Laver and Hunt (1992), and Taylor and Laver (1973).

is simply no reason to suppose that the American parties are structurally immune to developing coherent programs when facing the general electorate nor to implementing those programs once elected to office.

True, the bounds of thinkable thought are more conservative in the United States than in most countries; but they are not narrower. We must not confuse the rightward drift of American political culture with the rejection of ideology. The absence of socialism means that party conflict has taken place on one end of the ideological spectrum in the twentieth century; it does not mean that such conflict has been any less intense.

American political culture might be thought of as a large, rambling mansion, one generally undergoing some sort of reconstruction. Ideologies are the blueprints, and political parties one of the primary instruments, with which this reconstruction is periodically carried out. The following chapters relate the story of these changing and contrasting blueprints.

PART II

The Whig-Republican Party

3

The National Epoch (1828–1924)

Notwithstanding the organizational death of one party and its replacement by another, a civil war virtually without precedent in modern Anglo-European history, and several realignments of partisan voting allegiances, the evidence collected in this study suggests that a fairly consistent view of the political world was carried over from the party of Clay to the party of Lincoln to the party of Calvin Coolidge, the last bearer of American Whiggism.

What did this ideology consist of? I argue that these parties embodied a view of politics and society best summarized by the appellation National. National Republicans embraced laborers as well as capitalists within a broader framework valorizing *work* and *social harmony*. They were *mercantilists*, believing that the state had a particularly important role to play in ensuring economic development. They were *statists*, believing in strong government and the dignity of government service, and believing that good government occurred when the voice of the masses was properly channeled through institutions, rather than directly expressed. They were a *party of order*, inveighing against the dangers of unrestrained individualism, violence, and parochialism. They were *Yankee Protestants*, believing that human beings had a responsibility to reform themselves and to reform society. They were, finally, *Nationalists*, believers in the preeminence of American interests and American ideals.

The Value of Work and the Necessity of Social Harmony

In 1844, a Whig party pamphlet forthrightly declared, "In this country, labor, since our independence was acquired, always has been and still is, not only an original and fundamental, but a controlling power in society, and in the state. We are characteristically and distinctively a nation of workers. . . . If no interruption should take place in its progress, it will be the true Millenium [sic] of labor."[1] "I believe we should look after and protect our American workingmen; therefore I am a Republican," declared Benjamin Harrison four decades later.[2] Eighty years later still, Coolidge offered the following encomium to a group of labor leaders: "You come here as representative Americans. . . . I cannot think of anything that represents the American people as a whole so adequately as honest work. . . . We are proud of work and ashamed of idleness. . . . All work is ennobling and all workers are ennobled. . . . America recognizes no aristocracy save those who work. . . . We never had a government under our Constitution that was not put into office by the votes of the toilers."[3] From the 1830s to the 1920s, Whigs and Republicans heralded their party as the party of work and the natural home of the workingman. Regardless of how the party's record may look to present-day observers, it is important to underline the fact that to party leaders – and, if their votes are any indication, to a majority of working-class electors – the National Republican party was the party of labor.

Republican party organizers actively courted working-class constituencies with pamphlets like *McKinley on Labor*, issued by the Republican National Committee during the 1896 election and composed solely of the candidate's comments relating to the "labor question." Republican

1. Colton (1844: 103–6). The revered voice of Daniel Webster claimed that "Labor is one of the great elements of the prosperity of our country – not menial servile, or slave Labor, but manly, independent and intelligent Labor – that which accumulates property, maintains workshops, and helps to sustain the great Fabric of Government" (speech, 10/24/1848, in *New York Tribune* 10/26/1848). William Seward, the great Whig (and later Republican) leader from New York, stated, "There are two antagonistical elements of society in America – Freedom and Slavery. . . . Freedom insists on the emancipation and elevation of Labor: Slavery on its debasement and bondage" (speech, 10/26/1848, in *New York Tribune* 11/1/1848). The same logic that contrasted the free North with the enslaved South was extended to explain the essential difference between economic relationships in the New World and the Old: "In our case, the value of capital and the price of labor are not forced and fictitious, but they are the prerogative of freedom. In the case of Europe, the laborers are not a party in arranging the price of their task. They have no choice. It is *forced*" (Colton 1844: 46).
2. B. Harrison, speech, 10/6/1888 (Harrison 1892: 169).
3. Coolidge, speech, 9/1/1924 (Coolidge 1926: 75–76). Even in the midst of the Dollar Decade, party leaders went to great lengths to maintain the image of the Republican party as a party of labor. "Over and over again," writes historian Robert Zieger (1969: 14), "open shop enthusiasts sought to commit the party to an aggressively antiunion program, only to be put off with rhetoric and blandishments. In all the national elections of the 1920s Republicans made serious efforts to attract worker and union support and to mute expressions of hostility toward organized labor. . . . [A]ll but a handful of professional Republican politicians attempted to smooth the ragged edges of labor controversies and to steer clear of confrontations with aroused unionists."

orators were always eager to point out their support for the principle of collective bargaining – even if actual policy was often at odds with these goals.[4] The "free labor" doctrine served to underline the contrast between American and "Asiatic" countries. It was the fact that labor was free in America, and elsewhere enslaved, that justified the exclusion of foreign goods.[5] The key economic inducement offered to the urban working class was the promise of vigilant tariffs, which would exclude "unfair competition of contract labor from China" and from other countries with lower wage scales.[6] As we shall see, Republicans' primary argument in favor of high tariffs – and their repeated scare tactic against the Democrats throughout the nineteenth and early twentieth centuries – was "the spectre of low wages."[7] Not surprisingly, commitment to free labor was also a key component of the party's antagonism to slavery, that is, to the South's "forced labor" system of production (which will also be discussed here).[8]

To Democrats, "labor" meant primarily agricultural labor (in the nineteenth century) or manual labor more generally (in the twentieth) and did not characteristically refer to bankers, speculators, capitalists, or the rich. Democratic invocations of the work ethic were for the purpose of denigrating the "drones" of the mercantile classes, who lived idly off the labor of others. Republican laborism, on the other hand, included all types of labor and valorized the essential role of entrepreneurial and financial "labor" in the functioning of the economy. The National Republican version of the work ethic held that great property, far from being proof of idleness, was proof of industriousness.[9]

4. In any case, the success of labor organization was tied to the success of a protectionist trade policy. "The power of your labor organizations to secure increased wages is greatest," claimed Harrison, "when there is a large demand for the product you are making at fair prices" (speech, 9/27/1888, in Harrison 1892: 150).

5. "The Republican party," explained the 1884 party platform, "having its birth in a hatred of slave labor and a desire that all men may be truly free and equal, is unalterably opposed to placing our workingmen in competition with any form of servile labor, whether at home or abroad" (1884 platform, in Johnson 1958: 73). The specific reference here is to the "importation of contract labor," namely, the Chinese.

6. Blaine, acceptance letter, 7/15/1884 (Schlesinger 1973, 2: 1464).

7. B. Harrison, speech, 9/19/1888 (Harrison 1892: 133). See, as well, the 1888 party platform (Johnson 1958: 82) and Huston (1983).

8. See Foner (1970). Foner fails to note, however, that the free-labor doctrine characterized Whig-Republican ideology well before, and long after, the Civil War epoch.

9. "[T]he law of life is work," declared Theodore Roosevelt in the midst of McKinley's reelection bid, "and . . . work in itself, so far from being any hardship, is a great blessing. . . . The idler, rich or poor, is at best a useless, and generally a noxious, member of the community. . . . Woe to the man who seeks or trains up his children to seek

Poverty, through the same logic, was evidence of a lack of application.[10] Thus, although both parties drew upon the American work ethic, the doctrine performed quite different ideological and political functions, Democrats focusing on the idle rich, Whig-Republicans on the idle poor.

The political significance of laborism to the Republican party can hardly be overstated. Without it the party was susceptible to the repeated Democratic charge that it was a businessman's party. But as defenders of labor writ large, Republican orators managed to make credible their claim to represent a broad range of producer groups – those who supplied industrial labor, those who supplied agricultural labor, and those who supplied capital.[11] Labor was the grand equalizer, bestowing equal political and social status on all those who worked. "There is no royal blood among us," William McKinley reminded his audience. "There are no descended titles here; there is no way in the world of getting on and up, or earning money, except by work. There are just two ways in the United States to acquire money; one is to steal it, the other is to earn it, and the honorable way is to earn it; and you earn it by labor, either the labor of the hand or the labor of the brain."[12] It is a measure of the depth of the party's belief in the philosophy of work, and in the identity of America as a workers' republic, that women attending a rally held on McKinley's front porch were given the honorary appellation "working-women."[13]

Whig and Republican popularity among the working classes, however, was not simply a matter of manipulating symbols of status. There was, in addition, a straightforward appeal to material gain. "[Y]our interest in the [election] is apparent," Benjamin Harrison said to one of the many delegations of workingmen to visit his Ohio home. "The party that favors such discriminating duties as will develop American production and secure the largest amount of work for our American shops is the party whose policy will promote your interests."[14] During

idleness instead of the chance to do good work" (speech, 9/3/1900, in *New York Times* 9/4/1900).

10. "Wants make work, and work makes profit," read the popular *Junius Tracts*, by Calvin Colton. "This is the advantage of civilization over the natural state. It multiplies wants, sharpens invention, promotes industry, and thereby creates wealth" (Colton 1844: 42). "The mandate of God to his creature man is, Work!" (Colton 1844: 105). "Wherever labor is rising . . . we observe both the physical and moral healthfulness which it diffuses all around. It is good for man and woman to work, and neither can find the greatest comfort and happiness attainable in the human state, without employment. . . . Idleness is the curse of the human state, and diligent occupation, in a lawful and useful calling, the consummation of its blessedness" (ibid.).
11. Foner (1970: 15).   12. McKinley (1896b: 2).
13. B. Harrison, speech, 9/19/1888 (Harrison 1892: 133).
14. B. Harrison, speech, 9/15/1888 (Harrison 1892: 123).

the Civil War period, the party successfully pushed for the Morrill tariff, the Homestead Act, and the Morrill Land Grant College Act. "Together," writes James Huston, "these three pieces of legislation constituted a labor program, one that was designed specifically to create a better material condition for the worker."[15] Republican party leaders affirmed that "every workingman ought to have such wages as would not only yield him a decent and comfortable support for his family, and enable him to keep his children in school and out of the mill in their tender age, but would allow him to lay up against incapacity by sickness or accident, or for old age, some fund on which he could rely."[16] "[I]t is essential," Harrison continued, that American wageworkers "be kept free from the slavery of want and the discontents bred of injustice."[17] Whig and Republican orators from Clay to Coolidge proclaimed the gospel of wealth loudly to their working-class audiences. The 1872 campaign handbook crowed that "In no other country of the world have the workers so much political influence; nowhere, and at no time have they enjoyed so many elements of material, intellectual and moral development as here. The day's work of the mechanic buys fully twice as much as a day's work . . . upon the continent of Europe; so that here, if anywhere, the experiment must be worked out of making the laboring classes the equals in the enjoyment of the comforts of life, and of advancement in culture, to the professional and commercial classes."[18]

Issues of social class loomed large in national politics during the nineteenth and early twentieth centuries. The world's first labor movement emerged during the 1830s, and from the 1870s to the 1920s the United States endured some of the most violent and protracted labor disputes in the Western world. One of the apparent puzzles posed by the Whig and early Republican parties is that, despite a legislative and judicial record of actions hostile to organized labor,[19] these parties continued to

15. Huston (1983: 54).
16. B. Harrison, speech, 10/3/1888 (Harrison 1892: 158).
17. B. Harrison, speech, 10/4/1888 (Harrison 1892: 161).
18. *Campaign Documents Issued by the Union Republican Congressional Executive Committee* (1872: 3, 6). The same line cropped up repeatedly in Republican rhetoric. Garfield declared, "It is our glory that the American laborer is more intelligent and better paid than his foreign competitor" (acceptance letter, 7/12/1880, in Schlesinger 1971, 2: 1536). Coolidge, in the midst of 1920s prosperity, was moved to proclaim, "We have here in the United States not only the best paid workers in the world, but the best paid workers that ever lived in this world" (speech, 9/1/1924, in Coolidge 1926: 78).
19. Taft, for example, was popularly known as the "injunction judge" for his rulings (while a federal court judge) upholding the right of contract. The preemptive judicial weapon of the injunction was perhaps the most significant obstacle to unionization in the early twentieth century.

poll large numbers of working-class votes. How did party leaders reconcile the demands of labor (narrowly understood) with the demands of capital? Part of the answer can be found in the party's inclusive definition of labor. But there was more to it than a simple denial of conflict. Consider McKinley's tirade against the menace of Bryanism in 1896:

> [A]n effort is being made by those high in the counsels of the allied parties to divide the people of this country into classes and create distinctions among us which, in fact, do not exist and are repugnant to our form of government. . . . Every attempt to array class against class, "the classes against the masses," section against section, labor against capital, "the poor against the rich," or interest against interest in the United States, is in the highest degree reprehensible. It is opposed to the National instinct and interest, and should be resisted by every citizen. We are not a nation of classes, but of sturdy, free, independent and honorable people despising the demagogue and never capitulating to dishonor. This ever-recurring effort endangers popular government and is a menace to our liberties. . . . We meet the sudden, dangerous and revolutionary assault upon law and order . . . with the same courage that we have faced every emergency since our organization as a party, more than forty years ago. Government by law must first be assured; everything else can wait. The spirit of lawlessness must be extinguished by the fires of an unselfish and lofty patriotism.[20]

In this speech one can observe many of the party's trademark responses to the question of social class, which was vilified as dishonorable, divisive, and un-American. It is interesting to note that the classic encounter between a party of national order and a party representing the ideals of social equality occurred as early as 1896 – well before the onset of the New Deal (or even the New Freedom). I would take this argument one step further: the same set of responses to the ideal of social equality evident in McKinley's attack on William Jennings Bryan can be found, albeit usually in more moderate form, throughout the nineteenth and early twentieth centuries. To the concept of class the Whig and Republican parties repeatedly counterposed the notion of social harmony.

"Capital and labor are friends and not enemies," stressed Blaine in 1884. "In co-operation they can produce prosperity, but in hostility they can produce only adversity."[21] Rather than engendering an antagonistic relationship, National Republican orators showed how "all of us, whether we are wage-earners, professional men, farmers or business men, are in one boat with respect to prosperity."[22] A symbiotic relationship existed between the two dominant classes of industrial society:

20. McKinley, speech, 8/26/1896 (Schlesinger 1971, 2: 1866, 1870–71).
21. Blaine, speech, 10/30/1884 (Blaine 1887: 461).
22. Taft, speech, 9/8/1908 (Taft 1910: 53).

Labor needs capital to secure the best production, while capital needs labor in producing anything. . . . The capitalist . . . should be regarded with favor by the workingman, because, while his motive is merely one of accumulation, he is working not only for himself but for labor and for society at large. . . . I . . . hope that labor unions may be induced to assist the cause of honest industry by bringing to bear the moral force of . . . the union to improve the sobriety, industry, skill, and fidelity to the employer's interests of the employee.[23]

In setting forth this ideal, Taft referred specifically to the Civic Federation, an organization representing employers and labor leaders (prominent among them Samuel Gompers) established to foster cooperation and compromise between the feuding classes. This project of "mutual dependence" was a model of National Republican social philosophy.[24]

As to the role of government, National Republicans held to a simple proposition: equal treatment for labor and capital. "Our Government is not a government by classes or for classes of our fellow-citizens," Harrison stressed. "It is a government of the people and by the people. Its wise legislation distils its equal blessings upon the homes of the rich and the poor."[25] As Taft would say, with respect to the issue of legal injunctions, "there ought to be no favored class in litigation at all. . . . A man who has property and a man who has labor to sell [should] stand on an equality in court."[26] Thus did equal citizenship serve as a melting pot for class distinctions within civil society, as well as for ethnic, racial, and regional identities. In a striking example of how the exceptionalist argument could be applied to the question of class, McKinley declared:

This assemblage thoroughly typifies the National idea of a great American commonwealth in this, that it represents the equality of all which lies at the basis of popular government. It emphasizes the American spirit. Here are workingmen in every department of industry, professional men, newspaper

---

23. Taft, speech, 1/10/1908 (Taft 1908a: 2, 4, 7).
24. Colton (1844: 103). For further examples, see the fifth national platform of the party, which declares: ". . . The Republican party recognizes the duty of so shaping legislation as to secure full protection and the amplest field for capital, and for labor – the creator of capital – the largest opportunities and a just share of the mutual profits of these two great servants of civilization" (1872 platform, in Johnson 1958: 47). For a later example, one might observe Harding's acceptance speech, in which he declared, "I want the employers in industry to understand the aspirations, the convictions, the yearnings of the millions of American wage-earners, and I want the wage-earners to understand the problems, the anxieties, the obligations of management and capital, and all of them must understand their relationship to the people and their obligation to the Republic" (7/22/1920, in Harding 1920b: 26).
25. B. Harrison, speech, (10/6/1888 (Harrison 1892: 167).
26. Taft, speech, 8/29/1908 (Taft 1910: 46).

men – the native born and the naturalized citizen – all equal in privilege and power before the law; all alike interested in the government of the country, and with equal voice in controlling and shaping the destiny of our great Republic. Here is a striking protest against the unworthy effort on the part of those who would divide our citizenship into classes, and a striking condemnation of such an un-American appeal to passion and prejudice.[27]

Each citizen would receive justice, Theodore Roosevelt stressed, "no more and no less."[28]

National Republicans' repeated denunciation of "class politics" was grounded, therefore, not in the belief that social divisions were absent but rather in the belief that they were inevitable and were, for this reason, a futile subject for political agitation. Those who raised the politics of class were irresponsible demagogues, because they were asking government to address problems that government could not solve. "It is not possible," Taft said, "to have a condition of things by which wage-earners shall earn large wages, business men shall earn large profits from their business, farmers large profits . . . , and the man who has the money, who is investing it, gets no profit at all. . . . [T]herefore what we wish is fair treatment to all in order that the boat may sail on and give comfort and the enjoyment of happiness to all classes, wage-earners, business men, farmers and capitalists alike."[29]

Neo-mercantilism

The debate over Whig and early Republican social and economic policy is confused by the fact that at times the party argued against governmental intervention in economic matters and at other times in favor of such intervention. I shall argue, however, that it is possible to generalize about National Republican economic policy across the first hundred years, and that this policy is most neatly encapsulated in the term *neo-mercantilism*.[30]

27. McKinley, speech, 9/5/1896 (*New York Times* 9/6/1896).
28. Roosevelt, acceptance speech, 7/26/1904 (*Republican Campaign Textbook, 1904* 1904: 537). Hayes, along the same lines, promised that the government would "protect *all classes* of citizens in their political and private rights" (acceptance letter, 7/8/ 1876 [Schlesinger 1971, 2: 1449]). Taft reiterated, "Wherever we can see a statute which does not deprive any person or class of what is his, and is going to help many people, we are in favor of it" (acceptance speech, 8/2/1912, in Schlesinger 1971, 3: 2209–10).
29. Taft, speech, 8/29/1908 (Taft 1910: 50). "No one pretends to deny the inequalities which are manifest in modern industrial life," declared Harding a decade later (speech, 7/22/1920, in Harding 1920b: 26).
30. Although the concept of mercantilism has often been applied to the Whig party, it is rarely associated with the Republican party. One exception to this historiographic pattern can be found in Calhoun (1996), who argues – much along the lines of this

Neo-mercantilism can be defined as a general economic philosophy mandating the subordination of economic activity to the interests of the state and the nation; the intermingling of geopolitical, military, and economic policies in the international arena (with the general understanding that the achievement of status within the international community is inextricably linked to the achievement of material wealth); a vision of the international market as a competitive, zero-sum game (in which one country's winnings are another's losses); an industrial perspective on economic policy making; a favorable view toward the concentration of capital; and a vision of economic development emphasizing the attainment of national independence and self-sufficiency.[31] These general precepts could be seen behind most National Republican economic policies during the 1828–1924 period – high tariffs or restrictive quotas (primarily on manufactured goods), export subsidies, infrastructural development, the provision of credit or capital for new industries, the chartering of joint-stock companies with monopoly rights, the maintaining of supplies of raw materials for domestic industries, an import substitution strategy of development, the search (by military as well as diplomatic means) for export markets, and tight monetary policies calculated to maintain a strong currency.

The party took a distinctly statist approach to most economic questions. "Government can facilitate or embarrass, revive or destroy the trade of a nation," Calvin Colton's *Junius Tracts* instructed readers. "It is fair to hold the Government responsible in this matter. The maxim of Mr. Van Buren, 'Let the people take care of themselves, and the Government take care of themselves,' is as destructive as it is fallacious. It is subverting the design of Government."[32] "Smithian economics" was

chapter – that Republican economic policies of the Gilded Age constituted an "industrial policy."

31. The foregoing definition is drawn from Appleby (1992: ch. 1), Gilpin (1987: 31–34), McCraw (1986), Schlesinger (1963), and Viner (1948; 1968: 435–42). Although the mercantilist roots of American economic policy in the eighteenth century (Crowley 1993) and the nineteenth century (McCraw 1986; Schlesinger 1963) have been widely noted, the partisan nature of economic policy debates in the nineteenth century are rarely acknowledged. The mercantilist roots of National Republican economic policy can be seen at many points. Colton's *Junius Tracts* emphasize, for example, the critical role of gold and silver reserves, and the balance of trade, in party calculations: "In the absence of a suitable Tariff, specie is withdrawn from the country" (Colton 1844: 27). The Whig party would "enact such regulations for the government of our foreign trade, as will counteract and prevent this everlasting excess of imports over exports, and turn the tide of foreign commerce in our favor" (Colton 1844: 39). See also Larson (1990) on the neomercantilist aspects of John Quincy Adams's political philosophy.

32. Colton (1844: 19). The *Junius Tracts* were a multivolume set of campaign tracts issued by the Whig party during the election of 1844. They were written by Calvin Colton,

derided by Whig and Republican orators as a set of "visionary theories" concocted by persons "whose knowledge of Political Economy was obtained in the closet."[33] Laissez-faire, it is important to remember, arrived as a radical challenge to an old and well-established set of mercantilist principles, principles that dominated American political and intellectual circles through the early nineteenth century.[34] For National Republicans, as well as for most economists of the day, it was axiomatic that the art of government involved successful intervention into the marketplace.[35] In fact, this older worldview did not recognize a clear dividing line between politics and economics – usually referred to jointly as "political economy."

According to mercantilist tradition, the marketplace required state intervention in order to function at optimal levels. Society was perceived as functionally divided into different economic groups (variously defined), each of which played a different role in the national economy. Capital, finally, was to be provided by corporations, banking concerns, and the government itself, rather than simply by individual entrepreneurs. Unlike their Democratic colleagues, National Republicans believed that large-scale, organized production and distribution networks were necessary to the efficient functioning of the national economy. Corporations could provide the order and harmony otherwise lacking in an anarchic marketplace. National Republican views of the corporation stemmed from the early and mid-nineteenth century, when corporations were commonly issued charters by state governments "as a means by which the commonwealth could guide and promote economic growth."[36] The missions of the corporation and of government itself

whom Daniel Walker Howe credits as being "one of the leading progandists and theoreticians of the Whig party" (Howe 1973: 89).

33. Clayton, speech, 6/15/1844 (*New York Tribune* 6/18/1844). *Private enterprise, private sector, free enterprise*, and various other terms implying a separation of governmental and economic spheres did not become common features of Republican rhetoric until the 1920s. When, in 1924, Coolidge declared, "That tax is theoretically best which interferes least with business," and "that system is best which gives the individual the largest freedom of action, and the largest opportunity for honorable accomplishment," this was a fundamentally new ideological tack (acceptance speech, 8/14/1924, in Coolidge 1924: 13, 15).

34. Schlesinger (1963: 109).

35. Viner writes, "Mercantilism was a doctrine of extensive state regulation of economic activity in the interest of the national economy. . . . It accepted as axiomatic that if individuals were in their economic behavior left free from tight regulation, the consequences for the community would be disastrous" (1968: 439).

36. Thus, Schlesinger continues, "Early corporations were set up by specific legislative enactment and, in the main, to provide social overhead for quasi-public purposes" (1963: 112).

were thus intertwined from the start, a history that helps explain why Republicans continued to view no strict separation or necessary antagonism between the private and public sectors.[37]

National Republican attitudes toward business monopolies can also be seen as a product of their mercantilist perspectives. Whereas monopolies became a prime subject of abuse in Democratic rhetoric, Republican party leaders equivocated. The evils of monopoly, for example, rate only a brief mention in Benjamin Harrison's 1892 letter of acceptance. "I greatly regret that all classes of labor are not just and considerate and that capital sometimes takes too large a share of the profits," wrote the incumbent president blandly. McKinley, in 1900, restricted his treatment of the subject to two paragraphs (in a ten-page acceptance letter), concluding simply that combinations of capital "should be made the subject of prohibitory or penal legislation."[38] Roosevelt, without doubt the most enthusiastic opponent of monopoly among Republican presidential candidates, hardly measures up against Democratic trustbusters like Bryan and Wilson. In fact, even in his most radical phase, as a crusading third-party Progressive, Roosevelt was much less concerned about the dangers of the concentration of capital than his Democratic opponent. Roosevelt stated, almost complacently: "There is every reason why we should try to abate those evils and . . . make men of wealth bear their full share of the country's burdens, and keep as scrupulously within the bounds of equity and morality as any of their neighbors."[39] It was simply a matter of making them behave themselves. Bigness, in business as in government, was characteristically a Democratic anxiety.

Thus, although pro forma "antimonopoly" statements were fairly commonplace components of Republican acceptance addresses from 1888 to 1912, they expressed opposition not to the aggregation of capital per se but simply to *illegal* actions that might have been taken by corporations. Republican leaders took a legalistic view of the marketplace, a perspective that contrasted sharply with the Democrats' essentially *moral* posture. "We don't wish to destroy these great organizations that have a large wage fund when they are prosperous and that add greatly to the prosperity of the country," said Taft. "What we wish to do is to keep them within the law. . . . The combination of capital is absolutely essential so that we should progress."[40] Thus, whereas Bryan proposed to limit all companies to 50 percent of market share, declaring

37. Schlesinger (1963: 112).
38. McKinley, acceptance letter, 9/8/1900 (*Boston Sunday Globe* 9/9/1900).
39. Roosevelt, speech, 9/7/1900 (*New York Times* 9/8/1900).
40. Taft, speech, 9/8/1908 (Taft 1910: 41, 55).

all those above this margin to be "monopolies," the Republican party's general position was that firms could grow horizontally or vertically to whatever extent they were capable, as long as trade was not illegally restrained.[41] National Republicans emphasized that only a few corporations were naughty and that the good should not suffer for the indiscretions of a few.[42]

Mercantilist philosophy was most directly expressed in the recurrent partisan disputes over tariffs. The grand old tariff debates of the nineteenth and early twentieth centuries seem overblown to many contemporary observers and have often been taken as an example of the triviality of partisan conflict in America.[43] Yet it must be remembered that taxes on imports were not only the main instrument of economic policy through the 1930s but also the main source of federal government revenue until the introduction of the income tax in 1913. According to Morton Keller, "The tariff was the most prominent and persistent category of nineteenth-century American economic policymaking."[44] This was the single point of policy on which industry, agriculture, labor, and consumers would be directly affected by the partisan battles for the control of government, and each mobilized accordingly. National Republicans from the age of Clay to the age of Hoover were solidly on the side of "Protection," as it was fondly called, creating one of the most consistent and enduring partisan issue-divisions in American history. On the one hand, amid the profusion of high-tariff arguments from 1828 to

41. Coolidge, speech, 10/11/1924 (*New York Times* 10/12/1924).
42. Root, after noting Bryan's attacks against the growing influence of trusts, responded: "Yes, the great industrial enterprises which are opening the whole world to American markets, [a list of exploits follows], have grown beyond precedence" (speech, 10/24/1900, in *New York Times* 10/25/1900). Those few that were really monopolies should, of course, be suppressed, he said, but "Most of them have no element of monopoly whatever" (ibid.). A sense of Whig-Republicans' enthusiasm for the marketplace and for the productivity of aggregated capital can be seen in the following passage from the *Junius Tracts*: "By vested capital is commonly understood money put to use for what is called interest or income. The most common forms of vested capital, are bonds, mortgages, negotiable notes, silent partnerships in business firms, stocks in banks, insurances offices, turnpike and railroads, canals, . . . and any undertaking that is beyond the ordinary means of individuals, and which requires the combined and aggregate capital of numerous persons having money to put to use. . . . They are well adapted to a democratic state of society, by bringing down the powers of government, distributing them among the people, and vesting them in the hands of all persons who can raise twenty, or fifty, or a hundred dollars. . . . There are many important objects indispensable to the interests of the country, which can not be accomplished, except by the power of associated capital" (Colton 1844: 99, 102).
43. See Dobson (1972), and Nugent (1970).
44. Keller (1990: 193). See also Rogowski (1989), for a discussion of the tariff issue in other polities.

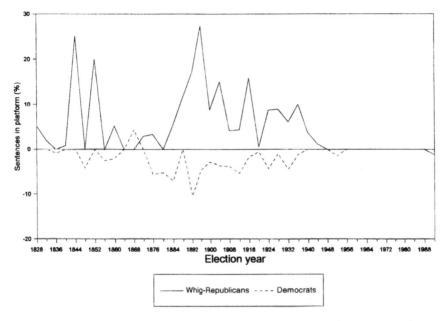

Figure 1. Support for tariffs, as measured by the percentage of sentences within Whig-Republican and Democratic party platforms proposing the proctection of labor and industry through the tariff *minus* the percentage of sentences in opposition to high tariffs, tariffs for revenue only, tariff reform, and so forth

1936, not a single sentence could be found in National Republican oratory arguing for the benefits of a more liberal trade regime. Democratic party platforms, on the other hand, scarcely had a pleasant word to say on the subject (see figure 1).

National Republican leaders promised to pursue foreign markets with the same zeal with which they closed off their own, a policy instituted by John Hay's "Open Door Notes," issued during the McKinley administration. The willingness of National Republicans to employ American military might for the sake of foreign trade illustrates another mercantilist premise, namely, that money and power are intimately linked in the international arena.[45] In addition to aggressive trade policies, National Republicans pursued specific industrial policies to stimulate economic growth. Primary among these were "internal improvements" – in contemporary lingo, "infrastructural development."[46] The first Republi-

45. See Viner (1948).
46. Industrial policies applied not only to the economy at large but also to particular industries, such as railroads and carrying ships, which were targeted – much as today's industrial policy advocates recommend – for special governmental support (cf. B.

can party platform declared that "a railroad to the Pacific Ocean . . . is imperatively demanded by the interests of the whole country, and that the Federal Government ought to render immediate and efficient aid in its construction."[47] That same platform argued for "appropriations by Congress for the improvement of rivers and harbors, of a national character, required for the accommodation and security of our existing commerce."[48]

National Republican economic policy was strongly tilted toward the development of industry, and manufacturing in particular, rather than toward the subsidy of agriculture or the service sector. Hamilton, the patron saint of mercantilism and the party's intellectual touchstone, declared, "Not only the wealth but the independence and security of a country appear to be materially connected to the prosperity of manufactures."[49] William Seward, in much the same vein, stated, "The Whigs . . . are in favor of the Protection to National Industry, knowing that no merely agricultural nation can be permanently prosperous. We must be also a commercial people, and the consequences will be most disastrous if our own workshops are not protected."[50] It is important to remember

Harrison, acceptance letter, 9/3/1892, in Schlesinger 1971, 2: 1517; Hughes, acceptance speech, 7/31/1916, in Schlesinger 1971, 3: 2306).

47. Republican platform, 1856 (Johnson 1958: 28).
48. Republican platform, 1856 (Johnson 1958: 28). For examples of federal aid for railroad construction, see Keller (1977: 165). On the campaign trail in 1908, Taft courted a Virginia audience with the following partisan boast: "The Republican Party has improved the waterways, is building the Panama Canal, . . . has started the movement for the reclamation of swamp lands, . . . and is taking many other steps that are for the development of the South" (speech, 8/21/1908, in Taft 1910: 11).
49. Quoted in Gilpin (1987: 33).
50. Seward, speech, 9/22/1848 (*New York Tribune* 9/25/1848). To the common Democratic objection that industrial methods of production benefited the rich rather than the poor, the *Junius Tracts* responded: "It is the labor of the country that is first and chiefly benefited by the investment of capital, or the setting up of business, that employs labor. . . . Investments in a large manufacturing establishment, existing in the shape of stocks, are not usually made so much for speculation, as for a reasonable and steady income. . . . To oppose manufactures, is therefore to oppose every man who depends on handy-craft for a livelihood – it is to oppose the march of civilization. . . . It has been said, that agriculture is our natural calling, and that our best national policy is to foster that chiefly. But what is agriculture good for, beyond the natural wants of the producer, without a market? . . . It is the multiplicity of industrial pursuits, that creates a market for the products of each" (Colton 1844: 41–42). The marriage of capital and labor was achieved with the dowry provided by industrial production.

The same reconciliation was offered to the South in the wake of the devastation of the Civil War (and as Republicans began to troll for votes in the defeated territories). Under the label of "the New South," Republicans encouraged the erstwhile

that the low cost of American commodities – unparalleled in the world throughout most of this period – meant that a high-tariff policy would, perforce, favor manufactured goods.[51]

A multitude of slogans regarding monetary policy cluttered the nineteenth-century political landscape – hard money, soft money, sound money, free banking, greenbackism, gold bugs, free silver, resumption, and so forth. On the whole, such slogans have been accorded very little significance in the ideological life of the two parties. The parties seemed to straddle the fence on most issues and were inconstant in their support of others.[52] Yet in focusing on specific issue-positions – which were, admittedly, often in flux – authors have missed the connecting threads among those issues. National Republican monetary policy was oriented toward providing a strong, uniform, and stable national currency. The means to this end were severalfold: a federal banking system, a balanced (though not necessarily austere) federal budget, and a paper currency backed by government stores of precious metals. "Gold and silver, weighed in the scales, and assayed by Chemistry," crowed the *Junius Tracts* in 1844. "This is the currency of the world at large, or international currency, established from time immemorial. The stamp they bear is that of the Creator, and the tests applied to them are the Creator's laws. . . . They constitute the bases and are the test of all other currencies."[53]

Although the issue of the national bank faded by the end of the 1840s – having been resolved in favor of the "Subtreasury" system – it was of such critical significance to partisan debate in the formative decades of the 1830s and 1840s that it deserves some notice. The Bank of the United States became a campaign issue of primary importance when President Andrew Jackson decided to veto a congressional bill for its rechartering in 1832. Those loosely assembled under the "National Republican" banner in 1832 (a precursor to the Whig party) were solid

rebels to part with their seditious – and seditiously "agrarian" – past. The South, Harrison predicted, would now "open her hospitable doors to manufacturing, capital, and skilled labor" (speech, 9/22/1888, in Harrison 1892: 142). The 1864 party platform pledged the party "to encourage the development of the industrial interests of the whole country" (Johnson 1958: 33). So firm was Clay's devotion to the ideal of a manufacturing economy that he prophesied in 1844 that "the day will come when the Cotton region will be the greatest *manufacturing* region of Cotton in the world," for "every part of the country possesses a capacity to manufacture, and every part of the country more or less does manufacture" (speech, 4/13/1844, in *New York Tribune* 6/29/1844).

51. In fact, agricultural tariffs would have done little to help farmers, since the United States was already producing the cheapest commodities in the world.

52. See Jones (1964) and Nugent (1970).   53. Colton (1844: 18).

supporters of the Bank, for it was through this mechanism that the currency could, they felt, be effectively controlled. The Bank represented a federal solution to a problem that Democrats preferred to resolve through a loose network of state and regional banks (the "subtreasury" system, which ultimately prevailed).[54] The 1832 address of the National Republican Convention explained the benefits of the Bank in the following terms: "This great and beneficial institution, by facilitating exchanges between different parts of the union, and maintaining a sound, ample, and healthy state of the currency, may be said to supply the body politic, economically viewed, with a continual stream of life-blood, without which it must inevitably languish."[55] Since the absence of central monetary control meant that states could issue separate notes, and thereby expand the quantity of credit available, the national bank was considered a "sound money" policy. It is worth noting that although the bank issue faded by the end of the 1840s, when it did resurface in later years, Republicans were generally to be found on the side of national banking institutions, and Democrats in opposition.[56]

National Republican currency policies followed a similar mercantilist logic. Whether "hard" (metallic) or "soft" (paper), the currency was to be backed by reserves of precious metals held by the government treasuries at fixed exchange rates such that the currency would retain a high value. This central goal of maintaining a strong currency makes sense of the party's gyrations on the question of gold and silver in the nineteenth and early twentieth centuries. National Republicans supported a bimetallic standard (reserves held in silver and gold) through 1873 for the simple reason that silver was in comparatively short supply and was consequently the more expensive of the two metals. Bimetallism prior to the 1870s conformed to the "sound money" ideal. The motivation behind the Grant administration's reversal of the traditional American policy of bimetallism (in 1873) was to protect the Treasury from an expected surge in the production of silver (which would have automatically devalued the gold- and silver-backed currency). Silver did indeed

---

54. Of the American banking system the *Junius Tracts* declared, "We had great resources, but wanted means to develope [sic] them, and thus to augment our wealth.... With the exuberance of our resources and enterprise, it [a national bank] affords the means of multiplying wealth in a manifold degree. Instead of one dollar to trade with, we have several, and they are all good, being convertible into specie on demand" (Colton 1844: 21).

55. Address of the National Republican Convention, 1832 (Schlesinger 1971, 1: 561).

56. The government, declared Roscoe Conkling in 1880, "has the right to charter National banks, if it sees proper" (speech, 10/9/1880, in Conkling 1880: 2).

become the cheaper metal in the subsequent decades, and in due course of time, the Republican party committed itself to gold.

However, even prior to 1896, the mantra of sound money (*aka* "strong money," or "honest money") was spoken more persistently and more fervently by National Republicans than it was by Democrats.[57] The significance of such apparently obscure points of currency policy as whether greenbacks issued during the Civil War would be retired or kept in circulation was vividly illustrated by Daniel Webster several decades *before* the War. Webster likened the currency to "fluid in the human system," which was "indispensable to life." When it "becomes disordered, corrupted, or obstructed in its circulation, not the head or the heart alone suffers, but the whole body. The analogy between the human system and the social and political system is complete, and what the life-blood is to the former circulation, money, currency, is to the latter; and if that be disordered or corrupted, paralysis must fall on the system."[58] The currency, from a National Republican perspective, was the lifeblood of the body politic. Whatever government institutions and policies were necessary to preserve this circulative medium would be supported by party leaders.[59]

Of course, the enthusiasm with which National Republicans endorsed

57. The following discussion is based, in part, on Nugent (1970) and Unger (1964), though I draw somewhat different conclusions than they about the long-term significance of the issue.

58. Webster, speech, 8/19/1840 (Norton 1888: 227). Along identical lines, the *Junius Tracts* advised that currency was "as blood to the animal economy. Disturb it, or vitiate it, or impair it, or tie up its veins, or overcharge it, or drain it, . . . or in any way treat it rudely and unskillfully, the effect is precisely the same on the health and wealth of the nation, as is produced by a like treatment of the vital current, functions, and organs of the human body" (Colton 1844: 24).

59. The Republican platform in 1880 boasted of having achieved an entirely gold-backed currency; the Democratic platform offered, instead, to create a bimetallic currency, thus foreshadowing the issues of 1896. The reasons for this devotion to a monetary orthodoxy are not difficult to locate. Whereas the Democratic party was riven by splits between the inflationist demands of the South and West in the late nineteenth and early twentieth centuries, the Republican party maintained a much greater share of its total vote from the Northeast, where creditors outnumbered debtors. It is true that western Republicans often voted with Democrats in Congress to support soft-money alternatives (Nugent 1970: 124). However, this obstreperous bunch was generally contained by the Republican stalwarts who controlled the party's congressional delegation and national conventions – assuring that the presidential party would always be "safe" on currency and monetary questions. Monetary and currency lines became much more clearly drawn after 1896, when the Democrats committed themselves to an obviously inflationary set of policies for the first time.

state intervention in economic matters was not matched in the area of social welfare. After an address at Cooper's Institute in New York, where workers were undoubtedly numerous, Taft was asked, "What do you advise the workingmen who are out of work for a considerable time and who are starving with their families on account of the present crisis to do?" To this he responded, "God knows. They have my deepest sympathy."[60] Not surprisingly, this sort of attitude has led many historians to question the party's statist credentials. My contention, however, is that the party's negative position on most aspects of social policy adhered to its more general mercantilist perspective on socioeconomic matters.

National wealth, not redistribution, was the sine qua non of state intervention in the economy. Child labor restrictions, legislation facilitating unionization, and most social welfare laws were all rejected on the grounds that they would impinge on the productivity of business. Whig-Republicans of this period, as of later periods, were interested in raising the social aggregate, not the least advantaged members of society. In fact, on the few occasions when Republicans could be found arguing for "welfare state" initiatives, the rationalization was often that such policies would foster economic growth. William Seward supported a greatly enhanced federal education policy on the grounds that such a set of expenditures would "develop the intellectual power of the nation," a resource that he considered to be as significant in the long-term economic success of the new country as the physical resources with which it was so magnificently endowed.[61] Generally, however, National Republicans opposed egalitarian-minded social policies, which offended "the principle and institution of private property."[62] Arguments for so-

---

60. Taft, speech, 1/10/1908 (Taft 1908a: 5).
61. Seward, speech, 9/22/1848 (*New York Tribune* 9/25/1848).
62. Taft, acceptance speech, 8/2/1912 (Schlesinger 1971, 3: 2204–5). This general picture of National Republican ambivalence with respect to social policy has been challenged in recent years by the rediscovery of an extensive program of soldiers' pensions set in place during Reconstruction and enduring through the first decades of the next century (cf. Skocpol 1992). How can we square this program with National Republican penury on other distributive policies? There were several unique features of the Civil War soldiers' pension program that militate against considering it a program of "social welfare," and that explain Republican enthusiasm for the scheme. First, governmental pensions, despite their prodigious expense (at least by the standards of the latter nineteenth century), imposed no direct cost on industry. The program was funded almost entirely by excise taxes (which themselves were conceived of as measures to enhance the growth of American industry). Second, soldiers' pensions were not redistributive. They were framed by Republican politicians throughout the period as re-

cial justice carried little currency with National Republicans. "[I]nsofar as the propaganda for the satisfaction of unrest involves the promise of a millennium, a condition in which the rich are to be made reasonably poor and the poor reasonably rich by law, we are chasing a phantom," concluded Taft.[63] It was the creation of wealth, not its redistribution, that concerned National Republicans.

Neo-mercantilism was not simply an economic philosophy but also a political philosophy that served a larger purpose within National Republican ideology. Inherent in the mercantilist project was an optimistic view of industrialization and of the workings of the marketplace in general, which contrasted starkly with the Democratic party's misgivings and (by 1896) its condemnations. Distrusting the realm of "specula-

wards for services rendered to the nation and to the state. The "Grand Army of the Republic," which had reestablished the legitimacy and reach of the central state apparatus, was being recompensed for its sacrifices. National Republicans remained uniformly uninterested in the theme of equality – whether phrased as "equal opportunity" or "equal distribution." It was only at the end of the 1920s that this latter goal entered Republican campaign discourse.

Third, veterans' pensions served a partisan function. Since pensions were awarded only to former members of the Union army – most of whom "voted as they shot" – and since the qualification requirements were loose, and loosely administered (and could always be overcome by special legislation to include worthy individuals not otherwise covered), the distribution of pensions became a primary tool of Republican patronage in the late nineteenth and early twentieth centuries. National Republicans were not opposed to government spending per se, nor to "big government." In fact, it was under their rule that the so-called patronage state reached its acme. Last, Republican arguments for soldiers' pensions made every effort to distinguish the program from anything that could be construed as charity or poor relief. It was the immense suffering of Union army veterans that justified this expenditure of government funds, not the present pecuniary needs of the recipients. McKinley, speaking in support of the Dependent Pensions Bill (which President Cleveland had recently vetoed), spent most of his time before the assembled House detailing the bravery of the men to be covered by the bill, concluding that "they were soldiers of the country, the rank and file, fighting for the maintenance of the Union," and therefore deserving of special appreciation from the U.S. Congress. "Between private charity or the poorhouse this bill says neither, but in lieu of both the generous bounty of the Government" (speech, 2/24/1887, in McKinley 1896a: 172). Pensions were, as the term implied, to be an extension of the minimal wages that Union soldiers received during their stint in the Grand Army of the Republic. Indeed, Skocpol (1992: 151) concludes, "The Civil War pension system was . . . not really a 'welfare state' in any objective or subjective sense. It was, rather, an unabashed system of national public care, not for all Americans in similar work or life circumstances, but for the deserving core of a special generation. No matter how materially needy, the morally undeserving or less deserving were not the nation's responsibility."

63. Taft, acceptance speech, 8/2/1912 (Schlesinger 1971, 3: 2204–5).

tion," of "monopoly," and of all the moral ambiguities inherent in relationships established by the marketplace, Democrats naturally opposed its incursion into the realm of politics. Such an incursion, they believed, could lead only to the corruption of the public sphere. National Republicans, feeling more at ease with marketplace transactions, felt more comfortable crossing the line that separated politics from economics. National Republicans' opposition to laissez-faire should not, therefore, be taken to indicate a fundamental distrust of market forces, for their intervention into the marketplace was spurred by a desire to *foster* market relationships, not to inhibit them. In a fundamental reversal of today's economic rhetoric, it was the Democrats' policy of laissez-faire that derived from an essentially negative view of the marketplace, and the opposing party's policy of interventionism that derived from a positive view of capitalism.

Antibusiness sentiment remained at negligible levels throughout the history of the Whig-Republican party (see figure 2). Although party platforms occasionally contained derogatory statements about capitalism, corporations, monopolies, industry, or the rich, such statements rarely matched the vehemence of commentary on such subjects within Democratic platforms. Indeed, National Republicans were positively enamored with the idea of economic growth, industrialization, and the associated processes and institutions attendant upon economic development. Whereas Democrats distrusted the speculative elements of the marketplace, many National Republicans openly embraced the principle of credit. "It is to th[e] system of a sound credit currency, that, as a nation, we owe our unrivalled march to prosperity and wealth," the *Junius Tracts* counseled. "By the use of the *principle of credit*, thus modified and guarded, it has anticipated means, and produced incalculable wealth out of resources which otherwise must have lain dormant. Credit is morality, and the exact measure of the soundness of the social state. To think of living without it, is turning the eye and footsteps back to a state of barbarism. Credit is the moral peculiarity of civilisation."[64]

The neo-mercantilist idea also implied that government bore responsibility for promoting economic growth, and the apparent success of National Republican policies in doing so was, not surprisingly, a constant feature of campaign rhetoric. National Republicans were the party of prosperity, not simply during the Dollar Decade (the Twenties) but throughout the nineteenth century as well. Of course, Democrats also jumped on the prosperity bandwagon when it suited their electoral advantage, but it did not suit them nearly so often. National Republicans,

---

64. Colton (1844: 21).

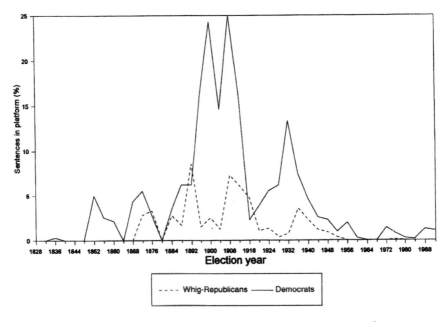

Figure 2. Antibusiness sentiment, as measured by the percentage of sentences within Whig-Republican and Democratic party platforms that include derogatory comments on business (e.g., entrepreneurs, corporations, monopolies, industry, capital) or the rich. (Does not include policy opposition to public ownership of private enterprises, public land ownership by monopolies and corporations, business regulation, boards of arbitration for labor disputes, equivocal antimonopoly statements, or antimonopoly statements in which the problem is defined only as a threat to small business.)

through the good fortune of electoral politics and the economic blessings of the New World, were more often in a position to toot the prosperity horn. Every election was an occasion to impress upon the voters what financial destruction Democracy would wreak if entrusted with national power. "This question," said Blaine, "is not one of mere sentiment. . . . It is a question of material interest. The triumph of the South in this contest would mean the triumph of Free Trade and the destruction of the Protective system."[65] Republicans prided themselves as the party that could be trusted with the complex task of managing the affairs of state and economy. "The struggle in all human society is first for bread," Blaine declared, in suitably blunt manner. "It is idle to propound fine theories to a man who is hungry. . . . [T]o secure [food and

65. Blaine, speech, 10/27/1884 (Blaine 1887: 454).

clothing] you must put the people in the way of earning good wages. ... To move [a man] you must make him feel that he can win prosperity himself."[66]

Economic boosterism was the stock-in-trade of the Republican party, which popularized the "full dinner pail," "two chickens in every pot," and, much later, "two cars in every garage." The standard pocketbook appeal so characteristic of Republican rhetoric took its classic form in one 1884 address by James Blaine: "[T]he question is whether over a given series of years there has not been a larger degree of prosperity to the people under the policy of Protection than under the policy of Free Trade."[67] In case the point was not entirely clear, Blaine asked rhetorically, "What agency was it that nerved the arm of industry to smite the mountains and create this wealth in West Virginia?"[68]

National Republicans offered voters a calculus of interest upon which they imagined the vote would be decided. As Coolidge said, without apparent cynicism, of the American electorate, "They have faith but they want works."[69] Thus, the perennial question of the tariff was "one of expediency, to be determined not on abstract academic grounds, but in the light of experience."[70] American workmen, wrote Benjamin Harrison, "may be roused by injustice, or what seems to them to be such, or to be led for the moment by others into acts of passion; but they will settle the tariff contest in the calm light of their November firesides and with sole reference to the prosperity of the country of which they are citizens."[71] Campaign talk was of work, prosperity, jobs, idleness, good ("American") wages, production, consumption, grain prices, and so forth. If ever there was a time when the business of America was business, it was the post–Civil War period. And the Republican party was preeminently the party of business.

Statism

National Republican politicians almost unanimously upheld the federal government's constitutional right to regulate and to spend.[72] Although they proclaimed the virtues of economical government (along with po-

---

66. Blaine, speech, 10/18/1884 (Blaine 1887: 445).
67. Blaine, speech, 10/1/1884 (Schlesinger 1973, 2: 1471).
68. Blaine, speech, 10/1/1884 (Schlesinger 1973, 2: 1472).
69. Coolidge, speech, 9/21/1924 (Coolidge 1926: 111).
70. Roosevelt, acceptance letter, 9/12/1904 (Roosevelt 1910: 72).
71. B. Harrison, acceptance letter, 9/3/1892 (Schlesinger 1973, 2: 1524).
72. This was not the position of the Republican-dominated federal court system through most of this period, but the courts' "strict constructionist" arguments were not prominent in the campaign rhetoric of party leaders.

litical parties everywhere) in the nineteenth century, National Republicans were not obsessed with the goal of fiscal austerity. Indeed, within the context of partisan debate in the nineteenth century, the National Republican party was militantly statist. "We live," proclaimed Francis Lieber, "in an age when the word is Nationalization, not Denationalization."[73] The state functioned as the symbol around which newly arrived immigrants were to rally. Lieber, a prominent Republican spokesperson for the German-American community and a political theorist of some note, promised, "We . . . adhere to our country, to her institutions, to freedom, and her power, and to that great institution called the government of our country. . . . Loyalty is pre-eminently a civic virtue in a free country."[74]

As many have pointed out, American identity has been defined largely by its form of government.[75] This was particularly the case for National Republicans. Rarely did a Whig or Republican speech wind down without some tribute to the American system of "self-government." "What a spectacle, my fellow-citizens, to the world, is this Government of 70,000,000 free people, governed by themselves and governing themselves, changing their Chief Executive every four years and their law-making power every two years," said McKinley during the 1896 campaign. "More than 120 years have passed since the Government was founded, and in every trial of our history we have demonstrated our capacity for self-government and shown to all mankind the blessings and advantages of the great republic."[76] The instrument of government held an almost mystical attraction for National Republican orators.[77] Garfield assumed that his audience shared a "reverence . . . for Government, . . . for its laws, . . . for its institutions."[78] Harding spoke evocatively of "the majesty of just government."[79] The federal government was commonly referred to as the "National authority," and in matters of foreign policy the identified national agent was the U.S. government (rather than "America," or "the nation").[80] For National Republicans, nation and

---

73. Lieber, speech, 4/11/1863 (Schlesinger 1971, 2: 1184).
74. Lieber, speech, 4/11/1863 (Schlesinger 1971, 2: 1183).
75. See, e.g., Arieli (1964).
76. McKinley, speech, 9/26/1896 (*New York Times* 9/27/1896).
77. Occasionally the European term *state* entered Whig-Republican discourse (cf. Roosevelt, acceptance letter, 9/15/1900, in *New York Times* 9/17/1900), but the preferred term was *government*.
78. Garfield, speech, 6/16/1880 (Garfield n.d.: 449).
79. Harding, speech, 1/10/1920 (Harding 1920a: 107).
80. Taft, speech, 8/21/1908 (Taft 1910: 4). In the face of continued foreign provocation on the eve of American entry into World War I, Hughes stated, "American government has seemed to mean naught but impotence and unavailing words" (speech, 10/25/1916, in *New York Times* 10/26/1916).

state were intimately intertwined. "My countrymen," began Benjamin Harrison, "this Government is that which I love to think of as my country."[81]

The virtues of strong government were advertised with missionary zeal by party orators. In a pamphlet issued during the 1876 campaign, the anonymous authors declare that "the first duty of a civilized government is to protect the interests of those over whom it exercises its guardianship. It is the duty of the head of a family to provide for his household, and to use every legitimate means to advance the interests and improve the condition of each individual under his protection. It is the same with the national government."[82] The parental metaphor was in full flower throughout the National Republican era. Henry Clay, who, following Hamilton's blueprint, articulated a comprehensive defense of protectionist trade policies, stated that although American industries would, like children, eventually learn to walk of their own accord, "in both instances, great distress may be avoided, and essential assistance derived, from the kindness of the parental hand."[83] Webster declared, "We want a Government of guardian kindness, of parental care."[84] All suffering classes – emancipated slaves, American Indians, the immigrant, former rebels – were to feel the parental care of government.[85] Clay argued that "the state has the right to assist an honest and unfortunate debtor . . . , borne down by a hopeless mass of debt, . . . and rendered utterly incapable of performing his duties to his family or his country. To say nothing of the dictates of humanity; nothing of the duties of a parental Government to lift up the depressed, to heal the wounds, and cheer and encourage the unhappy man who sees in the past, without his fault, nothing but ruin and embarrassment, . . . I maintain that the pub-

---

81. B. Harrison, speech, 2/22/1888 (Harrison 1892: 11).
82. "High and Low Tariffs, and their Effects," in *Documents Issued by the Union Republican Congressional Committee* (1877:1).
83. Clay, speech, 4/13/1844 (*New York Tribune* 6/29/1844).
84. Webster, speech, 5/5/1844 (*New York Tribune* 5/6/1844).
85. The "colored man," declared one campaign handbook, "owes every thing – liberty, security and enfranchisement to the Republican party" (*Campaign Documents issued by the Union Republican Congressional Executive Committee*, 1872: 5). Toward the Indians, "kindness, consideration and justice" were to be shown to "the most benighted and unfortunate inhabitants of the Republic" (*Campaign Documents Issued by the Union Republican Congressional Executive Committee* 1872: 6). The immigrant, too, would "feel the protecting care of the government of the United States" (ibid. 7). And the former rebels – "notwithstanding their persistent hostility and treasonable practices" – had been "clothed, fed and protected" (6). They should, the pamphlet counseled, "take hold of the National Government, and regard it as their best friend and protector" (6).

lic rights of the State, in all the faculties of its members, moral and physical, is [sic] paramount to any supposed rights which appertain to a private creditor."[86]

A tone of noblesse oblige ran through many stump speeches and after-dinner orations. "It is practically the duty of the educated and influential to help the ignorant and weak when possible," asserted Harrison, with respect to the (lawless and ignorant) immigrant.[87] Although the philanthropic side of National Republican rhetoric did not loose an avalanche of social legislation, it did establish the party's moral mission in the world:

> To whom much has been given, from him much is rightfully expected; and a heavy burden of responsibility rests upon the man of means to justify by his actions the social conditions which have rendered it possible for him . . . to accumulate and to keep the property he enjoys. He is not to be excused if he does not render full measure of service to the State and to the community at large. There are many ways in which this service can be rendered in art, in literature, in philanthropy, as a statesman, or as a soldier – but in some way he is in honor bound to render it, so that benefit may accrue to his brethren who have been less favored by fortune.[88]

Thus spake Theodore Roosevelt, whose life embodied the ideal of public service. "To do our duty; that is the summing up of the whole matter," Roosevelt informed his listeners on another occasion. "We must do our duty by ourselves and we must do our duty by our neighbors. Every good citizen . . . owes . . . service to the State, which is simply a form of expression for all his neighbors combined."[89] National Republican leaders were proud bearers of a rather deferential political culture that imposed the burdens of leadership upon the well-to-do.[90] The high-minded

---

86. Clay, speech, 6/4/1840 (Clay 1988: 419). It is perhaps clear that Clay is not advocating debt relief as a policy but simply asserting the government's right to intervene in such matters.

87. B. Harrison, acceptance letter, 9/3/1892 (Schlesinger 1973, 2: 1529). "We believe in the law of service," said Coolidge several decades thereafter, "which teaches us that we can improve ourselves only by helping others" (speech, 8/14/1924, in Coolidge 1924: 7).

88. Roosevelt, speech, 9/3/1900 (*New York Times* 9/4/1900).

89. Roosevelt, speech, 9/3/1900 (*New York Tribune* 9/4/1900).

90. Of the vice presidential nominee in 1844 (Theodore Frelinghuysen), the Whig platform claimed, "As a private man, his head, his hand, and his heart have been given without stint to the cause of morals, education, philanthropy, and religion" (Johnson 1958: 9). Of Grant, one party orator said, "Clothed with authority he has striven to protect the weak against the cruelties of the strong" (Henry Wilson, speech, 2/24/1872, in *Campaign Documents Issued by the Union Republican Congressional Executive Committee* 1872: 7). Henry Wilson harangued his audience to work for "the

ideal of political leadership, exerted through courts, bureaucracies, legislatures, and the presidency, was rooted in the presumption that the government would assemble the best and the brightest Americans, a true leadership class. Government was "to render [the Union's] institutions just, equal and beneficent, the safeguard of liberty and the embodiment of the best thought and highest purpose of our citizens."[91]

State-bashing, which would become the trademark of modern Republicanism, was virtually absent from Whig and Republican election appeals throughout the nineteenth and early twentieth centuries. In fact, the rhetorical center of gravity seems to have been very much on the side of the state. Henry J. Raymond argued against the Democratic notion that "the best government was the government which governed least." "No maxim," responded Raymond, "could be more dangerous or more false. . . . The Republican Government of the United States was created and exists for the express purpose of *aiding* the efforts of the people to improve their condition and to advance steadily toward greater prosperity and more complete well-being."[92]

National Republicans were state builders, working within the constitutional confines of a weak state. Pointing to the rise of the Italian nation-state (and thinking, presumably, of his divided homeland), Lieber saw unification as the predominant tendency among peoples of the Western world and the appointed task of his own party. The Civil War, viewed by many historians as a war whose primary accomplishment was the formation of the American state,[93] was similarly viewed by its protagonists. National Republicans were notoriously loose in their construction of the Constitution. "The Republican Party," Taft told his listeners, "has always been in favor of a liberal construction of the constitution to maintain the National power."[94] Although the Federalists were never referred to by name, the National Republican party maintained a spirited defense of Federalist principles. Contrasting the 1789 Constitution with the previous Articles of Confederation, the National Republican Convention issued the following manifesto in 1832:

> The great improvement made by the adoption of the present constitution in the political system of the old confederation, was the extension of the power of the union over the persons of the individual citizens, through the

elevation and protection of the poor and the lowly, the black men of the South and the poor white men of the whole country" (ibid. 8).
91. Republican platform, 1884 (Johnson 1958: 72).
92. Raymond, speech, 10/27/1852 (*New York Tribune* 10/29/1852).
93. See, e.g., Bensel (1990).   94. Taft, speech, 8/21/1908 (Taft 1910: 13).

action of the federal courts, including . . . a right of appeal to these courts from the decisions of those of the states. The adoption of this single salutary provision raised us from the situation of a cluster of poor, imbecile, and, for all substantial purpose, mutually dependent states, oppressed with debts, disturbed by insurrections, and on the verge of absolute anarchy, into our subsequent condition of one great, powerful, prosperous, glorious, free and independent federal republic.[95]

The evidence of party platforms portrays a stark and unremitting partisan struggle over the issue of government throughout the nineteenth century, with National Republicans adopting a posture of Federalism, and Democrats of Antifederalism (see figure 3).[96]

Where did this remarkably statist political philosophy originate? As has been discussed, National Republican views on political economy fed the party's appetite for government. The National Republicans were the "do something" party, the party that would shoulder the burden of economic development, defend American jobs and American products from foreign competition, defend and extend American commercial interests abroad, and carefully husband the country's natural resources. "Without sound governmental policy and wise and efficient governmental administration," Elihu Root assured his listeners, "the blessings [of prosperity] . . . would have been impossible."[97] Moreover, by the mid-nineteenth century such policies were increasingly the prerogative of the federal government, rather than the states, which gradually lost the capacity to regulate corporations.[98]

In this intimate government-business relationship, mercantilist doctrine emphasized that government was the senior partner. "The supervisory and regulatory power of society, exercised through the processes of government," Coolidge intoned, was "the supreme authority. No business may hold itself above consideration of the public interest and recognition of public authority. . . . If it will not fully and voluntarily adapt itself to these conditions, then they will be imposed upon it by the force of law."[99] This did not mean, of course, that party leaders were eager to impose this "force of law." National Republicans, seeing the interests of government and the interests of business as essentially complementary, were not ardent regulators, but they did adamantly maintain the supremacy of the state in business-government relations.

95. Address of the National Republican Convention, 1832 (Schlesinger 1971, 1: 563)
96. Virtually no exceptions could be found to this pattern.
97. Root, speech, 10/24/1900 (*New York Times* 10/25/1900).
98. See Dunlavy (1992).
99. Coolidge, speech, 10/11/1924 (*New York Times* 10/12/1924).

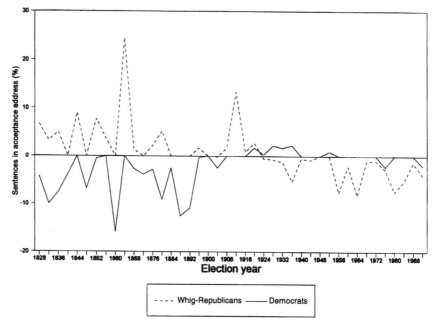

Figure 3. Statism, as measured by the percentage of sentences within Whig-Republican and Democratic nomination acceptance addresses devoted to the supremacy of the law, the virtues of the established authorities (legal and political) as brakes on popular passions, norms of social deference, the duties and responsibilities of the people vis-à-vis the government or society at large, strong and active government, government ownership, loose construction of the Constitution, or the supremacy of the federal government vis-à-vis the states and localities *minus* the percentage of sentences criticizing the supremacy of the federal government vis-à-vis the states and localities, or of government in general. (Does not include endorsements of good government or condemnations of bad government, endorsements of specific programs that may themselves have a statist effect but are not linked explicitly to the need for government interventionism, themes supporting social order, criticism of government ownership proposals that are advanced on purely pragmatic grounds, criticism of government capture by special interests [issues of government performance not intrinsic to government itself], and criticism of lower taxes or calls for public economy.)

Mercantilist theory was not incidentally statist, it was intentionally so. In fact, mercantilism may be viewed as the economic corollary of a more basic postulate, that of state building. "Protection," opined Clay, "was not merely called for by the substantial independence of our country, but it was a *parental duty of government*."[100] Tariff barriers, a uniform federal banking system, infrastructural improvements in transportation and communication, industrial development, and a strong national currency were proposed not simply for the purpose of achieving material wealth but also for the purpose of unifying the fractious country and constructing a strong and durable seat of power in the national capital. The formidable sectional biases of the United States would, according to orators from Hamilton to Coolidge, be overcome by the overriding concern for national prosperity that necessitated mutual cooperation among the states. The unsettled West, the underdeveloped South, and the financial and industrial centers of the eastern seaboard would all be linked together, to each section's mutual benefit. Whig and Republican orators endlessly repeated a line of argument adopted from Hamilton's *Report on Manufactures* – that the resulting surge in interstate commerce would "efface all lingering estrangements between our people."[101]

Underlying the two parties' differing views of the state was a contrasting view of political power. Whereas nineteenth-century Democrats viewed aggregations of power as inherently corrupt, National Republicans were less fearful. The party's long tenure in office, the 1904 platform declared, was not due to chance; it was, instead, "a demonstration that the Republican party has . . . a high capacity for rule and government," a fact all the more significant in light of "the incapacity and infirmity of purpose shown by its opponents."[102] The Republican party was the natural party of government, and government was seen as much more than simply a protector of individual liberties. In his characteristically terse style, Coolidge declared that "a government without power is a contradiction in terms" – a statement with which Democrats heartily concurred, but which they found worrisome.[103]

The party's attachment to government was not just a product of its economic philosophy but also a product of its anxieties. Government,

100. Clay, speech, 8/26/1828 (*New York Evening Post* 9/9/1828); emphasis added.
101. B. Harrison, speech, 9/26/1888 (Harrison 1892: 142).
102. Republican platform, 1904 (Johnson 1958: 137). "Unity of action and concentration of power should be our watch-word and rallying cry," said Johnson, campaigning for Lincoln in 1864 (acceptance letter, 7/2/1864, in Johnson 1986: 11).
103. Coolidge, speech, 9/6/1924 (Coolidge 1926: 92).

and its associated political institutions, was calculated to act as a brake on the passions of the electorate. Indeed, far from conforming to the populist strains of American liberalism, the dominant party between the Civil War and the Great Depression was frequently an outspoken foe of what it viewed as irresponsible and impractical notions of "rule by the people." Admittedly, the party never openly opposed the extension of suffrage rights, an issue that was largely settled in America by the 1820s; this much separated American conservatism from conservative parties elsewhere.[104] However, the fact that the democracy question had been settled early on should not obscure the very real differences that remained over the next century between the two parties on the central question of democracy.[105]

National Republican rhetoric, to begin with, contains scant mention of the term *democracy*. (The preferred terms were *republic*, or *American system of government*.) When *democracy* made an appearance, it was generally accompanied by the adjective *constitutional* or *representative*.[106] National Republicans referred to "our plan of popular government" – a plan that "contemplates such orderly changes as the crystallized intelligence of the majority of our people think best."[107] Democracy, for National Republicans, still contained its classical connotation of rule by the demos. In discussing the Russian Revolution, Harding refers to that cataclysm as a transition from one extreme to the other, from autocracy to "bolshevist democracy."[108] The clear implication is that only by maintaining an intermediate position between totalitarian control and democratic-inspired chaos had the United States managed to preserve the preeminent goal of liberty. National Republicans referred constantly to the dangers of "Demagogy." When the subject of popular sovereignty was raised, National Republicans were apt to stress its limits, its dysfunctionality. Coolidge warned, "The ability for self-government is arrived at only through an extensive training and education. In our own case it required many generations, and we cannot yet say that it is wholly perfected."[109]

National Republicans, like their Federalist forebears, tended to look askance at the prospect of the masses engaging directly in political af-

---

104. However, opposition to further democratization was occasionally expressed openly (e.g., Taft, acceptance speech, 8/2/1912, in Schlesinger 1971, 3: 2208).
105. See Ashworth (1983/1987).
106. See, e.g., the 1912 Republican platform (Schlesinger 1971, 3: 2178).
107. Harding, acceptance speech, 7/22/1920 (Harding 1920b: 27).
108. Harding, speech, 1/10/1920 (Harding 1920a: 111); speech, 2/23/1920 (Harding 1920a: 182).
109. Coolidge, speech, 10/15/1924 (Coolidge 1926: 150).

fairs. Virtually no statements in support of a majority-rule interpretation of democracy can be found in Whig-Republican rhetoric until the 1920s. (This was, of course, a staple of Democratic rhetoric by the end of the nineteenth century.) Public opinion, said National Republicans, was to be listened to only so long as it was "dependable," and "uttered through the representatives of the people," rather than self-appointed tribunes.[110] With respect to the pressing issue of nullification, Webster appealed to "the force of reason, . . . the progress of enlightened opinion, . . . the natural, genuine patriotism of the country, and . . . the steady and well-sustained operations of law," not simply "the people's will."[111] "Most certainly, I do not approve of appeals to the passions of the people, or of the use of disgusting or unworthy means to operate on their senses," said Henry Clay, in what was to become the party's stereotypical response to the threat of popular upheaval.[112] Of the Jacksonians, the National Republicans exclaimed, "Never was there a more direct appeal to those prejudices and passions, which, on all occasions, the good should disdain, and the wise should repress."[113] It was not to popular sovereignty per se that Republicans appealed, but to "intelligent and considered" public opinion, to the "enlightened conscience" of the public.[114] Accused on all sides of having "betrayed the people" during the three-cornered 1912 campaign, Taft wondered, "Who are the people? . . . [T]hey have not any of them given into the hands of any one the mandate to speak for them as peculiarly the people's representatives."[115]

Viewing the public as a generally passive body, National Republicans looked to parties, legislatures, bureaucracies, and courts to provide the political leadership necessary to conduct the affairs of government in a rational and considered manner. Whereas the Democratic party (particularly in its Populist phase) embodied the popular-will tradition of Rousseau and Paine, National Republicans stood squarely for *representative* democracy embodied in the Federalist Papers. National Republicans believed that public servants, once chosen, served as trustees, not delegates, of the people; that their responsibility was to the good of the whole community, not to a particular constituency; and that, to this end, legislatures were to be deliberative bodies, not conveyor belts for public opinion. The National Republicans' 1828 address to the people of Virginia dwelled at some length on the proper relationship between the

110. Harding, speech, 8/19/1920 (Harding 1920b: 64).
111. Webster, speech, 7/11/1832 (Webster 1986, 1: 566).
112. Clay, speech, 4/13/1844 (*New York Tribune* 6/29/1844).
113. Address to the People of Virginia, 1/17/1828 (Schlesinger 1971, 1: 465).
114. Coolidge, speech, 9/21/1924 (Coolidge 1926: 108).
115. Taft, acceptance speech, 8/2/1912 (Schlesinger 1971, 3: 2219).

legislator and his district: "The faithful Representative will obey the in-structions of his constituents whenever constitutionally given. He will pay a respectful attention to their wishes, and every evidence of their wishes. But, when not bound by instruction, he will look beyond the imperfect evidences of their will, informally conveyed: he will rest upon the conclusions of his own mind, formed from the best lights he can obtain: will consult his country's good, and firmly meet the responsibility of those acts, he deems proper for its attainment."[116] The "executive authority" had a clear duty, National Republicans felt, to stand up to pressures from civil society, to perform according to "principle," rather than popular acclaim.[117] As Roosevelt put it, lawmakers had a respon-sibility to act "in the interest of the people."[118]

The National Republican view of government fits comfortably into what would today be called an elite theory of democracy – democracy as an institutional arrangement in which citizens choose between com-peting teams of political elites. Foreshadowing Joseph Schumpeter, Wil-liam Seward declared, "By our individual suffrages, we express our choice whether one class of citizens, with a peculiar policy and peculiar principles, shall rule the country directing it in a course of their own, or whether a different mass with different policy and principles shall con-duct it in a different direction."[119] Democracy existed during elections; at other times the electorate was to sit and be silent.[120]

116. Address to the People of Virginia, 1/17/1828 (Schlesinger 1971, 1: 466). This point was echoed several decades later in a campaign speech given by James Garfield. His constituents, he claimed, "have not always approved my judgment, nor the wisdom of my public acts. But they have sustained me because they knew I was earnestly following my convictions of duty, and because they did not want a representative to be the mere echo of the public voice, but an intelligent and independent judge of public questions" (speech, 9/19/1874, in *Documents Issued by the Union Republican Congressional Committee* 1880: 13).
117. See, e.g., Hughes, speech, 10/9/1916 (Schlesinger 1971, 3: 2329–30).
118. Roosevelt, acceptance letter, 9/12/1904 (Roosevelt 1910: 94).
119. See Schumpeter (1942/1950) and Seward, speech, 10/21/1856 (Seward 1884, 4: 277).
120. Taft elaborated what amounts to a textbook statement of retrospective voting the-ory: "You ordinarily test the question whom you shall select by what they have done in the past, and if there be a party in power that has specifically met with efficiency and success the problems to be solved, the conclusion you will come to is that that party ought to be continued, rather than that another party should be put in power, whose policy you may be uncertain about" (speech, 8/29/1908, in Taft 1910: 37). The implication here is that it is rather difficult for the voters to involve themselves in the day-to-day running of government, or even to provide potential leaders with a comprehensive program for action once elected. "Uncle Joe" Cannon, Republican stalwart and, for several years, the dictatorial Speaker of the House of Representa-

Such attitudes were reflected in the different styles of campaigning adopted by nominees of the two major American parties. The Democrats, embodying their more plebiscitarian view of politics, were the first to issue an official letter of acceptance (Van Buren, in 1836), the first to accept the party nomination before a mass public (Grover Cleveland, in 1892, at Madison Square Garden), and the first to establish the precedent of open campaigning by a presidential candidate (Bryan, in 1896).[121]

Whigs and Republicans, by contrast, cultivated an antipopulist stance toward the general electorate. Party leaders administered paternal admonitions to the voters in which warnings and predictions of imminent disaster were followed by stern calls to duty.[122] Taft, throwing down the gauntlet before the American electorate in 1908, declared, "That is what the Republican party stands for, and that is what the Republican party intends to do, if you give them an opportunity by your mandate to take the power."[123] Voters were asked to vote up or down, not to question the party's programs. "We intend in the future to carry on the Government in the same way that we have carried it on in the past," Roosevelt asserted defiantly in 1904.[124] It was a defiant challenge to vote for the party of right, and far removed from the vox populi approach of the Democratic party.

The unreliable passions of the masses would be moderated, educated, and, if necessary, kept at bay by strong leaders, strong laws, and a functionally differentiated state apparatus. There was, to begin with, the U.S. Senate, a firm conservative bulwark against instability and popular revolt throughout most of the nineteenth and early twentieth centuries. Harding called senators "designated sentinels on the towers of constitutional government."[125] The upright statesmanship of the Senate's mem-

tives, is supposed to have remarked, "The best kind of government is where one party rules while the other watches."

121. Less well known are the previous canvassing efforts reviewed in the appendix. However, these proved to be isolated examples of candidate activism, lessons in what *not* to do for later nominees. All Democrats following after the Great Commoner took to the stump.

122. In schoolmarmish fashion, Coolidge lectured his listeners on the eve of the 1924 election: "The immediate and pressing obligation for tomorrow is that each one of us who is qualified shall vote. . . . If the individual fails to discharge that obligation, the whole nation will suffer a loss from that neglect" (speech, 11/3/1924, in *New York Times* 11/4/1924).

123. Taft, speech, 10/28/1908 (*New York Times* 10/29/1908).

124. Roosevelt, acceptance letter, 9/12/1904 (Roosevelt 1910: 48).

125. Harding, acceptance speech, 7/22/1920 (Harding 1920b: 21).

bers, coupled with its tradition of unrestricted debate and informed deliberation, assured the "security of stable, popular government."[126] It is important to point out that Harding spoke at a time when the Senate and the court system were under sustained attack, the former for its indirect process of election and nonmajoritarian rules of procedure and the latter for its unpopular and (it was charged) undemocratic decisions.[127] Until at least 1913, when the Seventeenth Amendment was passed, mandating the direct popular election of U.S. senators, the U.S. Senate retained its original mandate as an upper chamber, where bills passed by the direct representatives of the people (members of the House) would receive a more calm and reflective hearing. The Senate was perceived as an assembly of best men, those who were financially secure and who therefore could act on matters of public policy from a disinterested perspective, suitably removed from the pressures of popular election and from commercial pressures. Not coincidentally, the Senate was also a bastion of Republicanism. Whereas the House fell into Democratic hands fourteen times between 1861 and 1929, the Senate left Republican control during only five sessions.[128] Republican representation (as a percentage of total seats) was greater in the Senate than in the House in every congressional session except two during this period.[129]

More important than the Senate, however, was the independent judicial branch and the Constitution it was expected to uphold. From the very beginning, National Republicans looked upon the judicial system as an ally, a bulwark against the impulses of mass opinion. The judiciary, according to the 1832 Address of the National Republican Convention, was "an institution . . . more important than any one can be that merely affects the economical interests of the union."[130] Taft, the sitting president and future chief justice, explained it this way:

> The chief reason why the State devotes so much time and effort in the administration of justice is to promote the cause of peace and tranquillity

126. Harding, speech, 8/18/1920 (Harding 1920b: 61).
127. Harding, speech, 8/18/1920 (Harding 1920b: 64).   128. Stewart (1991: 206).
129. See Stewart (1991: 214). This persistent advantage in the upper chamber was not entirely accidental, Stewart has argued, since it was to some extent the product of the strategic admission of western states by Republican administrations and Republican-controlled Congresses. These low population areas contributed little to either party's representation in the House, but significantly bolstered Republican presence in the Senate, thus "ensuring the existence of a Republican enclave in the federal government that would be constitutionally capable of vetoing Democratic proposals when the Democrats captured the presidency and the House" (ibid.: 215).
130. Address of the National Republican Convention, 1832 (Schlesinger 1971, 1: 563). See also Webster, speech, 7/11/1832 (Webster 1986, 1: 528).

in the community. Speaking theoretically and ideally, of course, our aim is to secure equal and exact justice; but practically, the object sought is peace. ... The power of the courts to declare invalid laws of the Legislature ... has much contributed to the smooth working of our Constitution and to the supremacy of law and order in our community.[131]

Law, for National Republicans, was the first and foremost weapon in the fight against social disorder. The 1904 Republican platform praised McKinley for his rigorous "enforcement of the laws" and for his understanding that "to permit laws to be violated or disregarded opens the door to anarchy, while the just enforcement of the law is the soundest conservatism."[132] National Republican party leaders were involved with a juristic cast of mind, a fact rooted in their own personal histories. Adams, Clay, Scott, Lincoln, Hayes, Benjamin Harrison, McKinley, Roosevelt, Taft, Hughes, Harding, and Coolidge all came to politics with legal educations.[133] Indeed, every National Republican nominee except Garfield, Blaine, and those who rose to public prominence through military ranks was associated with the law in some fashion.[134]

The Constitution remained a beacon of National Republican ideology, "the ark of the covenant of American liberty."[135] "No other lesson short of the Lord's Prayer is so important," emphasized one minor Whig spokesperson in the election of 1844, referring to the task of inculcating respect for and knowledge of the U.S. Constitution.[136] The main theme of Webster's keynote address to the 1832 National Republican Convention was "whether the Constitution ... itself shall be preserved and maintained," a concern that was to preoccupy Republican orators through the Civil War, Reconstruction, and the diverse challenges of the late nineteenth and early twentieth centuries.[137] McKinley impressed upon his audience that "Standing by Constitutional authority and law is the highest obligation of American citizenship."[138] The Constitution embodied the force of prescriptive authority, particularly significant in a country with few symbols or myths legitimating the value of tradition.

---

131. Taft, speech, 8/6/1908 (Taft 1910: 3, 5).
132. Republican platform, 1904 (Schlesinger 1971, 3: 2006).
133. Roosevelt briefly attended law school at Columbia. Taft was a judge throughout most of his professional life. Hughes was a Supreme Court justice at the time of his nomination. Harding underwent a brief legal education.
134. The military men alluded to are William Harrison, Zachary Taylor, John Fremont, and U. S. Grant.
135. Harding, speech, 1/10/1920 (Harding 1920a: 104). Harding also referred to "the torch of constitutionalism" (speech, 7/22/1920, in Harding 1920b: 21).
136. Botts, speech, 4/12/1844 (*New York Tribune* 4/13/1844).
137. Webster, speech, 10/12/1832 (Webster 1986, 1: 531/69).
138. McKinley, speech, 9/12/1896 (*New York Times* 9/13/1896).

"The maintenance of the authority of the courts is essential unless we are prepared to embrace anarchy," said Taft in 1908, at the height of the Progressive era.[139]

As further protection for social order and private property, National Republicans appealed to statutory law. "Here is the volume of our laws," said Garfield, in the grandiloquent fashion of nineteenth-century oratory.[140] "More sacred than the twelve tables of Rome, this rock of the law rises in monumental grandeur alike above the people and the President, above the courts, above Congress, commanding everywhere reverence and obedience to its supreme authority."[141] The fascination that the concept of "rule of law" exercised over National Republicans was the product of two worries: first, the perceived threat of social anarchy, as represented by political acts of terrorism, violent labor/management conflicts, and the spread of socialistic and communistic societies in nineteenth- and early-twentieth-century America; and, second, the arbitrary and capricious nature of legislatures and executives when impelled by popular currents.

Thus, National Republicans endorsed a host of constitutional and institutional restrictions on the exercise of majority rule – an indirectly elected Senate, an independent judiciary, a written Constitution, and an accumulated body of statutory and common law. Such antimajoritarian features were not viewed as weakening the power of government. What worried members of the party was the specter of a radical, plebiscitarian executive, on the model of "King Andrew" Jackson, in tandem with a directly elected, nondeliberative House of Representatives. Checks and balances within the federal government were thus intended to thwart not the capacity of government but, rather, the possibility of popular

139. Taft, acceptance speech, 7/28/1908 (*Republican Campaign Text-book, 1908* 1908: 18). "The Republican party," the 1920 platform assured its readers, "will resist all attempts to overthrow the foundations of the government or to weaken the force of its controlling principles and ideals, whether these attempts be made in the form of international policy or domestic agitation" (Schlesinger 1971, 3: 2403). "Our Constitution has raised certain barriers against too hasty change," Coolidge emphasized. "Stability of government is a very important asset, . . . [yet a] deliberate and determined effort is being made to break down the guarantees of our fundamental law" (speech, 9/6/1924, in Coolidge 1926: 96). The Constitution was to guarantee not only governmental stability but also civil liberty and private property (ibid.).

140. Garfield, speech, 3/17/1880 (*Documents Issued by the Union Republican Congressional Committee* 1880: 3).

141. Garfield, speech, 3/17/1880 (*Documents Issued by the Union Republican Congressional Committee* 1880: 3). Except for a brief period in the 1920s when the federal enforcement of the Volstead Act became a major political issue, ordinary street crime remained in the background of national politics.

misrule. As long as popular prejudices were institutionally channeled, however, democracy would be kept safe, and government strong.

Order versus Anarchy

The theme of "order" loomed large in all National Republican pronouncements. Warnings of anarchy and social disorder, as well as endorsements of the necessity of restraints on individual freedom, were persistent from 1828 to 1932 and marked party leaders apart from their Democratic brethren (see figure 4).[142] The party phrased its public appeals in terms calculated to prey upon fears of wholesale change and instability. Valorized concepts included *history, tradition, conservation,* and *stability.* Terms of abuse included *experiment, innovation, radical,* and *revolution.* With the Revolution safely stowed away in the country's past, liberty was referred to as something to be preserved rather than sought after. "Friends of peace! Lovers of liberty!" the Maryland National Republicans declared in 1828, "We invoke you one and all to make one great and glorious effort, and *Preserve your country!* Recollect that the heritage we enjoy is a rich and precious one, and cost our fathers many years of sacrifice, of toil, and of danger – that it has been handed down to us to preserve inviolate. The trust is a sacred one – as its conservators we conjure you by the blood of our Fathers!"[143] "We want to give stability – to settle questions of national importance and give them repose," said the great Daniel Webster. "Every thing will be prosperous if we put down this everlasting agitation and adopt sound conservative Whig principles."[144]

Throughout the Gilded Age, Republicans continued to sing from the

142. The only election years showing significant traces of these themes in the modern Republican period occur in the late 1960s – a time when "law and order" had an obvious appeal to the conservative party. Such themes were, however, restricted to the issue of "crime," which had been recently discovered by Nixon. Party nominees did not leap to draw general conclusions about the disintegration of society and the need for a more energetic exertion of federal power in the interests of preserving social order.

143. Address to the people of Maryland, 11/6/1828 (Schlesinger, 1971, 1: 481).

144. Webster, speech, 5/2/1844 (*New York Tribune* 5/4/1844). Of Jackson's veto of the rechartering of the U.S. Bank, Webster had this to say: "We are entering on experiments, with the government and the Constitution of the country, hitherto untried, and of fearful and appalling aspect. This message calls us to the contemplation of a future which little resembles the past. Its principles are at war with all that public opinion has sustained, and all which the experience of the government has sanctioned. It denies first principles; it contradicts truths, heretofore received as indisputable" (speech, 7/11/1832, in Webster 1986, 1: 528).

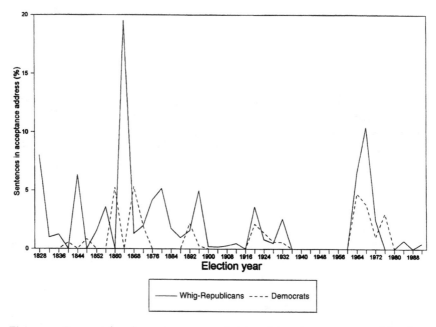

Figure 4. Support for the maintenance of the social order, as measured by the percentage of sentences within Whig-Republican and Democratic nomination acceptance addresses proposing the necessity of restraint on individual freedom; warning of the danger of anarchy and social disorder; or asserting the supremacy of the law, "liberty and order," and the necessity of tougher law enforcement

Whig songbook. Blaine attacked the Democrats' proposed tariff reductions by invoking the conservative values of his party: "Experiment in the industrial and financial system is the country's greatest dread, as stability is its greatest boon."[145] Three months later, Blaine declared, "I . . . remind you that if you do your duty on Tuesday next as becomes men of your lineage and your inheritance, the Republican adminstration of this Government will be continued; the Protective tariff will be upheld; the patriotism and the fruits of the civil struggle will be maintained, and the Government of the Union, preserved by the loyalty of the Union, will continue to be administered in loyalty to the Union."[146] One cannot help but be struck by the frequency of synonyms and near-synonyms of conservatism (*lineage, inheritance, continued, upheld, maintained, preserved, loyalty*) in this single sentence. The party was on a mission of

145. Blaine, acceptance letter, 7/15/1884 (Schlesinger 1973, 2: 1465).
146. Blaine, speech, 10/11/1884 (Schlesinger 1973, 2: 1474).

maintenance. McKinley implored his listeners to "be faithful to the acts, traditions, and teachings of the fathers. Make their standard of patriotism and duty your own. Be true to their glorious example, and whatever the difficulties of the present or problems of the future may be, meet them in the same spirit of unflinching loyalty to country and to public morals, family, the same acknowledgment of dependence upon God that has always characterized those grand men who builded [sic] the Republic."[147] The Republican party, as always, stood for "the preservation of law and order" and, in a memorable phrase, for "the reign of domestic quiet."[148]

Even at the height of the Progressive Era, the party identified itself as an agent of stability. In 1908, Taft pledged "nothing but safe and sane policies."[149] In 1912, in the face of overwhelming pressures for reform, he resolutely opposed "these innovations." The Republican party, Taft insisted, "refuses to make changes simply for the purpose of making a change, and cultivating popular hope that in the change something beneficial, undefined, will take place."[150] In 1916, Hughes portrayed Republicanism as "a party of stability; . . . a party of constructive force; . . . a party of rational progress. We look to the future, but we are inspired by a consideration of the record of the past."[151] In the Twenties, the presidential wing of the party could boast, "We have maintained our ancient traditions."[152]

How, then, was the threat of radicalism defined? In the case of the National Republican party, I argue that this threat, and the more general evil that motivated the party on all ideological fronts, was encapsulated in the concept of anarchy. What I mean by anarchy is something considerably more specific, and hence more descriptive, than simple opposition to revolution and radical change. To begin with, it is important to appreciate that the twin terms *socialism* and *communism* carried very little weight in National Republican rhetoric before the 1920s. In the midst of one of Taft's plodding, legalistic addresses during the 1908 campaign, the presidential nominee discussed his actions in a court case resulting from the 1894 Pullman Strike, led by Eugene Debs. Since Debs was also running for the presidency in 1908, the case was of more than historical interest. What is striking is how *in*significant Debs's ideology

147. McKinley, speech, 9/5/1896 (*New York Times* 9/6/1896).
148. McKinley, speech, 9/1/1896 (*New York Times* 9/2/1896).
149. Taft, speech, 8/21/1908 (Taft 1910: 29).
150. Taft, acceptance speech, 8/2/1912 (Schlesinger 1971, 3: 2209–10).
151. Hughes, speech, 9/28/1916 (Hughes 1916c: 3).
152. Coolidge, speech, 10/24/1924 (Schlesinger 1971, 3: 2554), and speech, 11/3/1924 (*New York Times* 11/4/1924).

seems to have been to the Republican candidate. One might expect that Taft would have jumped at the opportunity to lambaste the socialist threat. But his only concern was with the upholding of public order, and with the legal question – the proper use of injunctions – that he attempted to settle. Either Debs's peculiar ideology was entirely immaterial to him or Taft had good reason to pretend that it was; in either case, the peripheral nature of socialism in the party's public discourse is revealing.[153]

To make sense of the party's studied avoidance of socialism, as well as of communism, one must consider what these terms meant in pre–World War I America. In the context of the Transcendentalists' Brook Farm, Bellamy's utopian nationalism, George's single tax, Gronlund's cooperative Commonwealth, and countless other experiments in communal social organization[154] – many of them wildly popular among middle-class audiences – Republican orators from Clay to Hughes responded to the question of socialism with mild condescension, not rabid attacks. To one question about the prospects for creating cooperatively run business enterprises, posed after a lecture at New York City's Cooper's Institute, Taft responded: "It isn't possible to carry on a business as economically and with the same production of profit by a Government as it is under the motive of private gain. I am sorry that is the answer to the very humane and very kindly theories, many of which bear the name of socialism."[155] Later Republicans, needless to say, would take a less dispassionate tack. I do not mean to suggest that early Republicans were open to the ideas of socialism, but rather that they found it expedient to muffle their opposition and that they were infinitely more concerned with the threat of social collapse than with the threat of social reconstruction.

Taft considered the socialist solution equivalent to "confiscation," the abolition of "the principle and institution of private property," and the "taking away of the motive for acquisition, saving, energy, and enterprise," thereby destroying "the mainspring of human action that has carried the world on and upward for 2,000 years."[156] The objection is wholly pragmatic, the implication being that the socialistic state is very close to a state of anarchy, where property and contractual obligations are disregarded. What distinguishes the antiradicalism of Clay, McKin-

---

153. Taft fell back upon the familiar Republican refrain of maintaining governmental powers. "The authority of the courts must be upheld. If they are not, we might as well go out of the governing business" (speech, 10/28/1908, in Taft 1910: 215–16).
154. See, e.g., Nordhoff (1965).   155. Taft, speech, 1/10/1908 (Taft 1908a: 8).
156. Taft, speech, 8/2/1912 (Schlesinger 1971, 3: 2208).

ley, and Harding from that of Hoover, Eisenhower, Reagan, and associates is the conceptualization each era had of the dangers of the left. In an age prior to the development of the welfare state in Western Europe and state socialism in Russia, "radicalism" meant primarily disorder, anarchy. It was *too little* government that was to be feared, not too much. A reasonably vigorous state was considered necessary to uphold public order against the impending chaos of unchecked humanity. The National Republican party was thus a "law-and-order" party. ("We stand for enforcement of the law and for obedience to the law," said Roosevelt in 1904.)[157] But it is essential to understand that law and order carried a very different meaning from that understood in the present day. The primary enemy of society, according to National Republican belief, was anarchy and rebellion, not crime. (Crime became an issue of national importance for the first time in the 1920s, a more or less direct consequence of Prohibition.)

The most threatening instance of radicalism in the nineteenth and early twentieth centuries was neither socialism nor communism, but anarchism. There were, to be sure, relatively few adherents of anarchism. The movement owed its high profile largely to the mediaworthy nature of its cause (a provocative philosophical position, if ever there was one), its colorful and articulate protagonists, and its methods (most famously, "propaganda by the deed"). Anarchism made wonderful copy for mass-circulation tabloids, and with only several assassinations per decade it was possible to maintain a political "movement" of apparent magnitude. There was more to American anarchism than met the public eye (including efforts devoted to various working-class causes of the day and a principled stand for civil liberties), but these efforts, alas, were little noticed. The whole world was watching instead for signs of anarchistic dissolution.[158] No doubt, Republican sentiment on the matter was also affected by the assassination of one of their own (McKinley, in 1901) by a man claiming to follow the philosophical dictates of Emma Goldman.

The significance of anarchism in National Republican political philosophy can hardly be overstated. Anarchism was, logically speaking, the polar opposite of everything the party stood for – order, authority, and tradition. Some sense of the origins of this party-of-order perspective can be uncovered in the long history of domestic revolts that American nationalists had faced since the Revolution. By the mid-nineteenth cen-

---

157. Roosevelt, acceptance letter, 9/12/1904 (Roosevelt 1910: 94).
158. This is a paraphrase of the title of Gitlin's (1980) work on the interaction between the media and social protest during the 1960s.

tury, the nation had survived six armed or unarmed insurrections – in 1786 (Shays's Rebellion), 1794 (the Whiskey Rebellion), 1799 (Fries Rebellion), 1814 (the Hartford Convention), 1831 (the Nullification Crisis), and 1841–42 (Dorr's Rebellion) – as well as countless skirmishes with "rebellious" Native American tribes. National Republican statism was driven, in part, by the many internal rebellions afflicting the young republic, a danger partly real and partly fanciful, but in any case greatly feared. Not surprisingly, when the Civil War broke out, National Republicans looked upon the struggle as another outbreak in a long line of domestic insurrections.[159] "[W]e pledge ourselves," promised the 1864 platform, "to do everything in our power to aid the Government in quelling by force of arms the Rebellion now raging against its authority, and in bringing to the punishment due to their crimes the Rebels and traitors arrayed against it."[160] It was the government that was at war, and Government that was at stake.

It requires some effort from the contemporary reader to recapture the sense of horror that *anarchy* and its associated terms (*chaos, radicalism, agitation, rebellion, class*) evoked among National Republicans. If "Dorrism"[161] were to predominate, Clay thought, "Any unprincipled adventurer would have nothing to do but to collect around him a mosaic majority, black and white, aliens and citizens, young and old, male and female, overturn existing governments and set up new ones, at his pleasure or caprice! What earthly security for life, liberty or property, would remain if a proceeding so fraught with confusion, disorder and insubordination, were tolerated and sanctioned."[162] Several decades later, as pitched battles were played out across the country between labor and

---

159. Henry Clay's declaration of 1828 – that the Union was, "competent to suppress all . . . domestic insurrections" – foreshadowed the party's response to the Civil War (speech, 8/26/1828, in *New York Evening Post* 9/9/1828). For a work that takes this perspective on the Civil War, see Paludan (1972).

160. Republican platform, 1864 (Johnson 1958: 35).

161. This was a reference to Dorr's Rebellion, in the 1840s, which sought, unsuccessfully, to revise the Rhode Island Constitution in a more democratic direction. With respect to this rebellion, the *Junius Tracts* declared: "It has all along been but too apparent, that this new 'Democracy' was not overcharged with respect, either for Constitutional or Statute law, or any law whatever, that might happen to come in its way. But the outbreak in Rhode Island unmasked the party, . . . and evinced how much more they are swayed by passion . . . than by law. . . . The peace and welfare of our country, and the stability of our Government and its institutions, demand, that we should know who will sustain them, or who will consent to overturn them in an unpropitious hour" (Colton 1844: 89).

162. Clay, speech, 4/13/1844 (*New York Tribune* 6/29/1844).

management – the labor struggles of 1877, culminating in the deaths of three dozen persons; the Haymarket Riot (1886); the Homestead Strike (1892); the Pullman Strike (1894); and the Steel Strike and Policeman's Strike (1919) – the scale and ferocity of social violence seemed uncontainable.[163] Garfield wondered whether it was safe to disregard the authority of law when:

> In all quarters the civil society of this country is becoming honeycombed through and through by disintegrating forces – in some States by the violation of contracts and the repudiation of debts; in others by open resistance and defiance; in still others by the reckless overturning of constitutions and letting "the red foolfury of the Seine" run riot among our people and build its blazing altars to the strange gods of ruin and misrule. All these things are shaking the good order of society and threatening the foundations of our Government and our peace. In a time like this, more than ever before, this country needs a body of law-givers clothed and in their right minds, who have laid their hands upon the altar of the law as its defenders, not its destroyers.[164]

In 1896, with the Populist menace apparently rising, McKinley was moved to declare:

> ... the platform of the Democratic National Convention [is] an assault upon the faith and honor of the Government and the welfare of the people. ... We meet the sudden, dangerous and revolutionary assault upon law and order ... with the same courage that we have faced every emergency since our organization as a party, more than forty years ago. Government by law must first be assured; everything else can wait. The spirit of lawlessness must be extinguished by the fires of an unselfish and lofty patriotism.[165]

Skipping ahead another two decades, we find Harding wrestling with similar anxieties. "Humanity is restive," commented the future president. "Much of the world is in revolution, the agents of discord and

163. One might also consider the significance of vigilantism in nineteenth-century America. One historian estimates that more than 190 vigilante organizations populated the United States between 1861 and 1890 – groups that were dedicated to combating such diverse problems as horse thievery, toll turnpikes, the price of commodities, and the competition of Negro labor (Keller 1977: 487). The 1912 platform favored the condemnation and punishment of lynching not on the basis of its immorality or cruel effects, but rather because it was a form of "lawlessness," which, along with all other forms, should be suppressed (Republican platform 1912, in Schlesinger 1971, 3: 2185).

164. Garfield, speech, 3/17/1880 (*Documents Issued by the Union Republican Congressional Committee* 1880: 4).

165. McKinley, acceptance speech, 8/26/1896 (Schlesinger 1971, 2: 1863, 1870–71).

destruction have wrought their tragedy in pathetic Russia, have lighted their torches among other peoples, and hope to see America as a part of the great Red conflagration."[166] Harding's lecture, no doubt heartfelt, seems an eerie repetition of Garfield, of McKinley, and indeed of Henry Clay and Daniel Webster – who responded to the French revolutions of their day with much the same distaste. Long after the last embers of the Civil War had been extinguished, the perceived threat of internal revolt remained.

Even the Democratic party was suspect. Indeed, the Democratic party was viewed through National Republican eyes as treasonous, boss-ridden, immigrant-dominated, and prone to dangerous experimentation. The Democrats, along with third parties and protest movements, were subtly tarred with the anarchist brush. When facing the indomitably conservative Grover Cleveland, Benjamin Harrison declared that the Democratic party offered "a program of demolition."[167] William Jennings Bryan, a Populist in Democratic clothing, as far as McKinley and Roosevelt were concerned, only confirmed party leaders' long-standing fears.

Such responses were, I would argue, the reiteration of a long-standing sensitivity to threats against government and country among National Republican leaders. "The American Union is valuable in every respect," declared a party tract in 1876, "and because of all this, we cannot afford to close our eyes to the promulgation of any political creed or principle which may impair its power, or endanger its perpetuity, or ultimately accomplish its overthrow."[168] "The power to coerce," this document continued, "is ... clearly expressed in the Constitution, so clearly an incident of its authority, ... [and] essentially 'the first law of nature,' exercised by all nations."[169]

166. Harding, acceptance speech, 7/22/1920 (Harding 1920b: 25).
167. B. Harrison, acceptance letter, 9/3/1892 (Schlesinger 1973, 2: 1530).
168. *The People a Nation* (*Documents Issued by the Union Republican Congressional Committee* 1877: 1).
169. *The People a Nation* (*Documents Issued by the Union Republican Congressional Committee* 1877: 8). The significance of anarchy within National Republican thought can be glimpsed as well in the realm of foreign affairs. "Should our power by any fatality be withdrawn," McKinley warned, "the Commission believes that the government of the Philippines would speedily lapse into anarchy, which would excuse, if it did not necessitate, the intervention of other powers, and the eventual division of the islands among them" (speech, 9/8/1900, in *Boston Sunday Globe* 9/9/1900). Whether fighting Indians, the Mexican government, or various colonial powers, National Republicans tended to emphasize the superior capacity of the American government to provide order among indigenous people who were assumed to be incapable of doing so themselves. "[T]he most miserable failure which a Gov-

Born of revolution, the only democracy in the world with unrestricted (white) male suffrage, a settler society that had no fixed national identity and was rent by incessant and often violent conflict along class, racial, ethnic, and sectional lines, the United States posed a difficult challenge to state builders. But it was a challenge they understood and were well prepared to face. Perhaps more than any other value, *order* – and its antithesis, *anarchy* – defined Whig and Republican ideology between 1828 and 1924.

The Moral Order of Yankee Protestantism

The virtually unanimous opinion of those who have studied the Republican party is that, whatever else the party may have stood for, it also represented the values of "individualism."[170] It is easy to locate the sources of this common interpretation, for party orators harped on the virtues of personal autonomy, liberty, and the work ethic. Yet National Republican individualism was of a distinctive sort, one most aptly characterized as *Victorian*, since it emphasized the limits and duties of the individual rather than his or her unfettered freedom of action.[171]

For National Republicans, the Protestant ethic was a code of conduct more than a charter of rights. Citizens were implored to exercise self-restraint, self-control, self-mastery – to behave in a "civilized" fashion. Party leaders' preoccupation with the issue of character bordered on the obsessive. "The necessity of a careful discrimination among the emigrants seeking our shore becomes every day more apparent," Benjamin Harrison remarked. "We do not want and should not receive those who, by reason of bad character, are not wanted at home. The industrious and self-respecting, the lovers of law and liberty, should be discriminated from the pauper, the criminal and the anarchist, who come only to burden and disturb our communities."[172] German character was praised for "its steadiness, its industry, its fidelity, its integrity, its truth in friendship, its loyalty to Government."[173] The ever-popular term *self-*

---

ernment can inflict upon the people," thought Coolidge, two decades later, "is a lack of order and security. Unless a Government be strong enough to maintain public confidence in the observance of the orderly processes of law, we not only have no economic development but an immediate cessation of all enterprise and a substantial destruction of all values" (speech, 10/24/1924, in Schlesinger 1971, 3: 2554).

170. See, e.g., Keller (1977: 558).
171. The anti-individualistic – indeed, openly hierarchical – nature of Republican "mugwumpery" (referring generally to Republican reformers in the late nineteenth century) is nicely brought out in Ellis (1993: 110–14).
172. B. Harrison, acceptance letter, 9/3/1892 (Schlesinger 1973, 3: 1529).
173. Blaine, speech, 10/27/1884 (Blaine 1887: 453).

government held a double meaning for National Republicans, being understood on a national as well as an individual level.[174] The Lincoln myth was constructed as a model of manliness and self-restraint. "[H]ow lofty is the nature of Mr. Lincoln," began Blaine. "How he keeps himself free from the ordinary passions by which even great men are swayed beyond the confines of discretion. . . . He has gained control over others by constantly maintaining it over himself and has established the highest standard of personal and official bearing by refraining from the pettiness of resentment and being too magnanimous to indulge in revenge."[175]

The party was distinctly unenthusiastic about "individualism," a term associated with selfishness, greed, and licentious behavior. In only four nomination acceptance addresses in the nineteenth and early twentieth centuries did the "individual" (as noun or adjective) receive favorable treatment. More typical was the following commentary from Teddy Roosevelt. "Each section of the community will rise or fall as the community rises or falls," he said on the dais in 1900.[176] "While we should, so long as we can safely do so, give to each individual the largest possible liberty, . . . yet we must not hesitate to interfere whenever it is clearly seen that harm comes from excessive individualism."[177] Taft, when addressing the problem of antitrust violations, responded: "We are dealing with an incident of human progress and with some unfavorable condition produced by the operation of individualism."[178] The sort of individualism the early Republican party stood for was aptly summarized as "a wise and *regulated* individualism."[179]

The multitude was not to be trusted. "The worst evil that could be inflicted upon the youth of the land would be to leave them without restraint and completely at the mercy of their own uncontrolled inclinations," counseled Coolidge. "We know too well what weakness and depravity follow when the ordinary processes of discipline are neglected. . . . One of the greatest needs of the present day is the establishment and recognition of standards, and holding ourselves up to their proper observance."[180] A general fear of bodily appetites informed the National Republican view of humanity. Coolidge reminded his audience of the character who "refused to recognize or obey any authority, save his own

---

174. "Self-government" as applied to an individual might be translated in a contemporary context as "individual autonomy."
175. Blaine, speech, 9/5/1864 (Blaine 1887: 50).
176. Roosevelt, speech, 9/3/1900 (*New York Times* 9/4/1900).
177. Roosevelt, speech, 9/3/1900 (Roosevelt 1911: 306).
178. Taft, speech, 8/21/1908 (Taft 1910: 27).
179. Republican platform, 1908 (Schlesinger 1971, 3: 2110); my emphasis.
180. Coolidge, speech, 9/21/1924 (Coolidge 1926: 105).

material inclinations. . . . Vice and misery, were the . . . natural and inevitable consequences."[181] National Republicans, in keeping with their Protestant moorings, viewed human nature with an abiding mistrust.[182] Seeing the individual as inherently sinful, National Republicans concluded that a certain degree of self-imposed, and state-imposed, repression was necessary. When Republican politicians invoked "the individual," they meant not that one should do as one *would*, but rather that one should do as one *should*. "The *true theory* is, that it is the duty of every citizen to 'submit to the powers that be,' and that as the national authority is supreme, so is the national claim of allegiance to it supreme," declared one party tract in 1876.[183]

Duty and obligation were frequent themes of Republican campaign oratory, which bore more than a casual resemblance to sermons. "The feelings are to be disciplined, the passions are to be restrained, true and worthy motives are to be inspired, a profound religious feeling is to be instilled, and pure morality inculcated under all circumstances," said Daniel Webster in the 1840 presidential campaign. "All this is comprised in education. Mothers who are faithful to this great duty will tell their children that neither in political nor in any other concerns of life can man ever withdraw himself from the perpetual obligations of conscience and of duty; that in every act, whether public or private, he incurs a just responsibility, and that in no condition is he warranted in trifling with important rights and obligations."[184]

Liberty was, indeed, a paramount ideal of the National Republican party. However, the party's emphasis was usually on the problems posed by unrestricted liberty, rather than its blessings:

> What a wide difference between the American position and that imagined by the vagabond who thought of liberty as a glorious feast unprotected and unregulated by law. This is not civilization, but a plain reversion to the life of the jungle. Without the protection of the law, and the imposition of its authority, equality cannot be maintained, liberty disappears and property vanishes. This is anarchy. The forces of darkness are travelling in that direction. But the spirit of America turns its face towards the light.[185]

Liberty usually appeared in campaign rhetoric in conjunction with "order," as in "orderly liberty under the law" or the ubiquitous "liberty

181. Coolidge, speech, 9/21/1924 (Coolidge 1926: 106).
182. See, e.g., Taft, speech, 1/10/1908 (Taft 1908a: 8); and Coolidge, speech, 9/21/1924 (Coolidge 1926: 105).
183. *The People a Nation*, 1876 (*Documents Issued by the Union Republican Congressional Committee* 1877: 3).
184. Webster, speech, 10/5/1840 (Norton 1888: 339).
185. Coolidge, speech, 9/21/1924 (Coolidge 1926: 110).

and order."[186] Liberty, said Harding, "lies in the supremacy of law, and orderly government is humanity's best inheritance."[187] Liberty was a "temple," and the party's appointed task was to "save the Temple of Liberty from pollution."[188] Liberty and freedom, thus, referred to the freedom of the *community* more often than the freedom of the individual.[189] "Here is a temple of liberty no storms may shake," ran a typically florid passage from Harding. "Here are the altars of freedom no passions shall destroy. It was American in conception, American in its building, it shall be American in its fulfillment."[190]

From this perspective one can understand why governmental repression was often justified in the name of preserving liberty. "We do hold the right to crush sedition, to stifle a menacing contempt for law, to stamp out a peril to the safety of the Republic or its people, when emergency calls," asserted Harding, "because security and the majesty of the law are the first essentials of liberty. He who threatens the destruction of the Government by force or flaunts his contempt for lawful authority, ceases to be a loyal citizen and forfeits his rights to the freedom of the Republic."[191] Implying to members of the Church of Jesus Christ of Latter-day Saints that their religious practices might not receive protection under the First Amendment, Blaine stressed that, like other members of the national community, "the Mormons must learn that the liberty of the individual ceases where the rights of society begin."[192] "[T]he rights of freedom," emphasized Harding, "impose the obligations which maintain it."[193] Roosevelt asserted, "Whoever claims liberty as a right must accept the responsibilities that go with the exercise of the right."[194] On First Amendment matters, Harding asserted, "We have held the freedom

186. McKinley, speech, 10/13/1900 (*New York Times* 10/14/1900).
187. Harding, speech, 2/25/1920 (Harding 1920a: 205).
188. Address to the people of Virginia, 1/17/1828 (Schlesinger 1971, 1: 474).
189. Harding, speech, 8/4/1920 (Harding 1920b: 46).
190. Harding, acceptance speech, 7/22/1920 (Harding 1920b: 36).
191. Harding, acceptance speech, 7/22/1920 (Harding 1920b: 27). The 1920 Republican platform echoes the same refrain: "The Republican party . . . reaffirms its unyielding devotion to the Constitution of the United States, and to the guaranties of civil, political and religious liberty therein contained. It will resist all attempts to overthrow the foundations of the government or to weaken the force of its controlling principles and ideals, whether these attempts be made in the form of international policy or domestic agitation" (Schlesinger 1971, 3: 2403).
192. Blaine, acceptance letter, 7/15/1884 (Schlesinger 1973, 2: 1468).
193. Harding, acceptance speech, 7/22/1920 (Harding 1920b: 27). "If any man seeks the advantages of American citizenship," Harding said earlier in 1920, "let him assume the duties of that citizenship" (speech, 1/10/1920, in Harding 1920a: 106).
194. Roosevelt, acceptance letter, 9/12/1904 (Roosevelt 1910: 52).

of speech which the Constitution guarantees more sacred than the guaranteeing instrument. . . . There isn't room anywhere in these United States for any one who preaches destruction of the government which is within the Constitution."[195]

Liberty, in National Republican terms, meant the freedom to participate in American society according to the rules of government and the norms of society. It meant, first and foremost, the right of citizens "to work and enjoy the products of their labor."[196] Claiming that he would gladly free his slaves (in 1864) Andrew Johnson added: "If they do not like [me] and [my] pay, they can go where they can do better. This is the great principle of liberty in its true sense. Man must work – man must earn his living by the sweat of his brow."[197] Within the context of the Puritan-Protestant ethic, freedom was virtually a disciplining exercise, in which individuals would learn – by trial and error, if necessary – to apply themselves to the tasks that life imposed.[198]

The National Republican critique of Democratic populism was occasionally quite cogent. Coolidge addressed the question directly and at some length during one address at the beginning of the 1924 campaign:

> They [the libertines and libertarians of the world] seem to think that authority means some kind of an attempt to force action upon them which is not for their own benefit, but for the benefit of others. . . . They misinterpret the meaning of individual liberty, and therefore fail to attain it. They do not recognize the right of property, and therefore do not come into its possession. They rebel at the idea of service, and therefore lack the fellowship and cooperation of others. Our conception of authority, of law and liberty, of property and service, ought not to be that they imply rules of action for the mere benefit of someone else, but that they are primarily for the benefit of ourselves. The Government supports them in order that the people may enjoy them. . . . When each citizen submits himself to the authority of law he does not thereby decrease his independence or freedom, but rather increases it. By recognizing that he is a part of a larger body which is banded together for a common purpose, he becomes more than an individual, he rises to a new dignity of citizenship. Instead of finding himself restricted and confined by rendering obedience to public law, he finds himself protected and defended and in the exercise of increased . . . rights. . . . Primitive life has its freedom and its attraction, but the observance of the

195. Harding, speech, 1/10/1920 (Harding 1920a: 105).
196. Johnson, speech, 10/4/1864 (Johnson 1986: 226).
197. Johnson, speech, 7/19/1864 (Johnson 1986: 42).
198. "[O]ne of the most important things in the relationship of men," Harding reminded his audience, "is the keeping of contracts. We must perform our legal obligations with great fidelity, and we must always hold our moral obligations as inviolable" (speech, 9/11/1920, in Harding 1920b: 151).

restrictions of modern civilization enhances the privileges of living a thousandfold.[199]

This, as political rhetoric goes, is a truly gifted passage, arguing that freedom was more than a zero-sum game in which the individual vied with social and political authorities, that the construction of individuality was itself dependent upon social forms (such as government), and that within a democratic political system this authority emanated from the people themselves. Coolidge here points to a broader, more "positive" conception of freedom and liberty. "Underneath and upholding political parties," he asserted at another point in the 1924 campaign, "is the enduring principle that a true citizen of a real Republic can not exist as a segregated, unattached fragment of selfishness, but must live as a constituent part of the whole of society, in which he can secure his own welfare only as he secures the welfare of his fellow men."[200]

One way of viewing the party's oft-expressed ambivalence on questions of personal liberties and rights is that members of the party simply did not view the latter – with the exception of very basic civil liberties and right to property – as existing prior to society or to governmental institutions.[201] Harrison, quoting Washington, affirmed the party's general position, that " 'Liberty is indeed little less than a name where the Government is too feeble to withstand the enterprises of factions, to confine each member of society within the limits prescribed by the law, and to maintain all in the secure and tranquil enjoyment of the rights of persons and property.' "[202] "Natural rights" was the calling card of the Democratic party, and it could seldom be found in National Republican rhetoric. Rights, for this party, were thought to be definable only within the context of political institutions. "All that we have of rights accrue from the Government under which we live," emphasized Coolidge.[203]

199. Coolidge, speech, 9/21/1924 (Coolidge 1926: 106); and speech, 5/30/1924 (Coolidge 1926: 21–22).
200. Coolidge, acceptance speech, 8/14/1924 (Coolidge 1924: 3).
201. Speaking of the British Conservative party, O'Gorman writes: "Men had basic social rights – to the unhindered possession of their goods and labour, to order, justice and security – but their political rights depended upon the constitution of the state as it existed. . . . The will of the people . . . was not the origin of political rights. Men were obliged to obey legitimate (i.e. prescriptive) and legal authority so long as the state did not itself threaten its own legitimacy" (1986: 14).
202. B. Harrison, speech, 2/22/1888 (Harrison 1892: 11).
203. Coolidge, speech, 5/30/1924 (Coolidge 1926: 22). However, the more usual approach to these questions was simply to contrast "order" and "chaos." "There can be no peace save through composed differences, and the submission of the individual to the will and weal of the many. Any other plan means anarchy and its rule of

Throughout the nineteenth and early twentieth centuries, Whigs and Republicans were much more likely than their Democratic opponents to support sumptuary laws, temperance (or outright prohibition), and state-supported public education (rather than sectarian schools). It must be acknowledged that these issues did not appear with great frequency in the speeches and platforms of the presidential party. However, when they did, a contrast between "libertarian" Democrats and "moralistic" Republicans usually was apparent.[204] The 1888 platform, for example, asserts that "The first concern of all good government is the virtue and sobriety of the people and the purity of their homes. The Republican party cordially sympathizes with all wise and well-directed efforts for the promotion of temperance and morality."[205]

National Republicans are rightly understood as the party of American Protestantism, in its "pietistic" form. From the traditions of Yankee Protestantism the party derived its didactic tone and its sense of mission. "Elevate, educate, make moral and free the basis of society, and not only is the safety of the State ensured, but all other classes will be prosperous and contented." So counseled a partisan tract during the 1872 election.[206] It was an atmosphere as much as an agenda that Protestantism brought to the party. The Whigs were influenced directly by the Second Great Awakening, and their Republican successors carried forth, in scarcely attenuated form, a belief in the perfectibility of humanity and the consequent necessity of moral reform. Against the secular tradition of nineteenth-century Democracy (things would change in the twentieth century with the advent of William Jennings Bryan), National Republicanism counterposed a tradition of moral reform.[207] Whigs and Republicans believed in "efficiency, education, rationality, and uniformity," not just the achievement of prosperity.[208] They were, as historians have aptly pointed out, the party of uplift.

force," said Harding – a truly surprising statement, even for him (acceptance speech, 7/22/1920, in Harding 1920b: 25).

204. Although I build self-consciously on the work of other historians in the following account, my description of National Republicanism differs in substance and temporal range from the standard ethnocultural account. See Jensen (1971), Kelley (1979), Kleppner (1970; 1979), and Silbey (1985).

205. Republican platform, 1888 (Johnson 1958: 82–83).

206. "The Republican Party: The Workingman's Friend" (1872), in *Campaign Documents Issued by the Union Republican Congressional Executive Committee* (1872).

207. Kleppner (1981b: 134).

208. Howe (1979: 9). National Republicans were sensitive to those Democrats who accused them of committing the sin of greed. In response, party leaders appealed to the higher principle of patriotism. The nation was the higher good that would justify materialistic activities carried on in the marketplace.

Thus, although issues of a socioeconomic or political nature often seemed to preoccupy party officials, National Republicanism also represented a distinct cultural order. In the National Republican party, Protestantism met the spirit of capitalism. Despite the party's constant appeal to material interest, party leaders could be found just as often touting the significance of morality, spirituality, and (nonmaterial) devotion to country. Indeed, their invocations to thrift, hard work, cleanliness, sobriety, good character, social responsibility, and fair play drew as much from biblical sources as from marketplace experiences. The party's cultural agenda dovetailed with its economic agenda to such an extent that it is difficult to differentiate between the two (and, by all indications, National Republicans did not).

It is precisely because the marketplace was seen as an arena of moral activity, not simply of self-interest, that the occasional and inevitable transgression of the rules of the game struck National Republicans so profoundly. A moralistic perspective on such matters as unfair trade practices did not mean that party leaders were anticapitalist; they evaluated such events as pathologies, the product of individual sin rather than systemic injustice. (Democrats, by contrast, were more apt to take a systemic approach to the problem of monopoly.) It was therefore considered essential that all transgressors be promptly and firmly dealt with and that order and justice be restored. It is true that National Republicans identified themselves with an industrial system that wrought revolutionary change in the social structure and in popular lifestyles. But because National Republicans identified with these forces from the outset, there was no perceived disjuncture between economic progress and the dictates of morality. As long as the market was properly regulated and moral infractions consistently punished, prosperity would "promote that comfort and contentment at home which conduces to good citizenship, good morals, and good order."[209] The image of Ben Franklin rightly belongs on the National Republican mantel.

Similarly, there is no way of making sense of the nineteenth-century debate over slavery without an understanding of the National Republican party's moralistic approach to politics. To many Whig leaders, and to virtually all Republican leaders, slavery represented a moral blight. Even party centrists, like Lincoln, were convinced of the odiousness of this system of involuntary, abject, and permanent servitude. Indeed, the thrust of the party's arguments seemed to have more to do with cleansing white souls of evil than with helping their black brethren. It should be noted that at no time did the presidential wing of the Republican party

209. See McKinley, speech, 9/1/1896 (McKinley 1896a: 158–60).

advocate anything beyond civil and political rights for the oppressed black population. As Grant declared in 1873, "Social equality is not a subject to be legislated upon, nor shall I ask that anything be done to advance the social status of the colored man, except to give him a fair chance to develop what there is good in him, give him access to the schools, and when he travels let him feel assured that his conduct will regulate the treatment and fare he will receive."[210]

The issue of slavery poses evident problems for a thesis positing continuity between the Whig and Republican parties, since this is one issue on which they are usually considered quite distinct. The Whig party, with loyal constituencies in the South, could not articulate a strong aversion to chattel slavery without alienating those sections. Thus, the party's presidential candidates generally remained silent on this question, observing the so-called gag rule. At the same time, behind the veneer of indifference was a core of intense dislike for a system that jarred fundamentally with the free-labor ideal – a feeling shared by Clay, Webster, and virtually all Northern Whigs.[211] Even Clay, from the border state of Kentucky, was to declare to the Senate in 1833 that slavery was "the darkest spot in the map of our country."[212] During the 1844 election, the widely distributed *Junius Tracts* declared that its author was "a Northern man, born and educated in a free State, always opposed to slavery, still opposed to it, judging it to be wrong, and desiring to see it abolished, as well in this country, as in all others. . . . We, therefore, of the free States (we speak for the great body of the people), do not yield to the Abolitionists a whit in our opposition to slavery; we differ from them only as to the mode of getting rid of the evil."[213] It was no accident, therefore, that so many old-line Whigs eventually found their way into the newly formed Republican party.

A content analysis of party platforms that focuses on the broader issue of equal rights for African Americans reveals three salient points (see figure 5). First, scarcely a single statement in support of Negro rights

---

210. Grant, inaugural address, 3/4/1873 (Richardson 1897, 6: 4175).
211. Whigs, according to most scholars, cultivated a much stronger antislavery image than their Democratic opponents throughout the North during the 1840s. During the Jacksonian period, Silbey writes, "whatever support for intervention [in matters pertaining to slavery] there was came from the Whigs" (1991: 85). See also Ershowitz and Shade (1971: 611–12), Formisano (1971: 120–21; 1983: 299–300), Holt (1978: 149), Howe (1979: 17, 37), Kohl (1989: 174), Foner (1970: 189–90), Reiter (1996b: 217), Sundquist (1983: 53–55), and Watson (1990: 246).
212. Quoted in Foner (1970: 189). According to Foner, "Many western Whig-Republican leaders, including . . . Abraham Lincoln, learned their anti-slavery convictions as well as their staunch Unionism from Clay" (1970: 190).
213. Colton (1844: 66).

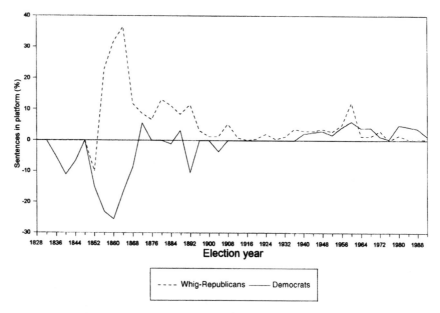

Figure 5. Support for civil rights for African-Americans, as measured by the percentage of sentences within Whig-Republican and Democratic party platforms advocating civil rights or civil liberties *minus* the percentage of sentences opposing civil rights, "Negro Supremacy," abolition, and so forth, or supporting states' rights and opposition to federal power in such contexts as would obviously impede civil rights

can be found in Democratic party platforms and scarcely a word of reproach in National Republican platforms. Second, although differences between the parties were most marked at mid-century, the question of civil rights (in particular, the voting rights of blacks in the South) continued to divide the parties through the entire period under consideration. Finally, it is important to note that civil rights dominated partisan discourse only during one brief period, immediately preceding and following the Civil War. Indeed, the banner under which Lincoln and other party leaders chose to conduct their campaigns – electoral and military – was the banner of nationalism. Republicans depicted themselves as protectors of the sacred Constitution and saviors of the union, not as protectors of black men and women. For several decades, the party formally renamed itself the Union and Republican Party. In Lincoln's pronouncements as a candidate and later as president, he would constantly insist that his mission and his duty was to save the Union, not – or at best only coincidentally – to free the slaves.

In light of the momentary and rather peripheral nature of antislavery

sentiment within the presidential wing of the Republican party, arguments for ideological continuity are all the more compelling. Republican
presidential candidates were just as keen to duck questions of civil rights
for black citizens at the end of the nineteenth century as Whigs had been
at the beginning of that century. It was simply not profitable to champion the cause of a group of citizens who were not numerous in the
North and could not vote in the South. Abolitionist rhetoric was popular
in New England, and sometimes in New York and Pennsylvania, but it
was not the logical rhetorical choice for a party seeking to win over the
West, the Midwest, and the border states. Abolitionists were already
ideological captives of the party anyway, having no place else to turn.
They remained on the fringes of the Republican party, a strong force
only within Congress and only through the end of Reconstruction. In
1868, Carl Schurz fashioned the Republican agenda as one of "peace,"
based upon "a restored Union, . . . results already accomplished and . . .
a state of things already existing."[214]

Thus, in matters of slavery, sobriety, schooling, and work, National
Republicans championed the values of Yankee Protestantism. The issues
of morality changed somewhat from era to era, but the image of crusading Whigs and Republicans chasing unregenerate Democrats endured. "[E]very political community and neighborhood has a character
of its own, a moral character, as well as every man and every woman,"
suggested Benjamin Harrison, "and it is exceedingly important . . . that
our communities should maintain a good reputation for social order,
intelligence, virtue, and a faithful and willing obedience to law."[215]

Americanism

America, said Teddy Roosevelt, was "the greatest Republic upon which
the sun has ever shone."[216] "They [the Democrats] serve the interests of
Europe; we will support the interests of America," promised the 1888
Republican platform.[217] "We propose to have an American Administra-

---

214. Schurz, speech, 9/19/1868 (Schurz 1913, 1: 419).
215. B. Harrison, speech, 10/6/1888 (Harrison 1892: 164). The moralistic side of Whig
    ideology is emphasized by Howe (1979). For the early Republican party, see Gien-
    app (1987: 430), and for mugwump and progressive Republicans, see Hofstadter
    (1955).
216. Roosevelt, speech, 10/6/1900 (*New York Times* 10/7/1900).
217. Republican platform, 1888 (Johnson 1958: 80). The 1892 platform commended "the
    able, patriotic and thoroughly American administration" of President Harrison
    (Johnson 1958: 95). Harrison claimed, on a similar note, that "the policies of the
    administration have . . . been distinctively and progressively American and Repub-
    lican policies" (acceptance letter, 9/3/1892, in Schlesinger 1973, 2: 1516). "[I]t has
    always been a source of profound gratification to me," he said, "that, in peace and

tion, which . . . will unflinchingly maintain American rights on land and sea," said Charles Evans Hughes. "We shall not tolerate the use of our soil for the purpose of alien intrigues. We shall not permit foreign influences or threats from any quarter to swerve our action."[218] "Nationalism," claimed Harding (who popularized the phrase "America First"), "was the vital force that turned the dearly wrought freedom of the republic to a living impelling power. Nationalism inspired, assured, upbuilded."[219]

With numbing regularity, National Republicans identified their party as the American party and their policies as American policies. Although such patriotic outbursts reached a shrill crescendo in the first several decades of the twentieth century, they were characteristic of the National Republican party throughout the nineteenth century. In virtually *all* epochs of party history, Whig-Republicans were more likely to appeal to patriotic sentiment than were their Democratic colleagues. (The only major exception to this pattern could be found in the 1840s, when the Whig party, reticent in the face of further westward expansion, briefly opposed the Polk administration's prosecution of the Mexican-American War.) Whether expansionist (throughout most of the nineteenth century), imperialist (during the country's brief venture into overseas territories in the 1890s), or isolationist (during the 1920s), the Republican party was sure to present its position on matters of foreign policy as the only true *American* position, the only position that would adequately defend American rights and interests. During the election of 1900 – one of the few American presidential elections to be waged primarily over matters of foreign policy – TR challenged his audiences to "look on all sides of [the imperial question] – the material side, the moral side, [and] the side of the greatness and honor of the Nation."[220] Monetary and currency questions in the nineteenth century were considered

war, a high spirit of patriotism and devotion to our country has always pervaded and dominated the party" (speech, 10/4/1888, in Harrison 1892: 160).

218. Hughes, speech, 10/25/1916 (*New York Times* 10/26/1916). Worried as ever about the debilitating effects of unrestrained marketplace practices, National Republicans responded: "It is love of country, not love of dollars, that will make America great" (Hughes, speech, 10/29/1916, in *New York Times* 10/30/1916).

219. Harding, speech, 9/11/1919 (Harding 1920a: 94). See also Harding, speech, 1/10/1920 (Harding 1920a: 113). The foregoing quotation recalls William McAdoo's evaluation of the president's speech-making capabilities: "His speeches leave the impression of an army of pompous phrases moving over the landscape in search of an idea. Sometimes these meandering words would actually capture a straggling thought and bear it triumphantly a prisoner in their midst until it died of servitude and overwork" (quoted in Harris 1966: 228).

220. Roosevelt, speech, 10/4/1900 (*New York Times* 10/5/1900).

inseparable from questions of "national honor."[221] "We do not need to import any foreign economic ideas or any foreign government," said Coolidge. "We had better stick to the American brand of government, the American brand of equality, and the American brand of wages. America had better stay American."[222] Thus, although also a figure of speech, homilies to the American form of government performed real political work, positioning National Republicans on a wide variety of foreign and domestic issues.

The Civil War provided one of the primary reference points for Republican patriotism. In winning the war, Republicans considered themselves to have saved the Union, reconsecrated the Republic, and renewed American virtue. Garfield, speaking to a crowd of veterans, waxed eloquent: "These very streets heard the measured tread of your disciplined feet, years ago, when the imperiled Republic needed your hands and your hearts to save it, and you came back with your numbers decimated; but those you left behind were immortal and glorified heroes forever; and those you brought back came, carrying under tattered banners and in bronze hands the ark of the covenant of your Republic in safety out of the bloody baptism of the war."[223]

National Republicans evinced a dedication to the ideals of state service, athleticism, and militarism that is without parallel in American party history. Waving the bloody shirt was not simply a vote-catching device. Fourteen times the party nominated men with military careers for the office of the presidency (the Democrats did so only five times during the same 1828–1924 period).[224] The most prominent interest group within the Republican party during the Gilded Age was an organization of veterans from the Civil War called the Grand Army of the Republic, a name that was to become synonymous with Republicanism in the Gilded Age. The idea that the victors in the battlefield should be the victors in the political field was common sense for members of this party, who did not suffer the Democrats' civic republican anxieties about standing armies and the prospect of military tyranny.[225]

221. McKinley, speech, 10/1/1896 (*New York Times* 10/2/1896); and Hughes, speech, 9/19/1916 (Hughes 1916a: 7).
222. Coolidge, speech, 9/1/1924 (Coolidge 1926: 81).
223. Garfield, speech, 6/16/1880 (Garfield n.d.: 449–50).
224. Taft, Roosevelt's successor, although not having served in the military himself, at least had the distinction of having been president of the Philippines Commission (the acting authority in what was then effectively a U.S. colony) and Roosevelt's secretary of war.
225. This fear could occasionally be found during the 1828 and 1832 elections, in response to the figure of General Jackson, but quickly died out as Whigs gained power

In many ways, however, it was a defensive sort of nationalism that party leaders articulated in the nineteenth and early twentieth centuries. National Republicans were convinced of the exceptional nature of American history and American institutions.[226] Yet the American experiment was fragile, and the autarchic ideal loomed large:

> If there be a nation on the face of the earth which might, if it were a desirable thing, build a wall upon its every boundary line, deny communication to all the world, and proceed to live upon its own resources and productions, that nation is the United States. There is hardly a legitimate necessity of civilized communities which can not be reproduced from the extraordinary resources of our several States and Territories. . . . This circumstance, taken in connection with the fact that our form of government is entirely unique among the nations of the world, makes it utterly absurd to institute comparisons between our own economic system and those of other governments, and especially to attempt to borrow systems from them.[227]

These were the words of John Logan, accepting the vice presidential nomination in 1884. The same line of reasoning could be seen in party rhetoric throughout the nineteenth and early twentieth centuries. Speaking in support of Clay's American System, several decades earlier, the *Junius Tracts* declared: "It is [British] policy to make and keep us *dependent on them*; it is our policy to be *independent of all the world*."[228] "Our country," the pamphlet crowed, "[is] a world in itself."[229] Protectionism, perhaps the preeminent economic issue of the National Republican period, was explained as the "protection of *American interests* against the hostile machinations of foreign commercial systems."[230]

and established themselves as the primary proponents of military men and military values.

226. The superiority of American over European citizenship, and especially over the less civilized territories of the world, was a favored theme. Coolidge, for example, declared that the holder of American citizenship was a "peer of kings" (speech, 5/30/1924, in Coolidge 1926: 23). "This country," thought McKinley, "differs in many and essential respects from other countries" (speech, 9/1/1891, in McKinley 1896a: 159).

227. Logan, acceptance letter, 7/21/1884 (*Proceedings of the Eighth Republican National Convention, 1884* 1884: 195).

228. Colton (1844: 37).   229. Colton (1844: 48).

230. Colton (1844: 39). Protectionism would "preserve the American market for American producers and . . . maintain the American scale of wages" (B. Harrison, speech, 9/11/1888, in Schlesinger 1971, 2: 1692). The war of independence was invoked with every tariff dispute, with National Republicans fighting for "the preservation of our commercial independence" (B. Harrison, speech, 10/13/1888, in Harrison 1892: 174). Harding argued along similar lines for a reforestation program that

Some of the force behind the party's patriotism can be found in the following passage from a speech by Charles Evans Hughes: "In this land of composite population, drawing its strength from every race, the national security demands that there shall be no paltering with American rights. The greater the danger of divisive influences, the greater is the necessity for the unifying force of a just, strong, and patriotic position. ... We are unreservedly, devotedly, whole-heartedly, for the United States, ... for the unflinching maintenance of all American rights on land and sea."[231] Whereas British Tories could stand upon a tradition with connections to medieval England, Whigs and Republicans were standard-bearers of a national identity still struggling to assert itself within a European-dominated world. It was not simply history that Americans lacked but also a distinctive race, ethnicity, and religion. In a country under siege, it seemed, from the forces of immigration, it is no wonder that a whole range of shields was erected to guard "Americanism" from foreign subversion. Isolationism would shelter the country from foreign diplomatic and military entanglements, high tariffs would shut out foreign goods, developmental economic policies would ensure that the country could produce all necessary goods and services itself, and restrictive immigration laws (at first of Asians, and subsequently of Europeans) would exclude those deemed incapable of assimilating to American ways.[232]

The National Republican party was considerably more prone to xenophobic reaction than were its Democratic opponents. Benjamin Harrison warned, with reference to "Asiatic" intruders, that "We are ... clearly under a duty to defend our civilization by excluding alien races whose ultimate assimilation with our people is neither possible nor desirable."[233] During the election of 1896, McKinley declared his support for "such extension of the laws as will secure the United States from invasion by the debased and criminal classes of the Old World."[234] "[E]very object of our institutions of society and government will fail," Coolidge assured his listeners several decades later, "unless America be kept American."[235] "If we want to get the hyphen out of our country," he added several months later, "we can best begin by taking it out of our own minds."[236]

would "leave us independent of the resources or the activities of the remainder of the world" (speech, 8/18/1920, in Harding 1920b: 54).
231. Hughes, acceptance speech, 7/31/1916 (Schlesinger 1971, 3: 2299).
232. See Silbey (1991: 89).
233. B. Harrison, acceptance letter, 9/11/1888 (Schlesinger 1971, 2: 1693–94).
234. McKinley, acceptance speech, 8/26/1896 (Schlesinger 1971, 2: 1869–70).
235. Coolidge, acceptance speech, 8/14/1924 (Coolidge 1924: 5).
236. Coolidge, speech, 9/6/1924 (Coolidge 1926: 100).

National Republicans wished all foreign races and languages, once in the country, might dissolve in a thorough process of "Americanization."[237] As Hughes stated the case, "We are a composite population, drawing our strength from every race and every clime, and the test of Americanism is not a test of race or of blood or of ancestry; the test is supreme devotion to our country, supreme love of the United States."[238] Americanism was also looked upon as a solution to sectional strife, with the National Republican party parading itself as the "National" party (versus the "Sectional" Democratic party). Patriotic feeling, finally, was the common ground upon which all social classes could meet; a healthy patriotism would help preserve the ideal of social harmony in the face of discordant material interests. To class politics – those "un-American appeals to passion and prejudice" – McKinley counterposed "a grander sentiment," that of patriotism.[239]

Whatever the source of their nationalism, it is indisputable that Whigs and Republicans were masters of patriotic bombast. It would be a gross mistake, however, to assume that the language and symbolism of patriotism were adopted by party leaders for purely instrumental reasons. The concept of nationhood was central to the entire project that I have labeled National Republicanism. For American conservatives, as for their British counterparts, patriotism was "a celebration not merely of individuals and institutions but of a way of looking at society and history, a way of feeling about public life."[240] The Oneida County proceedings of the Republican Party Convention held at Rome, New York, on September 26, 1862, proclaimed, "The Republican organization, in all its principles, in all its practices, and by all its members, is committed to the preservation of the Union and the overthrow of the Rebellion. It is the power of the State and the power of the Nation."[241] Whigs and Republicans saw themselves as bearers of a national tradition; there was nothing more sacred to party leaders from Henry Clay to Calvin Coolidge (or, for that matter, Ronald Reagan) than the preservation of American sovereignty, American ideals, and the American way of life.

237. Hughes, speech, 10/25/1916 (*New York Times* 10/26/1916). "I believe," said Harding, "that every man who dons the garb of American citizenship and walks in the light of American opportunity, must become American in heart and soul" (acceptance speech, 7/22/1920, in Harding 1920b: 33).
238. Hughes, speech, 11/4/1916 (*New York Times* 11/5/1916).
239. McKinley (1896b: 8).   240. O'Gorman (1986: 6).
241. Published originally in the *Utica (NY) Morning Herald*; quoted in Skowronek (1993: 202).

Conclusions

I have argued that the ideology of the Whig and early Republican parties is most accurately summarized by the label National, and most accurately periodized between the elections of 1828 and 1924. My debts to the work of others in helping construct this synthesis are numerous and, I hope, well referenced. At this point it may be useful to underline some of the differences between this synthesis and previous approaches to the subject, which may be broadly described as *Progressive, liberal, ethnocultural,* and *realignment.* Without descending into a great deal of detail, I shall now attempt to outline these various approaches, as well as their limitations.

The Progressive take on the Whigs and Republicans, as parties representing the interests of business classes, has apparently survived the demise of the Progressive school of historians.[242] These parties' determined opposition to labor organizing and to redistributive or market-regulative legislation has offered plenty of fuel for neo-Progressive fires. Although not manifestly false, the Progressive version of Whig and Republican history is rather limited in what it can explain. One finds, as Progressivism would predict, an open defense of the interests and prerogatives of business, of the industrial system of production, and of state-led programs to aid production, in tandem with a continuing suspicion of need-based social welfare programs. Whigs and early Republicans were clearly "probusiness." But this, in itself, only begins to explain these parties' political rhetoric and legislative program. Did the business class consist only of high finance and industry, or also of small entrepreneurs and farmers? What were the interests of this class? Was the party the direct representative of business in government, or did it merely support, more or less of its own accord, probusiness measures? To complicate matters further, Whigs and Republicans were persistent and eloquent defenders of the "rights of labor," and proposed a set of programs to do just that.[243] Progressive understandings of Whiggism and Republicanism, in addition to oversimplifying the economic agendas of these two parties, have little to say about their perspectives on *non*economic questions.

A more common understanding of the Republican party (though less often of the Whig party) is to be found within the broad rubric of lib-

242. See, e.g., Burnham (1981: 116, 164), Clubb (1981: 112), Josephson (1934; 1940: 8), Ladd (1970), Schattschneider (1956: 197), and Schlesinger (1945: 503).
243. To this, one should add that Republicans were more successful than their Democratic counterparts in gaining working-class votes during the periods under discussion.

eralism. Hartz, for example, finds his Republican exemplar in Edward Everett, who declared, "In this country . . . [the] wheel of fortune is in constant revolution, and the poor, in one generation, furnish the rich of the next."[244] Clinton Rossiter, in much the same vein, argues that Republicans have been prisoners of the American tradition, echoing the same libertarian, individualistic, antistatist, optimistic, business-oriented, and achievement-oriented doctrine set forth by the country's founders.[245] Republicans, in a word, were liberals, to be located somewhere in the nineteenth-century tradition of Mill, Gladstone, and Spencer. Eric Foner's widely influential work on the free labor ideology of the early Republican party fits neatly into this liberal rubric. Early Republicans, writes Foner, "embraced social mobility and competitive individualism, and rejected the permanent subordination of any 'rank' in society" in favor of a society of free and equal laborers.[246] It is perhaps already clear that as a general label for the ideology of the Whig and early Republican parties, liberalism falls short.[247] These parties were openly hostile to the doctrine of laissez-faire, supporting statist solutions to a whole range of economic problems. National Republicans, moreover, were far from individualistic, in the usual sense of that term. If they were liberals, then it is an extremely broad definition of liberalism that one is forced to adopt.

According to a third account of party ideology, the Whig and Republican parties derived their weltanschauung and issue-agenda from the ethnic and religious orientations of their constituents. Seeing in cultural allegiances the key to Whig and Republican ideology, the ethnocultural historians have brought an entirely different fulcrum to bear on the nature-of-the-parties debate. Whigs and Republicans, at least through the end of the nineteenth century, have been portrayed as "political churches," expressing the moralistic and pietistic views of their predominantly Protestant voting bases. Republicanism within the third electoral system (1850s–1890s), for example, is said to have embodied "an activ-

---

244. Quoted in Hartz (1955: 112). See also Foner (1970) and Keller (1977: 558).
245. Rossiter (1960: 62, 68–71).
246. Foner (1970: 40). See also Gienapp (1987), for further elaborations on the significance of "free labor" to the early Republican party.
247. As Foner implicitly admits toward the end of his classic study of the mid-nineteenth-century Republican party, the ideology of the party was not based *solely* on the concept of free labor: "Resentment of southern political power, devotion to the Union, anti-slavery based upon the free labor argument, moral revulsion to the peculiar institution, racial prejudice, a commitment to the northern social order and its development and expansion – all these elements were intertwined in the Republican world-view" (1970: 320).

ist and interventionist disposition, a defense of righteousness, and a government willing and able to use its powers to compel cultural homogeneity as nothing less than a requirement of God's own will."[248] This argument is probably much closer to the mark than Progressive and liberal formulations. However, the ethnocultural account goes only so far in explaining the varied programmatic concerns of these parties. Although ethnocultural themes may explain voting behavior at mass levels, they seem to have made relatively few inroads into party life at presidential levels. One is struck by the paucity of references to churches, schools, temperance, and immigration in the party's platforms and in speeches given by party leaders on the campaign trail. Prohibition, for example, draws barely a squawk from *any* presidential candidate in the period. Finally, the ideological transformation that ethnoculturalists claim occurred in the 1890s – from a politics of "pietism" to a secular discourse of "social harmony" – is difficult to locate in national party rhetoric.[249] In short, the ethnocultural features of Whig-Republicanism, which I have summarized as Yankee Protestantism, must be considered only a part of that party's overall agenda.

A fourth answer to the ideology question is the realignment, or traditional-historical, perspective. For many historians and realignment theorists, the Whig and Republican can be understood only within the context of particular eras. During the Jacksonian era the U.S. Bank, the tyrannies of "King Andrew," and the defense of internal improvements served as rallying cries for Whig supporters. The critical issue in the decline of Whiggism and the rise of the Republican party was antislavery and the free-labor ideology. By the end of Reconstruction, slavery, civil

---

248. Kleppner (1981a: 97). The party's constituency consisted of "pietist" groups – "native Baptists, Congregationalists, Methodists, and Presbyterians," as well as Norwegian, Swedish, British, and "less confessional" German Lutheran ethnic groups (Kleppner 1981a: 96). Hofstadter, though not an ethnoculturalist, nonetheless arrives at similar conclusions about the character of the party. Republicanism, he thought, was an outgrowth of "indigenous Yankee-Protestant political traditions, and . . . middle class life." The party "assumed and demanded the constant, disinterested activity of the citizen in public affairs, argued that political life ought to be run . . . in accordance with general principles and abstract laws apart and superior to personal needs, and expressed a common feeling that government should be in good part an effort to moralize the lives of individuals while economic life should be intimately related to the stimulation and development of individual character" (quoted in Harbaugh 1973: 2071). For further research in the ethnocultural vein, see Benson (1961), Formisano (1971), Holt (1969), Jensen (1971), Kelley (1977; 1979), Kleppner (1970; 1979; 1981b; 1987), and Silbey (1967a; 1967b; 1977; 1985; 1991).

249. See Jensen (1971: 308) and Kleppner (1981a: 95, 103).

rights, and the "bloody shirt" were supplanted by a variety of interconnected monetary, currency, and trade issues. The Progressive era and the Twenties brought in their train similar transformations in the issue-agenda of the party. There are, of course, many different ways of telling this story, but most period-specific accounts describe a party that changed in fundamental ways from decade to decade (whether or not these corresponded exactly to realignment periodizations).[250] Yet case studies of particular epochs miss the remarkable continuities in Whig and Republican ideology from the nineteenth to the early twentieth centuries.

Two periods in Whig-Republican history have discouraged political scientists and historians from considering the nineteenth and early twentieth centuries as a single ideological unit. First, there is the obvious discontinuity between Whig and Republican party organizations. Recent research has shown, however, that the organizational and electoral ties between these two parties in the North were actually quite intimate, particularly at elite levels, where the Republican party inherited a whole generation of Whig leaders, including Horace Greeley, William Seward, and Abraham Lincoln.[251] Our concern, in any case, is with the ideological baggage carried by these two labels, and here it would seem that early Republicans conformed to Whig principles on most political issues of the day.[252] True, Republicans adopted a stronger stance on the issue

250. Most period-specific work on the Whig and Republican parties does not fall neatly into any of the foregoing categories (Progressive, ethnocultural, liberal). The following list of sources, although nowhere close to comprehensive (it includes, for example, rather few state-level studies), should offer a solid introduction to the literature in each historical period. For the Jacksonian era, see Ashworth (1983/ 1987), Brown (1985), Ershkowitz and Shade (1971), Kohl (1989), Latner (1975), McCormick (1966), Meyers (1957/1960), Schlesinger (1945), Silbey (1967a; 1967b), Watson (1990), Welter (1975), and Wilentz (1982). For mid-century, see Foner (1970), Gienapp (1987), and Silbey (1967a; 1967b). For the Gilded Age, see De Santis (1963), Dobson (1972), Gould (1970), Keller (1977), and Morgan (1973). For the Progressive era, see Gould (1974) and Harbaugh (1973). For the 1920s, see Hicks (1960) and Weed (1994). For works dealing with these parties' histories in a more synoptic fashion, see Mayer (1967), Moos (1956), and Shade (1981).

251. See, e.g., Howe (1979) and Neely (1993).

252. Connections between the Republican and Whig parties were particularly noticeable during the 1888 campaign, led by Benjamin Harrison – the grandson of William H. Harrison (the first successful Whig candidate for the presidency). Republicans, notes Jensen, "emphasized the symbols of continuity with the Whig tradition," including Tippecanoe clubs, which were formed across the country to support Harrison's campaign. In an address to the Indianapolis club, Harrison boasted that the current Republican party defended the "principles which were dear to you as Whigs . . .

of domestic slavery, a more interventionist perspective on matters of foreign policy, and a more favorable disposition toward the presidency. Yet in other respects the ideological birth of Republicanism is most appropriately traced to the 1830s – or perhaps back to the Federalist administrations of Washington and Adams – not to 1854 (the nominal birth date of the Republican party).

The second major challenge to the endurance thesis arrives in the Progressive era, when the party appeared to turn away from its traditional image of stalwart conservatism. Certainly, Robert La Follette, William Borah, and other western Progressives were far removed from – and often openly at war with – the party's eastern contingent. However, Progressive tendencies found expression mostly within the two houses of Congress. In presidential politics, the party's right wing was generally successful in suppressing all but the blandest Progessive tendencies.[253] Not once after TR, writes James Holt, did the Progressive wing of the party "succeed in electing or even nominating a presidential candidate of whom they wholly approved, and for all their brilliance as legislators, they were never able to match the legislative achievements of the Democrats under Woodrow Wilson."[254] Indeed, the mainstream of the Republican party looked very similar before, during, and after the Progressive era.

Theodore Roosevelt is a key figure in this ongoing historical debate. It is worth noting at the outset that this upstart politician with Progressive sympathies never would have attained the White House were it not for the accident of McKinley's death. Moreover, Roosevelt was actually a lot *less* Progressive through most of his tenure at the helm of the Republican party than his popular legacy suggests. His published writings and speeches (most of which were distributed for campaign purposes) reveal a leader who, up until he left the Republican party to run as a third-party candidate in the 1912 election, retained a deeply conservative political consciousness. What antitrust, anticapital rhetoric one finds in Roosevelt's speeches is to be found, by and large, within the last year of his second term.[255] During the 1900 and 1904 campaigns – which

chief among these . . . a reverent devotion to the Constitution and the flag, and a firm faith in the benefits of a protective tariff" (Jensen 1971: 15).

253. Even within Congress, it is worth noting that the Progressives remained a distinct minority within the Republican caucus, incapable of thwarting party leadership without the aid of allies in the Democratic party.

254. Holt (1967: 2).

255. See Cooper (1983: 113). The Square Deal, according to this historian, "contained more show than substance" (1983: 77). "[T]he measurable domestic legislative

is to say, while bearing the Republican party standard – his public pronouncements were strong statements of National Republicanism as described here.[256] The trustbusting Roosevelt came into full bloom only
after he had been denied the nomination by party regulars in his bid for
a third term. Feeling betrayed by those who had once obediently followed him, Roosevelt turned to the radical doctrines of Progressivism
for solace as well as for electoral support in the campaign of 1912.
Moreover, it should be noted that when he returned to the Republican
party, several years later, he occupied an ideological niche that was virtually indistinguishable from the views of party stalwarts.[257] At this
point, he became a bitter opponent of his erstwhile Progressive allies.
Thus, TR was only slightly more "progressive" (in any sense of the term)
than McKinley before him or Taft after him *while a spokesperson for
the Republican party.*[258] In sum, the Progressives got no further in their
quest to transform the Republican party than the radical abolitionist
wing of the party had in the previous century. Both are rightfully viewed

achievements of the Square Deal were few; outside of his [Roosevelt's] conservative
measures, which he effected by executive orders, there were only the Elkins Act
(1903); the Hepburn, Pure Food and Drugs, Meat Inspection, and Employers' Lia-
bility acts (1906); the 1907 act prohibiting corporation contributions to campaign
funds; and the 1908 law limiting trainmen's hours. Despite his prosecutions, trusts
were more numerous and powerful at the end than at the beginning of his term"
(Coletta 1971: 2054). See also Harbaugh (1973).

256. "On issue after issue he deferred to all that was conventional, all that was safe and
     reassuring," notes one campaign chronicle (Schlesinger 1971, 3: 1985).
257. In foreign policy, TR was distinguished from his confreres by his great enthusiasm
     for joining the European war.
258. A recent biographer writes, "Not only did [Roosevelt] approve of and seek to uphold
     the existing distribution of power and privileges in society, but he began with the
     aristocratic assumptions of one who believed he was or ought to be part of the
     'governing class' " (Cooper 1983: 33). The underlying conservatism of most Repub-
     lican Progressives is nicely illustrated in a letter written in 1910 by Henry Stimson
     – soon to be appointed secretary of war in the Taft administration – to TR. "To
     me," writes Stimson, "it seems vitally important that the Republican party which
     contains, generally speaking, the richer and more intelligent citizens of the country,
     should take the lead in reform and not drift into a reactionary position. If instead,
     the leadership should fall into the hands of either an independent party, or a party
     composed like the Democrats, largely of foreign elements and the classes which will
     immediately benefit from the reform, and if the solid business Republicans should
     drift into new obstruction, I fear the necessary changes could hardly be accomplished
     without much excitement and possible violence" (quoted in Rae 1989: 20). With
     respect to the monopoly issue, Cooper concludes, Roosevelt "stood closer to the Old
     Guard than to the progressives" (1983: 83). McKinley, as Roosevelt's own notes
     indicate, was likely to have instituted much the same sort of reforms (the issue of
     conservation excepted) had he lived through the Progressive era (Cooper 1983: 77).

as minority factions within the Grand Old Party. Once this peripheral position is acknowledged, a greater sense of consistency emerges within the 1828–1924 period.

The unity of the National Republican period is perhaps most visible in light of this party's incessant search for social, political, and moral *order* – a search that animated its Protestant, mercantilist, laborist, nationalist, and statist perspectives. A symbiotic relationship was thus established between the demonology of anarchy and the mission of state building, in which the vice of the first suggested the remedy of the latter. In certain ways, the National Republican party represented a Hobbesian moment in American politics. Realists in war and at home, their preeminent fear was of social collapse. The *Junius Tracts* offered the following fable to its readers during the course of the 1844 campaign:

> The head of a great family saw the big old Newfoundland family dog in his path, and cried out unto his sons – "Mad Dog!" Whereupon the youngsters seized their rifles, gave chase, and shot him down. But it turned out that he was in no wise mad at all, and the loss was grievous. He had been especially useful in keeping the numerous pack of small dogs in order. The moment he was dead, the small dogs broke loose, many of them ran mad and bit numbers of the family.[259]

The point at issue in this case was the chaotic situation imposed on the country since Jackson's slaughter of the National Bank (a financial leviathan if ever there was one), but the analogy could be more generally applied: the federal government was the mad dog that, by dint of its overwhelming size, would preserve order and justice against the smaller – and, cumulatively, more destructive – predators within civil society.

From this perspective, little separated Lincoln the Whig from Lincoln the Republican. Consider the following passages from Lincoln's famous address to the Springfield Young Men's Lyceum in 1838. His subject: "the perpetuation of our political institutions."

> I hope I am over wary; but if I am not, there is, even now, something of ill-omen amongst us. I mean the increasing disregard for law which pervades the country; the growing disposition to substitute the wild and furious passions, in lieu of the sober judgement of the Courts; and the worse than savage mobs, for the executive ministers of justice. . . . Having ever regarded Government as their deadliest bane, they [the lynch mobs] make a jubilee of the suspension of its operations; and pray for nothing so much, as its total annihilation. While, on the other hand, good men, men who love tranquility, who desire to abide by the laws, and enjoy their benefits, who would gladly spill their blood in the defence of their country; seeing their

259. Colton (1844: 25).

property destroyed; their families insulted, and their lives endangered; their persons injured; and seeing nothing in prospect that forebodes a change for the better; become tired of, and disgusted with, a Government that offers them no protection; and are not much averse to a change in which they imagine they have nothing to lose ... Whenever this effect shall be produced among us; whenever the vicious portion of population shall be permitted to gather in bands of hundreds and thousands, and burn churches, ravage and rob provision stores, throw printing presses into rivers, shoot editors, and hang and burn obnoxious persons at pleasure, and with impunity; depend on it, this Government cannot last. . . . [H]ow shall we fortify against it? The answer is simple. Let every American, every lover of liberty, every well wisher to his posterity, swear by the blood of the Revolution, never to violate in the least particular, the laws of the country; and never to tolerate their violation by others. As the patriots of seventy-six did to the support of the Declaration of Independence, so to the support of the Constitution and Laws, let every American pledge his life, his property, and his sacred honor; – let every man remember that to violate the law, is to trample on the blood of his father, and to tear the character of his own, and his children's liberty. Let reverence for the laws, be breathed by every American mother, . . . – let it be taught in schools, in seminaries, and in colleges; – let it be written in Primmers [sic], spelling books, and in Almanacs; – let it be preached from the pulpit, proclaimed in legislative halls, and enforced in courts of justice. And, in short, let it become the *political religion* of the nation.[260]

Not surprisingly, when it came time to face the central issue of his presidency, Lincoln declared, "Plainly, the central idea of secession, is the essence of anarchy."[261] This, rather than the evils of slavery, animated the party's public relations campaigns in the eras of the Civil War and Reconstruction. Indeed, throughout the Whig-Republican period, one finds reiterated the same basic opposition of anarchy and order. Garfield's response to the Paris Commune, McKinley's response to Bryanism, Taft's response to the more radical strains of Progressivism, and party leaders in the Twenties as they faced the Bolshevik revolution abroad and widespread unrest at home were linked together by a common conceptual paradigm. Liberty, if it was to be preserved at all, could survive only if the licentious elements of the general public could be effectively controlled. This could be accomplished either through internal discipline ("character") or through societal regulation. In the final analysis, strong government was both proof of a virtuous citizenry – which would faithfully respect its laws and its authority – and its guarantee.

260. Lincoln, speech, 1/27/1838 (Lincoln 1989a: 28–32).
261. Quoted in Foner (1980: 25).

4

The Neoliberal Epoch
(1928–1992)

The previous chapter focused on the remarkable continuities in Whig-Republican doctrine from the 1830s to the 1920s, a period that I have referred to as the National epoch. This chapter focuses on the second epoch in Whig-Republican history, stretching from the 1920s to the 1990s and denominated *Neoliberal*.

Freedom, for the older generation of American conservatives, meant freedom from foreigners' intrusion – their arms, their goods, their peoples, and their ways – and from civil disorder. It meant a state that was strong enough, and insulated enough from public pressures, to protect private property, nourish American industry, and preserve the American way. Beginning in the 1920s, the threat to liberty was reconceptualized; the danger was no longer anarchy, but rather the *state*. The federal government, for a century the party's ally, was now identified as a public enemy. The party's social policy shifted rhetorical ground as well. Where previously Whig-Republicans represented themselves as a party of laborers, modern Republicans championed the undifferentiated unity of society and the equal opportunity of all individuals.

To be sure, Republicans of the Neoliberal epoch had their differences. However, such differences are better viewed as matters of emphasis rather than of principle. "Radicals" like Barry Goldwater and Ronald Reagan adhered to the same general precepts as their more moderate colleagues – Herbert Hoover, Alfred Landon, Wendell Willkie, Thomas Dewey, Dwight Eisenhower, Richard Nixon, Gerald Ford, and George Bush. Consider, for example, General Eisenhower, the icon of the party's liberal wing in the postwar era. As described by one historian, Eisenhower was:

> very conservative in fiscal affairs and devoted to the principle of local responsibility in power and resource development. . . . President Eisenhower acquiesced in certain New Deal programs, but did nothing to expand them, and . . . remained philosophically opposed to much of the spirit of both the

New and Fair Deals. His acquiescence in programs like social security and limited public housing reflected political inevitability by the 50s, not the triumph of a "moderate" or "liberal" wing within the Republican party.[1]

Similarly, it may make sense to look at the ideology of Ronald Reagan not as the product of a "neoconservative" movement (stemming from Goldwater) but rather as the continuation of an older, more established ideological tradition. During the 1984 campaign, for example, Reagan was noted for running *against* government while running the government. Yet the same ingenious technique was employed by Eisenhower and by other Republican incumbents in the Neoliberal era.[2]

Although Hoover, Eisenhower, and Reagan were separated by many decades and faced very different political challenges, their public philosophies were remarkably congruent. Indeed, the ideology now associated with the Republican party can be found, full-fledged, in a slim volume of Hoover's speeches published in 1922 (and later popularized in his two presidential campaigns).[3] Herbert Hoover and, to a lesser degree, Calvin Coolidge deserve to be considered the founding fathers of modern Republicanism.

The argument of this chapter, therefore, is that Republican presidential campaigns from 1928 to 1992 reveal a consistent ideology – an ideology that differed in important respects from the party's previous (National) incarnation. Neoliberalism valorized small business (rather than labor), equal opportunity (rather than the social harmony of different classes), and individual freedom (rather than social order). It demonized government, political elites in general, and communism (which, in its myriad guises, constituted the new threat from the left). This chapter investigates these defining characteristics of modern Republicanism, concluding with ruminations on the surprising endurance of the 1920s transformation.

From Labor to Small Business

When addressing the "social question," National Republican rhetoric relied on the free-labor ideal. America was portrayed as a laborers' paradise, where work was plentiful, well rewarded, and "free" (freely contracted). It was an inclusive view of labor that could accommodate virtually every occupation, manual or nonmanual. Only sloth was excluded from this vision of economic virtue. In the 1920s and 1930s,

---

1. Reichard (1975), quoted in Rae (1989: 39).
2. See, e.g., Eisenhower, speech, 10/1/1956 (Eisenhower 1957: 828–37).
3. See Hoover (1922/1989).

however, the terminological axis of labor began to change. Protectionist trade policies were no longer justified as a mechanism to protect American labor but were, instead, a means of protecting the "average family."[4] Labor Day addresses by Republican candidates roamed far and wide among domestic and foreign policy issues, often having little to do with their purported subject matter.[5] The party's declining interest in labor becomes particularly evident when contrasted with its attention to agriculture: equal treatment was granted to these two blocs in 1928, but by 1940 the Republican platform devoted five times as much prose to the needs of agriculture as to the needs of labor.[6]

Not only did attention to labor themes diminish, but the party's position vis-à-vis the demands of organized labor also became markedly antagonistic. "We are making progress toward social peace and contentment with the preservation of private industry, of initiative, and full development of the individual," Hoover assured his audiences in 1928. "Working out of this ideal cannot be attained by compulsory settlement of employee and employer conflicts by the hand of the government. It cannot be attained by placing the government in business and reducing our people to bureaucracies."[7] *Organized* labor became particularly obnoxious to modern Republicans insofar as such oligopolistic "combinations" violated the natural workings of the marketplace. The rhetorical transformation of labor from universal interest to special interest was complete.[8]

Republicans thus refashioned themselves from a party representing

4. Republican platform, 1924 (Schlesinger 1971, 3: 2508).
5. See, e.g., Nixon, speech, 9/3/1972 (Nixon 1974: 849). Eisenhower's speech before the Brotherhood of Carpenters and Joiners during the 1956 campaign ignored domestic labor issues altogether, dealing instead with the cold war and the blessings of freedom (10/23/1956, in Eisenhower 1957: 996).
6. Explicit appeals on behalf of agriculture in Republican party platforms began in 1916 and remained at fairly high levels through the 1980s. In 1920, the platform declared, "The farmer is the backbone of the nation," a sentiment that would be repeated, in various forms, in virtually all subsequent platforms (Schlesinger 1971: 2407). The agricultural pitch was particularly prominent in the 1928 campaign (e.g., Hoover, speech, 8/11/1928, in Singer 1976: 8).
7. Hoover, speech, 9/17/1928 (Hoover 1928: 84).
8. Although Republicans were never enamored of labor unions, it was only in the late 1920s that they began to articulate an explicitly antilabor response. Republican spokespersons frequently asserted the party's support for the "right to collective bargaining" through the early decades of the century, but by 1928 these assertions began to fade out of party rhetoric or were accompanied by the right of workers to organize "freely," i.e., without having union membership thrust upon them through closed-shop bargaining. The end point in this long transformation was the passage of the Taft-Hartley Act (over Truman's veto) in 1946, which allowed states to pass "right-to-work" laws.

labor and capital, the two primordial social orders of the National Republican era, to a party representing the undifferentiated mass known by the end of the 1930s as the middle class. Hoover, turning to the youth of America in 1932, celebrated "the starting of business and professional careers."[9] Landon appealed to the working man "who would like to become his own boss – the average American."[10] Nixon promised "a chance not just to be a worker but to be an owner and a manager."[11] Although the value of work and the corresponding evils of idleness continued to preoccupy Republican politicians in the modern era, the value of labor was no longer connected with the laboring classes, but rather with such vaguer social denominations as "working men and women of the United States," "American workers," "working families," or simply the ubiquitous "American people."[12]

The history of American labor, claimed Ike, was one of "individual freedom, rooted in human dignity and in human responsibility."[13] All connotations of class had been excised.[14] Whereas in the previous era the party's didactic attachment to the work ethic was directed at immigrants, potential ne'er-do-wells, and American citizens at large, in the modern Republican period the work ethic provided another bludgeon to hit over the head of bureaucrats and the poor, the two sectors of

---

9. Hoover, speech, 10/31/1932 (Singer 1976: 120).
10. Landon, acceptance speech, 7/23/1936 (Singer 1976: 139).
11. Nixon, speech, 9/10/1968 (typescript, obtained from the Richard Nixon Library and Birthplace).
12. Eisenhower, speech, 9/3/1956 (Eisenhower 1957: 730); and Nixon, speech, 10/7/1972 (Nixon 1974: 964).
13. Eisenhower, speech, 10/23/1956 (Eisenhower 1957: 993).
14. Implicit in Republican campaign rhetoric was the illegitimacy of interest-based politics (which would array "class against class"). Rather than emphasizing the mutual benefits enjoyed by labor and capital and the reciprocal nature of their relationship, latter-day Republicans tended simply to ignore that there were any such divisions. Eisenhower's self-declared political philosophy (as articulated in his bid for reelection in 1956) was as follows: "We have rejected all concept of a nation divided into sections, groups or factions. We have insisted that, in the American design, each group in our nation may have special problems, but none has special rights. Each has peculiar needs, but none has peculiar privileges. . . . The supreme concern . . . is the justice, the opportunity, and the unity shared by 168 million Americans" (9/19/1956, in Eisenhower 1957: 781). As the 1972 party platform declared, "We must not divide and weaken ourselves by attitudes or policies which would segregate our citizens into separate racial, ethnic, economic, religious or social groups" (Johnson 1978: 886). The role of citizen was self-consciously substituted for that of worker (e.g., Eisenhower, speech, 10/23/1956, in Eisenhower 1957: 993). Whereas the Democrats saw people "only as members of groups," reiterated Ronald Reagan a decade later, a Republican government would "serve all the people of America as individuals" (speech, 8/23/1984, in Bush 1985: 310).

American society portrayed as idle or wasteful (unproductively employed). The party's traditional commitment to labor as a social category was also undermined by its increasingly consumerist outlook, a transformation that began in the 1920s and accelerated as the century progressed.[15] Where National Republicanism held a production-oriented view of the economy, featuring large-scale manufacturing enterprise, latter-day Republicanism was more likely to tilt toward the needs and interests of the individual consumer.

The decline of labor was accompanied by the rise of the "business man," or the "small business man," an innovation of great (though little-noticed) ideological significance.[16] Business thus became the universal social signifier of the modern Republican party, just as labor had been for the Whig and early Republican parties. Under this label, all respectable elements of society were henceforth subsumed. Thus did the party redefine itself from a party of labor and capital to a party representing the emergent middle classes.

The Equal Opportunity Society

Equal opportunity, when it entered National Republican discourse at all, usually referred to the equality of social classes, not of individuals. Thus, Taft promised "to secure for the wage-earner an equality of opportunity and such positive statutory protection as shall place him on a level in dealing with his employer."[17] Hughes declared his desire "to see throughout this land contented workingmen, realizing in their lives the equality of opportunity which our institutions promise."[18] In this context, equality of opportunity meant little more than equal treatment before the law, or "fair play." Whigs and early Republicans betrayed some doubt as to whether complete equal opportunity existed or could exist.[19] In any case, they did not make such themes the centerpiece of their

---

15. See, e.g., Republican platform, 1920 (Schlesinger 1971, 3: 2410); and Harding, speech, 9/6/1920 (Harding 1920b: 117).

16. In one of its last appearances in Republican party rhetoric, "capital" was defined by Hoover as "the savings of the people" (speech, 11/2/1928, in Hoover 1928: 181). Alf Landon was the first Republican nominee to adopt the small business man as emblematic of the party's constituency, and in this first instance the implication of the term for succeeding generations of Republican orators was clearly set. Landon told his campaign audience the lengthy story of how government abused small business men, who could not easily compete under the "monopolistic conditions" established by New Deal regulations (speech, 10/20/1936, in *New York Times* 10/21/1936).

17. Taft, speech, 7/28/1908 (*Republican Campaign Text-book*, 1908: 12).

18. Hughes, speech, 9/19/1916 (Hughes 1916a: 10).

19. See, e.g., Taft, acceptance speech, 8/2/1912 (Schlesinger 1971, 3: 2209).

campaign appeals. The prosperity of the laboring classes was a favorite theme, but "prosperity" did not signal equal opportunity across class boundaries. It meant that American workers would earn better wages and secure more regular employment than their counterparts in Europe and Asia would. "The wages of labor," explained McKinley, "should be adequate to keep the home in comfort, educate the children, and, with thrift and economy, lay something by for the days of infirmity and old age."[20] Economic success was defined as "contentment and independence" and the avoidance of "penury and want."[21]

Modern Republicans redefined success in bourgeois terms – the possession of a business and the achievement of substantial economic reward. "At one time we demanded for our workers a 'full dinner pail,' " said Hoover at the height of the 1920s economic boom. "We have now gone far beyond that conception. Today we demand larger comfort and greater participation in life and leisure."[22] Every man and woman was a potential entrepreneur. Dewey proclaimed the existence of "a free, open door for every man who wants to start out in business for himself."[23] "America became great," he continued in the throes of the wartime election of 1944, "because in this country there was unlimited opportunity."[24] Reagan referred to the Republican party as the "Great Opportunity Party," and America as the "opportunity society."[25] A tremendous spurt in "equal opportunity" themes appeared during Hoover's 1928 campaign. It was Hoover who proudly proclaimed "the emancipation of the individual" and the "ideal of equal opportunity."[26] Whereas previously the goal of equal opportunity was understood simply as a rejection of "class politics," now its purpose was to emancipate the individual:

> Equality of opportunity is the right of every American – rich or poor, foreign or native-born, irrespective of faith or color. It is the right of every individual to attain that position in life to which his ability and character entitle him. It tolerates no privileged classes or castes or groups who would hold opportunity as their prerogative.... Only from confidence that this right will be upheld can flow that unbounded courage and hope which stimulate each individual man and woman to endeavor and to achievement.

20. McKinley, acceptance letter, 9/8/1900 (*Boston Sunday Globe* 9/9/1900).
21. McKinley, acceptance letter, 9/8/1900 (*Boston Sunday Globe* 9/9/1900).
22. Hoover, acceptance speech, 8/11/1928 (Singer 1976: 12).
23. Dewey, speech, 9/7/1944 (Dewey 1946: 728).
24. Dewey, speech, 9/22/1944 (Dewey 1946: 746).
25. Reagan, speech, 8/25/1984 (Reagan 1987: 1190); and speech, 9/19/1984 (Reagan 1987: 1321).
26. Hoover, acceptance speech, 8/11/1928 (Singer 1976: 19).

... Th[e] ideal of individualism based upon equal opportunity to every citizen is the negation of socialism. It is the negation of anarchy. It is the negation of despotism. It is as if we set a race. We, through free and universal education, provide the training of the runners; we give to them an equal start; we provide in the government the umpire of fairness in the race. The winner is he who shows the most conscientious training, the greatest ability, and the greatest character. Socialism bids all to end the race equally. It holds back the speedy to the pace of the slowest. . . . Equality of opportunity is a fundamental principle of our nation. With it we must test all our policies. The success or failure of this principle is the test of our government.[27]

Perhaps no passage in twentieth-century Republican rhetoric better expresses the essence of the modern party's neoliberal perspective. In the 1920s, Republicans began trumpeting the rags-to-riches story as never before. "My parents and my grandparents came to Iowa in the covered wagon," confessed Hoover.[28] Willkie advertised himself as a descendant of "humble people – not members of the ruling or wealthy classes."[29] The presidency, the most exalted office in the republic, became the apotheosis of the self-made man. The United States was "a country in which any young man might become President."[30] Horatio Alger themes would continue to characterize Republican rhetoric through the 1990s (see figure 6).[31]

From Social Order to Individual Freedom

In 1908, the Republican platform promised that "the Republican party stands for a wise and regulated individualism,"[32] for, at this time, *unre*-gulated individualism was a harbinger of social disorder. By the 1920s, however, a more liberatory notion of individualism began to creep into party rhetoric. Henceforth, Republican speeches praised the "energy, determination and self-reliance" of the American pioneers.[33] "We don't celebrate dependence day on the Fourth of July, we celebrate Independence Day," Reagan pointed out during his bid for reelection, "the right of each

27. Hoover, acceptance speech, 8/11/1928 (Singer 1976: 19–20).
28. Hoover, speech, 10/4/1932 (Hoover 1977: 459).
29. Willkie, acceptance speech, 8/17/1940 (Singer 1976: 172).
30. Willkie, acceptance speech, 8/17/1940 (Singer 1976: 172).
31. Isolated examples of the Algerist myth in the National Republican period can be found in the 1890s in the speeches of McKinley (1896b: 3) and the 1908 party platform (Schlesinger 1971, 3: 2110). See also Foner (1970).
32. Republican platform, 1908 (Schlesinger 1971, 3: 2110).
33. Landon, speech, 11/2/1936 (*New York Times* 11/3/1936).

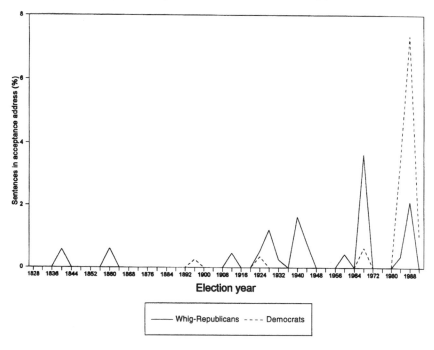

Figure 6. Algerism, as measured by the percentage of sentences within Whig-Republican and Demoncratic nomination acceptance addresses devoted to the success ethic, self-help, the American dream, the log cabin myth, or the existence of a classless society

individual to be recognized as unique, possessed of dignity and the sacred right to life, liberty, and the pursuit of happiness."[34] The Supreme Court, the Constitution, and the separation of powers remained staples of the Republican diet in the second period, but now they were bastions not of public order and government but rather of "the liberty of the individual."[35] The age of modern individualism had arrived (see figure 7).

The theme of order – the necessity of restraints on individual freedom and warnings of the danger of anarchy and social disorder – declined in tandem (see figure 4). Only the isolated issue of crime, accounting for a

34. Reagan, speech, 8/23/1984 (Bush 1985: 317).
35. Landon, speech, 10/30/1936 (*New York Times* 10/31/1936). It is perhaps noteworthy within this context that the American people were referred to, on many occasions, on an individual (rather than a collective) basis – as in Eisenhower's claim to have cut taxes "with about two-thirds of the cut going directly to individuals" (speech, 10/1/1956, in Eisenhower 1957: 843).

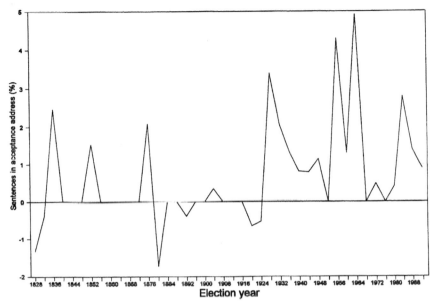

Figure 7. Individualism, as measured by the percentage of sentences within Whig-Republican nomination acceptance addresses positively portraying the "individual" (as noun or adjective – e.g., "individual rights," "the rights of the individual"), using *personal* as an adjective (e.g., "personal rights"), or invoking theses of self-help, self-reliance, and individualism *minus* the percentage of sentences portraying the foregoing in a critical light

brief resurgence of order themes in the 1960s, served as a reminder of the party's past. By the end of the 1920s, Republicans had metamorphosed into avid libertarians. "Liberty," always a favored term within Republican discourse, formerly referred to the American system of government, not to individual Americans. Now, just about anything was a candidate for liberation – most commonly "American initiative," but also "the effects of an arbitrary and uncertain monetary policy" and, for workers, "interference from any source."[36] "We, the people, defy entrenched political power!" proclaimed Willkie grandly. "A free people now arise to write a single word across the vast American sky: Liberty. Liberty. Liberty."[37] Of American labor Dewey opined, "In this free land, as in no other land, labor is free; free to organize, to bargain collectively, to strike; free to choose jobs and to change jobs; free to speak up and

36. Landon, acceptance speech, 7/23/1936 (Singer 1976: 138–39, 142).
37. Willkie, speech, 11/2/1940 (Schlesinger 1971, 4: 2999).

to talk back."[38] Every conceivable policy was hung on the freedom tree. "We hold that the protection of the freedom of men requires that budgets be balanced, waste in government eliminated, and taxes reduced," declared the party's platform in 1956.[39] Dewey suppported "the fundamental freedom of choice of occupation, even of the right to own a car or a home or a farm."[40]

It was, of course, the restricted or *liberal* sense of liberty or freedom that Republicans were attracted to – "freedom from" rather than "freedom to."[41] Freedom, for Landon, meant that "men may live free to pursue their happiness, safe from any kind of exploitation."[42] "[T]hat system is best," averred Coolidge, "which gives the individual the largest freedom of action."[43] In words that could be mistaken for self-parody, the 1980 platform declared its fealty to "the right of personal mobility and freedom as exemplified by the automobile and our modern highway system."[44] The phrase "possessive individualism" fit latter-day Republicanism to a tee.[45] The goal of government, stated Coolidge, was that of "protecting the freedom of the individual, of guarding his earnings, his home, his life."[46] "[W]e must build up men and women in their own homes, on their own farms, where they may find their own security and express their own individuality," added Hoover.[47] Eisenhower saw an America "in which every man can eat his own bread in peace, raise his own family in security, and strengthen his own spirit and mind in dignity."[48] Dewey spoke for "the God-given right of the individual to be his own master."[49]

The freedom of the individual, it was clear, usually referred to freedom from governmental coercion. On the "wrecking" of free enterprise by four successive Democratic administrations, the 1952 platform charged, "It has sought to curb, regulate, harass, restrain and punish."[50] "[O]ur medical profession is free," claimed Nixon, which was to say,

38. Dewey, speech, 10/30/1948 (Dewey 1950: 709).
39. Republican platform, 1956 (Schlesinger 1971, 4: 3388).
40. Dewey, speech, 9/20/1948 (Dewey 1950: 640).   41. See Berlin (1967).
42. Landon, acceptance speech, 7/23/1936 (Singer 1976: 143).
43. Coolidge, speech, 8/14/1924 (Coolidge 1924: 15).
44. Republican platform, 1980 (Johnson 1982: 180). Eisenhower, on the issue of compulsory arbitration, is unequivocal: "If you want the basic, irreconcilable difference between his [Stevenson's] position and mine, there it is. He and his Party embrace compulsion. I reject compulsion!" (speech, 9/17/1952, in Eisenhower 1952).
45. See Macpherson (1962).   46. Coolidge, speech, 9/6/1924 (Coolidge 1924: 93).
47. Hoover, speech, 10/4/1932 (Hoover 1977: 482).
48. Eisenhower, speech, 10/1/1956 (Eisenhower 1957: 840).
49. Dewey, acceptance speech, 6/28/1944 (Dewey 1950: 724).
50. Republican platform, 1952 (Schlesinger 1971, 4: 3286).

"they aren't working for the Federal Government."[51] Striking a jubilant note, the 1992 platform declared, "The self-governing individual has overcome the paternalistic state."[52] Although considerably less optimistic about the outcome, Goldwater could certainly agree on the terms of this debate. "The individual, the private man, the whole man – you! – " warned Goldwater ominously, "today stands in danger of becoming the forgotten man of our collectivized, complex times. The private man, the whole man – you! – must and can be restored as the sovereign citizen, as the center of the family, the state, and as the prime mover and molder of the future."[53]

Against the State

Whereas the National Republican party engineered a wide variety of neo-mercantilist policies to encourage the growth of native industries, the later Republican party eschewed all governmental involvement in economic affairs, except where necessary to preserve competition. Traditional Republican high-tariff policies were gradually relinquished in the 1940s (see figure 1). Platforms from the 1930s to the 1990s urged "the removal of restrictions" on business, rather than governmental policies to develop American economic production.[54] Whereas the National Republican party believed in the necessity of large-scale aggregations of capital, modern Republicans espoused the virtues of small business and independent entrepreneurship. Despite the fact that for the past century the party had been busy heralding the rise of the industrial order, in the 1920s and 1930s party leaders began to speak longingly of the family farm and its plight at the hands of modern centralized agribusiness, of the small business man and his plight at the hands of corporate monopolies.

In the 1930s, Republicans suddenly discovered the virtues of antitrust legislation, which Landon referred to as "laws protecting the little fellow from monopoly."[55] The logic behind this about-face is explainable by the

---

51. Nixon, speech, 10/29/1960 (U.S. Senate 1961b: 885).
52. *The Republican Platform 1992* (1).
53. Goldwater, speech, 9/3/1964 (*New York Times* 9/4/1964). It should have been no great surprise that "empowerment," once a key term in the liberal-left lexicon, was adopted by the conservative party in the 1980s. "Republicans," the 1988 party platform read, "want to empower individuals, not bureaucrats" (Republican party 1988: 52A).
54. See, e.g., Republican platform, 1936 (Schlesinger 1971, 4: 2858).
55. Landon, speech, 10/29/1936 (*New York Times* 10/30/1936). See also Landon, acceptance speech, 7/23/1936 (Singer 1976: 144); and speech, 10/20/1936 (*New York Times* 10/21/1936). Dewey, several elections later, agreed that "We must protect our enterprise system from monopoly" (speech, 9/20/1948, in Dewey 1950: 642).

party's turn from economic nationalism to economic liberalism. Whereas from the former perspective the concentration of capital was a sign of economic vitality, the party now viewed economic growth as the product of competition among small- and medium-sized firms. "The prosperity of the American nation," proclaimed the 1924 party platform, "rests on the vigor of private initiative which has bred a spirit of independence and self-reliance."[56] Identifying themselves with *small* business, Republicans charged that this constituency was being victimized by government-imposed monopolies and by government itself – the quintessential monopoly. Shifting the focus of attention from the marketplace to the state, Republicans removed the onus of monopoly from American business and placed it squarely upon the back of government. Business, in its newfound incarnation as "small," was portrayed as the fragile victim, and government the aggressor. By 1936 it was possible for Landon to assert that he was "against the monopoly of an all-powerful central government."[57] Slander of the left had become slander of the right.

Crucial to the monumental redefinition of economic and governmental activity occurring in the 1920s and 1930s within the Republican party was the identification of laissez-faire policies with those traditional American goods – freedom, self-government, and democracy. Thus, the American System – the term that Henry Clay chose to label his comprehensive blueprint for governmental intervention in the economy – became, in the words of the Republican party's 1936 platform, "the American system of free enterprise, private competition, and equality of opportunity."[58] Landon spoke of the American system of government as one that guaranteed "economic freedom, political freedom, and personal liberty."[59] Willkie defended the American system of "democracy and free enterprise."[60] "What do we find standing between our free enterprise and the totalitarian method of production by slavery?" he inquired.[61] One plank of the 1936 platform was given the title "Constitutional Government and Free Enterprise."[62] The prestige of American business was further bolstered by the historic task that now devolved upon the private

---

56. Republican platform, 1924 (Schlesinger 1971, 3: 2413).
57. Landon, speech, 10/29/1936 (*New York Times* 10/30/1936).
58. Republican platform, 1936 (Schlesinger 1971, 3: 2857).
59. Landon, speech, 10/20/1936 (*New York Times* 10/21/1936).
60. Willkie, speech, 10/31/1940 (*New York Times* 11/1/1940).
61. Willkie, speech, 10/17/1940 (Singer 1976: 187). Eisenhower, in virtually identical terms, described free enterprise as "the indispensable economic support to human liberty" (speech, 9/4/1950, in Eisenhower 1970: 33).
62. Republican platform, 1936 (Schlesinger 1971, 3: 2857).

sector, the defeat of communism. A whole free-market vocabulary was invented to illustrate the virtues of private enterprise – *competition, initiative, the release of energy, private sector* – words that could scarcely be found in Republican rhetoric prior to the 1920s. "New methods and new ideas are the outgrowth of the spirit of adventure, of individual initiative, and of individual enterprise," Hoover assured his audiences in 1928.[63] Landon, following in Hoover's wake, declared that "American initiative is not a commodity to be delivered in pound packages through a governmental bureau. It is a vital force in the life of our nation and it must be freed! . . . The time has come to unshackle initiative and free the spirit of American enterprise. We must be freed from incessant governmental intimidation and hostility. We must be freed from excessive expenditures and crippling taxation. . . . We must be freed from private monopolistic control."[64]

Republicans responded to a whole range of social policy questions with noble forbearance. The 1936 platform protested that the New Deal would. "regiment and ultimately eliminate the colored citizen from the country's productive life, and make him solely a ward of the federal government."[65] Three decades later, in the wake of the civil rights movement and a slew of programs directed at poverty within the urban ghetto, Nixon reiterated essentially the same argument:

> Black Americans – no more than white Americans – do not want more Government programs which perpetuate dependency. They don't want to be a colony in a nation. They want pride and the self-respect and the dignity that can only come if they have an equal chance to own their own homes,

---

63. Hoover, speech, 10/22/1928 (Singer 1976: 26).
64. Landon, acceptance speech, 7/23/1936 (Singer 1976: 138–40). According to Willkie, "The greatest threat to the American system today comes from the effort to restrict free competitive enterprise" (article, 12/1939, in Willkie 1940: 46). See also Dewey, speech, 10/28/1948 (Dewey 1950: 707). "We shall encourage a healthy, confident, and growing private enterprise, [and] confine Government activity to essential public services," declared the party platform in 1940 (Schlesinger 1971, 4: 2964). Eisenhower expressed the view that "the great American potential can be realized only through the unfettered and free initiative, talents and energies of our entire people" (speech, 10/1/1956, in Eisenhower 1957: 829).

    Even the label "capitalism" was occasionally embraced; the 1972 party platform pledged support "for the basic principles of capitalism which underlie the private enterprise system of the United States" (Johnson 1978: 861). The party's 1988 platform declared, "The restoration of our country's tradition of democratic capitalism has ushered in a new age of optimistic expansion, [b]ased on free enterprise, free markets, and limited government" (Repulican party 1988: 46A).
65. Republican platform, 1936 (Schlesinger 1971, 3: 2863).

to own their own businesses, to be managers and executives as well as workers, to have a piece of the action in the exciting ventures of private enterprise.[66]

Nixon, appealing to the principle of American liberalism, wondered, "Will discrimination and quotas limit their [black Americans'] horizons?"[67] By the end of the nineteenth century, civil rights issues had receded in importance; despite a slight resurgence in the late 1930s and the 1940s, such issues never returned to their former prominence (see figure 5).

The party's treatment of social welfare issues partook of the same general logic. Republican leaders vacillated between ambivalent support for social policies, when it was politically provident – but with noticeably few issue-commitments that would cost taxpayers money – and veiled attacks. With Nixon, the contrast between the work ethic and the "welfare ethic" became an accepted Republican trope.[68] "[N]one of us has the right to expect a free ride – to remain idle," he emphasized during the 1972 campaign, "to take advantage of other men's labor."[69] As a rule, however, Republican presidential candidates avoided any direct attack on the poor. Instead, they preferred to talk about the dangers of governmental bureaucracy and of taxation – which, of course, portrayed quite a different set of victims. "The Government," Eisenhower insisted, "must not deprive the individual of his just reward,"[70] which was "the rights of working men and working women to be productive, the rights of each of us to earn what he can and to save it as far as taxes will let him."[71] Throughout the twentieth century, it was the Democrats who acted as the spokespersons for greater equality in the distribution of wealth, and the Republicans who demurred (see figure 8).

As the century wore on, Republican candidates were increasingly inclined to blame the ills of society on excessive interference of government (see figure 3).[72] "I want the people of America to be able to work less for the Government and more for themselves," vowed Coolidge, striking

---

66. Nixon, speech, 8/8/1968 (Schlesinger 1971, 4: 3838). Racism, Nixon declared, wasn't "a Government problem" but, rather, "a personal problem" (Nixon, speech, 8/2/1960, in U.S. Senate 1961b: 1137).
67. Nixon, speech, 11/5/1972 (Nixon 1974: 1135).
68. Nixon, speech, 9/3/1972 (Nixon 1974: 850–51).
69. Nixon, speech, 10/28/1972 (Nixon 1974: 1057).
70. Eisenhower, speech, 9/4/1950 (Eisenhower 1970: 36).
71. Eisenhower, speech, 8/20/1952 (Eisenhower 1970: 40).
72. See, e.g., Hoover, speech, 11/19/1925 (Podell and Anzovin 1988: 435); Republican platform, 1924 (Schlesinger 1971, 3: 2413); and Hoover, speech, 10/22/1928 (Singer 1976: 27).

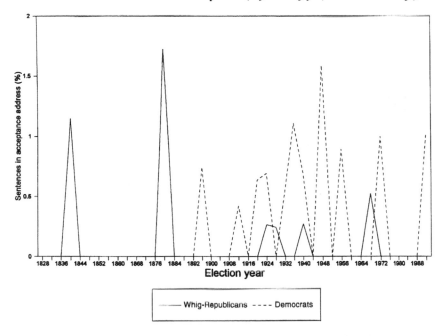

Figure 8. Support for the redistribution of wealth, as measured by the percentage of sentences within Whig-Republican and Democratic nomination acceptance addresses endorsing social equality or progressive taxation

a theme that would be recycled time and again in Republican rhetoric. "I want them to have the rewards of their own industry. That is the chief meaning of Freedom. Until we can reestablish a condition under which the earnings of the people can be kept by the people, we are bound to suffer a very distinct curtailment of our liberty."[73] Platform planks in the 1920s began to feature headings like "Taxation," "National Economy," and "Public Economy." "[T]he budget idea," Coolidge admitted, "is a sort of obsession with me. I believe in budgets. I want other people to believe in them. . . . Yes, I regard a good budget as among the noblest monuments of virtue."[74]

73. Coolidge, acceptance speech, 8/14/1924 (Coolidge 1924: 13). "Public economy," in fact, is virtually the only issue of any prominence to be found in Coolidge's 1924 addresses, in which he was fond of declaring that "the practice of public economy and insistence upon its rigid and drastic enforcement is a prime necessity of the people of the United States" (speech, 10/24/1924, in Schlesinger 1971, 3: 2556).
74. Coolidge, speech, 10/26/1924 (Coolidge 1926: 169). Moderate taxation was a theme at least as old as the American republic, and a more or less continuous presence in

For modern Republicans, fiscal austerity was next to godliness. Coolidge pointed out that "the power to tax is the power to destroy, and . . . the power to take a certain amount of property or of income is only another way of saying that for a certain proportion of his time a citizen must work for the Government." The noble citizen's fight against arbitrary government was played out through the struggle over taxation, in which property rights (and, ultimately, personal liberty) were held in balance against the government's will to expand and to coerce. "One of the first signs of the breaking down of free government is a disregard by the taxing power of the right of the people to their own property," continued the indefatigable Coolidge. "Unless the people can enjoy that reasonable security in the possession of their property, which is guaranteed by the Constitution, against unreasonable taxation, freedom is at an end";[75] "I am for economy. After that I am for more economy. . . . So far as it is within my power I will not permit increases in expenditures that threaten to prevent further tax reduction or that contemplate such an unthinkable thing as increase in taxes."[76] Read his lips. The 1920s thus saw the Republican party moving away from the notion of the state as dispenser of political patronage, and toward the goal of neutral and frugal administration.

The first wide-ranging philosophical attack on the state was also led by "Silent Cal" (who was, in fact, quite voluble during the 1924 campaign). In a classic statement of the virtues of limited government, Coolidge clarified,

> The Government can help to maintain peace, to promote economy, to provide a protective tariff, to assist the farmers, to leave the people in the possession of their own property, and to maintain the integrity of the courts. But after all, success must depend on individual effort. It is our theory that the people make the Government, not that the government makes the people. Unless there abides in them the spirit of industry and thrift, of sacrifice and self-denial, of courage and enterprise, and a belief in the reality of truth and justice, all the efforts of the Government will be in vain.[77]

The Republican party's long-standing and visceral dislike of big government, therefore, had its origins in the 1924 and 1928 campaigns, not in the party's response to the New Deal, as is so often claimed. The

campaign rhetoric emanating from both parties. Not until the 1924 campaign, however, does this theme emerge as a centerpiece of Republican ideology.

75. Coolidge, speech, 6/30/1924 (Coolidge 1926: 40).
76. Coolidge, speech, 6/30/1924 (Coolidge 1926: 47).
77. Coolidge, speech, 10/24/1924 (Schlesinger 1971, 3: 2562).

1928 party platform insisted, "There is a real need of restoring the individual and local sense principles; there is a real need for the people once more to grasp the fundamental fact that under our system of government they are expected to solve many problems themselves through their municipal and State governments, and to combat the tendency that is all too common to turn to the Federal Government as the easiest and least burdensome method of lightening their own responsibilities."[78]

By the 1920s, the state had become a truly mythic entity, capable of assuming many guises and imposing tyranny in countless insidious ways. "I do not want to see any of the people cringing suppliants for the favor of the Government," declared the normally solemn Coolidge, "when they should all be independent masters of their own destiny."[79] The sprawling state apparatus sapped the people of their autonomy, their individuality, their strength. "Bureaucracy," insisted Hoover, "does not tolerate the spirit of independence; it spreads the spirit of submission into our daily life and penetrates the temper of our people not with the habit of powerful resistance to wrong but with the habit of timid acceptance of irresistible might. Bureaucracy is ever desirous of spreading its influence and its power. You cannot extend the mastery of the government over the daily working life of a people without at the same time making it the master of the people's souls and thoughts."[80] It is noteworthy that Republican orators stopped referring simply to "government" – substituting, whenever possible, "big government," or "the bureaucracy."

Not surprisingly, the vast expansion of governmental prerogatives sponsored by Roosevelt and the Democratic party elicited general panic from the Republican opposition during the 1930s. The 1936 platform began ominously: "America is in peril. The welfare of American men and women and the future of our youth are at stake. We dedicate ourselves to the preservation of their political liberty, their individual opportunity and their character as free citizens, which today for the first time are threatened by Government itself."[81] The New Dealers, warned Landon in the same campaign, "believe in the concentration of political and economic authority."[82] "Our liberties," he insisted, "can be lost. . . .

---

78. Republican platform, 1928 (Schlesinger 1971, 3: 2640).
79. Coolidge, speech, 9/1/1924 (Coolidge 1926: 85).
80. Hoover, speech, 10/22/1928 (Singer 1976: 27). Landon protested that the federal government's attempt to collect payroll taxes would necessitate a large bureaucratic police force of snoopers (speech, 10/31/1936, in *New York Times* 11/1/1936).
81. Republican platform, 1936 (Schlesinger 1971, 3: 2856).
82. Landon, speech, 10/26/1936 (*New York Times* 10/27/1936).

This administration wields the same ax which has destroyed the liberties of much of the Old World."[83] "There can be only two systems of government: the one where the government is the master of the people and the other where it is the servant of the people."[84] Willkie quoted Spencer approvingly: "If men use their liberty in such a way as to surrender their liberty, are they thereafter any less slaves?"[85] Listening to Wendell Willkie during the 1940 campaign, an uninformed auditor might be excused for concluding that revolution was just around the corner.

It is interesting to note that the figure of Herbert Spencer – now "one of the greatest of the English liberals"[86] – was scrupulously avoided by previous generations of Republicans. As late as 1924, Republicans were at pains to distance themselves from the "night watchman" theory of the state with which Spencer was associated. Yet by 1940, Spencer had become a safe, and evidently desirable, reference point for Republican orators.

Republicans began to look at the apparatus of the state as a power to be divided rather than conquered. The purpose of the Constitution, Coolidge discovered in 1924, was to assure that "the minority, even down to the most insignificant individual, might have their rights protected."[87] After fighting with states'-rights Democrats all through the nineteenth century, Republicans were finally discovering the virtues of the Bill of Rights. Their concern for the "rights of the individual" or "minority rights" grew into an all-abiding faith.[88] In a precise reversal of his party's historic role, Eisenhower declared in 1952, "This country is a Federal organization, an organization of sovereign states."[89] Republican speech makers now recycled Jefferson ("Eternal vigilance is the price of liberty") like a mantra.[90]

Populism from the Right

The turn from statism to antistatism was accompanied by a parallel shift in political style within the Republican party. Whereas earlier Whig-

---

83. Landon, speech, 10/26/1936 (*New York Times* 10/27/1936).
84. Landon, speech, 10/26/1936 (*New York Times* 10/27/1936).
85. Willkie, speech, 12/8/1939 (Willkie 1940: 179).
86. Willkie, speech, 12/8/1939 (Willkie 1940: 179).
87. Coolidge, speech, 9/6/1924 (Coolidge 1926: 94–95).
88. See, e.g., Republican platform, 1936 (Schlesinger 1971, 3: 2863); Landon, speech, 10/20/1936 (*New York Times* 10/21/1936); and Dewey, speech, 6/30/1948 (Dewey 1950: 638).
89. Eisenhower, speech, 8/20/1952 (Eisenhower 1970: 38).
90. See, e.g., Landon, speech, 10/20/1936 (*New York Times* 10/21/1936); and Dewey, speech, 9/22/1948 (Dewey 1950: 647).

Republicans had upheld a stately, nineteenth-century vision of politics in which a tacit division between leaders and followers was observed, modern Republicans adopted a strident populism. Republicans now attacked special privileges, special interests, and various other expressions of elite control with a persistence that rivaled Bryanite Democrats. Hoover warned repeatedly against the demands on the Treasury made by "special groups and special sections" and the "pressures of minorities."[91] He pilloried Democratic welfare measures as "pork-barrel legislation," and "logrolling, selfishness, and greed."[92] Tired of bearing the "special interest" onus, Republicans now hoisted the Democrats on their own populist petard.[93] "I know that we have been called a party of special privilege," acknowledged Eisenhower, "but I tell you . . . that of all the special privileges that are dangerous in this country the most dangerous is the special privilege of big government."[94] Taking up the outsider theme with alacrity, Eisenhower railed against "political expediency in Washington, D.C.," against the "special favoritism, [and] cronyism" of the Democrats, which he contrasted with "an America where no politician any longer can treat the farmer himself as a product to be bid for in the political marketplace."[95] To the "pressure of groups" represented by the Democratic party, Republicans counterposed "the conscience of the individual."[96] The "interest-group liberalism" tag thus became attached to the Democratic party long before it became fashionable within academic circles. The Republican party, by contrast, was "a one-universal-interest party."[97]

Amid all the talk of unity and togetherness, there were hints early on in the second Republican period that all Americans were not equally deserving. The "forgotten American" theme, which can be traced back to William Graham Sumner's writings in the late nineteenth century, began to appear in Republican rhetoric in the Twenties and Thirties. During the 1936 campaign, for example, Landon made special appeals to the "solid citizenry of America."[98] There were good, decent, deserving Americans, and then there were others that, by implication at least, were not so good.

---

91. Hoover, speech, 10/31/1932 (Singer 1976: 110).
92. Hoover, speech, 10/4/1932 (Hoover 1977: 472).
93. In election after election the Democratic party was tagged the party of "special privileges." See, e.g., Dewey, speech, 11/1/1944 (Dewey 1946: 782).
94. Eisenhower, speech, 10/9/1952 (Eisenhower 1952).
95. Eisenhower, speech, 9/25/1956 (Eisenhower 1957: 797); speech, 10/1/1956 (Eisenhower 1957: 836); speech, 10/1/1956 (Eisenhower 1957: 840).
96. Goldwater, speech, 9/3/1964 (*New York Times* 9/4/1964).
97. Eisenhower, acceptance speech, 8/23/1956 (Schlesinger 1971, 4: 3423).
98. Landon, acceptance speech, 7/23/1936 (Singer 1976: 139).

The classic and most memorable form of this rhetoric was reached during the divisive 1968 campaign, in which Nixon regularly admonished his audiences to listen to "another voice, . . . a quiet voice in the tumult of the shouting. It is the voice of the great majority of Americans, the forgotten Americans, the non-shouters, the non-demonstrators. They're not racists or sick; they're not guilty of the crime that plagues the land."[99] Central to modern Republicanism was the perception that certain Americans were being shut out of the political process.

There was, therefore, an edge to Republican rhetoric in the period. The party played directly on democratic norms of social equality and popular sovereignty to demonstrate the oppression of the middle class at the hands of forces beyond its control. The David and Goliath story assumed countless forms. The Neoliberal period saw the adoption of a whole cast of characters who had never before appeared in Republican scripts, including the "average man," the "small man," the "little fellow," the "small farmer," the "little taxpayer," and of course, the "small business man." The hallmark of virtue within the Republican liberal mind-set was to be little, and diminutive status was bestowed upon all manner of political groupings.[100] Landon accused the Roosevelt administration of making "large payments to big landowners," thereby worsening the situation of small farmers.[101] In taxation policy, "again we see, . . . the small man is penalized for the benefit of the big fellow."[102] Speaking for the party's traditional policy of public economy, Landon appealed not to the nineteenth-century shibboleths of "sound finance" and "thrift" but to the sufferance of the little fellow: "It is the little fellow who pays. It is the little fellow who suffers from government extravagance."[103] "We need an administration," thought Dewey, "that cares more about little business than it does about big government."[104] "I am against the big tax spender and for the little taxpayer," added Ford, three decades later.[105]

People power took on government power. Mincing no words in his attempt to strike a democratic pose, Coolidge declared, "The voice of the people is the voice of God."[106] "America's most priceless resource

99. Nixon, acceptance speech, 8/8/1968 (Schlesinger 1971, 4: 3833).
100. Witness Landon's reference to the "small independent oil producer" (acceptance speech, 7/23/1936, in Singer 1976: 144).
101. Landon, speech, 10/23/1936 (*New York Times* 10/24/1936).
102. Landon, speech, 10/23/1936 (*New York Times* 10/24/1936).
103. Landon, speech, 10/26/1936 (*New York Times* 10/27/1936).
104. Dewey, speech, 11/4/1944 (Dewey 1946: 791).
105. Ford, acceptance speech, 8/19/1976 (Bush 1985: 247).
106. Coolidge, speech, 11/3/1924 (*New York Times* 11/4/1924).

. . . is its people," crowed Dewey in 1948.[107] "[W]e can have a Government that does not grow complacent," promised Ike, "that does not grow away from the people and become indifferent to them, that does not become arrogant in the exercise of its powers, but strives to be the partner and the servant of the people and not their master."[108] Whereas National Republicans had looked to government as a disciplinary force within an inherently chaotic and unruly society, modern Republicans championed the citizenry, whose job it was to flail government into obedience on a regular basis.

The term *democracy*, a scarce reference in National Republican propaganda, became a constant point of departure for Republican speakers in the 1930s and 1940s, eclipsing *republic*. The implications of this terminological shift were far-reaching. Republic, as invoked by National Republicans, implied a nonmonarchical, constitutional form of government. It was an expression of support for the institutions and authority of the American national government, in contrast to European monarchies and Asian despotisms. "Democracy," in contrast, had more populist connotations. "I learn that democracy is not what we call the government. Democracy is the people," clarified Willkie.[109] By separating the American system of government from the government proper, the concept of democracy allowed the speaker to attack the state without attacking the hallowed Constitution or the American way of life. Majoritarian themes, which had been played down by a century of Whigs and Republicans, now became regular features of Republican nomination acceptance addresses (see figure 9). FDR was criticized for having "lost faith in the American people."[110] "Just look at the men surrounding him," cried Willkie passionately. "They are all cynics who scoff at our simple virtues, particularly those simple virtues that you and I learned here in the Midwest. They think that the people and most of us are too dumb to understand. Their idea is that they, the intelligentsia, can govern us. . . . Give our country back to us. It belongs to us. We want it."[111] "We, the people," he shouted, without any apparent trace of self-consciousness, "defy entrenched political power."[112]

If William H. Harrison (of hard cider and log cabin fame) or Benjamin Harrison (several generations later) were "common," they were common in the sense that they sprang from simple folk, *not* that they

107. Dewey, speech, 9/28/1948 (Dewey 1950: 667).
108. Eisenhower, speech, 8/20/1952 (Eisenhower 1970: 41).
109. Willkie, speech, 9/16/1940 (Schlesinger 1973, 3: 2346).
110. Willkie, speech, 9/16/1940 (Schlesinger 1973, 3: 2348).
111. Willkie, speech, 9/16/1940 (Schlesinger 1973, 3: 2348).
112. Willkie, speech, 11/2/1940 (*New York Times* 11/3/1940).

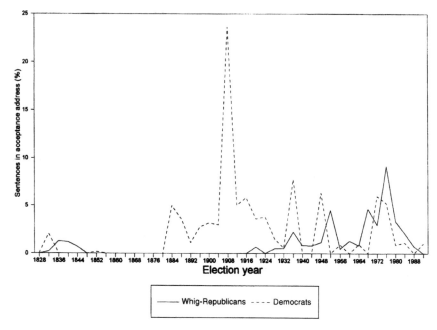

Figure 9. Support for majority rule, as measured by the percentage of sentences within Whig-Republican and Democratic nomination acceptance addresses devoted to popular sovereignty, direct election of senators, direct primaries, campaign finance reform, congressional reform, or encomiums to the virtue and intelligence of the people. (Does not include the use of the term *democracy* without any of the foregoing connotations.)

themselves were common. The subtext of every Republican rhetorical quip, and of the speeches that often rambled on for several hours, was that the speaker was an *extra*ordinary specimen of humanity. He, as a champion of the party, was the strongest, most "bully" fighter the party could find to send into battle against its bitter partisan opponents. Presidential nominees were generals in an ongoing political war. Such leaders were not considered – nor did they portray themselves as – one of the boys. National Republicans prided themselves on their competent management of the affairs of state, in contrast to their bumbling and overtly partisan opponents. After the 1920s, however, the party ceased to advertise its excellence and began instead to emphasize its commonness. Self-deprecation was de rigueur. Bush's preference of pronouns to nouns, as well as his general aversion to verbs, was not simply a personality trait; it appears even in prepared speeches he recited from teleprompters. Bush-speak was the product of a calculated attempt to overcome the effete and vaguely aristocratic image resulting from the candidate's wealth, East Coast origins, and Yale education. In one speech, Bush's life was related in a diary-like list of everyday events – "high school football on Friday nights, Little League, neighborhood barbecue, . . . kids and a dog and a car" – a slice of Americana establishing the candidate's regular-guy credentials.[113]

Part and parcel of this newfound populist style was a general reaction against experts and expertise – formerly a major rhetorical prop of Republicanism. Hoover's 1928 campaign marked the first departure from the standard facts-and-figures style of National Republican oratory. Later, in the 1932 campaign, he apologized for a reference to "economics," a term that would have been a point of pride to earlier Republican campaigners, who reveled in lengthy discourses about the merits and demerits of various currency and monetary policies.[114] Later Republican orators, beginning with Landon, would eschew statistics whenever given the chance, in favor of analogies, anecdotes, and rhetorical turns of phrase. Modern Republicanism thus retreated from the dignity and majesty of government to the common people and the commonplace. "It is well for the country to have liberality in thought and progress in action," thought Coolidge, "but its greatest asset is common sense. In the commonplace things of life lies the strength of the Nation. It is not in brilliant conceptions and strokes of genius that we shall find the chief reliance of our country, but in the home, in the school, and in religion. America will continue to defend these shrines. Every evil force that seeks to desecrate or destroy them will find that a Higher Power has endowed the people with an inherent spirit of resistance."[115]

A virtual cult of civil society was erected on the ruins of big government in the 1920s and 1930s. In the creed of antistatism, certain key words – among them *community, participation, local, state, the personal element, voluntary associations, citizens, the people, private*, and, perhaps most prominently, *family* – gained talismanic status (see figure 10).[116] Humanity fought the machine of government. Against the power of organized groups, Republicans sang the virtues of voluntary associations – churches, united funds, community chests, voluntary hospitals,

---

113. Bush, speech, 8/18/1984 (*Vital Speeches of the Day* 55:1, 10/15/1988).
114. Hoover, speech, 10/4/1932 (Hoover 1977: 464). Hoover, however, succumbed to the old facts-and-figures rhetoric in the 1932 campaign, when – much to his discredit – he sought to defend the Republican legislative record in the face of the Great Depression.
115. Coolidge, acceptance speech, 8/14/1924 (Coolidge 1924: 16).
116. See, e.g., Hoover, speech, 11/2/1928 (Hoover 1928: 196); and Nixon, speech, 10/6/1968 (press release of Nixon/Agnew Campaign Committee 10/6/1968).

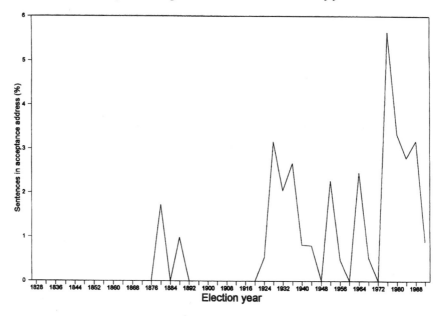

Figure 10. Support for the family, as measured by the percentage of sentences within Whig-Republican nomination acceptence addresses devoted to the family or the home (not the house)

private foundations, voluntary welfare agencies, and fraternal and service organizations.[117] To avoid the regimentation of federal lawmaking, Hoover offered self-help programs of public service based on "individual, community, and state responsibility."[118] "In people helping people, we can find the spiritual cement to put our country together again, and to make our nation whole by making its people one," proclaimed Nixon at a time when the nation was distinctly lacking in unity.[119] Individual citizens, he pointed out, can "reach what government cannot: the qualities of heart, of caring, that are the difference between impersonal bureaucracy and personal concern."[120] In local communities it was possible to preserve traditional values of the heart, person-to-person relationships (rather than faceless bureaucratic ones), and self-worth and dignity

117. See, e.g., Nixon, speech, 10/6/1968 (press release of Nixon/Agnew Campaign Committee 10/6/1968).
118. Hoover, acceptance speech, 8/11/1932 (Schlesinger 1971, 3: 2795).
119. Nixon, speech, 10/6/1968 (press release of Nixon/Agnew Campaign Committee 10/6/1968).
120. Nixon, speech, 10/6/1968 (press release of Nixon/Agnew Campaign Committee 10/6/1968).

(rather than the selfish desire for power that animated the political system in Washington). On the other side, in the Washington beltway, lay the heartless, machine-like bureaucracy, with its controls, its regulations, and all the loss of freedom and individual autonomy that such rules entailed. "We must not allow [children] to be used as pawns in the hands of social planners in Washington," insisted Nixon, "many of whom basically believe that children should be raised by the Government rather than by their parents."[121]

Hoover was the first Republican campaigner to extol at length the simple virtues of home and family: "The American home . . . is the sanctuary of our loftiest ideas, the source of the spiritual energy of our people. . . . Successful democracy rests wholly upon the moral and spiritual quality of its people."[122] The end and aim of all government, Hoover claimed, was "the comfort and welfare of the American family and the American home. The family is that unit of American life and the home is the sanctuary of moral inspiration and of American spirit. The true conception of America is not a country of 110,000,000 people but a nation of 23,000,000 families living in 23,000,000 homes."[123] "This is a land of homes, family life and the rearing of children in an atmosphere of ideals and religious faith."[124] A half-century later, the themes of home and family remained a centerpiece of Republican rhetoric.[125] The party had turned inward to the private sector, to private associations, and to private life. Freedom was "the freedom that men and women cherish from raising their children in family loyalty – choosing their jobs or their freinds and associates – to practicing their religious faith without fear."[126] The 1972 platform promised "to defend the citizen's right to privacy."[127]

Republicans also referred to religion as the bulwark of civil society against an ever-encroaching state. "There is no way by which we can

---

121. Nixon, speech, 9/3/1972 (Nixon 1974: 852).

122. Hoover, acceptance speech, 8/11/1932 (Schlesinger 1971, 3: 7–8).

123. Hoover, speech, 8/21/1928 (Hoover 1928: 60). See also Hoover, speech, 10/15/1932 (Hoover 1977: 528).

124. Hoover, acceptance speech, 8/11/1932 (Schlesinger 1971, 3: 2804).

125. Ford spoke in support of a tax structure that favored "the family home, the family farm, and the family business" (acceptance speech, 8/19/1976, in Bush 1985: 250). Reagan emphasized that "work and family are at the center of our lives; the foundation of our dignity as a free people" (acceptance speech, 7/17/1980, in Bush 1985: 268). Bush described the family as an "essential unit of closeness and of love," the institution that "communicates to our children . . . our culture, our religious faith, our traditions and history" (speech, 8/19/1984, in *Vital Speeches of the Day* 55:1, 10/15/1988).

126. Eisenhower, speech, 10/23/1956 (Eisenhower 1957: 994).

127. Republican platform, 1972 (Johnson 1978: 877–78).

substitute the authority of law for the virtue of man. . . . Peace, justice, humanity, charity – these cannot be legislated into being. They are the result of a Divine Grace," declared Coolidge.[128] The 1956 platform invoked the same secular/spiritual contrast, to the effect that "the freedom and rights of men came from the Creator and not from the State."[129] Thus, when the 1992 platform described the ultimate agenda of socialism as the liberation of "youth from traditional family values by replacing family functions with bureaucratic social services," it played on a long rhetorical history of defending home and hearth against the intrusions of government.[130]

The party's heightened treatment of "social issues" in the 1980s and 1990s marked a significant extension of this home-and-hearth rhetoric. It is noteworthy that in the wake of the intensely watched Scopes trial of 1925, neither Hoover nor Al Smith felt it necessary to take a public position on the matter. The 1992 Republican platform, by contrast, declared the party in support of the proposition that "schools should teach right from wrong."[131] This prominent aspect of contemporary American politics was simply not considered political (not, at least, in national politics) until the latter half of the twentieth century.

However, the place of social issues within the contemporary Republican party is easily exaggerated. Although it is of immense interest to a small and vocal constituency of party members, the social values theme has not played well with national audiences,[132] and social issues have

---

128. Coolidge, speech, 10/15/1924 (Coolidge 1926: 153).
129. Republican platform, 1956 (Schlesinger 1971, 4: 3386). In light of communist "paganism," Eisenhower urged his audience to "preach and practice the truly revolutionary values of man's dignity, man's freedom, man's brotherhood under the fatherhood of God" (speech, 8/25/1952, in Schlesinger 1971, 4: 3301). Nixon railed against the "atheistic Communist system of education" (speech, 10/18/1960, in U.S. Senate 1961a: 887). Relatively abstract references to God were common in all periods of Whig and Republican campaigning, but it was quite unusual for Republicans of the modern period to use direct scriptural quotations or extended metaphors. God served mostly as a touchstone, an invocation, and was usually inserted in the introduction or peroration of the speech. Such spiritual references generally carried a ritualistic quality with little immediacy. Eisenhower, for example, declared that "free government is the political expression of a deeply felt religious faith" (speech, 9/4/1950, in Eisenhower 1970: 37).
130. *The Republican Platform 1992* (6). For a pre-Reagan example of the "family values" genre, see Nixon, speech, 9/3/1972 (Nixon 1974: 852).
131. *The Republican Platform 1992* (9).
132. Pat Buchanan's tirades against homosexuality and "abortion on demand" at the 1992 National Republican Convention, to cite one example, were generally noted for their alienating effects on the national television audience.

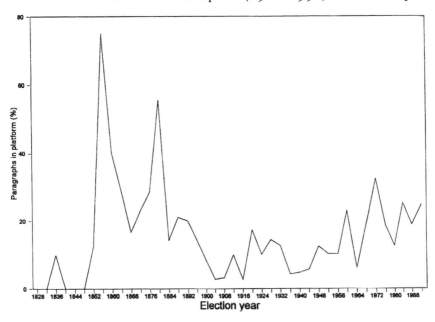

Figure 11. Attention to social-cultural issues, as measured by the percentage of paragraphs within Whig-Republican party platforms dealing with abortion, the arts, crimes, drugs, family values, immigration, minorities, pornography, Prohibition, temperance, the value of neighborhoods, school prayer, and women

never constituted more than a small fraction of the party's general election rhetoric.[133] Candidates have tended to avoid reference to the contentious matters of abortion and homosexuality, unless addressing special audiences where position-taking on such topics is obligatory.[134] In fact, the present era shows *no* increase of any significance in social-cultural campaign themes – including the arts, crime, drugs, immigration, minorities, abortion, alcohol, temperance, prohibition, family values, the value of neighborhoods, pornography, school prayer, and women – as judged by their presence in party platforms (see figure 11). Despite vigorous prodding from the "Pat" wing of the party (named for Buchanan and Robertson), social issues have been granted only a small place in the party's official pronouncements.

133. Primary election rhetoric, evidently, caters to a different audience and is likely to be more oriented toward social issues.
134. The National Religious Broadcasters convention, which regularly draws the Republican presidential candidate, is one such audience.

Anticommunism

In one significant respect, modern Republican ideology did *not* deviate from the path set by National Republicanism. The Whig-Republican party always defined itself as the bearer of a national tradition. Whig and Republican orators were passionately, self-consciously, and ubiquitously patriotic. Democrats, of course, also invoked national symbols to justify their partisan programs, but they did not do so with the overtness, insistence, and frequency of Republican speakers. "The American way of life," "the American form of government" – these were constants of Whig and Republican rhetoric from Clay to Bush.[135]

America was represented by Republican speakers as a creed, not simply a nation-state. Willkie titled one speech "The Faith That Is America."[136] Republican orators in the liberal period talked proudly of their country as the greatest of all nations – not simply of the present time but of all time. "The world," Eisenhower promised, "will again recognize the United States of America as the spiritual and material realization of the dreams that men have dreamt since the dawn of history."[137] With reference to John Winthrop's well-known sermon, the party's 1992 platform declared, "We are a shining city on a hill, the last best hope for man on earth."[138] Nixon asserted, "We have a divine destiny, . . . not simply to hold our own, not simply to keep freedom for ourselves, but to extend freedom throughout the world."[139] Reagan referred to "this vast continent which God has granted as our portion of his creation."[140] Thus, in one respect at least – as the party of forthright Americanism – modern Republicanism built unapologetically on its own partisan traditions.

Taking a closer look, however, one can discern a significant change in the definition of patriotism between the two periods of Whig-Republicanism. From the 1830s to the 1920s, the party acted to preserve America from an influx of foreign goods, foreign persons, and foreign ways. Of course, the specific ethnic and racial content of foreigners was never entirely stable; but it usually referred to persons of Catholic heritage and swarthy appearance.[141] In the 1930s and 1940s, the definition

---

135. The only partial exception to this pattern could be found during the Mexican-American War (as noted in chapter 3).
136. Willkie, article, 12/1939 (Willkie 1940: 47).
137. Eisenhower, speech, 8/25/1952 (Schlesinger 1971, 4: 3302).
138. *The Republican Platform* 1992 (2).
139. Nixon, speech, 11/6/1960 (U.S. Senate 1961b: 1060).
140. Reagan, acceptance speech, 7/17/1980 (Bush 1985: 272).
141. Asians, of course, were undubitably foreign, but immigration from Asia was not substantial enough to have an impact on party ideology in the way European im-

of otherness – of un-Americanness, that is – changed in fundamental ways. No longer embodied in a religion, an ethnicity, a language, or a readily distinguishable lifestyle, it was now an ideology. The battle against communism, which composed a large portion of Republican rhetoric in the Neoliberal period, fit handily within the reigning dichotomy of freedom/slavery. As the party's 1952 platform put it, "We are threatened by a great tyranny – a tyranny that is brutal in its primitiveness. It is a tyranny that has brought thousands, millions of people into slave camps and is attempting to make all humankind its chattel."[142] "Unless the individual accepts governmental mastery of his life and soul," Ike explained, "he can be convicted without trial; . . . he can be banished to live out his life in a slave camp. That is what the Soviet planners contemplate for all the world, including America."[143]

Three things are worth commenting on with respect to the much-studied anticommunist crusade. First, the antiradical theme arrived in Republican rhetoric well before the McCarthy hearings in the early 1950s.[144] The party's 1940 platform devoted an entire section to the subject of "un-American activities," declaring, "We vigorously condemn the New Deal encouragement of various groups that seek to change the American form of government by means outside the Constitution. We condemn the appointment of members of such un-American groups to high positions of trust in the national Government. The development of the treacherous so-called Fifth Column, as it has operated in war-stricken countries, should be a solemn warning to America. We pledge the Republican Party to get rid of such borers from within."[145] Nor could the adoption of anticommunism be chalked up simply to the party's opposition to the New Deal and to the flowering of communism among union members and certain sections of the intelligentsia during the 1930s, for the same themes could be found during the previous decade. "The question," suggested Coolidge in 1924, "is whether America will allow itself to be degraded into a communistic and socialistic state, or whether it will remain American."[146]

migration did. Moreover, both major parties registered their disapproval of "Mongol" immigration, so there was no partisan differentiation on this score.

142. Republican platform, 1952 (Schlesinger 1971, 4: 3298).

143. Eisenhower, speech, 9/4/1950 (Eisenhower 1970: 30). For a general discussion of anticommunism's impact on American political culture, see White (1997).

144. The House Committee on Un-American Activities was established in 1938. Its focus was not simply on communists but also on fascist and other "un-American" groups.

145. Republican platform, 1940 (Schlesinger 1971, 4: 2964). See also Willkie, speech, 10/31/1940 (*New York Times* 11/1/1940).

146. Coolidge, speech, 9/6/1924 (Coolidge 1926: 96–97). Along identical lines, the main theme of the 1940 campaign was articulated as "whether or not America shall embrace State socialism, or State capitalism, or communism, or whatever you choose

National Republicans, to be sure, were just as anxious about the radical threat as modern Republicans, but this threat assumed an entirely opposite form, as indicated by Harding's warning during the 1920 campaign. "Humanity is restive," observed Harding, "much of the world is in revolution, the agents of discord and destruction have wrought their tragedy in pathetic Russia, have lighted their torches among other peoples, and hope to see America as a part of the great Red conflagration."[147] *Revolution, discord,* and *destruction* are the key words in this passage, indicating National Republicans' primary concern with the maintenance of social order. Anarchism – the result of too *little* political organization – was the bête noire of the early Republican party. Clearly, the new fight against communism suggested a different set of policy priorities than the old fight against anarchism had.

Finally, it is worth noting that, although it was shared by some Democratic candidates (Truman, Stevenson, and Kennedy in particular), anticommunism as an electoral theme was not entirely bipartisan. Democrats, while warning against the communist threat, frequently tempered their tirades against radicalism with an emphasis on the importance of preserving civil liberties at home. Anticommunism was a less prominent theme in Democratic than in Republican rhetoric in most election years and tended to be focused on foreign, rather than domestic, policy. Democrats tended to call attention to the country's international responsibilities, whereas Republicans emphasized the country's internal peril. Subversion and conspiracy themes were correspondingly more common in Republicanspeak than in Democratspeak.[148] The tenor of the

to call it. These are merely different names for the same thing – absolute and arbitrary power in the hands of government" (Willkie, speech, 10/21/1940, in *New York Times* 10/22/1940). The 1944 campaign was, in this respect, virtually a repeat performance. Acknowledging in 1944 that "Nazism and Fascism are dying in the world," Dewey warned that "the totalitarian idea is very much alive and we must not slip to its other form – Communism" (speech, 11/1/1944, in Dewey 1946: 784). Each would "make the State supreme, give political power only to those who deny the supremacy of God and use that power to force all men to become cogs in a great materialistic machine" (ibid. 784). "Little by little," said Dewey, "the New Deal is developing its own form of corporate state. It becomes clear why the twice convicted Comrade Browder and his friends are so eager for the re-election of my opponent" (speech, 10/7/1944, in Dewey 1946: 753). "The Democratic party," he charged several weeks later in the 1944 campaign, "had been kidnapped by "the Communists and the Political Action Committee" (speech, 10/20/1944, in Dewey 1946: 763). See also speech, 10/7/1944 (Dewey 1946: 753); and speech, 11/1/1944 (Dewey 1946: 781–85).

147. Harding, acceptance speech, 7/22/1920 (Harding 1920b: 25).
148. Eisenhower referred to the "world conspiracy" during his first campaign, which was perhaps the most virulently anticommunist of the entire modern Republican period

subversion theme is well illustrated by a passage from one speech during the 1952 Eisenhower campaign:

> Their efforts behind the Iron Curtain are accompanied by virulent subversion and propaganda inside the free world. . . . And though we say it in shame, as we say it in anger, they have penetrated into many critical spots of our own country, even into our Government. . . . [L]et us tolerate nobody in our whole society who attempts to weaken and destroy the American constitutional system. Especially let us be watchful for those who by stealth attempt subversion and treasonable betrayal in government.[149]

The cancer metaphor was also common. "Because of Communist penetration, the Castro regime has now exposed itself within the Western Hemisphere as an intolerable cancer," said Nixon in 1960. "It will endlessly fester until we and the other freedom-loving nations in the Western Hemisphere move and do so promptly and authoritatively, to prevent further Soviet penetration. . . . I say that our goal must be to quarantine the Castro regime in the Americas."[150] Even after the fall of the Soviet Union, Republicans continued to warn against communism, the "dogmas of the Left," and the "bureaucratic millennium" (associated with "ivory towers").[151]

Conclusions

Usually, the ideology of the contemporary Republican party – the ideology, let us say, of Ronald Reagan – is viewed as the outgrowth of postwar conservatism, a conservatism personified in the figure of Barry Goldwater and in the movement designated the New Right.[152] All recent studies emphasize the Republican party's dramatic shift to the right and the attendant demise of "liberal Republicanism" over the past several decades.

The *longue durée* of party history, I have argued, reveals a rather different picture of ideological development. Reagan, it is true, followed in the ideological footsteps of Goldwater. What is missed in this conventional narrative, however, is the sense in which Goldwater himself was the intellectual stepchild of Hoover. Indeed, Hoover was the first

(speech, 8/16/1952, in Eisenhower 1970: 49). Its one possible rival was Nixon's first presidential campaign, in 1960.

149. Eisenhower, speech, 8/25/1952 (Schlesinger 1971, 4: 3299–3301).
150. Nixon, speech, 10/18/1960 (U.S. Senate 1961b: 661).
151. *The Republican Platform 1992* (1).
152. See Brennan (1995), Erickson (1985), Himmelstein (1990), Rae (1989), and Reinhard (1983).

voice to cry out against the creeping forces of state socialism. (Of the Great War, Hoover explained, "We were challenged with a peacetime choice between the American system of rugged individualism and an European philosophy of diametrically opposed doctrines – doctrines of paternalism and state socialism."[153]) Thus, Goldwater and Reagan, though appearing to represent a new brand of Republicanism, in fact propagated a set of ideas and ideals that had been characteristic of their party for quite some time – but not from time immemorial. Modern Republicanism, I have argued, is only distantly related to William McKinley and William Howard Taft; the party's recent moves to the right complete a trajectory begun in the 1920s, not the 1960s.

By the end of the Twenties, the Republican party had reinvented itself in the image of democratic capitalism, appropriating many of the symbols that had heretofore characterized its partisan opponents. The party embraced an essentially Jacksonian political ideal – that "no group can dominate the nation" – and assumed the Democratic party's traditional role as standard-bearers in the fight against "autocracy of economic power."[154] "[S]alvation," wrote the indefatigable Hoover in *American Individualism*, will not "come by any device for concentration of power, whether political or economic, for both are equally reversions to Old World autocracy in new garments."[155] This ideal was coupled with an aggressive embrace of democracy, which "arises out of individualism and prospers through it alone."[156] Hoover, finally, introduced the modern party's reverence for the individual person: "[I]ntelligence, character, courage, and the divine spark of the human soul are alone the property of individuals. These do not lie in agreements in organizations, in institutions, in masses, or in groups. They abide alone in the individual mind and heart. . . . Individualism insists upon the divine in each human being."[157]

---

153. Hoover, speech, 10/22/1928 (Singer 1976: 23).
154. Hoover (1922/1989: 49, 53).   155. Hoover (1922/1989: 59).
156. Hoover (1922/1989: 51).
157. Hoover (1922/1989: 36, 42). For some, like Joan Wilson (1975), Hoover is a "forgotten progressive" – a political leader far in advance of his time, who tried to nudge the Republican party toward a more progressive vision of politics and toward an intermingling of business and politics. In his work during World War I and throughout the Twenties (in various Republican administrations), Hoover attempted to forge an "associational democracy," a partnership between private and public sectors. (See also Hart 1998.) Two points need to be added to this picture, however. First, Hoover always insisted that any moves toward cooperation be *voluntary* (except, of course, in wartime). He could favor an associational democracy and still hold an individualistic view of society and politics because he was convinced that businesses would find it in their interest to unite together and to forge compromises with labor, government, and community leaders. Government's role would be informational (through, e.g., the Commerce and Labor Departments) and hortatory. Second, the

The reasons for the fundamental yet scarcely noticed transformation of the 1920s were complex. Among the contributing factors, one might mention the decline of the tariff as an instrument of social and economic policy, the decline of mercantilism as a general philosophy of political economy, the redefinition of labor as *organized* labor and as a Democratic constituency, the parallel growth of a sizable middle class, the events of 1919 at home and abroad, the virtual disappearance of anarchism and the astonishing spread of socialism in Europe and Russia, the growth of federal governmental power during the war years, and the use of that power to discipline the private sector.[158] By the late 1920s, it was also becoming increasingly evident that the Republican-backed prohibition amendment – the culmination of a century of Protestant-inspired social reform – was not achieving its objectives. From the Republican perspective (though not, of course, from the Democratic perspective), all of these developments delegitimated government and led to a parallel rediscovery of the virtues of civil society.

Party constituencies were also evolving. As the twentieth century wore on, Republicans drew less from the Northeast and more from the West and South, less from urban areas and more from rural and suburban areas. These regional and demographic shifts bespoke a shift from labor, financial, and manufacturing constituencies to small business and middle management. The transformation from mercantilist to neoliberal economic policies might indeed be understood as a shift from "big bourgeois" to "petty bourgeois" elements within the party.[159] Many of these

progressive-associational Hoover worked largely behind the scenes; when campaigning for office, he assumed a more Neoliberal guise. For an account accenting Hoover's individualism, see Best (1975). For a rundown on historiographic questions, see Hawley (1981).

158. In the last category, one might mention the War Industries Board (1917), which was to oversee the conversion of industry to wartime production, to eliminate waste and duplication, to fix prices, and to purchase supplies for the United States and the allies; the Lever Food and Fuel Control Act (1917), which empowered the president to make regulations pertaining to the production and distribution of products deemed necessary for the war effort; the War Revenue Act (1917), which made the income tax the chief source of revenue during the war and which imposed higher burdens on the rich, on corporations, and, in particular, on persons and corporations earning "excess" profits; the president's takeover of the entire railroad industry (1917); the National War Labor Board (1918), which, as a last resort, would resolve labor/management disputes by government fiat; and the Overman Act (1918), which authorized the president to consolidate bureaus, agencies, and offices to achieve greater administrative efficiency in matters relating to the conduct of the war. See Morris (1953: 278–79) for brief explanations of these wartime measures.

159. This is not to say that big business deserted the Republican party; however, its place within the party was probably less important in the latter twentieth century than it had been in the days of McKinley, Hanna, Taft, and Roosevelt.

changes followed, rather than preceded, the party's shift in the 1920s, and so must be viewed as consolidating factors rather than initiating ones.

For the same reason, the common claim that postwar "liberal" Republicanism owes its origins to the New Deal realignment must simply be discarded.[160] No significant differences in basic values and beliefs separated Hoover from Landon, Willkie, or Dewey, although these unfortunates were forced by the tenor of the times to accept a good portion of the New Deal. Of course, the events of the 1930s surely reinforced the party's ideological realignment, as did the onset of the cold war.[161] But the party's conversion to populism, libertarian individualism, and antistatism occurred well before the onset of the Great Depression and the New Deal. The specter of Democratic radicalism *already* haunted Republican party leaders.

At the same time, it should be stressed that the central ideals of Whig-Republicanism (adumbrated in chapter 1) held steady throughout the transformation of the 1920s. Indeed, one might argue that the transformation was driven by party leaders' steadfast adherence to these core values. Changing attitudes toward state and society, which I have summarized in the terms *National* and *Neoliberal*, occurred in response to a new set of challenges to liberty, prosperity, and the American nation. This reevaluation constituted the most fundamental rethinking of American conservatism since the acceptance of mass democracy by New England Federalists.[162]

160. See, e.g., Beer (1965) and Ladd (1970: 203).
161. For a discussion of the Republican party's response to the New Deal, see Weed (1994).
162. See Fischer (1965).

PART III

The Democratic Party

5

The Jeffersonian Epoch
(1828–1892)

What was the ideology of the nineteenth-century Democratic party – the party of Andrew Jackson, Stephen Douglas, and Grover Cleveland? A variety of scholarly work has addressed this question, at least tangentially, and it is not surprising to find a good many propositions pertaining to that party over this long and tumultuous historical period. Three overarching perspectives, however, have dominated contemporary research on the ideology of the Democratic party. To some, the nineteenth-century party is quintessentially liberal, in the classic nineteenth-century sense of the term – enamored of free trade, free markets, laissez-faire, industrial development, philosophical individualism, and the task of protecting civil liberties and civil rights.[1] To others, the party appears to be the embodiment of the democratic populist ideal. This perspective, initiated by the Progressive historians and revised and reformulated in various recent accounts, interprets the party's mission as the defense of the rights of farmers and urban laborers against financial and industrial elites.[2] Still others have rechristened the Democratic party as a coalition of ethnic and religious minorities. Accordingly, the Democratic party is said to have developed an ideology centered on personal liberty – "a toleration and defense of alternative life-styles and values, of laissez-faire social ethics, and of a government whose powers were circumscribed so as to preclude positive intervention in the daily lives of its citizens."[3] All three of these major perspectives – liberal, democratic-populist, and ethnocultural – tend to highlight *discontinuities* in Democratic dogma through the course of the nineteenth century, dividing the party's history

---

1. See Kelley (1969).
2. See Beard (1929), Croly (1909), Holcombe (1924), Sait (1927), Schlesinger (1945). See also Ashworth (1983/1987), Bailey (1968), Hofstadter (1955), and Ladd (1970).
3. Kleppner (1981a: 97). See also Benson (1961: 332) and Silbey (1991: 89).

into two or three periods (typically, the Jacksonian era, the Civil War–Reconstruction era, and the Gilded Age).[4]

I argue that we are better served by focusing on the remarkable continuities within this first century of Democracy. Despite the strains induced by westward expansion, wars foreign and domestic, a continuous inflow of European immigrants, rapid industrialization and urbanization, and fundamental alterations in constituencies, the party of Cleveland retained much the same essential values and beliefs upon which it had been founded. From 1828 to 1892, Democratic leaders steadfastly defended a preindustrial economic order, limited government, and the liberties of white people. Forged from the unlikely combination of racism, antistatism, and civic republicanism, this ideology is most accurately and concisely described as Jeffersonian.

To be sure, the party founded in the 1830s by Andrew Jackson and Martin Van Buren had weak organizational links to the factional alignment led by Thomas Jefferson in the 1790s and 1800s. Indeed, there were no political parties at all (in the usual sense of the term) in Jefferson's day.[5] Moreover, the direct heir of Jefferson's factional alignment would appear to be John Quincy Adams – the founder, I have argued, of the Whig-Republican party – not Jackson. Nonetheless, from an *ideological* perspective, the party of Jackson trod carefully and respectfully in Jefferson's footsteps.

One tends to think of the founding of a new party as a move into the future. This, arguably, was the first mass party in the Western world, and thus represented an organizational breakthrough of world-historic proportions. But this particular party was established with the explicit purpose of defending a tradition – specifically, the American revolutionary tradition. Indeed, early Democrats were fond of referring to themselves as Old Republicans, a label that emphasized their links with the generation of 1776. Their utopia looked backward to the republic as it stood in 1789, rather than forward to the twentieth century. They were radical in the sense that the American revolutionaries were radical,

---

4. Democratic populism is usually discussed in the context of the 1830s and 1840s, and liberalism in the context of the Gilded Age, whereas ethnocultural accounts emphasize shifts in party ideology from the second party system to the third. To this it should be added that the vast bulk of the work conducted on party history takes the form of period-specific studies, which also tend to emphasize the fragmented nature of Democratic party ideology during the nineteenth century, partitioning that history into increments of one or several decades. Partial exceptions to this general trend can be found in Kelley (1969) and Silbey (1991).

5. See Formisano (1974). For further discussion, see the appendix.

which is to say, they were alert to every encroachment of power that might threaten their cherished liberties.[6]

As exemplary of this traditionalism and testamentary of the party's ideological continuity over the long nineteenth century, one might consider the words of the party's national platform in 1892:

> The representatives of the Democratic party of the United States . . . do reaffirm their allegiance to the principles of the party, as formulated by Jefferson and exemplified by the long and illustrious line of his successors in Democratic leadership, from Madison to Cleveland; we believe the public welfare demands that these principles be applied to the conduct of the Federal Government, through the accession to power of the party that advocates them; and we solemnly declare that a need of a return to these fundamental principles of free popular government, based on home rule and individual liberty, was never more urgent than now, when the tendency to centralize all power at the Federal capital has become a menace to the reserved rights of the States that strikes at the very roots of our Government under the Constitution as framed by the fathers of the Republic.[7]

Nineteenth-century Democrats were radical preservationists.

Racism

No one doubts the significance of the issue of slavery in the southern wing of the Democratic party, especially during the years of the Civil War and Reconstruction, but it has been difficult to resolve the relationship of this issue to the national wing of the party. Was slavery and the broader question of Negro civil rights a passing issue of purely sectional importance, or was it a vital part of Democratic ideology during the nineteenth century? The evidence provided by presidential campaign rhetoric supports the latter view, though in a modified form.

Not before, during, nor after the Civil War did the party ever explicitly condone the institution of slavery. Yet its position was far from ambiguous. In the Lincoln-Douglas debates of 1858, the future Democratic presidential candidate remarked, "We here do not believe in the equality of the Negro socially and politically. Our people are white people; our state is a white state, and we mean to preserve the race pure without any mixture with the negro."[8] In the subsequent presidential

---

6. For discussion of radicalism during the American Revolution, see Gordon Wood's brilliant synthesis (1991). For discussion of Jefferson's political philosophy, see Banning (1978), Elkins and McKitrick (1993), and McCoy (1980).
7. Democratic platform, 1892 (Johnson 1958: 86).
8. Quoted in Baker (1983: 185).

campaign, Douglas declared, "In my opinion, this government was made by white men for the benefit of white men and their posterity for ever, and should be administered by white men, and by none other whatsoever."[9] Whereas Whig and early Republican politicians in the North (including Lincoln) frequently declared a personal abhorrence of slavery (see chapter 3), similar sentiments are virtually impossible to discover among Democratic election statements, northern or southern. Indeed, the repeated insistence by Democrats that slavery should be kept off the political agenda constituted a more than implicit defense of the institution.[10]

Moreover, the party's position on racial questions was well established by the landmark election of 1860. In 1836, for example, party members supported the recent extension of the franchise in New York but noted approvingly that it "did not extend to persons of color." Congress, the writers of this address added, "has no right to interfere with the question of slavery in any state of the Union." As for the abolition of slavery in the District of Columbia, it would tend "to produce in the [slaveholding sections of the population] a degree of uneasiness and excitement, which would disturb the feelings of harmony now happily subsisting between the different states of the Union."[11]

In short, greater continuity can be found in the Democrats' position on matters of race than historians have generally acknowledged. Douglas's principal slogan during his Illinois senate contest against Abraham Lincoln (and during his run for the presidency two years later) was "popular sovereignty" – a term that referred to the right of states to decide political matters by democratic choice rather than by the (implicitly undemocratic) intervention of the federal government. This same principle, labeled "local sovereignty" by Lewis Cass, the Democratic

9. Douglas, speech, 2/29/1860 (Flint 1860: 175).
10. Actions of a more than rhetorical sort were also taken by local party functionaries – as in Charleston, when a local postmaster allowed a mob to burn abolitionist literature held within the post office, or in the North, where similar mobs of Democrats were doing their best to forcibly disperse abolitionist meetings. "Almost unanimously, the Jacksonian political coalition sought to defend slavery against abolitionist attack," judges historian Harry Watson (1990: 203).
11. New York State Convention, "Address to the Republican Electors of the State of New York" (*New York Evening Post* 9/20/1836). (During this period, Democrats were often referred to as Republicans, or Democratic-Republicans.) The importance of these issues to Democratic party leaders may be gauged by the following events. In 1831, the first issue of Garrison's *Liberator* appeared and Nat Turner's slave rebellion broke out in Virginia. Two years later, the American Anti-Slavery Society was founded and began pressuring Congress to abolish slavery in the District of Columbia. The tide of abolition sentiment seemed to be rising, and it was evidently a hostile tide.

standard-bearer in 1848, was just another way of expressing the party's traditional stance of "states' rights." From the 1830s on, it was considered critical to select as the party's presidential candidate a northern leader who was "safe" on the slavery issue – "a northern man with southern principles," as the phrase went.[12] Indeed, this was the primary purpose for the institution of the two-thirds rule at the party's 1836 convention.[13]

Racial issues informed Democratic ideology not only in the antebellum, Civil War, and Reconstruction periods but also throughout the Gilded Age – this time in the form of arguments over civil rights. The 1892 party platform, for example, focused its ire on the so-called Force bill, a proposed (but never passed) piece of legislation that would have provided for the supervision of elections by the federal government to ensure the voting rights of African American voters in the South.[14] Since the issue remained one of how far the federal government would, or could, intervene in southern affairs to protect the rights of Negroes, the tenor of these Gilded Age debates remained remarkably consistent with those of an earlier vintage. The war was lost, but the battle continued. A comprehensive count of civil rights issues in Democratic platforms, charted in figure 5 demonstrates the early origins of this theme, its brief upsurge in the 1850s and 1860s, and its return to a peripheral position within party rhetoric in the Gilded Age, as well as the stark contrast between the two parties on this congeries of issues.

Taking a broader view of the matter, it is worth observing that virtually every aspect of the Democratic party's rhetorical and programmatic agenda supported the cause of white supremacy. Its opposition to federal voting rights laws, its all-pervasive antistatism, its constitutional fundamentalism (centered on the Tenth Amendment), its "minoritarian" view of democracy and general distrust of power, its defense of property rights, its praise for the virtues of tolerance and a pluralistic society, its proto-Marxist critique of capitalism, and its embrace of the interests of agriculture – all bolstered the legitimacy of the increasingly peculiar institution and, thereafter, of Jim Crow. It is important to note that even

12. To this end, each nonsouthern presidential hopeful was pressured to issue a written statement of his support for states' rights. Martin Van Buren, a New Yorker, was the first to undergo this litmus test.
13. This rule, unique to the Democratic party, meant that two-thirds (rather than a simple majority) of convention delegates would have to endorse a presidential candidate before that candidate could receive the party's nomination. The rule endured for a century, helping maintain the hegemony of the party's southern (and more overtly racist) wing.
14. Democratic platform, 1892 (Johnson 1958: 86–87).

with the bolting of the southern factions during the tumultuous election of 1860 and the domination of the party by northern Democrats during the 1860s and 1870s, national party spokespersons continued to reiterate the themes of a long-established ideological tradition. It is impossible, therefore, to interpret Democratic issue-positions on slavery simply as a bow to sectional demands. Although the issue of slavery rocked the nation for several decades, the party's position on the persisting issue of civil rights hardly varied during the nineteenth century, informing the political perspectives of every Democratic presidential candidate from Jackson to Cleveland.

Preserving Limited Government

Although one would not want to downplay the norm of white supremacy in Democratic party ideology, it would be equally fallacious to jump to the conclusion that it was the only key to the party's identity during the nineteenth century. Much of the party's programmatic consistency during this period is rightfully attributed to the forceful simplicity of a single perspective: antistatism. Throughout most of the century, Democratic leaders adopted tight fiscal, currency, and monetary policies: hard currencies (gold and/or silver), balanced budgets, little government borrowing (and quick repayment), low spending, and low tariffs.[15]

On the infamous banking issue that lit up the political sky in the 1830s and 1840s, the party embraced a weak regulation approach, one that would release industry from the corrupting hand of government. "We trust the day is coming when free trade principles will wholly prevail," wrote one party organ, "when the restraining law will be entirely swept away; and when men will be left to the enjoyment of their natural liberty to follow whatever pursuit their capacity may fit them for, or their inclination select."[16] The bank was denounced throughout the 1830s and 1840s as "unconstitutional, inexpedient, and dangerous to public liberty; and [a] . . . gigantic instrument of corruption."[17] As a substitute for the Federalist-Whig national bank, Democrats proposed something called the Subtreasury, by which banking policy would be put in the

---

15. I should note the fact that monetary policy was not always a partisan issue in the nineteenth century (Whigs and Republicans sometimes echoed the same "tight" policies of Democrats). However, monetary issues separated the nineteenth-century Democrats from their twentieth-century descendants and are, in this sense, an important ingredient of the party's "Jeffersonian" political philosophy.
16. Editorial (*New York Evening Post* 9/28/1836).
17. *Address of the National Democratic Party Convention to the People of the United States* (1840: 2).

hands of a whole series of state banks rather than, as formerly, consolidated in the hands of a single Bank of the United States.

Internal improvements were opposed on the same grounds, from Jackson's well-publicized veto of the Maysville highway construction bill in 1830 to Gilded Age opposition to Republican schemes to finance railroads, rivers, highways, and harbors. "Every day's experience teaches us . . . that public works of every description can be made at a much smaller cost by private enterprise, or by the local authorities directly interested in the improvement, than when constructed by the Federal Government," said Douglas.[18]

With regard to the preeminent economic issue of the nineteenth century – the tariff – Democrats were ardent opponents of Republican protectionism. "All restraints on the freedom of trade must be swept away," one editorial in the Democratic *New York Evening Post* read, implying the naturalness of free trade and the artificiality of tariffs.[19] After the 1830s, when the free trade label lost its political shine, the party still doggedly insisted upon tariffs established at minimal levels. The standard Democratic slogan was "Tariffs for revenue only," by which was meant that only that level of surcharges on imported goods should be tolerated which was absolutely necessary to sustain the normal operations of the federal government. Tariffs, in other words, were viewed as a tax, not an industrial policy (as was the Whig-Republican perspective).[20] A content analysis of party platforms, displayed in figure 1, reveals that just as Protection, more than any other single issue, defined Republicanism in the late nineteenth century, so Tariff Reform defined its opponents. Cleveland referred to the latter as "the shibboleth of true Democracy and the test of loyalty to the people's cause."[21] It is noteworthy that those Democrats who adopted the cause of a federal income tax in the 1890s did so because they perceived that such an overt tax would be more difficult to collect than the traditional excise tax. The income tax was an "honest" tax, because it was levied directly on the heads of taxpayers.

Taxes were the subject of a continuous Democratic harangue in the nineteenth century. "When the government, this instrumentality created and maintained by the people to do their bidding," wrote Cleveland, "turns upon them and, through an utter perversion of its powers, extorts

18. Douglas, letter to Governor Matteson, 1/2/1854 (Carr 1909: 241). See also, "Democratick State Convention Address to the Republican Electors of the State of New York" (*New York Evening Post* 9/20/1836).
19. *New York Evening Post* (10/28/1836).
20. Cleveland, acceptance letter, 9/8/1888 (Schlesinger 1971, 2: 1685).
21. Cleveland, speech, 4/2/1892 (Cleveland 1909: 331).

from their labor and capital tribute largely in excess of public necessities, the creature has rebelled against the creator and the masters are robbed by their servants."[22] Even in the Jacksonian era – prior, that is, to the expansion of revenue occasioned by the Civil War – Democrats complained, "Everything, except the light of heaven and the air we breathe, is burdened with a tax, in some form or other."[23] The early Democratic antitax philosophy went far beyond the pale of Whig and Republican calls for public economy. Although Republicans also professed an interest in saving money and in keeping "sound" businesslike practices, they did not look upon the government as an entity evil by nature. But, for the Democrats, more than money was at stake. Democrats subscribed to what might be called the original sin theory of government: the state was evil in and of itself, and the most it could do for its citizens was to attempt to restrain its greed. Democratic economic policy consisted of blaming all illnesses on governmental policy. If only tariff schedules could be reduced and government-sponsored favoritism eliminated, the market would be restored to its pristine state of equal competition, and all social classes would thrive once again in a happy state of social harmony.

Predictably, Democratic leaders vehemently opposed any enlargement of the federal bureaucracy. Civil service reform, for example, meant not the strengthening of the civil service so much as its streamlining and its removal from partisan politics. From Jackson to Cleveland, Democrats opposed any scheme of governmental distribution based on the principle of need, and in the latter part of the nineteenth century they spent a good deal of their political capital fighting the expansion of Union army pensions, which the Republicans were apt to distribute to anyone who could demonstrate sufficient political pull. Cleveland, the only Democrat to inhabit the White House from 1861 to 1913, argued tirelessly against the idea "largely prevailing among the people that the General Govern-

22. "[T]he continual withdrawal and hoarding by the Government," Cleveland continued, created a "tendency toward gross and scandalous public extravagance." A surplus of public moneys had a "demoralizing influence . . . upon the judgments of individuals" (acceptance address, 9/8/1888, in Schlesinger 1971, 2: 1684–86).

23. Editorial (*New York Evening Post* 9/21/1836). The address of the Democratick Republican Young Men's Convention asserted "the unconstitutionality of any law by which congress shall raise money for distribution" (*New York Evening Post* 10/5/1836). Jackson, one year later, wrote, "There is, perhaps, no one of the powers conferred on the Federal government so liable to abuse as the taxing power" (farewell address, 3/4/1837, in Richardson 1897: 1518). Cleveland, finally, wrote, "The right of the government to exact tribute from the citizen is limited to its actual necessities, and every cent taken from the people beyond that required for their protection by the government is no better than robbery" (speech, 10/26/1884, in Cleveland 1909: 56).

ment is the fountain of individual and private aid; that it may be expected to relieve with paternal care the distress of citizens and communities, and that from the fullness of its Treasury it should, upon the slightest possible pretext of promoting the general good, apply public funds to the benefit of localities and individuals." Cleveland professed outrage at the discovery that "gratuities in the form of pensions are granted upon no other real ground than the needy condition of the applicant."[24] "Though the people support the government," he said, "the government should not support the people."[25] To be sure, the party opposed any federal interference in the affairs of the several states – whether pertaining to slavery, civil rights, morality, or internal improvements – and strenuously upheld rights of individual liberty against the threat of governmental despotism. Party leaders were opposed not only to high taxation but also to the distribution of federal funds to the states (gained by selling public lands, by tariff duties, or by direct taxation), since this would put ultimate control in the hands of federal politicians.[26]

Democratic economic policy in the nineteenth century is impossible to understand without reference to the party's virulent opposition to the federal government. No other single issue was repeated as adamantly or as persistently. "States' rights," "home rule," "popular sovereignty," "That government is best which governs least"[27] – these were the party's mating calls from Jackson to Cleveland. Arguments over specific policies were conducted in the special dialect of eighteenth-century constitutionalism. Democrats held to the "compact" theory of constitutional origins, i.e., the federal government derived its authority from the constituent states, not the people at large. A manifesto from 1828 explained: "The states were left, as distinct sovereignties, not merely for the purpose of securing a better administration of our domestic concerns, but as an additional precaution against the growth of an absolute government."[28] Limited government referred not simply to the reserved power of the states but also to the division of power within the central government.

24. Cleveland, fourth annual address, 12/3/1888 (Richardson 1897: 5362).
25. Cleveland, quoted in Henning (1989: 91).
26. "Democratick State Convention Address to the Republican Electors of the State of New York," 9/1836 (*New York Evening Post* 9/20/1836).
27. The last clause was made famous for later generations by its inclusion in Thoreau's essay "Civil Disobedience." However, the quotation certainly did not originate with Thoreau. Indeed, it may have been adopted from the masthead of the *Democratic Review*, one of the more important party organs of the Jacksonian era (Stern 1970: 455).
28. "Address to the Republican [Dem] Electors of the State of New York from the New York Republican State Convention," 9/29/1828 (*New York Evening Post* 9/30/1828).

The 1880 party platform reaffirmed the party's now traditional opposition to "centralization and to that dangerous spirit of encroachment which tends to consolidate the powers of all the departments in one, and thus to create whatever be the form of government, a real despotism."[29]

Nineteenth-century Democrats exhibited a quasi-religious reverence for the words of the Constitution and took a fundamentalist approach to its interpretation. "Upon this country more than any other," declared Andrew Jackson, in a style that managed to be both plain and regal at once, "has . . . been cast the special guardianship of the great principle of adherence to written constitutions. . . . It is our duty to preserve for it the character intended by its framers."[30] The eighteenth-century Federalist/Antifederalist debate endlessly repeated itself, with Democrats fulminating against "liberal or latitudinarian construction" and the "doctrine of expediency and general welfare."[31]

This raises a central problem in early Democratic party history, namely, how are we to differentiate the party's stance toward the federal government from its stance toward state and municipal governments, where extensive economic regulation, as well as social policies, was commonly administered by Democratic regimes?[32] First, one must appreciate the profound gulf that nineteenth-century Democrats perceived between the distant federal government and the nearby state and local governments. Whereas the latter lay directly under popular control, the government at Washington was deemed too large, too removed, and too heterogeneous to be trusted with such important tasks. Democrats, second, perceived economic and social policies as pertaining to local groups,

---

29. Democratic platform, 1880 (Johnson 1958: 56). See also Seymour, acceptance letter, 8/4/1868 (Schlesinger 1971, 2: 1282–84). The one notable exception to this generalization could be found in the first decade of Whig rhetoric, when the party responded to the threat of "King Andrew" with a spirited defense of the separation of powers as a check on ambition in the executive branch.
30. Jackson, first annual message, 12/8/1829 (Richardson 1897: 1015).
31. "Statement by the Democratic Republicans of the United States," 7/31/1835 (Schlesinger 1971, 1: 624, 629). Democrats insisted upon "strict construction" of the "plain and honest language of the constitution" ("Address to the Republican Electors of the State of New York," in *New York Evening Post* 9/30/1828). A host of specific issues were opposed on constitutional grounds. Van Buren's main objection to the Bank of the United States, for example, was that "the Constitution does not give congress the power to erect corporations within the States" (letter to Elizabeth City County, 7/31/1840, in Van Buren 1840b: 3). See also *Address of the National Democratic Party Convention to the People of the United States* (1840: 5); and Cleveland, fourth annual message, 12/3/1888 (Richardson 1897: 5358).
32. See Bourgin (1989), Handlin and Handlin (1947), and Hartz (1948).

local businesses, and local problems. No single set of initiatives crafted in Washington could hope to address such a wide range of human needs and cultural demands. Most important, by entrusting such "household" matters to a distant federal source, the states would be granting an authority beyond their power to control. For all these reasons, many of which echoed the arguments of the original opponents of the U.S. Constitution, one must differentiate Democratic attitudes toward the federal government from the party's attitudes toward state and local government.

In the former case, Democratic attitudes were so austere that they can be said to approximate the mythic ideal of a night watchman state. Cleveland, quoting Jefferson, envisioned "a wise and frugal government which shall restrain men from injuring one another, shall leave them otherwise free to regulate their own pursuits of industry and improvement, and shall not take from the mouth of labor the bread it has earned." This, Cleveland insisted, was "the sum of good government."[33] Indeed, a comprehensive count of statist and nonstatist themes in Democratic acceptance speeches, displayed in figure 3, reveals the party's overwhelming opposition to federal activism in all its guises. (This, of course, was in marked contrast to Whig and Republican rhetoric during the period, which was cautiously supportive of the expanding role of government and which treated government with reverence.) Democrats were naysayers on virtually every significant economic and social policy of the day. The proper role of the national government, reiterated generations of Democratic orators, was simply to protect private property.[34] Governments were to uphold virtue in their own sphere, not go about corrupting the populace with vain and meretricious expenditures.

Preserving a Preindustrial Economy

Nineteenth-century Democrats have often been described as a party of liberalism. Yet, despite their attachment to an antistatist philosophy of government, to the protection of private property, and to individual liberties, Democratic leaders also gave voice to some remarkably *un*liberal ideas and ideals. One of the many curiosities posed by early Democratic history is that while apparently supporting a laissez-faire vision of eco-

33. Cleveland, speech, 4/27/1889 (Cleveland 1892: 247). Cleveland quotes from Jefferson's first inaugural address.
34. "The protection of the people in the exclusive use and enjoyment of their property and earnings concededly constitutes the special purpose and mission of our free Government" (Cleveland, acceptance letter, 9/26/1892, in Schlesinger 1971, 2: 1765).

nomic policy, the party was on many occasions quite hostile to the sign-posts of economic progress. Monopoly was a pro forma target of Democratic rhetoric from Jackson to Cleveland. The "despotic sway" of the National Bank, Jackson's bête noire, was described as a "great monopoly" that concentrated "the whole moneyed power of the Union, with its boundless means of corruption and its numerous dependents, under the direction and command of one acknowledged head."[35] Nor did the antimonopoly theme entirely disappear from Democratic party rhetoric after the 1830s. In 1888, with reference to its support of homestead legislation, the party boasted having "reclaimed from corporations and syndicates, alien and domestic, and restored to the people, nearly one hundred millions of acres of valuable land."[36]

We should also note that although occasional mention of "let-alone" and free trade policies could be found in the party's election rhetoric from the 1830s, Democratic politicians by and large avoided such an explicit avowal of free-market faith.[37] In short, the Democrats' de facto laissez-faire policy should not be interpreted as an embrace of free-market capitalism or, more generally, of a classic nineteenth-century liberal faith (à la Mills, Cobden, or Bright). The animating ideal of the Jacksonian Democrats was not that the market was so wonderful but rather that the state was so bad. Democratic economic philosophy, although it followed the tenets of Manchester liberalism, is probably more correctly viewed as the product of the older ideology of civic republicanism.

Civic republicanism, like its archrival, liberalism, is an abstract and ever-shifting concept.[38] We can best gain a sense of this term, and the mountains of historical work it has generated in the past several decades, by aggregating all those traits and ideals which have been commonly applied to it, namely, virtue, liberty, frugality, fraternity, community, citizenship, active participation in and responsibility for the common-

---

35. Jackson, farewell address, 3/4/1837 (Blau 1954: 15).
36. Democratic platform, 1888 (Johnson 1958: 77).
37. Cleveland declared, "The question of free trade is absolutely irrelevant, and the persistent claim made in certain quarters that all the efforts to relieve the people from unjust and unnecessary taxation are schemes of so-called free traders is mischievous and far removed from any consideration for the public good" (third annual message, 12/6/1887, in Richardson 1897: 5175).
38. In fact, historians have only recently agreed to adopt a common name for this political culture. Virtually synonymous with what I have called civic republicanism are the terms *civic virtue, civic humanism, Country, Commonwealth, neo-Whig*, and simply *republicanism*. The last word now seems to rule the terminological roost. I have used its older version, *civic republicanism* to differentiate this ideology from that of the Republican party.

weal (understood as part of the concept of patriotism), popular sovereignty (not to be confused with democracy), balance, order, an agrarian way of life, individual autonomy, the rights of property (on a small scale, and referring to land rather than to capital goods), a millennial vision of a regenerated society, self-sacrifice, a backward-looking view of time, a suspicion of power, and a fear of the corruption of the republic into some form of tyranny.[39] As we shall observe in the following pages, *all* of these descriptors might be profitably applied to the nineteenth-century Democratic party, though some are more apropos than others.

Indeed, the descriptors that used to be applied to the Populists and the early twentieth-century Democratic party – that they comprised a backward-looking class of anti-industrial Jeffersonians – could with much greater accuracy be applied to the nineteenth-century Democratic party. "What has been the financial history of this country for the last twenty-five years?" James Buchanan asked, in an election sermon notable for its anticapitalist bile.

It has been a history of constant vibration – of extravagant expansions in the business of the country, succeeded by ruinous contractions. At successive intervals many of the best and most enterprising men of the country have been crushed. They have fallen victims at the shrine of the insatiate and insatiable spirit of extravagant banking and speculation. . . . What effect has [a] bloated system of credit produced upon the morals of the country? In the large commercial cities it has converted almost all men of business into gamblers. Where is there now to be found the old-fashioned importing merchant, whose word was as good as his bond, and who was content to grow rich, as our fathers did by the successive and regular profits of many years of patient industry? . . . All now desire to grow rich rapidly. . . . If the speculator should prove successful, and win the golden prize, no matter by what means he may have acquired his wealth, this clothes him with honor and glory. Money, money, money, confers the highest distinction in society. The republican simplicity and virtue of a Macon would be subjects of ridicule in Wall street or Chestnut street. The highest talents, directed by the purest patriotism, moral worth, literary and professional fame, in short, every quality which ought to confer distinction in society, sink into insignificance when compared with wealth. Money is equivalent to a title of nobility in our larger commercial cities. This is the effect of our credit system. We have widely departed from the economical habits and simple virtues of our forefathers. These are the only sure foundations upon which our republican institutions can rest. The desire to make an ostentatious display of rapidly acquired wealth, has produced a splendor and boundless expense unknown in former times. There is now more extravagance in our large commercial

39. This constellation of traits is drawn from discussions of the subject in Appleby (1992), Bailyn (1967; 1968), Pocock (1975; 1972), Rodgers (1992), and Shalhope (1972).

cities, than exists in any portion of the world which I have ever seen except among the wealthy nobility of England. Thank Heaven, this extravagance has but partially reached the mountains and valleys of the interior. . . . Our system of banking is the very worst, and the most irresponsible that has ever existed on the face of the earth. The charters of these banks nowhere impose any efficient restraints upon the first instinct of their nature, which is to make as much money for their stockholders as possible.[40]

Such diatribes against speculation, mammon, gambling, and other figurative allusions to marketplace activity were not at all unusual in Democratic rhetoric – particularly when the economy was performing poorly.[41] Economic tidings, for good or ill, were interpreted as the product of virtuous or unvirtuous behavior. Any deviation from "sound" economic principles – particularly in the form of stock speculation or economic concentration – was bound to result, sooner or later, in economic collapse. The cycle of sin, suffering, and expiation was endlessly repeated. As a result, when the Panic of 1893 set in, Cleveland held firm, refusing to increase the supply of money or to extend government spending.[42]

Although Democratic orators were not so unwise as to openly deprecate industrial enterprise, it was clear where their sympathies lay. An editorial in the *New York Evening Post* expressed fear that Whig-sponsored legislation would confer "vested rights" on manufacturers.[43] The anti-industrial leanings of the party came into the open during the heat of the 1850s, when the party came under attack from abolitionists. The northern system of free labor, countered Douglas, was nothing more than "white slavery," since it deprived the workingman of the true value of his labor.[44] This proto-Marxist critique of the northern industrial economy, not uncommon for Democratic orators at mid-century, was drawn directly from Jacksonian rhetoric (and, on closer inspection, was not very Marxist).

Where the Whigs and Republicans were mercilessly portrayed as par-

40. Buchanan, speech, 1/22/1840 (Buchanan 1908–09, 4: 5–8).
41. Buchanan spoke in the immediate wake of the first serious nationwide economic downturn in the country's history, the Panic of 1837. See also editorial, *New York Evening Post* (9/14/1836) and *Address of the National Democratic Party Convention to the People of the United States* (1840: 4).
42. Democratic economic philosophy stuck close to common wisdom, as revealed by Tilden's declaration that "I would give all the legerdemain of finance and financiering, I would give the whole of it for the old, homely maxim: 'Live within your income' " (speech, 9/24/1868, in Tilden 1885: 437).
43. See *New York Evening Post* (9/28/1836).
44. See also Andrew Johnson, speech, 1/8/1856 (Johnson 1970: 355). (Johnson, at this point, was a Democrat.)

ties of mammon, the Democratic party was seen as the protector of the common people; where the Republicans cast themselves as harbingers of limitless industrial growth, Democrats were wont to emphasize the difficulties inherent in such a project. In the midst of the 1848 campaign, one of the party's broadsheets proclaimed, "We must count upon a host of presses . . . upon streams of money, contributed by the rich merchants and the greedy manufacturing capitalists, being poured out against us."[45]

As the foregoing quotations indicate, the economic philosophy of the early Democratic party is perhaps more accurately encapsulated in the terms *agrarianism, producerism,* or, as I have chosen, *civic republicanism,* than in liberalism. It was not the marketplace that nineteenth-century Democrats sought to protect, since they did not have a well-developed understanding of that mechanism. The despised term *laissez-faire,* as I have indicated, was entirely absent from Democratic discourse, and its correlate, *free trade,* beat a hasty retreat by the end of the 1830s. The party's concern was for the protection of civil society and the individuals therein. Democrats inhabited a moral economic universe in which hard work was, under normal market conditions, assumed to pay off in roughly equal quantities of money. The Ricardian overtones of Jacksonian rhetoric flowed in part from the common assumption that money should derive its value more or less directly from labor hours, that insofar as money became a value in and of itself (separate, that is, from its labor value) it was corrupt speculation. Andrew Jackson's farewell address formulated the classic statement of the civic republican economy:

> The planter, the farmer, the mechanic, and the laborer all know that their success depends upon their own industry and economy and that they must not expect to become suddenly rich by the fruits of their toil. Yet these classes of society form the great body of the people of the United States; they are the bone and sinew of the country; men who love liberty and desire nothing but equal rights and equal laws and who, moreover, hold the great mass of our national wealth, although it is distributed in moderate amounts among the millions of freemen who possess it.[46]

Labor may be considered one of the touchstones of Jacksonian economic thinking, the connecting thread between the party's yeoman ideal of the independent producer, its traditional agrarian economic model, and its distrust of the parasitic state, of paper money, of all speculative schemes, and of large concentrations of capital – all of which were thought to rob the virtuous laborer of his just rewards.

45. "The Moral Power of the Two Parties," the *Campaign* (6/21/1848) 56.
46. Jackson, farewell address, 3/4/1837 (Blau 1954: 17).

Far from championing the advances of the bourgeoisie, Jacksonian Democrats distrusted currencies, banks, monopolies, tariffs, and many other trappings of capitalist civilization. Within this context, the party's insistent defense of property rights is properly viewed as a defense of the rights of smallholders. Property required labor, since land would otherwise be unproductive, and also ensured individual autonomy. Van Buren, for instance, imagined that Native Americans could be "induced to labor and to acquire property, and [that] its acquisition will inspire them with a feeling of independence."[47]

Following Jefferson and Jackson, the example of the yeoman farmer loomed large in Democratic discourse. Samuel Tilden, in 1868, testified that "it was in the simple habits, moderate tastes, and honest purposes of the rural community that I was accustomed in my youth. . . . It is from [the farmers] that we must largely hope for whatever of future is reserved to our country."[48] Democrats throughout the century stood resolutely for an agrarian set of economic policies: cheap land, low taxes, minimal tariffs, stable and affordable currency, westward expansion on the American continent (but not overseas), and noninterference with slave labor (understood as necessary in the growing of tobacco and cotton).[49]

But the civic republican economy was meant to encompass not simply farmers – its original inspiration – but also urban artisans, as represented by the figure of the mechanic in Jackson's farewell address. Economic and political well-being (for the two were inseparable) were the product of "industry, morality, intelligence and republican habits."[50] It was these virtuous habits, and the smallness and independence of their protoindustrial operations, that bestowed virtue upon urban artisans.

Preserving the Republic

I have argued that Democratic views of the marketplace are more properly referred to as civic republican than liberal. I shall now argue

47. Van Buren, first annual message, 12/5/1837 (Richardson 1897: 1609).
48. Tilden, speech, 9/24/1868 (Tilden 1885: 423). Cass, in 1852, envisioned "the glorious light of a community, stretching along our vast inland frontier, each family keeping its own land, and every one with elements of prosperity within their reach. . . . What is more glorious for us, or more useful to the republican institutions of the world, than such a distribution of the public domain of this country?" (speech, 9/2/1852, in *Evening Post Documents* 1852: 3).
49. See Watson (1990: 114).
50. Van Buren, open letter to North Carolina constituents, 3/6/1836 (Schlesinger 1971, 1: 605).

that Democratic views of politics also stemmed from this classical ideal. To begin with, the concerns of the Jacksonian Democratic party were preeminently political, not economic. The occasional panic was duly registered in party rhetoric, but Democrats were simply not as oriented to monetary and financial concerns as were their Whig and Republican opponents; hence their rather lackadaisical approach to economic theory. Civic republicanism was an ideology whose primary concern was with the vices and virtues of government, and a substantial proportion of nineteenth-century party rhetoric concerned observations – often of a highly theoretical sort – on the rightful purposes of government, the construction of government, and so forth. Democrats of that era were simply more anxious about the health of the republic than about the health of the economy – or, for that matter, the social equality of its citizens. They assumed that a basic level of social equality would result if the state were modest in stature and virtuous in performance. Government, said Jackson, echoing Jefferson, should "measure out equal justice to the high and the low, the rich and the poor."[51] There was no condemnation of riches in this remark, simply an insistence upon the right to procedural justice.

The animating purpose behind the party's national ideology was the prevention of tyranny, rather than the achievement of anything in particular. Here we arrive at one of the most consistent themes of nineteenth-century Democratic oratory. The national convention of 1840 worried that "our Republican institutions, though they might preserve their form, would not long retain their purity, their simplicity, or their strength."[52] The "great moneyed institution" was a threat to the survival of republican government, and it was on these grounds primarily that it was attacked. The danger was spelled out in more explicit form by General Jackson himself. The Bank of the United States, he argued, was unjust because of the "great evils to our country and its institutions [that] might flow from such a concentration of power in the hands of a few men irresponsible to the people."[53] In truth, the party's attacks against predatory monopolies seemed to be motivated more by worries about political corruption than by any concern for the inequality such aggregations of wealth might produce within civil society.

Party pols spoke ecstatically of the people, the republic, and popular

---

51. Jackson, veto message, 9/10/1832 (Richardson 1897: 1141–42). See also Cleveland, acceptance letter, 9/26/1892 (Schlesinger 1971, 2: 1766).
52. *Address of the National Democratic Party Convention to the People of the United States* (1840: 11).
53. Jackson, veto message, 7/10/1832 (Richardson 1897: 1144).

sovereignty. The party's first official national platform, for example, included the following declarations: "That the will of the people is the only legitimate source of power. That all power thus derived, is a trust to be exercised only for the public good. That agents so entrusted with its exercise are responsible to the people for the performance of their duties. That this responsibility should be as direct and immediate as possible."[54] First, we should note the ritual affirmation of popular government. Democratic politicians were exceedingly fond of presenting issues as a contest between the people and some infamous element of tyranny (in the 1830s, this was the Bank of the United States). Second, we might note the direct and immediate relationship that was supposed to characterize the roles of lay citizen and elected citizen. Whereas Whigs and Republicans viewed representatives as *trustees*, Democrats insisted upon an unmediated *delegatory* relationship. Antifederalist principles of frequent rotation in office, of amateur rather than professional representatives, and of direct popular rule found their home in the Democratic party. Even in the Gilded Age, when such ideals are commonly assumed to have fallen by the wayside, Democratic orators often bemoaned the distance that separated the people from the officeholders.

The party's rejection of federal consolidation, I have argued, was not simply a knee-jerk rejection of government and a defense of slavery but also an impassioned defense of an older concept of politics. As much as they were concerned with rule by the people, Democrats were equally concerned with *virtuous* rule and with the maintenance of the republic. Although fears for the demise of the republic during the 1830s have been much remarked upon, it is noteworthy that this ancient political rhetoric survived through the late nineteenth century in Democratic election pronouncements.[55] In 1880, for example, vice presidential candidate William H. English warned that "the constant encroachments which have been made by that [Republican] party upon the clearly reserved rights of the people and the states will, if not checked, subvert the liberties of the people and the government of limited powers created by the fathers, and end in a great consolidated central government – strong, indeed, for evil – and the overthrow of republican institutions."[56]

The danger posed by the military was particularly great, for, as Buch-

---

54. *Address of the National Democratic Party Convention to the People of the United States* (1840: 1).

55. See Hubbard (1828); "Address to the Republican Electors of the State of New York from the New York Republican State Convention" (*New York Evening Post* 9/30/1828); and Van Buren (1836b: 21).

56. English, acceptance letter, 7/30/1880 (*The Campaign Text Book* 1880: 7).

anan reminded his audience, "The history of all ruined republics . . . teaches us this great lesson. From Caesar to Cromwell, and from Cromwell to Napoleon, this history presents the same solemn warning, – beware of elevating to the highest civil trust the commander of your victorious armies."[57] The fragility of the republic necessitated continued vigilance on the part of its citizens. The English Revolution – or, more accurately, the Whig version of the English Revolution – was thus relived several centuries later (and with no monarch in sight) in the hands of Democratic speechwriters. Platform resolutions urged "that the usurpations of Congress and the despotism of the sword may cease"[58] and warned against "a self-perpetuating oligarchy of office-holders." The conspiracy at hand, implied the party's 1892 platform, would "practically establish . . . monarchy on the ruins of the Republic."[59]

It was in the nature of power to insinuate itself into the hearts and minds of those it sought to direct. Thus, despite the apparent disappearance of overt repression (e.g., in the Alien and Sedition Acts), Van Buren warned, "the spirit of encroachment has . . . become more wary, but it is not a bit more honest. Heretofore the system was coercion, now it is seduction. Heretofore unconstitutional powers were exercised to force submission, now they are assumed to purchase golden opinions from the people with their own means."[60] The well-worn oppositions of the people and the interests, virtue and corruption, liberty and power, disinterestedness and ambition were replayed in Democratic speeches in virtually every nineteenth-century election.

Use of the term *democracy* confuses the ideology of that party insofar as it implies a devotion to majority rule. How are we to square this with the party's insistence on a governmental apparatus that was constitutionally handicapped? This has been a difficult feature for contemporary writers to digest, lending the party a conflict-ridden or nonideological air. As I have suggested, however, Democrats were much more comfortable with the principle of democratic responsiveness when this operated at a state or local level. In addition, Democrats conceived of a zero-sum political universe in which the power of government was achieved at the expense of the rights of the people. The majority-rule-versus-limited-government problem that has so exercised the modern era was simply not understood by nineteenth-century Democrats, who could

57. Buchanan, speech, 10/7/1852 (Buchanan 1908–09, 4: 464).
58. Democratic platform, 1868 (Johnson 1956: 38).
59. Democratic platform, 1892 (Johnson 1956: 86).
60. Van Buren, speech, 1827 (Van Buren 1836b: 24).

not foresee any circumstances in which right-minded citizens would grant their own privileges to the keeping of a national government. The Democratic sentiment, according to Van Buren,

> has its origin in a jealousy of power, justified by all human experience. It is founded on the assumption that the disposition of man to abuse delegated authority is inherent and incorrigible; it therefore seeks its only security in the limitation and distribution of those trusts which the very existence of government requires to be reposed somewhere. Hence the aversion of its supporters to grant more power than is indispensably necessary for the objects of society; and their desire, as an additional safeguard, to place that which is conferred in as many hands as is consistent with efficiency.[61]

Thus, the constitutional restrictions that Democrats lauded were intended to hem in the powers of government, not the powers of the people. Elections were viewed as an occasion for the people to rise up to smite the giant, else his rule deprive them of their most sacred liberties. Democracy was to serve as "the sheet anchor of [the people's] liberties"[62] against any "consolidation of unchecked, despotic power, exercised by majorities of the legislative branch."[63]

Left implicit was the notion that a virtuous exercise of the franchise would be moderate and restrained. A sentimentalized version of self-government was served up by party rhetors, one bound up in the patriotic duty of the citizen and the glorious Old Republican tradition. The following peroration, from a speech by Cleveland during the 1888 campaign, is typical of Democratic views on this score: "With firm faith in the intelligence and patriotism of our countrymen, and relying upon the conviction that misrepresentation will not influence them, prejudice will not cloud their understanding, and that menace will not intimidate them, let us urge the people's interest and public duty for the vindication of our attempt to inaugurate a righteous and beneficent reform."[64] Here it is "the people's interest and public duty" that is called upon, rather than simply "the people's demand" (a trope that was used with great regularity after Bryan's arrival). Cleveland and other Democratic orators of the time spoke as leaders unto the people, who were their charges. "We have undertaken," states Cleveland quite revealingly, "to teach the voters."[65] Government was a simple matter of following strict republican

---

61. Van Buren, speech, 1827 (Van Buren 1836b: 19).
62. *Address of the National Democratic Party Convention to the People of the United States* (1840: 9).
63. Polk, fourth annual message, 12/5/1848 (Richardson 1897: 2519).
64. Cleveland, acceptance letter, 9/8/1888 (Schlesinger 1971, 2: 1690).
65. Cleveland, open letter, 9/14/1888 (Cleveland 1892: 286).

principle, about which there could be little doubt. Politics was seen as a duty – "a patriotic performance of the duties of citizenship" – not a field of creative endeavor.[66]

Although champions of the people, Democratic candidates represented their constituencies in an aloof, almost Olympian manner. Again, the concept of democracy (or of populism) is misplaced. Political leaders were expected to rise from the common people but, at the same time, to embody *un*common virtue. The curiously distant quality of Democratic leaders was a stance intended to indicate their disinterestedness – and hence, their capacity for independent and virtuous judgment. Such a Sir Galahad, imbued with self-restraint, modesty, and forbearance, would thus remain one of the people while inhabiting, for a limited time, the most exalted position of the republic. The magic of Democratic candidates like Andrew Jackson and (in a more mundane fashion) Grover Cleveland was that they managed to capture the simplicity, as well as the nobility, of the Washington model. The nobility of the Democratic orator, it might be observed, sprang from his simplicity.

This congeries of eighteenth-century republicanism and nineteenth-century moralism is captured in particularly resplendent form in a speech by Grover Cleveland given in 1890:

> The intrigues of monarchy which taint the individual character of the subject; the splendor which dazzles the popular eye and distracts the attention from abuses and stifles discontent; the schemes of conquest and selfish aggrandizement which make a selfish people, have no legitimate place in our national life. Here the plain people of the land are the rulers. Here, our patriotism is born and entwines itself with the growth of filial love, and here our children are taught the story of our freedom and independence. But above all, here in the bracing and wholesome atmosphere of uncomplaining frugality and economy, the mental and moral attributes of our people have been firmly knit and invigorated.[67]

Government, according to Democrats, was instituted to serve basic principles like private property and liberty, which stood *prior* to government. Any infringement of these natural rights constituted an offense against nature. Some form of popular participation was necessary to preserve these rights, thereby countering the inherent corruption of political power; but the point of popular participation was to act as a preservative, not an agent of change. There were, in fact, few decisions open to adjudication, since most matters could be reduced to simple judgments of principle.

66. Cleveland, speech, 1/8/1891 (Cleveland 1892: 263).
67. Cleveland, speech, 11/13/1890 (Cleveland 1892: 250).

In the party's perpetual battle against the depredations of self-interest, Democrats called continually on the populace to enforce rigid republican norms. Greed became the focus of much Democratic opprobrium, particularly with regard to import taxes: "Though the subject of tariff legislation involves a question of markets, it also involves a question of morals. We cannot with impunity permit injustice to taint the spirit of right and equity which is the life of our Republic, and we shall fail to reach our National destiny if greed and selfishness lead the way."[68] Democrats defined themselves as the party of virtuous frugality, and their opponents as the profligate party of mammon.

The cry of corruption was one of the most consistent elements of Democratic rhetoric in the Gilded Age. It did not, of course, go unnoticed in Republican campaign rhetoric, but its volume and vituperance were stronger on the Democratic side. After all, Republicans had most of the federal patronage; Democrats had little to offer the voter but their virtue. This was in plentiful supply.[69] Every Democratic platform promised "the expulsion of corrupt men from office"[70] or "a thorough reform of the Civil Service."[71] Corruption, however, in the nineteenth-century political vocabulary, implied not simply illicit gain from public office but also the eventual downfall of the republic. Something of the charged nature of this omnipresent word is brought home by Cleveland's pledge to "preserve from perversion, distortion, and decay the justice, equality, and moral integrity which are the constituent elements of our scheme of popular government."[72]

Unsurprisingly, such a restricted view of the purposes of politics gave a distinctly conservative cast to Democratic rhetoric in the nineteenth century. Communism and socialism were equated with free love and the breaking of social taboos. Cass declared himself "opposed to all the isms of the day."[73] The 1832 address of the New York City and County Nominating Committee enjoined respondents to remember "that we have usages transmitted to us from the pure and simple days of our Republic; we have held fast to those usages in times of trial; we have conformed to them now."[74] The party that identified itself as the bearer

---

68. Cleveland, acceptance letter, 9/26/1892 (Schlesinger 1971, 2: 1766).
69. Cleveland, speech, 4/2/1892 (Cleveland 1892: 324). See also Cleveland's personal interview given to the New York *Commercial Advertiser* under the title "Moral Issues in Politics," 9/19/1889 (ibid. 343).
70. Democratic platform, 1868 (Johnson 1956: 37).
71. Democratic platform, 1872 (Johnson 1956: 42).
72. Cleveland, speech, 4/2/1892 (Cleveland 1909: 333).
73. Cass, speech, 9/2/1852 (*Evening Post Documents* 1952: 4).
74. *New York Evening Post* (10/30/1832).

of the Revolution was the most determined upholder of tradition throughout the nineteenth century.

Preserving Liberty

No doubt, Democratic suspicion of majority rule was strengthened by the humiliating position of the South during Reconstruction.[75] The advocacy of minority rights, however, cannot be chalked up simply to expedience. After all, this position had been staked out as early as the 1830s, when the party was dominant, and continued through the Gilded Age, when two-party competition returned. Throughout the nineteenth century, the Democratic party was much more likely to emphasize the significance of civil liberties and civil rights (as they pertained to white men) than was the Whig-Republican party. Freedom of the press and of religion, "personal or home rights," the abstract praise of liberty, and the ritual invocation of the Kentucky and Virginia Resolutions and the Bill of Rights were predominantly Democratic themes. This is perplexing, given the role of the Republican party in emancipation and its (at least tentative) support for civil rights in the post–Civil War South. Here it is helpful to remember that the Republican party did not fight the Civil War to free the slaves; rather, the party took it upon itself to fight a war it saw no way of avoiding if the nation and the constitution, in their present form, were to be preserved. This was a Union party, not an abolition party. In this capacity, Whigs and Republicans could view themselves as a party representing majority interests within American society (see chapter 3).

Democrats, however, as ethnocultural historians have keenly pointed out, saw many disadvantaged minorities in their midst – the South of course, but also agriculture (oppressed by industrial and financial interests) and various immigrant groups that composed the party's urban voting base. The reality of this geographic, economic, and/or cultural oppression matters less for our purposes than its perception. The Democratic party portrayed itself throughout the nineteenth century as a party of victims, and it is this rhetoric of victimization that gave Democratic ideology much of its minoritarian flavor.

Democrats, predictably, were more open to European immigration than were Republicans.[76] In matters of religion, Democrats were secular republicans, in both deed and rhetorical form. Although their campaign

75. Polk, inaugural address, 3/4/1845 (Richardson 1897: 2225).
76. No statements in opposition to European immigration could be found among party platforms. See also Watson (1990: 242).

oratory did begin to incorporate a Protestant moralism toward the end of the century, references to God and scripture were so rare as to be almost unnoticeable. When they did appear, they were casual, almost pro forma, and harkened more to the civic republican sense of the sublime than to the religious. Cleveland, for example, ended his acceptance address in 1892 with the promise of "humble reliance upon the Divine Being, infinite in power to aid, and constant in a watchful care over our favored Nation."[77] Sometimes Cleveland substituted "Supreme Being" for "Divine Being"; in either case, the effect was soporific.[78] In contrast to the evangelical tenor of the Bryan period and to the overwhelmingly Protestant ethos of the Whig-Republican party, the nineteenth-century Democrats occupied an island of secularism. The only persistent reference to matters of the cloth was to the separation of church and state, a Jeffersonian doctrine that found its most avid defender in the nineteenth-century Democratic party. Democratic party leaders – Protestants themselves, by and large – defended the rights of Catholics during a virulently anti-Catholic age. They were leery of Republican-sponsored legislation to prohibit the sale of liquor, to institute public schools (and thereby challenge the authority of parochial schooling), and to socialize newcomers in the doctrines of Americanism. Although many of these contests over social morality were played out at city and state levels, the presidential parties inherited an ethos that derived from these local struggles of pride and prejudice – an ethos of Protestant moralism for Whig-Republicans and of libertarianism for nineteenth-century Democrats.

Conclusions

Views of the early Democratic party have usually centered on one of three general frameworks, introduced at the beginning of the chapter: democratic populism, liberalism, and ethnoculturalism. The democratic view is probably most apt as a description of radical elements of the party during the 1830s, particularly in New York City. The presidential party, on the other hand, was less than enamored of the leveling pretensions of its supporters in the Locofoco movement.[79] Democracy and political equality were goals that had already been achieved by the 1830s. The party's obsession was to maintain these rights and liberties, not

---

77. Cleveland, acceptance letter, 9/26/1892 (Schlesinger 1971, 2: 1769).
78. Cleveland, acceptance letter, 9/18/1884 (Cleveland 1909: 55).
79. For work on this group of partisans, see Bridges (1984), Hugins (1960), and Wilentz (1984).

to venture into government regulation of property relations. Democracy and its correlates (equality, populism, popular sovereignty) must therefore be placed within the larger rubric of civic republicanism, for it was the republic and the natural rights of the people, not majority rule, that party officials were concerned to protect.

As for the familiar liberal label, I have shown how the impulses of the party were often quite *un*liberal. It explains a lot about American political culture that the impulse toward preserving civic republican traditions would culminate in a set of policies normally associated with the forward-looking, pragmatic, and economistic philosophy of liberalism. Yet it remains the case that the Democratic party stayed out of marketplace affairs not because of any faith in free enterprise but rather out of an abiding lack of faith in the federal government.

Like democratic and liberal views of the party, ethnocultural accounts are not so much incorrect as incomplete. The party's preference for liberty, states' rights, and limited government no doubt gained impetus from its coalition of white ethnics, who feared the dominance of an intolerant majority. However, these policies were not simply the product of constituency pressures, nor do they exhaust the nineteenth-century Democratic belief system.

In contrast, finally, to most previous work on the subject, I have argued that Democratic ideology remained remarkably constant over the long and tumultuous course of the nineteenth century and that this ideology is best described as the confluence of three intersecting values: white supremacy, antistatism, and civic republicanism. Most of what party leaders said and did from 1828 to 1892 could be connected to these three ideals.

In 1880, the party's vice presidential nominee, William English, tendered the traditional letter of acceptance to the party's nominating committee. The letter acknowledged the great honor the party had bestowed upon him and pledged his fealty to the timeless principles of Democracy. Though an obscure figure from an equally obscure campaign (which the Republican, Garfield, would win), English offers us a glimpse into the totalistic, rather dogmatic, and devotedly unreconstructed ideology that his party represented – a fitting coda to this chapter:

> Perpetuating the power of chronic Federal office-holders four years longer will not benefit the millions of men and women who hold no office; but earning their daily bread by honest industry, is what the same discerning public will no doubt fully understand, as they will also that it is because of their own industry and economy and God's bountiful harvests that the country is comparatively prosperous, and not because of anything done by

these Federal office-holders. . . . This contest is in fact between the people endeavoring to regain the political power which rightfully belongs to them, and to restore the pure, simple, economical, constitutional government of our fathers on the one side, and a hundred thousand Federal office-holders and their backers, pampered with place and power, . . . on the other.[80]

80. English, letter of acceptance, 7/30/1880 (*The Campaign Text Book* 1880: 7).

6

The Populist Epoch
(1896–1948)

The era of the First World War constituted the defining moment of most contemporary European party systems.[1] The most widespread and enduring aspect of this transformation from preindustrial to industrial cleavage structures was the gradual eclipse of centrist (liberal or agrarian) parties by socialist, social-democratic, and/or communist parties on the left.[2] That this did *not* occur in the United States has often been regarded as the defining feature of the American party system.[3] Others have suggested, somewhat to the contrary, that the Democratic party served as the functional equivalent of European social democracy such that there was nothing particularly exceptional about the development of the American party system.[4]

What was the character of the left party in America during the first half of the twentieth century? Writers portray the Democratic party prior to the 1930s as an organization periodically drawn and quartered by the demands of its disparate constituents – northerners and southerners, farmers and urban laborers, immigrants and natives, wets and drys, progressives and reactionaries. According to this view, the realignment of 1896 heralded not so much the arrival of a new ideological age as the revival of an older Jacksonian framework. "[F]irmly rooted in negativism, clinging to outdated ideals of states' rights, retrenchment, and limited government," one historian has written, "the Democratic party

---

1. See Lipset and Rokkan (1967).
2. In Britain, for example, the Liberal party was gradually squeezed out by the Labour party.
3. For overviews of this classic question, see Laslett and Lipset (1974), Lipset (1977), and Shafer (1991).
4. For comments supportive of this view, see Greenstone (1977), Harrington (1972: 251), Lipset (1977), Mowry (1968: 271–72), and Shannon (1968: 241). This question is addressed in chapter 2.

seemed a ramshackle, almost irrelevant array."[5] There was, in short, no single Democratic ideology but rather a great profusion of outlooks and interests.

After 1932 and through the next several decades, the Democrats finally achieved a modicum of ideological cohesion (at least on domestic affairs). The focus of this newfound sense of political direction was the welfare state and its associated public philosophy – pragmatism, statism, scientific expertise, Keynesian economic policies, and redistributive social policies. Sidney Milkis summarizes the standard view:

> The decisive break with American traditions of limited government . . . came with Franklin Roosevelt in the 1930s and his deft reinterpretation of the "liberal" tradition in American politics. Liberalism had always been associated with Jeffersonian principles and the natural rights tradition of limited government. . . . Roosevelt pronounced a new liberalism in which constitutional government and the natural rights tradition were not abandoned but linked to programmatic expansion and an activist national government.[6]

Thus, the identity of the early-twentieth-century Democratic party is usually seen as internally and temporally fragmented (between pre- and post-New Deal regimes).

I argue that there was more cohesion and continuity within Democratic ideology between 1896 and 1948 than is generally recognized. This ideology was not oriented on Jefferson, nor was it oriented on the technocratic management of the welfare state; rather, it was *Populist* in tone and in policy.[7]

Although not exactly statists, twentieth-century Democrats backed in-

---

5. Williams (1970: 146). See also Broesamle (1974: 83), Burner (1967/1968), Burnham (1981: 158), Clubb (1981: 120–22), Hofstadter (1955), Jensen (1971: 269), Ladd (1970: 161), and Milkis (1993: 21). Some writers extend this sectional fragmentation through the 1940s (e.g. Garson 1974). For general works on the Democrats through the nineteenth and twentieth centuries, see Chambers (1964), Goldman (1979; 1986), and Rutland (1979).

6. Milkis (1992: 109). For other analyses of Democratic ideology during the New Deal, see Brinkley (1995), Burns (1956), Clubb (1981), Ekirch (1969), Fraser and Gerstle (1989), Hawley (1966), Holt (1975), Jenkin (1945), Leuchtenberg (1963), Rotunda (1986), and Schlesinger (1957, 1959, 1960). Writers and contemporaries noted that the New Deal did not spring forth de novo in 1932. Antecedents have been located in the broad range of reform movements and parties of the late nineteenth and early twentieth centuries, and, to a lesser extent, in the Progressive-era Democratic party. See Burner (1967/1968), Cherny (1981), Craig (1992), Fine (1956), Goldman (1977), Gould (1978), Hofstadter (1955), Lichtman (1983), McCormick (1981), Rogin and Shover (1970), and Sarasohn (1989).

7. I shall use *Populism* to refer to the ideology of the Democratic party in the 1896–1948 period and *populism* to invoke the general (nonspecific) concept.

creasing government intervention in and regulation of the marketplace, the redistribution of wealth through government transfers, loose monetary policies, and demand-led economic growth. They were suspicious of monopolies and of big business in general. The moral bases of this political and social revolution spread from producerism to evangelical Christianity and crystallized on the notion of serving the public interest. Democrats' political philosophy could be encapsulated in the ideal of majority rule and in the populist narrative in which the people fought for their rights against an economic and political elite. I argue, therefore, that William Jennings Bryan is the rightful father of the Progressive–New Deal Democratic party, bringing to it a regulatory style and redistributive purpose found hitherto only outside the mainstream of American party politics. From 1896 to 1948, Democratic candidates sounded the bell of political and economic freedom and advocated for the rights of the common man.[8]

I should note that my analysis centers on the campaigns led by the most prominent of the party's leaders during this period – William Jennings Bryan (nominated in 1896, 1900, and 1908), Woodrow Wilson (1912, 1916), Al Smith (1928), Franklin Roosevelt (1932, 1936, 1940, 1944), and Harry Truman (1948). Alton B. Parker (1904), James Cox (1920), and John W. Davis (1924) receive comparatively short shrift. These were, of course, the more conservative candidates of the party during these years, so the following account is tilted in a more progressive direction than would have been the case had I treated all candidates equally.[9] However, there are compelling reasons for evaluating

8. Of course, populism did not arrive completely unannounced in the 1890s. Monopolies were a traditional target of Democratic oratory, and railroads were lambasted in party tracts beginning in the 1870s. The party platform of 1892 went still further. Here it was averred that another Republican administration might result in "the dominance of a self-perpetuating oligarchy of office-holders." The platform charged that Republican protectionist policies were "a robbery of the great majority of the American people for the benefit of the few," qualifying, therefore, as a piece of "class legislation" (Johnson 1958: 86–87). In terms even more stridently populist, the platform condemned "Trusts and Combinations, which are designed to enable capital to secure more than its just share of the joint product of Capital and Labor" (ibid. 87). This horror, however, was chalked up simply to "prohibitive taxes," which disturbed the course of the free market (ibid.). In his 1892 campaign, Cleveland draped himself in "The People's Cause," defending "the rights of every man, rich or poor," but he went no further than to invoke the usual nostrums of tariff reform and "the protection of just and equal laws" (speech, 4/2/1892, in Cleveland 1909: 331). Thus, despite these deviations, the 1892 campaign retained a nineteenth-century flavor. Indeed, the platform called for "a return to . . . fundamental principles of free popular government, based on home rule and individual liberty" (Johnson 1958: 87).

9. Each campaign is treated equally in the content analysis, of course.

the party through its most influential spokesmen: only three times during these fourteen presidential elections did avowedly conservative candidates get the party's nod; none were seriously considered for renomination; they were the least successful candidates during this period (judging by popular vote totals); and none of the three gained lasting influence within the party. Thus, when I speak of the Democratic party during its Populist period, I shall be speaking primarily of the party of Bryan, Wilson, Smith, Roosevelt, and Truman, not that of Parker, Cox, and Davis.

Plebiscitarian Democracy

The transformation of the Democratic party from the nineteenth to the twentieth century must be understood within the context not merely of policy but also of *style*. Changes in how the party stood were intimately related to what the party stood for. Democratic presidential hopefuls from Jackson to Cleveland, although referring to themselves collectively as the party of the people, maintained a civic republican sense of reserve when facing their constituents. Up until the landmark election of 1896, only two Democratic presidential hopefuls had dared address the people directly (in the disastrous attempts of Stephen Douglas in 1860 and Horace Greeley in 1872). Presidential campaigns were carried on by party organizations, while the candidates sat at home (or, if they were incumbents, in the White House) writing letters and entertaining visitors. Bryan's 1896 campaign broke decisively with the reserved manner of the nineteenth century, bestowing upon later campaigns a distinctly plebiscitarian air. In Bryan's 1896 marathon, the boy wonder managed to give more than six hundred speeches in twenty-seven states, averaging eighty thousand words per day. The civic republican model, in which the people courted the statesmen, now stood on its head. Henceforth, all Democratic presidential nominees would tour the country in an open and unabashed search for the American voter.[10]

It is important to recall that the presence of a presidential candidate on a railroad car platform or on the stage of a local assembly hall was something entirely new under the democratic sun. For the first time, the populace (a fairly sizable percentage of them, at any rate) listened to their champion directly, rather than to party spokespersons. Moreover,

10. Republicans were slower in reconciling themselves to the new, candidate-centered campaign; not until 1908 did a Republican presidential nominee forsake his front porch to stump through the countryside.

these campaigns were not the managed, routinized events they became in the latter twentieth century. Candidates bantered with the crowd, answered questions, dealt with hecklers, and rarely stayed with the written text of a speech – which, in any case, they had probably helped write. Thus, the plebiscitarian model of democratic politics, in which a candidate directly encounters the people (rather than encountering them through radio and television and through a phalanx of polls, reporters, and consultants) was more authentic at this historical moment than perhaps at any other time in American history.

"I rejoice," said Bryan, "to live in a land where the people can select one of their number and make him their public servant, and when he stands, not in his own strength, but in their strength, he does become the greatest man in the world. And yet he should never forget that he is their servant, and that he acts not for himself, but for them, that he is but the instrument by which they accomplish their sovereign will."[11] As Wilson explained to one audience, it was not the business of the statesman to judge *for* the nation but rather "to judge *through* the nation as its spokesman and voice."[12] For all the party's cant and posturing, one is obliged to take seriously its claim to be the vehicle of the people. Whereas the Jacksonian party viewed the question of government as having been settled, once and for all, at the Constitutional Convention of 1787, for the party of Bryan the principle of majority rule was pre-

11. Bryan, speech, 10/16/1900 (*New York Times* 10/17/1900). Bryan defined the "vital principle of republics," as "absolute acquiescence in the decision of the majority" (speech, 10/3/1896, in Bryan 1896: 520). "There is more virtue in the people than ever finds expression through their representative. To hold that a representative can act for the people better than they can act for themselves is to assert that he is as much interested in the people as they are in themselves, and that his wisdom is greater than the combined wisdom of the majority of the people. Neither proposition is sound" (Bryan, speech, 9/3/1900, in *New York Times* 9/4/1900). See also Bryan, speech, 7/8/1896 (Bryan 1900: 307); speech, late Sept./1896 (Bryan 1896: 499–501); acceptance letter, 9/18/1900 (*Official Proceedings of the Democratic National Convention . . .* 1900: 246); speech, 10/16/1900 (*New York Times* 10/17/1900); speech, 9/1909 (Bryan 1913: 366); Wilson, speech, fall/1912 (Wilson 1913: 31, 47, 50, 57, 59); speech, 9/30/1916 (Schlesinger 1971, 3: 2319); and Roosevelt, speech, 9/21/1932 (Roosevelt 1938a: 731).
12. Wilson, speech, fall/1912 (Wilson 1913: 54). What the country needed, Wilson said unself-consciously, was a leader on the order of Abe Lincoln, "who stood up declaring that the politicians did not see from the point of view of the people, . . . that tall, gaunt figure rising in Illinois, . . . a man free, unentangled, unassociated with the governing influences of the country, ready to see things with an open eye, . . . to see them as the men he rubbed shoulders with and associated with saw them . . . a leader who understood and represented the thought of the whole people" (speech, fall/1912, in Wilson 1913: 53).

eminent. Byran's third presidential acceptance speech, for example, was boldly titled "Let the People Rule."[13]

The standard view of American electoral history is that after the turn of the century, with the precipitous decline of voter turnout, party organization and party competition, presidential campaigns were increasingly dull affairs.[14] At the same time, however – and somewhat ironically – the presidential election came to occupy a place of greater prominence in American political life. From a policy perspective, to begin with, much more was at stake. Whereas in the nineteenth century, Democratic campaigns were organized for the purpose of celebrating and preserving the past, in the twentieth century the emphasis shifted toward the earnest search for political and social reform. It was no longer sufficient to invoke the ways of the founders or the patented truths of all republics. Populist campaigns were conducted with a sense of immediacy – in some cases, of perfectionism – rarely felt in the nineteenth century's "military style" of campaign organization.

Democratic campaigns in the first several decades of this century were great, apocalyptic events for those who took politics seriously. In part, this was the product of the newness of the candidate-centered campaign. Localized, machine-dominated campaigning was slowly being replaced by campaigns centered on the presidential candidate. (It would be several decades before this style of campaigning itself became routinized.) Rather than simply rallying the faithful, the purpose of the campaign in the twentieth century was to convert the unconverted.[15] This required a message of hope and of change, not simply a repetition of party platitudes and established traditions.

This was also a time of comparative innocence in American politics, a time when party leaders were looked upon as moral and intellectual leaders of the nation. Bryan, Wilson, and Roosevelt, in particular, saw themselves as educators who, with single-minded devotion and impassioned rhetoric, could mold public opinion and rouse an apathetic citizenry into action. Matters of organization and ideology thus combined to create the general atmosphere of a charismatic social movement, an atmosphere as absent from the party-led campaigns of the previous century as it would be from

13. Roosevelt, three decades later, declared, "Ever since 1776 th[e] struggle has been between two forces. On the one hand, there has been the vast majority of our citizens who believed that the benefits of democracy should be extended and who were willing to pay their fair share to extend them. On the other hand, there has been a small, but powerful group which has fought the extension of those benefits" (speech, 10/21/1936, in Roosevelt 1938b: 525).
14. See Burnham (1981), Jensen (1969), and McGerr (1986).
15. See Jensen (1969).

the bland, media-dominated affairs of the postwar period. The Populist era was, for several reasons, a heroic period in presidential politicking.

People versus Power

Inseparable from this new way of practicing democracy was a new way of thinking about democracy. Throughout the nineteenth century, Democratic orators painted themselves as the party of the people, yet popular sovereignty was to be limited by a strict interpretation of the U.S. Constitution. Democracy meant preserving the rights of the people against the depredations of the state, *not* the right of the people to rule. Beginning in 1896, the party reframed its understanding of democracy from minority rights to majority rule – a transformation that its Republican opponents were loath to follow (see figure 9).

Democrats, to begin with, were increasingly skeptical about the Constitution and the courts. No longer the bulwark of democracy, the Constitution became, for the first time, a source of irritation.[16] During the Progressive era, the party's efforts to create a national income tax, to help organized labor, to combat the power of economic monopolies, and to impose controls on worker health and safety were continually frustrated by the opposition of a federal court system (staffed largely by Republican appointees) acting in defense of property, contract, and state prerogatives.[17] (FDR's battle with the Supreme Court in the Thirties is rightly viewed as the last act in a long drama.) The Constitution, party leaders now said, was to be "liberally" interpreted, according to the *spirit* of the founders and the needs of the country.[18] "Living political constitutions," Wilson declared, "must be Darwinian in structure and in practice."[19] Nor did Democrats shrink from advocating reforms in the fundamental law of the land. Of antitrust regulation Bryan remarked,

16. Struggles over the jurisdiction of the federal government during the nineteenth century were considered by Democrats to be the result of a too-loose interpretation of the Constitution by Whigs and Republicans. It was not the Constitution that was at fault, therefore; indeed, Democrats felt that the words of the founders were not taken seriously enough.

17. Recent scholarship has confirmed the role of the independent judiciary as one of the primary obstacles in the path of organized labor during the late nineteenth and early twentieth centuries (Hattam 1990).

18. The Declaration of Independence, similarly, was "an eminently practical document, meant for the use of practical men; not a thesis for philosophers, but a whip for tyrants; not a theory of government, but a program of action. Unless we can translate it into the questions of our own day, we are not worthy of it" (Wilson, speech, fall/1912, in Wilson 1913: 43).

19. Wilson, speech, fall/1912 (Wilson 1913: 42).

"If such law be unconstitutional, and so declared by the Supreme court, I am in favor of an amendment to the constitution that will give congress power to destroy every trust in the country."[20]

The connection between the fight for democracy and the fight against economic elites could be seen in many issues of the period. Democrats complained, for instance, about employers' influence over the votes of workers, a charge that originated in the electoral brawl of 1896. Toward the end of this vicious and unscrupulous campaign, many corporations had sent voting "suggestions" along with regular paychecks mailed out to employees. The implication, thought Bryan, was that if workers did not support McKinley, they would lose their jobs. Henceforth, the accusation of illicit interference in the democratic process – via corporate contributions or employer coercion – would become a hallmark of Democratic campaigns.

The public/private distinction was central to the Populist idiom. Wilson referred disparagingly to "private monopolies," "private power," "private control," "private conferences," "private understandings," and "private purposes," evils that he contrasted with the "general good" or the "public interest."[21] "Common" interests were in eternal battle against "particular" interests.[22] Al Smith's demand for state ownership of utilities was carefully phrased as a campaign for "public power." Whereas the Republican party "adhere[d] to the policy of private development by private individuals for private profit and gain," the Democratic party believed "in public development under public ownership and under public control in the interest of the rank and file of the people, the rightful owners of the power."[23]

Much of the party's reform program in the Progressive era concerned opening up the processes of government to the public. As Wilson explained, governmental operations "have been too secret, too complicated, too round-about; they have consisted too much of private conferences and secret understandings, of the control ... by men who were not legislators, but who stood outside and dictated. Government

---

20. Bryan, speech, 9/16/1899 (Boyd 1900: 482).
21. Wilson, speech, 8/7/1912 (Schlesinger, 1971, 3: 2228–36). "What form does the contest between tyranny and freedom take to-day?" asked Wilson in 1912 (speech, fall/1912, in Wilson 1913: 43). "By tyranny, as we now fight it, we mean control of the law, of legislation and adjudication, by organizations which do not represent the people, by means which are private and selfish" (speech, fall/1912, in Wilson 1913: 43).
22. Wilson, speech, 8/7/1912 (Schlesinger 1971, 3: 2236)
23. Smith, speech, 11/3/1928 (Smith 1929: 293).

ought to be all outside and no inside . . . [since] corruption thrives in secret places."[24] "Publicity," Wilson concluded, "is one of the purifying elements of politics."[25] Unsurprisingly, Democratic presidential candidates were favorably disposed to Progressive reforms aimed at democratizing the political system – including direct primaries, initiatives, referenda, recall elections, trial by jury, the direct election of Senators, direct primaries, the eradication of election fraud, campaign finance disclosure laws, and the opening up of Senate and House procedures.[26] The public interest, Democrats emphasized, should override private interests. "[T]he interests of society are far superior to the interests of either debtors or creditors," Bryan would say.[27] The land was "the rightful heritage of all the people," said FDR in a phrase that might have been plucked from Henry George's *Progress and Poverty*.[28] Corporations, insisted Bryan, "are creatures of law. They have no rights except those rights granted by the people."[29] The people, therefore, "have the right to place upon them such limitations as may be necessary for the protection of the public welfare."[30]

Implicit in the demand for popular rule was the assumption of elite rule, and explicit in every Democratic campaign from 1896 to 1948 was "the avenging wrath of an indignant people" against the abuse of power perpetrated by these elites.[31] Bryan, quoting Wendell Phillips, declared,

"On the one side stand the Tories and the cowards, those who hate the people and those who honestly doubt their capacity and discretion; on the

24. Wilson, speech, fall/1912 (Wilson 1913: 76).
25. Wilson, speech, fall/1912 (Wilson 1913: 77).
26. See, e.g., Bryan, acceptance speech, 8/12/1908 (Schlesinger 1973, 2: 1126).
27. Bryan, acceptance speech, 8/12/1896 (Bryan 1896: 332). Wilson, reiterating this theme, remarked, "There are some things in which society is so profoundly interested that its interests take precedence [over] the interests of any group of men whatever" (speech, 9/23/1916, in Wilson 1982: 217). "[T]he interest of society is paramount to every other interest" (ibid.). The 1940 platform, similarly, advocated improvement in "the welfare of the people" (Schlesinger 1971, 4: 2847).
28. Roosevelt, speech, 11/2/1940 (Schlesinger 1971, 4: 2996). See also Roosevelt, speech, 9/21/1932 (Roosevelt 1938a: 728). Henry George, Jim Gregory reminds me, was originally a member of the Democratic party, as were Eugene Debs, Walt Whitman, and many other radicals of the late nineteenth century.
29. Bryan, speech, 1/20/1900 (Bryan 1900: 183).
30. See Bryan, speech, 1/20/1900 (Bryan 1900: 183). "The liberty of people to carry on their business," thought Roosevelt, "should not be abridged unless the larger interests of the many are concerned. When the interests of the many are concerned, the interests of the few must yield" (speech, 9/21/1932, in Roosevelt 1938a: 728; see also speech, 8/3/1936, in Roosevelt 1938b: 280).
31. Bryan, speech, 7/8/1896 (Bryan 1900: 308).

other side we see the men who still believe in the declaration of independence and are resolved that this shall be, as Lincoln said, a 'government for [sic] the people, by the people, and for people.' . . . I believe in the people, in universal suffrage. . . . If corruption seems rolling over us like a flood, it is not the corruption of the humbler classes – it is millionaires, who steal banks, mills and railways; it is defaulters, who live in palaces and make away with millions; it is money kings, who buy up Congress."[32]

At the heart of the Populist drama lay the poignant struggle between honest common folk and politicoeconomic elites.[33] "We are engaged," said Bryan, "in a great contest, which is to determine whether a few men banded together are more powerful than all the rest of the people."[34] Democratic candidates during the 1896–1948 period harped incessantly on "the control over the government exercised by Big Business." Wilson attempted to convince voters that "the masters of the United States are the combined capitalists and manufacturers of the United States."[35] Of the Hoover administration, Roosevelt said: "It was high-finance-minded – manned and controlled by a handful of men who in turn controlled and by one financial device or another took their tool from the greater part of all other business and industry." The government, he insisted, was "in the hands of one hundred or two hundred all-wise individuals controlling the purse-strings of the Nation."[36]

Whereas Jacksonian Democrats spoke of "the people" at large, Democrats from Bryan to Truman were more likely to speak for the "common people," "ordinary Americans,"[37] or the "struggling masses."[38] The clear implication, in any case, was that Americans were *not* all the same; some were unjustly privileged above others. Populist Democracy was thus distinguished from the previous century of Democratic rhetoric by its *implicit* class orientation. Themes of class resentment began to rise toward the end of the nineteenth century, reaching peaks in the 1896–1912 period and the 1930s and tapering off thereafter (see figure 2).

32. Bryan, speech, late Sept./1896 (Bryan 1896: 499).
33. "The issue presented in the campaign of 1900," Bryan said in his next effort at national office, "is the issue between plutocracy and democracy. All the questions under discussion will, in their last analysis, disclose the conflict between the dollar and the man" (speech, 6/1900, in Schlesinger 1973, 2: 1086).
34. Bryan, speech, late Sept./1896 in Tammany Hall (Bryan 1896: 510).
35. Wilson, speech, fall/1912 (Wilson 1913: 48).
36. Whereas nineteenth-century Democrats had long defined themselves against the center, twentieth-century Democrats campaigned against the periphery – the "special interests, illiberal minorities, [and] panic-stricken leaders" of the status quo (Roosevelt, speech, 10/14/1936, in Roosevelt 1938b: 482).
37. See, e.g., Roosevelt, speech, 7/19/1940 (Schlesinger 1971, 4: 2972).
38. See, e.g., Bryan, speech, 9/7/1896 (*New York Times* 9/8/1896).

(Not surprisingly, content analysis reveals the Democratic party to be the more vociferous champion of "class politics" in *all* periods of American history, even those eras in which class-based issues were not in the forefront of political debate.)

"The Republican Party," charged Bryan, "is forgetting the man from whom it collects while it takes care of the man who receives. All over this land are the homes of forgotten men, men whose rights are disregarded, men whose interests are neglected because of the demands made by combined capital."[39] "[T]he men I am interested in," added Wilson in the next decade, "are the men who never have their voices heard, who never get a line in the newspapers, who never get a moment on the platform, who never have access to the ears of . . . anybody who is responsible for the conduct of government, but who go silently and patiently to their work every day, carrying the burden of the world."[40] Roosevelt, in similar fashion, spoke of a program that rested on the "forgotten man," the man "at the bottom of the economic pyramid," the "little fellow."[41]

Thus, although the tocsin of class struggle was abjured, there was more than a trace of economic grievance in the populist-inspired appeals of Democratic candidates. Bryan, quoting Carlisle, conceived of the 1896 election as "a struggle between 'the idle holders of idle capital' and 'the struggling masses, who produce the wealth and pay the taxes of the country.' "[42] Two months later in the same grueling campaign, Bryan articulated a populist version of Marx's theory of immiseration: "As you sacrifice more and more, you will find that your debts virtually increase as your ability to pay your debts decreases, and in the long run, the capitalistic classes will devour all the property."[43] "Society," he raged, "is divided on the money question. On the one side you find the capitalistic classes and on the other side you find the struggling masses."[44] "The 'idle holders of idle capital' insist upon making the laws in time of peace while the 'struggling masses' are despised and spit upon."[45]

39. Bryan, speech, 10/8/1900 (*New York Times* 10/9/1900).
40. Wilson, speech, 9/2/1912 (Wilson 1956: 92).
41. Roosevelt, radio address, 4/7/1932 (Roosevelt 1938a: 625–26).
42. Bryan, speech, 7/8/1896 (Bryan 1900: 309).
43. Bryan, speech, 9/19/1896 (Bryan 1896: 463).
44. Bryan, speech, 10/15/1896 (Bryan 1896: 560).
45. See Bryan, speech, 10/15/1896 (Bryan 1896: 560). Bryan's ire did not cool in his two subsequent campaigns for the presidency. See speech, 6/1900 (Schlesinger 1973, 2: 1087, 1092). Perhaps no one in Democratic party history was more hostile to "the rich" than Harry ("Give-'em-hell") Truman, who declared, "The Wall Street reactionaries are not satisfied with being rich. They want to increase their power and their privileges, regardless of what happens to the other fellow. They are gluttons of priv-

Thus, although both parties appeared to propagate the same liberal-consensus view (negating the existence of social class), in fact there were important features separating the parties' treatment of this sensitive issue. Whig-Republicans, on the one hand, decried the dangers of class conflict, referring to those who raised such issues as "demagogues." Democratic leaders, on the other hand, decried the economic and political policies that created a class-divided society and pointed to privileges possessed by "monopolies" or "the rich." To Republican criticism of " 'paupers' who are not worth their salt," Roosevelt responded, "Can the Republican leaders deny that all this all-too-prevailing Republican sentiment is a direct, vicious, unpatriotic appeal to class hatred and class contempt?"[46] One of the Democrats' favored strategies was to accuse the Republicans of practicing "class politics" by excluding the common people from the halls of power and privilege. To Republican charges of communist sympathizing, Roosevelt responded, "This form of fear propaganda is not new among rabble rousers and fomenters of class hatred."[47] The Bryanite Democratic party thus presents us with the spectacle of a party practicing class politics while refusing to recognize the existence of social classes. There was a certain disingenuousness to Democratic protestations of innocence. "While I do not want to array one class against another," Bryan insisted, he was nonetheless willing to "array all the people who suffer from the operation of trusts against the few people who operate the trusts."[48]

Antimonopoly themes within party platforms show a strong upsurge at the turn of the century, followed by a second upsurge in the 1930s and 1940s (see figure 12). This criticism concerned the infamous "trust" or "monopoly," an entity that was difficult to define but that aroused universal opprobrium from Democratic candidates. Roosevelt explained the arrival of the Great Depression in the following terms: "Throughout the nation, opportunity was limited by monopoly. Individual initiative was crushed in the cogs of a great machine. The field open for free business was more and more restricted. Private enterprise be-

---

ilege. . . . Agriculture, labor, and small business played second fiddle, while big business called the tune. . . . They [the Republicans] want a return of the Wall Street economic dictatorship. . . . The Republican strategy is to divide the farmer and the industrial worker . . . so that big business can grasp the balance of power and take the country over, lock, stock, and barrel. . . . It's about time the people of America realized what the Republicans have been doing to them" (speech, 9/18/1948, in Schlesinger 1971, 4: 3199–201).

46. Roosevelt, speech, 11/1/1940 (Roosevelt 1941: 539).
47. Roosevelt, radio address, 10/5/1944 (Roosevelt 1946: 323).
48. Bryan, speech, late Sept./1896 (Bryan 1896: 510).

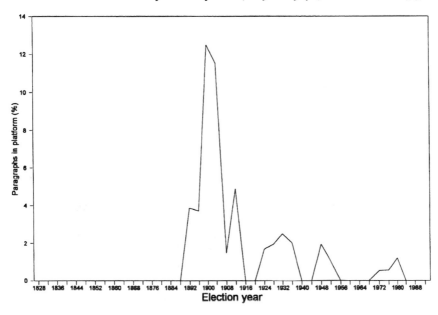

Figure 12. Antimonopoly sentiment, as measured by the percentage of paragraphs within Democratic party platforms devoted to trusts, monopolies, or economic concentration

came too private. It became privileged enterprise, not free enterprise."[49] Earlier, in the 1932 campaign, Roosevelt had sought to convince his audiences that "5,000 men in effect control American industry."[50] More, perhaps, than any other single theme, antimonopoly rhetoric tied the party of Bryan, Wilson, Smith, Roosevelt, and Truman together in the first half of the twentieth century.[51] Antitrust, like tariff

49. Roosevelt, acceptance speech, 6/27/1936 (Singer 1976: 127).
50. Roosevelt, speech, 10/31/1932 (Schlesinger 1973, 3: 1983).
51. In the late nineteenth century, the existence of private-sector monopolies was chalked up to the workings of the protectionist tariff (see, e.g., Cleveland, acceptance letter, 9/8/1888, in Schlesinger 1971, 2: 1688). If the marketplace were simply left alone, Democratic politicians from Jackson to Cleveland promised, monopolies would evaporate. In the twentieth century, by contrast, the consolidation of business power in America became the party's primary argument for government intervention. Thus, not only the prevalence but also the treatment of the antimonopoly theme changed radically after 1896.
    The significance of the trust in Democratic theorizing during the Progressive Era is well established; more controversial is its place within the New Deal (see, e.g., Brinkley 1995 and Hawley 1966). There were certainly many within the Roosevelt administration who felt that bigger business was sometimes better business and that

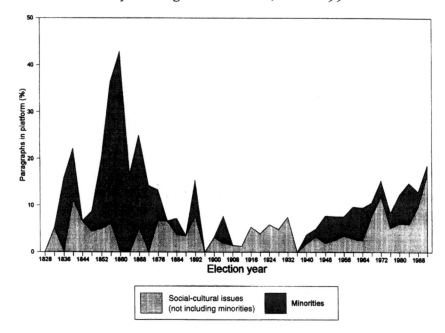

Figure 13. Attention to social-cultural and minority issues, as measured by the percentage of paragraphs within Democratic party platforms dealing with (1) social-cultural issues (abortion, the arts, crime, drugs, family values, immigration, minorities, pornography, Prohibition, temperance, the value of neighborhoods, school prayer, and women); and (2) minorities (predominantly African Americans, but also other groups with minority status)

reform for the previous generation, was the shibboleth of true Democracy.

Labor

Traditional views of Democratic ideology rest largely on evidence provided by voting constituencies, which, prior to the New Deal, were the product of ethnicity, race, and region more than of social class. Yet ethnic and religious issues were never particularly prominent in national party rhetoric, and the race issue dropped out of Democratic rhetoric almost entirely by the 1890s, remaining submerged for the next five

the federal government should therefore take a relaxed attitude toward its trustbusting obligations. Others maintained the Brandeis-Bryan line. For present purposes, the important point is that the party's *public* face – its legitimating ideology – was its antimonopoly face.

decades (see figure 13).[52] Here, as elsewhere, constituency behavior proves an unreliable indicator of party ideology (at least as revealed in campaign rhetoric).

Several circumstances conspired to suppress race-based rhetoric during the Populist period. By the end of the 1890s, the populist movement had been incorporated into the Democratic party, removing the immediate threat of a successful biracial coalition of blacks and poor whites.[53] During the same period, Jim Crow laws were successfully instituted, establishing a secure postbellum system of racial subordination.[54] Finally, by the end of the century, whatever lingering fears southerners had concerning a revival of Reconstruction had proved groundless. The wounds of the Civil War gradually eased. The much-heralded New South was showing remarkable resemblances to the Old South, particularly in its partisan allegiances. Thus, the absence of race from Democratic presidential rhetoric during the early twentieth century is hardly surprising: there was no longer an agenda of civil rights issues that the party needed to respond to and, with the South proving as solid as ever, it was no longer profitable to raise the divisive issue of race in a national context, where it might alienate potential constituents in other regions.[55]

52. Of course, this does not mean that Populist leaders were any less racist than their forebears; it simply means that policy issues involving race were less prominently featured than previously.

53. See Woodward (1951).

54. There is some dispute over precisely when blacks were disenfranchised in the South. Likely, it varied from state to state. See Cresswell (1995), Key (1942/1958), and Kousser (1974).

55. The predominant sense of an issue having been disposed of is brought out in the work of Arthur Holcombe, a prominent Harvard political scientist. Writing in 1924, Holcombe states confidently, "Racial, like religious, parties . . . have no place in national politics. Prior to the adoption of the Thirteenth, Fourteenth, and Fifteenth Amendments, discrimination against the African race was not prohibited by the federal Constitution, and was practiced in varying degrees in most of the states. But now all persons born or naturalized in the United States are entitled to all the privileges and immunities of American citizenship, and no state may make any law which will abridge these privileges and immunities or deny to any person the equal protection of the laws. It is still possible to make racial distinctions which may in practice amount to discrimination against the negro race, and proposals for such discrimination may play an important part in state and local politics. The Congress might make more effective provision for negro suffrage in federal elections than has yet been made, but with that exception national party leaders have no powers which they can easily utilize for the gratification of racial sympathies or antipathies" (1924: 37).
   In fact, the self-conscious exclusion of racial issues from the national political arena during the first half of the twentieth century was probably even more effective than previous efforts by the Whigs and Democrats during the antebellum period. Carmines and Stimson (1989: 30) remark, "While the Supreme Court led the retreat

In any case, the disappearance of racial themes, and the continued subordination of ethnic and religious themes, paved the way for a new partisan identity based primarily on socioeconomic concerns.

The year 1906 was a turning point in this developing relationship between labor leadership and the Democratic party, for it was at this time that Gompers's appeal to the Republican party was openly (and humiliatingly) rebuffed and that a tacit alliance was first struck between the American Federation of Labor (AFL) and the Democratic party.[56] Gompers's official stance of voluntarism was perhaps judicious, given the weakness of the Democratic party through most of the early twentieth century. However, continued Republican hostility to labor legislation, the stacking of the judicial system with antilabor judges, and the inability of sympathetic progressives within the Republican party to do much of practical importance for their would-be labor allies pushed the AFL leadership into Democratic ranks.[57] During Bryan's 1908 campaign, the ties between organized labor and the Democratic high command were intimate. Democrats, writes Sarasohn, "accepted bodily the first six demands of the AFL, including limitations on injunction, an eight-hour workday on all federal projects, and a separate Department of Labor. . . . Bryan personally contacted Gompers after the convention to make sure that the labor section was acceptable" and met repeatedly with Gompers to incorporate labor themes in his speeches.[58] "The labor organization helps those outside of it as well as its members," Bryan assured his listeners, "because the increased wages and improved

from the cause of racial equality, it was also joined by the other national political institutions. After Reconstruction Congress did not pass a single piece of civil rights legislation until the Civil Rights Act of 1957. No president until Harry Truman in 1948 had even sent a major civil rights program to the Congress. And both political parties, but especially Democrats, were also willing to see racial issues kept off the national agenda." See also Brinkley (1995: 165). One might note, in this context, that after the demise of the abolitionist movement, no social movement championing the rights of black Americans would arise until the mid-twentieth century.

56. See Coletta (1971: 2073–74), Greene (1996; in press), Karson (1958: 58–64, 70–78, 83–86), Keller (1990: 132), Mink (1986), and Sarasohn (1989). The increasingly close ties between organized labor and the Democratic party were given concrete illustration in 1911, when Alton B. Parker, the party's standard-bearer in 1904, defended Gompers in *Gompers v. Bucks Stove*, in which the head of the AFL was accused of criminal contempt for having ignored an antiboycott injunction. Mink (1986: 204–5) considers the "formal coalition" between the AFL and the Democratic party to have arrived in 1912 rather than 1908. However, she stresses, "the AFL's association with the Democrats stretched back to 1896, when the party . . . adopted anti-injunction and anti-immigration planks in its platform. Industrial workers may have repudiated Bryan's party of the 'toiling masses,' but union labor worked to promote it" (ibid.).

57. See Sarasohn (1989: xi).   58. See Sarasohn (1989: 45).

conditions are shared by non-union men as well as by union men."[59] This laborist rhetoric made good strategic sense. Winning the presidency required that Bryan move beyond his natural constituencies in the South and Midwest and focus instead on winning the urban-industrial states of the Northeast.[60] The excoriation of corporate capital and the adoption of prolabor planks were intended to identify the Democratic party as the party of industrial, as well as of agricultural, labor.[61]

Producerist norms, inherited from the party's Jacksonian past, provided the rhetorical scaffolding that brought agricultural and industrial workers together under the big tent of labor. Workers were valorized, and holders of power and privilege were stigmatized (as "idle parasites," "drones," and so forth). Ironically, labor faced a friendlier rhetorical setting in the early twentieth century than in the postwar era, for at this time, labor (writ large) was the primary measure of economic and social value in America.[62] Business was vulnerable to criticism, because businesses appeared to rely for their profits on the labor of others. "We are not opposed," said Bryan, "to that wealth which comes as the reward of honest toil. . . . We draw the line between honest wealth and predatory. We draw the line between that wealth which is a just compensation for services rendered and that wealth which simply measures the advantage which some citizen has taken over many citizens."[63] Wealth earned by labor was "honest"; that accumulated through speculation or investment was not. Labor was identified with manliness, strength, and American identity. American labor – highly paid, highly skilled, and autonomous – was repeatedly contrasted with foreign labor, which was cheap and degraded. Although the votes of working-class citizens did not appear in the Democratic column in large numbers until the 1930s, this transfer of allegiance must be seen as the culmination of decades spent cultivating links between organized labor and the Democratic leadership. The arrival of labor was thus the fulfillment of a dream long deferred.[64]

59. Bryan, speech, 9/7/1908 (Bryan 1913: 165).   60. See Sarasohn (1989: 53).
61. See, e.g., Wilson, speech, 9/2/1916 (Schlesinger 1971, 3: 2310–11).
62. See Rodgers (1974).
63. Bryan, speech, 10/16/1900 (*New York Times* 10/17/1900).
64. At the same time, it should be noted that at no time in American presidential politics were the rights of labor so openly defended as during the late 1930s and the 1940s. "We all know that certain people will make it a practice to deprecate the accomplishments of labor – who even attack labor as unpatriotic," began Roosevelt in 1944. "They keep this business up usually for three years and six months in a row. But then, for some strange reason, they change their tune – every four years – just before election day" (speech, 9/23/1944, in Schlesinger 1971, 4: 3077). To Republican attacks against the increasing influence of organized labor, Roosevelt responded by condemning such "labor-baiters." Truman made the antilabor Taft-Hartley Act –

Rehabilitating Government

Democratic ideology in the Bryan-Wilson-Roosevelt era was, to state the obvious, strongly egalitarian. Whereas "equality" in the party's previous era had referred mainly to matters of politics, by the turn of the century the equality ideal came to refer primarily to economic matters (see figure 14). In this sense, the American Democratic party underwent an ideological trajectory remarkably similar to that charted by the British Liberals during the same period – from "classic" liberalism to "social" liberalism, or, in T. H. Marshall's terms, from political rights to economic rights.[65] Nowhere was this transformation more directly manifested than in the party's switch from excise taxes to direct taxes on income. Bryan argued for a federal income tax on the grounds that "in our taxation we have been imposing upon the great struggling masses the burden of government, while we have been voting the privileges to a few people who will not pay their share of the expenses of the government."[66] "[W]e must choose," said Roosevelt, several decades later, "between democracy in taxation and special privilege in taxation. Are you willing to turn the control of the Nation's taxes back to special privilege?"[67] From being champions of "public economy," Democratic leaders came to embrace an expanding public sector. By the turn of the century, appeals for or against redistribution became one of the most predictable points of differentiation in the party system (see figure 8), and social welfare increasingly came to define the Democratic party (see figure 14).

Even more striking, perhaps, than this commitment to equality was the Democratic party's abandonment of a century of antistatism (see figure 3).[68] "We cannot serve posterity better," said Bryan, "than by

a "Republican onslaught against the rights of the working men in this country" – a major focus of his 1948 campaign (speech, 10/25/1948, in Truman 1948-49: 21).
65. See Marshall (1964).   66. Bryan, speech, 9/16/1899 (Boyd 1900: 484).
67. Roosevelt, speech, 10/21/1936 (Roosevelt 1938b: 529).
68. Democratic attacks on "paternalism" have been misinterpreted, for these attacks were directed only toward those structures of power which were thought to be undemocratically controlled. It was not a reaction against the state or against institutions in general but simply against the *illegitimate* exercise of political power. "Organization," said Wilson, "is legitimate, is necessary, is even distinguished, when it lends itself to the carrying out of great causes. Only the man who uses organization to promote private purposes is a boss." See Wilson, speech, fall/1912 (Wilson 1913: 134). The significance of the party's call for popular rule (discussed subsequently) becomes apparent; only insofar as the government was responsive could it be trusted. By the same token, a great degree of social control would be tolerated if it could plausibly be claimed that this control expressed the will of the people.

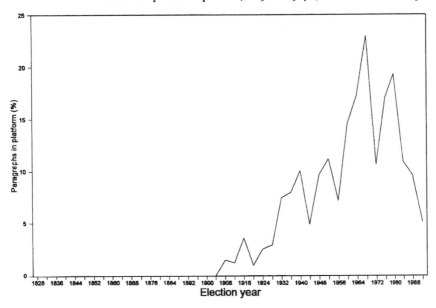

Figure 14. Attention to social welfare, as measured by the percentage of paragraphs within Democratic party platforms devoted to urban policy, cities, youth, children, the elderly, the poor, the underprivileged, the handicapped, welfare, and social policy. (Does not include treatment of home-ownership policies or education.)

contributing to the perfection of the Government, that each child born into the world may feel that it has here an opportunity for the most complete development, and a chance to secure, through service, the largest possible happiness and honor."[69] "We used to say that the ideal of government was for every man to be left alone and not interfered with," admitted Wilson forthrightly during the 1912 campaign. "That was the idea that obtained in Jefferson's time. But we are coming now to realize that life is so complicated that we are not dealing with old conditions, and that the law has to step in and create new conditions under which we may live."[70] FDR's celebrated speech to the San Francisco Common-

69. Bryan, speech, 9/7/1908 (Bryan 1913: 179–80).
70. Wilson, speech, fall/1912 (Wilson 1913: 27). Another speech snippet from the 1912 campaign brings home the same basic message: "There is one principle of Jefferson's which no longer can obtain in the practical politics of America . . . that the best government is that which does as little governing as possible, which exercises its power as little as possible" (quoted in Cooper 1983: 198).

wealth Club during the 1932 campaign – usually credited with being the first public disavowal of the party's Jeffersonian past – was in fact the second or third version of this disavowal, following Bryan and Wilson.[71] All three Democratic leaders tried hard to explain to Americans why they would have to part with traditional views of government and market. It was a story with a lesson that was quite familiar by the time of the New Deal: new forms of industrial organization necessitated new forms of governmental organization.

Federalism posed a particular problem for a party whose traditional mating call had been "states' rights." Bryan, as usual, was undaunted: "The predatory corporations have taken advantage of the dual character of our Government and have tried to hide behind State rights when prosecuted in the federal courts, and behind the interstate commerce clause of the constitution when prosecuted in the State courts."[72] To the perennial question of which constitutional authority should manage the regulation of private enterprise, Bryan answered, "Our platform demands that federal legislation be *added to, not subtracted for* [sic], State legislation."[73] "Jefferson," insisted Bryan, "believed in preserving the rights of the States, and yet he did not abate in the least the power and vigor of the Federal government which extends over all."[74]

The concept of laissez-faire – which, I have argued, was never particularly influential in Democratic counsels – functioned as the "straw man" argument of the twentieth century, an argument so obviously absurd that every candidate from Bryan through Truman delighted in mocking it.[75] To the charge that the government should leave banking to the banks, Bryan replied in 1896 that "the right to coin and issue money is a function of government[,] . . . a part of sovereignty, and can no more with safety be delegated to private individuals than we could afford to delegate to private individuals the power to make penal statutes or levy taxes."[76] This represented a historic departure from the party's trademark position that government and banking did not mix.

On occasion, Democratic statism was even more categorical. "When I find a man who is not willing to bear his share of the burdens of the

---

71. See Roosevelt, speech, 9/23/1932 (Roosevelt 1938a: 742–56).
72. Bryan, speech, 9/9/1908 (Bryan 1913: 184).
73. Bryan, speech, 9/9/1908 (Bryan 1913: 184); and speech, 9/16/1899 (Boyd 1900: 480).
74. Bryan, speech, 10/6/1896 (Bryan 1896: 520).
75. See, e.g., Wilson, speech, 10/19/1916 (Wilson 1982: 481); and Roosevelt, speech, 10/2/1932 (Roosevelt 1938a: 771).
76. Bryan, speech, 7/8/1896 (Schlesinger, 2: 1847).

government which protects him, I find a man who is unworthy to enjoy the blessings of a government like ours," stated Bryan forthrightly.[77] "I love government," said the irrepressible Bryan on another occasion during the 1896 campaign, "and I want to make it so good that there will not be one citizen in all the land who will not be willing to die for his government."[78] "The Democratic party favors the full exercise of the powers of the Government for the protection of the rights of the people," added the Commoner in his third, and final, campaign.[79]

At several moments Democrats agitated for government ownership of industry – not, of course, under the guise of establishing socialism but simply for the purpose of combating monopoly power over civil society. Bryan suggested this solution in a speech given in 1906, just after returning from Europe. "[R]ailroads partake so much of the nature of monopoly," he said, with little awareness of the stir such a position would create, "that they must ultimately become public property and be managed by public officials in the interests of the whole community."[80] The following public outcry was so great that no further word was heard from the Great Commoner on this subject.[81] The issue of government ownership came to the forefront of

---

77. Bryan, speech, 7/8/1896 (Bryan 1900: 306). Bryan, speaking in favor of the income tax, voiced concern that the lack of such a tax might, at some future time, "paralyze the arm of the government" (speech, 1/20/1900, in Bryan 1900: 166).

78. Bryan, speech, 9/19/1896 (Bryan 1896: 463).

79. Bryan, speech, 9/9/1908 (Bryan 1913: 184). "We are just upon the threshold of a time when the systematic life of this country will be sustained, or at least supplemented, at every point by governmental activity," said Wilson, in his more circumspect style (speech, fall/1912, in Wilson 1913: 129). There were, of course, exceptions to such statist sentiments, particularly during the elections of 1924 (see, e.g., Davis, speech, 9/1/1924, in Schlesinger 1971, 3: 2537–39) and 1928 (see, e.g., Democratic platform, 1928, in Schlesinger 1971, 3: 2616). But these campaigns must be measured against the standard set by Bryan, Wilson, and FDR. It was the last who asked, in 1932, "What is the State?" His answer: "It is the duly constituted representative of an organized society of human beings, created by them for their mutual protection and well being. One of the duties of the State is that of caring for those of its citizens who find themselves the victims of . . . adverse circumstances. . . . I assert that modern society, acting through its Government, owes the definite obligation to prevent the starvation or the dire want of any of its fellow men and women who try to maintain themselves but cannot . . . a matter of social duty" (speech, 10/13/1932, in Roosevelt 1938a: 788). "Your interests may be in your home," said FDR to a group of women, "but you now know that they are no longer disassociated from the interests of the State" (speech, 11/5/1932, in Roosevelt 1938a: 863).

80. Bryan, speech, 9/1906 (Bryan 1913: 93).

81. Bryan's statement is, nonetheless, an interesting indication of his *personal* ideology, which roamed freely into policy options that were considered rabidly socialistic in America. He was not, needless to say, constrained by an "agrarian" mentality during any of the years in which he carried the party's torch. (The Bryan of the 1920s is

presidential politics again in the 1928 campaign, when Al Smith championed the public ownership of utility corporations – an issue that would reappear, in somewhat attenuated form, in Roosevelt's prewar campaigns. Smith's (and later, Roosevelt's) arguments rested on the actions of railroad and utility corporations in restraint of trade, the special nature of these industries that made them peculiarly prone to monopolistic consolidation, the corrupting influence of their corporate-sponsored lobbies on the democratic process, the increased costs imposed by monopolies on consumers, and the illegitimate and scandalously high level of profit sustained by those businesses. "Public power," of course, had been an old war cry of Populism and western Progressivism, one that found its home, ultimately, in the Democratic party.

Yet Democrats were statists by necessity, not by choice. They adopted the federal government because, by the end of the nineteenth century, no other instrument was sufficiently powerful to challenge the power of corporate wealth. Populist Democrats were convinced, in Roosevelt's words, that "no business is above Government; and Government must be empowered to deal adequately with any business that tries to rise above Government."[82] Bryan, ever the brilliant polemicist, pointed out the absurdity of a government that could "take the son from his mother, the husband from his wife, the father from his child, and stand them up in front of the enemy's guns, but in an hour of danger . . . cannot lay its hands upon accumulated wealth and make that wealth bear its share of the expenses of the government that protects it."[83] In a land passionately devoted to civil society, Democrats were willing, if reluctant, defenders of the state.

Reconciling the Individual and the State

Confusing as it may seem, Democrats in the early twentieth century were more vigorous in their praise for free markets than were Republicans. "When there is competition," thought Bryan, "every employer has to get a good man to meet competition, but when there is no competition, anybody can sit in the office and receive letters and answer them, because everybody has to write to the same house for anything he wants."[84] "I believe," he continued, "the principle of monopoly finds its inspiration

---

quite another matter, as I will discuss.) Populism, one must conclude, does not lead inexorably to antistatism. In fact, the Populist movement of the 1890s imagined an even greater role for the state than did New Deal Democrats.

82. Roosevelt, speech, 9/11/1940 (Roosevelt 1941: 415).
83. Bryan, speech, 1/20/1900 (Bryan 1900: 167).
84. Bryan, speech, 9/16/1899 (Boyd 1900: 477).

in the desire of men to secure by monopoly what they cannot secure in the open field of competition."[85] "The struggle against private monopoly is a struggle for, and not against, American business. It is a struggle to preserve individual enterprise and economic freedom."[86] Antitrust rhetoric, as Hofstadter, Hartz, and many others have pointed out, was rooted in the philosophy of free markets.[87]

It was in this manner that "equal opportunity" became a primary weapon in the party's increasingly statist agenda. "America was created to break every kind of monopoly, and to set men free, upon a footing of equality, upon a footing of opportunity, to match their brains and their energies," opined Wilson.[88] "[W]e must make American individualism what it was intended to be," pledged Roosevelt, "equality of opportunity for all, the right of exploitation for none."[89] The party's 1936 platform, at the most radical phase of the New Deal, declared, "The American people are called upon to choose between a Republican administration that has and would again regiment them in the service of privileged groups, and a Democratic administration dedicated to the establishment of equal economic opportunity for all our people."[90]

There was seemingly no end to the hanky-panky that could be performed with traditional American norms. Roosevelt, for example, suggested that, in the interests of assuring the personal property rights of people of moderate means, it might be necessary to "restrict the operations of the speculator, the manipulator, even the financier."[91] To protect property rights, it would be necessary to infringe upon property rights;

---

85. Bryan, speech, 9/16/1899 (Boyd 1900: 478). To Wilson, America was no longer a place where "a man may choose his own calling and pursue it just as far as his abilities enable him to pursue it" (speech, fall/1912 in Wilson 1913: 24). "American industry is not free, as once it was" (speech, fall/1912, in Wilson 1913: 25).

86. Roosevelt, speech, 10/14/1936 (Roosevelt 1938b: 488). "[H]uge monopolies," thought Roosevelt, "were stifling independent business and private enterprise" (speech, 10/14/1936, in Roosevelt 1938b: 483).

87. See Hartz (1955) and Hofstadter (1955). Bryan was opposed to trusts not simply because they raised consumer prices but also because "the trust is closing the door of opportunity against our young men and condemning the boys of this country to perpetual clerkship" (speech, 10/16/1900, in *New York Times* 10/17/1900). The danger posed by trusts was that of "industrial despotism." "Give the boy a chance," said Bryan on another occasion, "and let success be the reward of merit" (speech, 9/15/1900, in *New York Times* 9/16/1900).

88. Wilson, speech, fall/1912 (Wilson 1913: 45). See also Bryan, speech, 9/7/1896 (Bryan 1896: 375–83); and Wilson, speech, 9/23/1916 (Wilson 1982: 212); speech, fall/1912 (Wilson 1913: 106, 109); and speech, 8/7/1912 (Schlesinger 1971, 3: 2230–31, 2233).

89. Roosevelt, speech, 8/20/1932 (Roosevelt 1938a: 681).

90. Democratic platform, 1936 (Schlesinger 1971, 3: 2851).

91. Roosevelt, speech, 9/23/1932 (Singer 1976: 86).

to protect the free market, it would be necessary to infringe on the freedom of economic competition; to protect the individual, it would be necessary to regulate the labor market.[92] "[E]ver since history began," Wilson argued,

> men were related to one another as individuals. To be sure there were the family, the Church, and the State, institutions which associated men in certain wide circles of relationship. But in the ordinary concerns of life, . . . men dealt freely and directly with one another. To-day, the everyday relationships of men are largely with great impersonal concerns, with organizations, not with other individual men. . . . There is a sense in which in our day the individual has been submerged. In most parts of our country men work, not for themselves, not as partners in the old way in which they used to work, but generally as employees . . . of great corporations. . . . You know what happens when you are the servant of a corporation. You have in no instance access to the men who are really determining the policy of the corporation. . . . Your individuality is swallowed up in the individuality and purpose of a great organization. . . . There is something very new and very big and very complex about these new relations of capital and labor.[93]

Wilson pointed forcefully to the impersonality, the coldness, and the undemocratic features of corporate forms of organization. The subtext of all these observations was that Americans had most to fear the increasing power and unscrupulousness of *business* tyranny – not the tyranny of government.

In this denunciation of business power, the ideal of autonomy, derived from some combination of the country's civic republican, Protestant, and classic liberal heritages, loomed large.[94] "Republicans, if you be here," said the prince of Populism, "I dare you to shut the door upon the humblest child and take away from it the possibility of being independent."[95] Of the "allied capitalists," Wilson said, "That is dependence, not freedom";[96] "It is a great deal better to shift for yourselves than to be taken care of by a great combination of capital. . . . I would rather starve a free man than be fed a mere thing at the caprice of those who are organizing American industry as they please."[97] Roosevelt, contrary

---

92. "I believe in the sacredness of private property," began Roosevelt in a typical refrain, "which means that I do not believe that it should be subjected to the ruthless manipulation of professional gamblers in the stock markets and in the corporate system" (speech, 8/20/1932, in Roosevelt 1938a: 680).
93. Wilson, speech, fall/1912 (Wilson 1913: 20–21).
94. See, e.g., the interpretation of the Revolutionary period offered by Kloppenberg (1987).
95. Bryan, speech, 10/16/1900 (*New York Times* 10/17/1900).
96. Wilson, speech, fall/1912 (Wilson 1913: 27).
97. Wilson, speech, fall/1912 (Wilson 1913: 114).

to most historians' estimations, did not herald the advent of a collectivist age; he referred, in his public rhetoric, to the "ideal of self-reliance" represented by the American farmer.[98]

Again and again individualistic norms came to the service of Democratic statism.[99] "Industrial independence is necessary to political independence," declared Bryan in 1908.[100] Where the burden of government rested on the decisions of the ordinary citizen, Bryan argued that the ordinary citizen would have to maintain a certain level of economic self-sufficiency such that his or her political decisions would not be conditioned by economic forces. Political equality, in short, necessitated a measure of economic equality. Individualism, and the associated ideals of liberty and freedom, meant "the realization of man's possibilities," including the full and free exercise of the mind.[101]

Here was a classic example of the plasticity of the American liberal tradition, for the meanings of all of these key terms – *liberty, freedom, humanity, the individual* – were fundamentally renegotiated in Democratic rhetoric at the turn of the century. "We all declare for liberty," Roosevelt pointed out several decades later, "but in using the same word we do not all mean the same thing. With some the word liberty may mean for each man to do as he pleases with himself, and the product of his labor; while with others the same word may mean for some men to do as they please with other men, and the product of other men's labor."[102] "Necessitous men are not free men," said Roosevelt, on another occasion. "Liberty requires opportunity to make a living – a living decent according to the standard of the time, a living which gives

---

98. Roosevelt, speech, 10/10/1936 (Roosevelt 1938b: 438).
99. "When there is industrial independence," thought Bryan, "each citizen is stimulated to earnest endeavor by the hope of being able to profit by his own genius, his own energy, his own industry, and his own virtue. But when private monopoly reaches its full development each branch of industry will be controlled by one or a few men, and the fruits of monopoly, like the divine right of rule, will be kept within the possession of a few from generation to generation, while the real producers of wealth will be condemned to perpetual clerkship or servitude" (speech, 9/15/1900, in *New York Times* 9/16/1900).
100. Bryan, speech, 8/25/1908 (Bryan 1913, 2: 141).
101. Bryan, speech, 9/7/1908 (Bryan 1913: 177). The rest of this interesting passage runs as follows: "The animal needs only food and shelter, because he has nothing but a body to care for; but man's wants are more numerous. The animal complains when it is hungry, and is contented when its hunger is appeased; but man, made in the image of his Creator, is a threefold being, and must develop the head and the heart as well as the body. He is not satisfied with mere physical existence. . . . His possibilities must be as unlimited as his aspirations" (speech, 9/3/1900, in *New York Times* 9/4/1900).
102. Roosevelt, speech, 10/29/1936 (Roosevelt 1938b: 557).

man not only enough to live by, but something to live for."[103] Without such, "life was no longer free; liberty no longer real; men could no longer follow the pursuit of happiness."[104]

Virtually any issue of equality could be justified according to notions of equal opportunity. "In other countries and other civilizations," said Bryan, "men have been condemned by birth to a particular occupation, place, or caste; in this country, each man, however or wherever born, can strive for the highest rewards in business, State, or Church."[105] This sounds initially like Republican rhetoric from the Neoliberal period (1928–1992). But Democratic appeals to the universally held ideal of the classless society were nearly always voiced in the context of the (actual or threatened) denial of this ideal. For Republicans the classless nature of American society was a reassurance that further social or labor legislation was unnecessary and that there was no need and no point to political action based on economic position; for Democrats it was a protest. When Republicans spoke of the classless state of American society, it was in the present tense; when Democrats did so, it was generally in the past, future, or conditional tense. A reality for one party, it remained an ideal for the other.[106] It was under the guise of restoring freedom to the individual that freedom was gradually stripped away from the private sector.

It is no surprise, therefore, that the most radical moments in the party's history were accompanied by an intensification of free-market capitalism and equal opportunity themes. Roosevelt, for example, frequently referred to the aims of the New Deal as a "democracy of opportunity."[107] Democrats might invoke the norms of a golden age of "natural" free enterprise, but they did not anticipate its return any time soon. In no sense, therefore, should Bryan be thought of as advocating a return to an agrarian or artisanal mode of production, though it may be argued that the model of independent entrepreneurship maintained a peculiar hold over the Democratic imagination.

---

103. Roosevelt, acceptance speech, 6/27/1936 (Singer 1976: 127).
104. Roosevelt, acceptance speech, 6/27/1936 (Singer 1976: 127). On an earlier occasion, he had resolved the matter in the following way: "I believe that the individual should have full liberty of action to make the most of himself; but I do not believe that in the name of that sacred word [*individualism*] a few powerful interests should be permitted to make industrial cannon fodder of the lives of half of the population of the United States" (speech, 8/20/1932, in Roosevelt 1938a: 680).
105. Bryan, speech, 9/3/1900 (*New York Times* 9/4/1900).
106. See, e.g., Roosevelt, speech, 8/3/1936 (Roosevelt 1938b: 280).
107. Roosevelt, speech, 8/3/1936 (Roosevelt 1938b: 280).

The Party of Humanity

No analysis of the Democratic party in the first half of the twentieth century is complete without an appreciation of the party's moralistic tone. The reform agenda of Democracy clothed itself in a language of righteousness derived from a diverse set of historical sources, including Protestantism, humanism, and civic republicanism. It was this heterogeneous mix of languages that provided a moral lever against the injustices of the marketplace and against the Republican party's pocketbook appeal.

What troubled Bryan and Wilson, to begin with, was the selling of human labor on the open market. The experience of slavery, as well as the virtue accorded to personal autonomy and the independent labor from which it derived, made contractual market relations seem more than a little sinful, relegating laborers to a weak and dependent existence. It was something less than what was intended for God's offspring. Workers were "not a mere marketable commodity."[108] Bryan, at greater length, explained, "The Republican Party assumes that the laboring man is all stomach, and has neither head nor heart. It tells the laboring man that he has plenty to eat, and that therefore he should not be interested in any question that concerns his Government. . . . [However,] the laboring man, made in the image of his Creator, wants more than a full dinner pail and a place to sleep." (This was followed by a long list of reforms for the benefit of labor.) The Populist perspective envisioned a world of Darwinian struggle, in which, unless otherwise restrained, the strong would "put the weak to the wall."[109] Democratic Populists identified themselves with the victims of this unnatural process of selection. They were shepherds of the oppressed.

To Republican "materialism," campaigners contrasted Democratic compassion. The Democratic party was great because "it had the real red blood of human sympathy in its veins and was ready to work for mankind."[110] "I am more interested," said Wilson, in ministerial garb, "in the fortunes of oppressed men and pitiful women and children than in any property rights whatever."[111] "The relation between labor and capital was

---

108. Wilson, acceptance speech, 9/2/1916 (Wilson 1982: 130).
109. Bryan, speech, 10/16/1900 (*New York Times* 10/17/1900).
110. Wilson, speech, 9/30/1916 (Schlesinger 1971, 3: 2320). The 1936 party platform explained that the party's success was due to the "humanizing policies of the Federal Government as they affect the personal, financial, industrial, and agricultural well-being of the American people" (Schlesinger 1971, 3: 2851).
111. Wilson, acceptance speech, 9/2/1916 (Schlesinger 1971, 3: 2314).

not "merely a contractual relationship" but "a relationship between one set of men and another set of men with hearts under their jackets and with interests that they ought to serve in common with persons whom they love and must support on the one side and on the other."[112]

To the rights of property, Wilson counterposed the rights of humanity: "[T]he states of America were set up to vindicate the rights of man and not the rights of property or the rights of self-aggrandizement and aggression. Property we have found to be the indispensable foundation of stable institutions, but the rights of humanity are the essence of free institutions, and nothing can take precedence of them."[113] Bryan went further than most in the direction of what might be called a "just wage." Starting from first principles, as he was so fond of doing, Bryan begins: "Let us see if we can agree upon the rules that should govern us in the accumulation of the money that we need. How much money can a man rightfully collect from society?" The answer: "[Not] more than he honestly earns." More than that Bryan considered, without any hint of exaggeration, to be "stealing."[114] "God made all men," said the Commoner, "and he did not make some to crawl on hands and knees and others to ride upon their backs."[115] A more moderate presentation of

112. Wilson, speech, 9/23/1916 (Wilson 1982: 214). "The labor question," said Bryan eight years earlier, "is more a moral than an intellectual one" (speech, 9/7/1908, in Bryan 1913: 164).

113. Wilson, speech, 10/5/1916 (Wilson 1982: 348). See also Bryan, acceptance speech, 8/12/1896 (Bryan 1896: 319); and speech, 6/1900 (Schlesinger 1973, 2: 1087).

114. Bryan (1909: 339–40). The labor question, said Bryan in 1908, "is chiefly a question of distribution, . . . [the] equitable distribution of the proceeds of toil. . . . The difficulty has been to divide the results fairly between the captains of industry and the privates in the ranks. As the dividing is done largely by the captains, it is not unnatural that they should magnify their part and keep too large a share for themselves" (speech, 9/7/1908, in Bryan 1913: 178–79). "There must," said Bryan the following year, "be a reasonable relation between the pay of the general and the pay of the enlisted man" (speech, 9/1909, in Bryan 1913: 412). Those who stood on the Chicago platform (1896), thundered Bryan, "do not defend the occupation of the highwayman who robs the unsuspecting traveler, but they include among the transgressors those who, through the more polite and less hazardous means of legislation, appropriate to their own use the proceeds of the toil of others. The commandment, 'Thou shalt not steal,' . . . is no respecter of persons" (acceptance speech, 8/12/1896, in Bryan 1896: 319). Again, one could observe how the value-orientation of the populist Democratic party derived from the basic American belief in the producerist ethic, "that each individual should receive from society a reward for his toil commensurate with his contribution to the welfare of society" (speech, 9/7/1908, in Bryan 1913: 179).

115. Bryan, speech, 9/16/1899 (Boyd 1900: 490–91). Occasionally, Bryan's producerist and egalitarian rhetoric echoed the quasi-socialist plans of Henry George. Bryan said at one point that there was only one just method of wealth distribution, one that

the same idea was to be found in Roosevelt's notion of a "living wage" – a wage, he explained, "which will insure the worker and the worker's dependents a living in accordance with American standards of decency, happiness and self-respect"[116] "[E]very one of our people is entitled to the opportunity to earn a living, and to develop himself to the fullest measure consistent with the rights of his fellow men."[117]

Democrats were fond of appealing to rights, "human" or "natural."[118] Not surprisingly, the Declaration of Independence and the Bill of Rights remained constant points of reference for Democratic orators, though to quite different effect than during the nineteenth century.[119] The argument from fundamental rights was much stronger – and infinitely more appealing – than the argument from charity. "We do not want a benevolent gov-

"measured justly each individual's share of the joint product. Every man who, by his brain or muscle, contributes to the sum total of this nation's wealth must have a part of that wealth as his reward" (speech, 10/7/1908, in Bryan 1913: 412).

116. Roosevelt, speech, 9/6/1936 (Roosevelt 1938b: 331).

117. Roosevelt, speech, 11/5/1932 (Roosevelt 1938a: 861). "I see an America," said the longtime president, "where the income from the land shall be implemented and protected by a Government determined to guarantee to those who hoe it a fair share in the national income" (speech, 11/2/1940, in Schlesinger 1971, 4: 2997). The 1940 platform promised "to work always for a just distribution of our national income among those who labor" (Schlesinger 1971, 4: 2951).

118. See, e.g., Wilson, acceptance speech, 8/7/1912 (Schlesinger 1971, 3: 2228). The Democratic party saw itself fighting for "the cause of humanity," and the "human element" remained, in slightly less apocalyptic form, central to the Democratic party's presentation of self. "[P]olitics," thought Wilson, "rest . . . upon the human soul" (speech, 11/2/1916, in Wilson 1982: 592). "Progressive legislation . . . merely means plowing that subsoil of human nature out of which all the influences must come which will produce the great crops of prosperity and national growth" (speech, 11/2/1916, in Wilson 1982: 596). The 1940 platform promised to "continue to emphasize the human element in industry [and to] place human resources first among the assets of a democratic society" (Schlesinger 1971, 4: 2951, 2954). "I believe," said Roosevelt, "that our industrial and economic system is made for individual men and women, and not individual men and women for the benefit of the system" (speech, 8/20/1932, in Roosevelt 1938a: 680). It was human against machine, the individual against the system. The human factor was what separated the trust from the other industrial combination, the labor union. "The trust," said Bryan, "is a combination of dollars; the labor organization is an association of human beings. . . . The trust deals with dead matter; the labor organization deals with life and with intellectual and moral forces" (speech, 9/7/1908, in Bryan 1913: 169). "We are all caught in a great economic system which is heartless," thought Wilson. "When we deal with [the modern corporation] we deal with an impersonal element, an immaterial piece of society" (speech, fall/1912, in Wilson 1913: 23). The "privilege of the government" was "to see that human life is protected" (speech, fall/1912, in Wilson 1913: 29).

119. See, e.g., Bryan, speech, 9/16/1899 (Boyd 1900: 488).

ernment," explained Wilson. "Every one of the great schemes of social uplift which are now so much debated by noble people amongst us is based . . . upon justice, not upon benevolence. It is based upon the right of men to breathe pure air, to live; upon the right of women to bear children, and not to be overburdened so that disease and breakdown will come upon them."[120] Populism was a struggle for justice, not a plea for government handouts. "We have rights that may be called natural rights; they are inherent; we have them because we are human beings. The Government did not bestow them upon us – the Government cannot rightfully withdraw them from us," claimed the Commoner.[121]

God, natural rights, the myth of creation – all were called into play in one particularly interesting piece of mythmaking by the three-time presidential nominee:

> When God made man as the climax of creation, he looked upon his work and said that it was good, and yet when God finished his work the tallest man was not much taller than the shortest, and the strongest man was not much stronger than the weakest. That was God's plan. We looked upon his work and said that it was not quite as good as it might be, and so we made a fictitious person called a corporation, that is in some instances a hundred times, a thousand times, . . . stronger than the God-made man. Then we started this man-made giant out among the God-made men. . . . My contention is that the government that created must retain control, and that the man-made man must be admonished: "Remember now thy creator in the days of thy youth," and throughout thy entire life. . . . What government gives the government can take away. . . . I insist that both the state government and the federal government must protect the God-made man from the man-made man.[122]

In this Rousseauian vision, individuals were deprived of their natural state of equality by the introduction of unnatural forms of economic organization. Bryan's implicit reference to the Frankenstein story was probably not lost on his audience: a monster had been unknowingly created and would continue its depredations unless forcibly remanded to human (read governmental) control.[123] Thus Bryan recalled the primacy of humanity over the artificial, *man-made* corporation, a primacy that derived, in one of Bryan's memorable phrases, from man's *God-made* connection to the Creator. Bryan recalled the authority of patri-

---

120. Wilson, speech, fall/1912 (Wilson 1913: 130).
121. Bryan, speech, 9/7/1908 (Bryan 1913: 167).
122. Bryan, speech, 9/16/1899 (Boyd 1900: 485–86).
123. "If these great aggregations of wealth take the side of the Republican party, then it seems to me that the God-made men had better look out for themselves" (Bryan, speech, 1/20/1900, in Bryan 1900: 184).

archy; the corporation, though now having reached its maturity and being in full possession of its formidable powers, still owed a debt of gratitude and respect to its creator. Bryan's ingenious symbolic dance managed to convey the primacy of government over the corporation as a matter of traditional patterns of authority. There was nothing new or innovative in the assertion that what the government gave the government could take away.

Democratic Populists like Bryan and Wilson made a valiant attempt to overcome the politics of self-interest – which they associated with the Republican party – with a politics based on fundamental principles. Bryan and Wilson, in particular, inveighed against materialism, "which makes man the slave of his possessions."[124] "We were born," said Wilson, "not to pile up material wealth, but to see that the spirits of mankind did not lose heart. We were born to prefer justice to power, humanity to any form of selfish achievement."[125] "[T]he love of money is the root of all evil," Bryan would say. "What shall it profit a man if he shall gain the whole world and lose his own soul?"[126] "The Republican party is concerned chiefly with material things," claimed the party's platform in 1924, whereas "the Democratic party is concerned chiefly with human rights."[127] It was yet another episode in the classic New Testament story of might versus right. "Our opponents," complained Bryan somewhat petulantly, "have appealed to the selfishness of nearly every class of society."[128] After listing at great length the material benefits to each class of society to be derived from bimetalism, Bryan got to the heart of the argument: "We do not live for ourselves alone. . . . Let those who are now reaping advantage from a vicious financial system remember that in the years to come their own children . . . may . . . be made to pay tribute to the descendants of those who are wronged today."[129] This brought the argument back to the Democrats' home court, social justice:

> Our opponents say that this money question is a business question; they try to rid it of sentiment. But there is not much business which is devoid of

124. Bryan, speech, 9/1909 (Bryan 1913: 347).
125. Wilson, speech, 10/7/1916 (Wilson 1982: 368).
126. Bryan, speech, 9/16/1899 (Boyd 1900: 479).
127. Democratic platform, 1924 (Porter and Johnson 1961: 243).
128. Bryan, acceptance speech, 8/12/1896 (Bryan 1896: 322). "Nothing is more important," said Bryan, gearing up for the 1900 presidential race, "than that we shall in the beginning rightly understand the relation between money and man. Man is the creature of God and money is the creature of man. Money is made to be the servant of man and I protest against all theories that enthrone money and debase mankind" (speech, 9/16/1899, in Boyd 1900: 474–75).
129. Bryan, acceptance speech, 8/12/1896 (Bryan 1896: 325–26).

sentiment. . . . When our opponents tell us that we are running a sentimen-
tal campaign and that they are running a business campaign, we reply to
them that we are simply placing the heart of the masses against the pock-
etbooks of a few. Some one has said that no one can write a poem in favor
of the financial policy of the present adminstration, and why? Because there
is nothing in it to appeal to the sentiment or to the heart.[130]

"[T]he only thing that moves life," said Wilson two decades later, "is
the impulse of actual, genuine, poetic sentiment. The world is not moved
by mind; it is moved by sentiment. It is moved by the impulses of the
heart; it is moved by sympathy."[131] Such moral didacticism was quite a
departure from the party's austere and secular demeanor in the nineteenth century.

An overriding sense of moral duty informed early-twentieth-century
Democratic reform. Bryan, naturally, was the primary instigator of this
do-rightism:

I believe that, in a civilized society, the question is not what is, but what
ought to be, and that every proposition must be arraigned at the bar of
reason. If you can prove that a thing is good, let it stay; but if you cannot
prove that it is good, you cannot hide behind the assertion that it is here
and that you cannot get rid of it. I believe that the American people can
get rid of anything that they do not want – and that they ought to get rid
of everything that is not good. I believe that it is the duty of every citizen
to give to his countrymen the benefit of his conscience and his judgment,
and cast his influence, be it small or great, upon the right side of every
question that arises. In the determination of questions we should find out
what will make our people great and good and strong rather than what
will make them rich. . . . Shall we decide the ethics of larceny by discussing
how much the man is going to steal or the chances of his getting caught?
No, my friends, we must decide questions upon a higher ground.[132]

Democratic candidates would attempt to arraign all issues before the bar
of justice, decide upon their morality, and then bring down all the forces
of righteousness in their behalf.[133]

Truth, it was believed, would win out over falsehood, light over dark-

---

130. Bryan, speech, 9/19/1896 (Bryan 1896: 463).
131. Wilson, speech, 10/7/1916 (Wilson 1982: 367). "The heart of a nation is just as
    pure, just as warm, just as genuine, as the hearts of its citizens. And outside of the
    heart, there is no life" (Wilson, speech, 10/19/1916, in Wilson 1982: 491). "It has
    been brought home to us," declared Roosevelt, "that the only effective guide for the
    safety of the most worldly of worlds is moral principle" (acceptance speech, 6/27/
    1936, in Singer 1976: 128).
132. Bryan, speech, 9/16/1899 (Boyd 1900: 487).
133. Justice, said Wilson, "consists of something more than refraining from wrong. It
    consists in organizing good, in making it effective, so that people will not only talk
    good, but also do good" (speech, 10/16/1916, in Wilson 1982: 449).

ness, virtue over evil, if only a frank and unbiased discussion of the issues could be brought before the people. "Truth," Bryan confidently asserted, "will vindicate itself; only error fears free speech."[134] A spirit of outrage pervaded party propaganda. Without financial resources, Bryan relied "upon the righteousness of our cause."[135] Wilson envisioned "a land of justice, . . . a land of brotherly love, . . . a land where men cooperated because they believed in each other's rights, . . . where all men were united together in a like comradeship and affection."[136] The Democratic party was surely the party of the Golden Rule.[137]

Republican candidates had a more limited view of their own mission and were, in any case, less temperamentally disposed to play this romantic part. Democrats of the day were heavily into healing. "I have seen poorly dressed women, tears streaming down their faces, holding up little children to me, as if they had discovered a friend," said Wilson, during the course of his second presidential campaign.[138] Of those who were in need, he said, "they come to us with tears on their faces and outstretched arms and thank God for a friend."[139] Roosevelt declared, "I see an America where factory workers are not discarded after they reach their prime, where there is no endless chain of poverty from generation to generation, where impoverished farmers and farm hands do not become homeless wanderers, where monopoly does not make youth a beggar for a job."[140]

Communicating with the common people required a revamped vocabulary, and, following Bryan, Democratic orators traded in their Olympian graces for a common touch. In a speech arguing for more stringent regulations on banking activity, Bryan explains the matter by reference to "a little boy at the table watching his father heap the plates."[141] Republican arguments in defense of trusts were likened to the man who attempted to return a cracked kettle: "[In the first place] . . . he never borrowed the kettle, in the second place, it was cracked when he got it, and third, it was good when he took it home."[142] The homely

134. Bryan, acceptance speech, 8/12/1896 (Bryan 1896: 320).
135. Bryan, acceptance speech, 8/12/1896 (Bryan 1896: 315).
136. Wilson, speech, 10/7/1916 (Wilson 1982: 368).
137. Bryan admonished his audience to "love thy neighbor as thyself" (speech, 9/1909, in Bryan 1913: 414).
138. Wilson, speech, 11/2/1916 (Wilson 1982: 596).
139. Wilson, speech, 11/2/1916 (Wilson 1982: 586). Wilson was the champion of togetherness, of social harmony. Instead of "exclusive combinations," Wilson advocated "universal cooperation," "spiritual organization," and an "organic connection" between members (speech, 10/16/1916, in Wilson 1982: 416, 448).
140. Roosevelt, speech, 11/2/1940 (Schlesinger 1971, 4: 2996).
141. Bryan, speech, 1/20/1900 (Bryan 1900: 181).
142. Bryan, speech, 1/20/1900 (Bryan 1900: 182).

anecdote had arrived. References to family filled the Great Commoner's addresses, often in the form of rose-tinted vignettes describing American life and Christian values – it was Norman Rockwell in prose, and part and parcel of the Democratic party's newfound celebration of common life and common people. Where once the Democratic speaker's task was to prove his mastery of rhetorical form, his command of facts, and his modesty, gradually Democratic rhetoric refocused around folksy sayings, fiery attacks, and sentiment – what an earlier generation of Democrats would have called demagoguery.[143]

Democratic campaigns during the Populist period were campaigns of political awakening and moral renewal, combining aspects of evangelical revivals with the newer chautauqua movement. *Emancipation*, and various near-synonyms, all of a sudden became key words in the Democratic lexicon. Candidates called for the liberation of children from wage labor, of working men from the commodification process, of small business from large business, of the citizen from special interests that controlled the government, and of peoples everywhere around the world who struggled for freedom against the forces of tyranny and injustice.[144] "It is our prayer," said Roosevelt, "that all lovers of freedom may join us – the anguished common people of this earth for whom we seek to light the path."[145]

The "human rights" strand of Democratic thought stretched from the 1890s to the 1940s. Recycling Progressive-era moralism, the New Deal president declared,

> The only effective guide for the safety of the most worldly of worlds is moral principle. We do not see faith, hope and charity as unattainable ideals. . . . Charity literally translated from the original means love, the love that understands, that does not merely share the wealth of the giver, but in true sympathy and wisdom helps men to help themselves. . . . In the place of the palace of privilege we seek to build a temple out of faith and hope and charity. . . . The immortal Dante tells us that divine justice weighs the sins of the cold-blooded and the sins of the warm-hearted in different scales. Better the occasional faults of a government that lives in a spirit of charity

---

143. "I propose," began Smith, in the first radio-broadcast campaign, "to speak on this subject in the plain, everyday language which makes it understood by the rank and file of our people" (speech, 9/22/1928, in Smith 1929: 61). Four years later, Roosevelt commented on a complicated policy measure: "This subject has been discussed so much in complex language, in terms which only a lawyer can understand, or in figures which only accountants can understand, that there is need for bringing it back into the realm of simple, honest terms understood by millions of our citizens" (speech, 9/21/1932, in Roosevelt 1938a: 728–29).
144. See, e.g., Wilson, acceptance speech, 9/2/1916 (Wilson 1982: 130).
145. Roosevelt, speech, 11/2/1940 (Schlesinger 1971, 4: 2996).

than the consistent omissions of a government frozen in the ice of its own indifference.[146]

Although Bryan's evangelical moralizing has frequently been observed, few have bothered to remark upon the presence of the same rhetorical modes in the speech making of so secular a personage as Franklin Roosevelt. Of those chastened by the experiences of the Depression and New Deal reform, Roosevelt admonished, "You stopped, once and for all, gambling with other people's money – money changing in the temple."[147] This sort of sermonizing on greed, gambling, and speculation was in fact quite typical of the public face of the New Deal. Roosevelt blamed the Depression on "selfish forces," on the "lone wolf, the unethical competitor, the reckless promoter, the Ishmael or Insull whose hand is against every man's."[148] The spirit of Christian charity, and Christian condemnation, ran strong in Democratic oratory.

Conclusions

I have argued that rather than dividing early-twentieth-century Democratic history into decade-long epochs (the Progressive era, the Twenties, the New Deal), this history fits into a single ideological frame stretching from 1896 to 1948. Throughout this period, Democratic presidential candidates (with a few exceptions) carried the torch of moral, political, and economic reform. The ethos of this egalitarian moment I have characterized as Populist, a term that emphasizes the party's ties to traditional elements of American political culture (Protestantism, civic republicanism, and free-market liberalism), its distance from socialism, and its distance, as well, from the Jeffersonian ideology purveyed by party leaders in the nineteenth century.

This period of Democratic history is dominated by three figures in the party's history – William Jennings Bryan (often considered an offshoot of the populist movement of the 1890s), Woodrow Wilson (the party's foremost Progressive), and Franklin Roosevelt (associated, of course, with the New Deal). The argument for continuity, therefore, rests on the notion that the careers of these politicians followed similar scripts. Since this goes against the grain of most historical interpretation, the

146. Roosevelt, acceptance speech, 6/27/1936 (Singer 1976: 128–29).
147. Roosevelt, speech, 11/2/1940 (Schlesinger 1971, 4: 2995). See also Roosevelt, speech, 8/20/1932 (Roosevelt 1938a: 680).
148. Roosevelt, speech, 10/14/1936 (Roosevelt 1938b: 483); and speech, 9/23/1932 (Singer 1976: 86).

remainder of this chapter will be devoted to a reevaluation of these key figures as exemplars of Democratic Populism.

Bryan

Until recently, historians generally viewed Bryan as an anachronism. "Though Bryan lived through one quarter of the twentieth century, in his thinking, his ideals, and in his political techniques he was always of the nineteenth century. [He was] . . . one of the last . . . men to give shape and voice to the agrarian political ideologies of Jefferson and Jackson," writes Stanley Jones.[149] Why has Bryan been looked upon as backward-looking rather than forward-looking? Why as a Jeffersonian and not a Progressive?

First, what made Populist appeals so resonant is perhaps to be explained by Populism's origins in the civic republican tradition. Tyranny, aristocracy, corruption – these Jeffersonian concepts were indeed carried over from the nineteenth to the twentieth century within the rhetoric of the Democratic party. This is undeniable and testifies to the strength of an ongoing Democratic tradition that seems at times to transcend the boundaries of time. What is missed in this familiar comparison, however, are the different uses and purposes that this ancient vocabulary served in these two historical contexts. Monopoly in the 1830s, for example, was looked upon as a product of undue governmental interference in the affairs of private citizens. By the turn of the century, the problem of monopoly was seen as engendered by the marketplace; its victims were workers rather than corrupted citizens, and government regulation was trumpeted as the only viable solution. Similarly, although the suspicion that private interests were corrupting the public good derived directly from a Jeffersonian view of political power,[150] the majoritarian and statist features of this revamped Democratic ideology were quite novel.[151]

Second, the distinction between Populism and Progressivism – and hence, by common analogy, between Bryan and Wilson – has been

---

149. See Jones (1964: 65), as well as Hofstadter (1955). For exceptions to this historiographic orthodoxy, see Koenig (1975) and Sarasohn (1989).

150. See, e.g., editorial (*New York Evening Post* 10/12/1836).

151. More to the point, if Bryan was a Jeffersonian, then so was Franklin D. Roosevelt, whose "many thousands of small business men and merchants" fought to free themselves from the iron grip of "industrial dictatorship" (acceptance speech, 6/27/1936, in Singer 1976: 127). At this point, one either assumes a Hartzian view of things – that little has *ever* changed within American party history – or looks more closely at the differences between Bryan, Wilson, and Roosevelt and their predecessors in the nineteenth century, as I have sought to do.

greatly exaggerated. Of course, there were differences separating these two movements, but then there were also great differences *within* each of these diffuse aggregations. Both movements drank from the broad waters of reform at the turn of the century. Although they drew from somewhat different constituencies, they shared common perspectives on politics and on the reform questions of the day. As Wilson emphasized in his first campaign, "We haven't just begun being progressive. We have been progressive for sixteen years and we saw the year 1912 half a generation before it came."[152]

Third, Bryan was a three-time loser, and nobody likes a loser, particularly members of the loser's own party. Wilson, for example, in the foregoing quotation, pointedly avoided mention of the paramount leader of the party during the pre-1912 period. The rejected parentage of William Jennings Bryan was a rejection not so much of Bryan's message but simply of his failure. Evidence in this regard can be adduced from the fact that when Franklin Roosevelt resuscitated the party's dormant Populist heritage, Bryan had to be brought back into the party by the back door, via Theodore Roosevelt. It was TR who originated the "malefactors of great wealth" quotation that became associated with the radical phase of the New Deal and that his cousin quoted with relish at every opportunity during the 1936 campaign. What is not often remarked upon is the fact that, several decades previously, Bryan had also attempted to appropriate TR, making one of the central points of his 1908 campaign the fact that Progressive elements within the Republican party were no longer welcome in their own party. The FDR-Bryan symmetry was close to perfect. The very same TR quotations – the "malefactors" and "representatives of predatory wealth" tags – were chosen by Bryan in 1908 and FDR in 1936.[153] Had Bryan won in any of his three attempts, one can be fairly certain that subsequent Democratic speeches would have been peppered liberally with Bryanisms, for he was the party's most brilliant rhetorician, a twentieth-century Tom Paine.

Last, Bryan's long career in the Democratic party – a career that spanned five decades – has been eclipsed in historical memory by his role in the Scopes trial and his identification with prohibition and isolationism in the 1920s. These, by any historical measure, were the *least* significant of Bryan's contributions to American politics.[154] For all these

---

152. Wilson, speech, 9/2/1912 (Wilson 1956: 98).
153. Bryan, acceptance speech, 8/12/1908 (Schlesinger 1973, 2: 1121).
154. Claude Bowers recalled in the 1950s, "Almost everything we've got today in the way of reforms originated with Bryan. . . . And yet everybody thinks of him now because of his prohibition views and on account of the evolution trial" (Oral History Memoir, Columbia University, 1954; quoted in Burner 1967/1968: 13). Moreover,

reasons, the name William Jennings Bryan has been expunged from the party's own record; his memory was almost never invoked by subsequent Democratic candidates – even those, like Wilson, Roosevelt, and Truman, who were so obviously following in his rhetorical footsteps.

Yet Bryan himself must be credited as a major creative force in the fashioning of twentieth-century Democratic ideology. It was he who first brought together the various religious and secular strands of Democratic reform in the 1896–1948 period. His eminence within the party might be judged by the fact he was nominated by that party on three separate occasions, a feat equaled by only three other men in the history of the American party system.[155] And his eminence did not fade with the end of the 1908 campaign; Bryan remained a formidable broker within the party through the end of the Progressive era.[156] Wilson remarked in 1911, "No Democrat can win [the nomination] whom Mr. Bryan does not approve."[157]

What are we to make, then, of Bryan's heroic defeat? Conventionally, Bryan's losses are blamed on his "agrarian" ideology, an ideology that alienated workers and easterners generally.[158] Bryan, it is true, did not win the labor vote, but neither did the Democratic party – until the country's gravest economic crisis dropped these voters into the party's lap. Alton B. Parker, the Clevelandesque conservative nominated by the party in 1904, managed to convince only 37.6 percent of the country's voters to cast their ballot for the Democratic ticket – one of the worst electoral drubbings ever sustained by a major American party.[159] In short, these were not happy times for the Democratic party, but there is no reason to suppose that Bryan was particularly at fault. Beyond remarking on one passage from Bryan's "Cross of Gold" speech, com-

> as I have argued throughout, a party's public ideology should be judged on the basis of the rhetoric produced and disseminated during the presidential campaign. The histories of the candidates before and after their moment in the sun are of significance only insofar as they may shed light on the moment in which they bore the party's standard. It is with the ideology of the party, not the persons, that I am primarily concerned.

155. I am speaking, of course, of only the major parties. The other three-time nominees are Grover Cleveland, Franklin Roosevelt (nominated four times), and Richard Nixon.
156. "If Wilson owed his election to any other man save himself it was to Bryan," writes Mowry (1971: 2056). See also Sarasohn (1989: 135).
157. Quoted in Cooper (1983: 181).
158. See Kleppner (1970: 303–4) and Sundquist (1983: 164). This thesis, one might recall, is more than a little reminiscent of those who blame the failure of socialism on the nonpragmatic, doctrinal approach of its leaders (Bryan being to the Democrats what De Leon was to the socialists). See Bell in Laslett and Lipset (1974: 3–29).
159. Bryan gained 46.8 percent (1896), 45.5 percent (1900), and 43.1 percent (1908) of the popular vote in his three campaigns.

mentators have given little attention to what Bryan said during this epic campaign. With one or two exceptions,[160] Bryan's three election campaigns were *not* advertisements for a rural paradise. Bryan – unlike William McAdoo, several decades later – had sense enough not to attack the party's eastern constituencies.[161] Bryan, conscious of his western roots, emphasized at every possible occasion that the fates of urban and rural classes were inextricably linked and that neither deserved preference above the other. "Farmers and wage-earners together" constituted the "considerable majority of the people of the country." These were the two class designations that laced virtually every Bryan speech. The producer ethic, reiterated by every Democratic candidate in the Populist period, united agrarian and urban interests together as workers.

Moreover, the blend of populism, progressivism, and laborism that the Democratic party developed in the 1896–1948 period was probably the most canny rhetorical strategy the party could have employed, given the Republican party's political dominance and its unassailably conservative ideology. By 1896, there was no longer sufficient ideological space for two conservative parties. Not to have appropriated the Populist-Progressive mantle would have left the party vulnerable to third-party challenges from the left. (The Populists, it is important to recall, achieved 9 percent of the Presidential vote in 1892 and were well positioned to overtake the Democrats in many western, midwestern, and southern states by the mid-1890s.) Within the constitutionally mandated two-party system, any reform party would have to attempt the joining of urban and rural constituents. As Bryan himself noted during the 1900 campaign, "Without a large percentage of the laboring vote no party can win an election in the United States."[162] The United States offered a historical situation in the late nineteenth and early twentieth centuries that was, in some ways, uniquely favorable to such an alliance. Unlike many northern European countries, rural/urban class divisions were not so clearly defined. Neither an industrial proletariat nor a traditional peasantry existed. The ideology of producerism, which made no distinction between agrarian and industrial labor and was deeply rooted in American political culture, was the logical rhetorical choice for a party with egalitarian goals.[163]

It is doubtful, in any case, that Bryan's three defeats had much to do

---

160. See Bryan, speech, 7/8/1896 (Bryan 1900: 309); and speech, 9/16/1899 (Boyd 1900: 489).
161. For details of this story, see Burner (1967/1968).
162. Bryan, speech, 9/3/1900 (*New York Times* 9/4/1900). Bryan uses "laborer" here to mean those "who work for wages" (not, that is, farmers).
163. For a history of the work ethic in late-nineteenth- and early-twentieth-century American political life, see Rodgers (1974).

with rhetoric. In fact, some evidence points to the desertion of eastern labor *before* the critical election of 1896.[164] The brute fact of the matter was that the Democrats were caught red-handed with the Panic of 1893 and, much like the Republican party in the wake of 1929, could do little to cover their tracks. Striking boldly in a new direction was an entirely appropriate response. Cleveland, by 1896, was a fat albatross around the party's neck, and Bryan rightfully did everything he could to distinguish himself from the goldbug wing of the party.

Wilson

In understanding the ideology of the Democratic party during the early twentieth century, the second great historical debate concerns whether the party may properly be considered "Progressive," in the sense of the times. Traditionally, Teddy Roosevelt and the western wing of the Republican party have been seen as the vanguard of reform. My argument, of course, focuses on the presidential wings of these parties.[165] Here, it seems fair to say that the Democratic candidate was more Progressive on issues of labor, social welfare, taxation, and business regulation than the Republican candidate in every presidential contest except 1904 (when TR faced off against Alton B. Parker).[166]

Wilson, to be sure, did not enter political life as a Progressive. However, his embarrassingly swift transformation from Cleveland Democrat to Bryan Democrat was relatively predictable once the New Jersey governor made the decision to enter national politics. "Wilson had no choice but to play reformist, antimachine, anticorporation cards," writes a recent biographer.[167] What he offered, in the words of another historian, was "Bryanism with a Princeton accent."[168] It is worth noting that TR, Wilson's principal opponent in the 1912 campaign, was obliged to form a third party after his conversion to the cause of progressivism. The differing nature of the two parties in the early twentieth century was such that in one party Progressivism was de rigueur, whereas in the other it was virtually proscribed.[169] To make the parallel even neater, the key

164. See Sundquist (1983).
165. Sarasohn (1989: 3) claims that during TR's second term, Democrats within Congress provided stronger support than Republicans for the president's increasingly heterodox initiatives.
166. Admittedly, "Progressivism" is a vague label (see Rodgers 1982), but it is also a label that is difficult to dispense with.
167. Cooper (1983: 181).   168. Sarasohn (1989: 123).
169. Admittedly, there were significant differences between New Freedom (Wilson's banner in 1912) and New Nationalism (TR's slogan), so the parallel is not perfect. But it is close enough. In fact, it is even *more* difficult to imagine Wilson's Populist brand

year in both these Progressive transformations was 1908. Roosevelt's lame-duck term was nearing its end, and the restless leader no longer had much to lose by antagonizing the party's old guard. After 1908 and for the next half-decade, both "the warrior" and "the priest" moved in the same leftward direction, Wilson into mainstream party politics and Roosevelt further and further away from that mainstream.[170]

Roosevelt

If, as I have argued, the 1896–1948 period marks a single ideological epoch in Democratic history, the third controversial element of that argument is the one that links Bryan and Wilson with Roosevelt – 1890s Populism and 1912 Progressivism with the New Deal. Evidently, the New Deal went well beyond Progressive-era reforms and was marked by a pragmatic, technocratic style of policy making that has led many to differentiate the 1930s from reform initiatives of the past.[171] In addition, the New Deal Democratic party was backed, for the first time, by a large majority of the working class. Finally, the pre-1930s Democrats are usually characterized as having maintained a traditional Democratic antipathy to a strong centralized government and, hence, to redistributive plans based upon central bureaucratic initiative.

This generally accepted view of the period has been fostered by several misperceptions. First, the position of organized labor (as opposed, that is, to labor constituencies) within the Democratic party was solidified, but by no means originated, in the 1930s. As I have argued, the party's courting of organized labor extended back as far as 1896, and ties between the AFL leadership and the Democratic party were begun shortly thereafter. On matters of industrial relations, the party reversed its long-standing hostility to the programs of organized labor, embracing a wide range of AFL-sponsored legislation and forming close ties with AFL

of progressivism gaining acceptance within the Republican party than it is to imagine Roosevelt's more statist – i.e., National Republican – brand of progressivism finding a home in that party.

170. TR's reabsorption into the Republican party with the approach of World War I coincided with his abandonment of Progressivism in favor of the nationalist doctrines that had attracted him initially to that party. See Cooper (1983).

171. See Hofstadter (1955), Ekirch (1969: viii), Fine (1956), and Milkis (1992: 109). Hartz's treatment of the New Deal (1955) is fraught with ambivalence. He clearly wants to defend it (New Dealer that he was), but at the same time he sees in it only a slight departure from the irrational Lockeanism of the American creed. The problem is answered by the deus ex machina of "pragmatism": New Dealers were doing un-Lockean things but were doing so within a Lockean frame of reference, whose evident contradictions they were able blithely to ignore.

leadership as early as 1906. The "labor" orientation of the New Deal, in other words, was not so new.

Second, although it is true that Democratic leaders from previous decades had not contemplated the expansion of government services on the scale of the New Deal, neither had Roosevelt. Most of what was new about the New Deal was a direct response to the dire economic circumstances of the time.[172] It was not until the 1940s that Roosevelt accepted the notion that the federal government should be handing out paychecks to those nonelderly citizens who could not provide for themselves. At the inauguration of the New Deal, FDR had argued that social welfare was "a narcotic, a subtle destroyer of the human spirit," concluding that the national government "must and shall quit this business of relief."[173] The welfare state as a theme within Democratic presidential rhetoric did not flower until the 1960s. Government intervention in the 1930s was sold as a temporary expedient, an emergency measure to restore the economy to health, after which the government would end deficit spending and return to its former position as regulator and guarantor of rights.

In other words, FDR's stance vis-à-vis the Great Depression was no more radical than might have been expected of his forebears Bryan and Wilson. I doubt whether they would have been held back by more antiquated ideas of the state's relation to the economy, since, as I have tried to show, there was a basic continuity in Democratic dogma on this point. Bryan, as we have seen, was *more* statist on all accounts than any other Democratic candidate of the period (perhaps in the history of the party). Moreover, the economic crisis of the Thirties fit comfortably into a populist worldview; it was the 1890s recession writ large. The same evils were blamed, and the government was asked, albeit on a rather different scale, to fix the problem. The relevant point is not that Bryan recommended free silver and Roosevelt, ultimately, a welfare state, but that Wilson (or Bryan, for that matter) would likely have resorted to the same sorts of fiscal remedies had he occupied the Oval Office in 1933. More pointedly, Roosevelt did not advance policies any different from those of Bryan and Wilson until it became apparent that such traditional economic methods (e.g., balancing the budget) would not do the job.

Certainly, the *quantity* of governmental proposals fostered in the 1930s could not be matched in any previous era. However, the alphabet soup agencies and the "try anything" approach of the New Deal were

172. Roosevelt was notoriously open-minded when it came to economic and social questions.
173. Quoted in Heclo (1994: 399).

largely a response to an emergency situation to which several centuries of American history do not provide a close parallel. Most of these policies are rightly viewed as the culmination of plans laid several decades previously. The New Deal is thus more properly seen as an end point, rather than a starting point, in Democratic party ideology. The "decisive break with American traditions of limited government"[174] occurred three decades earlier than scholars have usually determined. It was in 1896, not 1932, that the Democratic party first committed itself to a statist and redistributive vision of public policy. Although they occasionally reiterated the age-old pledge to "public economy," Bryanite Democrats were adamant about increasing the tax base of the federal government. Monetary policy, which for virtually a century had revolved around the defense of tight money policies, now shifted considerably in the opposite direction. In agricultural policy, the party retained its traditional affection but now was much more willing to back that affection with concrete programs of aid (particularly during the agricultural depression of the 1920s). Economic regulation, an occasional element in party rhetoric of the 1880s, made its full-blown entrance onto the party's agenda in the wake of the 1896 election. The most frequent entry in this spate of issues was, of course, the "Trust Question," a preoccupation that would haunt the party through the 1940s. Although these movements into public-sector management, economic regulation, and welfare spending paled by comparison with those proposed by socialist and social-democratic parties in Europe, we should not dismiss their significance within the American context. This was, after all, the only period in American history when schemes of nationalization were explicitly proposed and defended, and the period to which we owe the foundation of the current welfare state.

Finally, the programs of the New Deal were sold to the American public with the ideological weapons of Populism, not a philosophy of "pragmatism." There was nothing electorally appealing about the president's offer of "bold, persistent experimentation" (although it has held great appeal to academics). We must differentiate, that is, between the *public* philosophy of the New Deal and its *private* philosophy. Historical work on the period has relied mostly on private communications (letters, memos) and policy discussion among politicians and academics (e.g., the famed Kitchen Cabinet). With these data at hand, historians have asked, what were the president and his closest advisers thinking when they launched this historic episode in American politics? Of equal interest is the question that preoccupies this study, namely, how did they justify

---

174. Milkis (1992: 109).

these programs before the general public? For present purposes, it does not matter whether Roosevelt (or Tugwell or Perkins et al.) really believed what he said. What matters is whether he said it, and of this there can be little doubt. FDR found the rhetoric of Bryan, Wilson, and Theodore Roosevelt (the third-party TR of 1912) indispensable in his task of galvanizing public support for the New Deal. He led the battle against economic and political "dictatorship," a battle on behalf of the "anguished common people of this earth for whom we seek to light the path."[175] When FDR spoke of providing a "more equitable opportunity to share in the distribution of national wealth," he was echoing voices in the Democratic past.[176] When in 1940 he spoke of "a wider and more equitable distribution of wealth in our land" and of liberalizing the "control of vast industries lodged today in the hands of a relatively small group of individuals of very great financial power," he was again speaking in the idiom of Democratic Populism.[177]

Hoover once referred to the New Deal as "Bryanism under new words and methods," a phrase that hits the nail quite precisely on the head.[178] Thus, although the Great Depression catapulted this minority party into power and renewed (and to some extent redrew) its electoral base,[179] its effect on the party's public philosophy was merely to accentuate ideological predispositions already well established by the Great Commoner. The combined effects of economic catastrophe and partisan triumph produced a political environment in which it was possible, for the first time in American history, to implement at a federal level social programs that had been bandied about in progressive circles since the turn of the century.

"American traditions of political revolt," Hofstadter wrote in 1955, were "based upon movements against monopolies and special privileges in both the economic and the political spheres, against social distinctions and the restriction of credit, against limits upon the avenues of personal advancement."[180] Hofstadter focused primarily on protest movements, not mainstream party politics. However, his eloquent portrayal of the American reform tradition could, with a few minor adjustments, be comfortably applied to the national Democratic party during the Bryan-

---

175. Roosevelt, speech, 11/2/1940 (Schlesinger 1971, 4: 2996).
176. Roosevelt, acceptance speech, 7/2/1932 (Schlesinger 1971, 3: 2791).
177. Roosevelt, acceptance speech, 7/19/1940 (Schlesinger 1971, 4: 2971). See also acceptance speech, 6/27/1936 (Singer 1976: 125–29).
178. Quoted in Wilson (1975: 212).
179. Whether this electoral base changed, or merely deepened, remains a matter of some dispute (see appendix).
180. Hofstadter (1955: 10).

Wilson-Roosevelt epoch. Populism was not just a bubble of third-party radicalism that spilled over into the Democratic party in the late 1890s, it was the mainstay of the party's national election rhetoric from 1896 to 1948. From the moment Bryan won the party's nomination, Democratic candidates sounded the tocsin of class injustice and arraigned the special privilege of elites. During this period of half a century, the Democratic party functioned as the repository for an old and venerable tradition of American popular protest.

7

The Universalist Epoch (1952–1992)

From the perspective of most observers, Democratic ideology in the postwar period has followed on the heels of the New Deal. "[I]t is from the New Deal that liberalism in its contemporary American usage has acquired its principal meaning," writes Samuel Beer. "And the stress on economic balance and economic security that was characteristic of the New Deal remained essential to the meaning of liberalism in its later embodiments in Truman's Fair Deal and the programs of the Kennedy-Johnson administrations."[1] Of course, writers have noted differences between the New Deal and the party's contemporary agenda – its support for civil rights, "postindustrial" values, "new politics," and so forth – and there have been repeated attempts to define a "neoliberal" or "new Democrat" agenda for the party in the postwar decades.[2] However, in the opinion of most scholars, the party of Bill Clinton is still the party of FDR, albeit in a rather attenuated form.[3]

I shall offer two perspectives on Democratic ideology in the postwar period. Undoubtedly, the social justice elements of contemporary Democratic ideology mirror the ideals of the New Deal, but they also mirror

1. Beer (1965: 145–46).
2. Ladd (1981: 136), for example, emphasizes the postindustrial qualities of the new Democrats, their support for "new standards of personal morality, cultural values, and life-styles, a questioning of the merits of economic growth on the grounds that growth threatens the 'quality of life,' and a redefinition of the demands of equality in the direction of 'equality of result.' " For a discussion of the 1960s and 1970s "new politics" in the party, see Parmet (1976). Neoliberalism is often defined as a combination of fiscal conservatism and social liberalism (e.g., Grimes 1962), and many studies have indicated the fundamental significance of civil rights in establishing the party's contemporary identity (e.g., Carmines and Stimson 1989, and Edsall and Edsall 1992).
3. See, e.g., Fraser and Gerstle (1989), Ladd and Hadley (1973; 1975), Leuchtenberg (1983), Parmet (1976), Ross (1973), Rotunda (1986), Skocpol (1983), and Wade (1973).

the ideals of the Bryan-Wilson years. In short, if one looks at the party's commitment to welfare policy and wealth redistribution, as measured in content analyses of party platforms and nomination acceptance addresses, the postwar period looks like a continuation and extension of the Populist Democratic epoch (see figure 8 and figure 14). Since I have dealt with these aspects of Democratic ideology already, I shall not belabor the point in this chapter. Suffice it to say that contemporary Democratic thought – "liberalism" as a partisan philosophy – is as much a legacy of 1896 as of 1932.

Yet, in the wake of World War II, the party's egalitarian agenda was broadened to include a host of social groups and political issues that did not fit neatly into the socioeconomic perspective and the masses-versus-elites dichotomy of the Populist period. Equality in the 1890s or the 1930s did not mean the same thing as equality in the 1950s and 1960s. This is the perplexing story of the postwar Democrats. The second major turning point in a century and a half of Democratic party ideology occurred not in the 1930s, with Roosevelt, but rather in the 1950s, in the rather colorless form of Adlai Stevenson. In fact, it was the very colorlessness of Adlai Stevenson – his all-embracing, none-offending character – that was to stamp the postwar epoch in Democratic history. Forsaking the shrill polemics of Bryan, the party now adopted a soothing tone and reassuring demeanor. The rhetoric of reconciliation replaced that of resentment. The all-inclusive American People subsumed the figure of the Common Man. References to illicit business practices died out, to be replaced by a resolutely probusiness perspective. The organizing theme of Democratic ideology changed from an attack against special privilege to an appeal for inclusion. Party leaders rewrote the Democratic hymnbook; Populism was out, and Universalism was in.

Economic Issues

The campaign of 1948 was the last one of the Populist era, and Truman was one of its finest practitioners: "[T]he people know that the Democratic Party is the people's party, and the Republican Party is the party of special interest, and it always has been and always will be."[4] The "Republican rich man's tax bill," continued the irascible Truman, "sticks a knife into the back of the poor."[5] By the 1950s, however, Populist rhetoric had slowed to a trickle, a pat phrase or two, the oblig-

4. Truman, acceptance speech, 7/15/1948 (Schlesinger 1971, 4: 3187).
5. Truman, acceptance speech, 7/15/1948 (Schlesinger 1971, 4: 3190).

atory nod to tradition. In the mouths of most postwar Democrats the regenerative prose of Populism appeared trite, tired, and empty of conviction.

The sea change in the Democratic party's public philosophy was most noticeable, perhaps, in its treatment of the labor question. "Do you want to carry the Taft-Hartley Law to its full implication and enslave totally the workingman, white collar and union man alike," inquired Truman, "or do you want to go forward with an administration whose interest is the welfare of the common man?"[6] To Democratic candidates in the Populist era, labor was viewed as the advance agent of reform.[7] "[L]abor never had but one friend in politics, and that is the Democratic Party and Franklin D. Roosevelt," Truman declared proudly.[8] Yet in the 1950s, big labor appeared to be an electoral hindrance. In response to Republican charges that Democrats were hostage to the AFL and CIO, Stevenson, Kennedy, and their successors emphasized their "independence." At a Labor Day rally, an occasion that several generations of Democratic orators had used to profess their loyalty to the cause of the workingman, Stevenson declared defensively, "You are not my captives, and I am not your captive. . . . You are freeborn Americans – a proud and honorable station, carrying with it the right and the responsibility to make up your own minds – and so am I."[9] Of labor-capital conflict, Stevenson asserted the rights of labor in uncertain terms: "Democracy is working when free men solve their own problems in their own way and in their own political and industrial communities. The 80,000 private collective bargaining agreements today in effect are alternatives to laws – and better than laws. They are voluntary private solutions which make unnecessary involuntary government decisions."[10] Stevenson's opposition to the Taft-Hartley Act was muted when compared with his predecessor's, and by 1956 the issue had receded entirely from the party's presidential agenda.

The party's declining enthusiasm for labor was all the more noticeable in the context of its increasing affection for labor's traditional foe, business. "[T]he hostility of businessmen to Democrats and the New Deal is one of the absurdities of our time," remarked Stevenson in a 1952 interview.[11] Although it had been the case that the market derived its le-

6. Truman, speech, 9/6/1948 (Truman 1948–49: 120).
7. Roosevelt, speech, 10/5/1944 (Roosevelt 1946: 322–23). See also examples cited in chapter 6.
8. Truman, acceptance speech, 7/15/1948 (Schlesinger 1971, 4: 3188).
9. Stevenson, speech, 9/1/1952 (Stevenson 1953: 46).
10. Stevenson, speech, 9/1/1952 (Stevenson 1953: 48).
11. See Parmet (1976: 111).

gitimacy from labor – prices and profits being legitimate only to the extent that they reflected the amount of labor involved in the process of production – now, seemingly, labor was to derive its legitimacy from the logic of the market. "Collective bargaining," argued Stevenson defensively, "is a form of free competition."[12] In a parallel development, postwar Democrats reoriented their economic perspectives from production to consumption. "Our welfare," thought Stevenson, "is not measured by what we get from the payroll clerk, but by what we get at the store."[13]

In the Populist era, Democrats had sought to portray themselves as the friends of the businessman and the upholder of capitalism; however, this position was attenuated by the party's shrill cries against the depredations of "monopoly," "big business," and "usurious" business practices. In the postwar era, the party dropped its litany of economic protest themes (see figure 2),[14] and Populist-leaning candidates generally fared poorly in the candidate selection process. Only McGovern, Carter (in 1976), and Mondale integrated Populist themes into their rhetoric on a regular basis, and these occasional notes of protest were not nearly as vehement or shrill as those registered by their predecessors in the 1896–1948 period. It might also be pointed out that only one of these candidates made it to the White House. Thus, although Populists were the most successful candidates during the 1896–1948 period they were, by and large, the *least* successful candidates in the postwar period (McGovern's landslide loss being a primary case in point, and Carter's 1976 victory the only exception).[15]

12. See Parmet (1976: 51).
13. Stevenson, speech, 9/1/1952 (Stevenson 1953: 48). "Good incomes for our workers," declared the 1952 platform, "are the secret of our great and growing consumer markets" (Schlesinger 1971, 4: 1275). Not surprisingly, candidates increasingly took note of the rights of "consumers" while ignoring the traditional rights of "producers." This shift too was presaged in the election of 1944, where Roosevelt made the *un*populist statement that he looked forward "to millions of new homes, fit for decent living; to new, low-priced automobiles; new highways; new airplanes and airports; to television; and other miraculous new inventions and discoveries" (speech, 11/2/1944, in Roosevelt 1946: 388).
14. With reference to his party's traditional antibusiness rhetoric, Stevenson remarked during the 1952 campaign, "I think we must sweep out of the corridors of government . . . those lingering suspicions which are a holdover from an earlier and very different time" (speech, 10/30/1952, in Stevenson 1953: 295).
15. The exhaustion of Democratic Populism in the postwar period was illustrated in the 1992 Clinton campaign. Despite occasional references to "trickle-down economics" or "politics for the rich and powerful" (speech, 10/27/1992, in Federal News Service 10/27/1992: 4), Clinton was more likely to use the following rhetorical posture: "I want people with money in this country to make a lot of money but I want

The whole nature of the debate on economic questions changed after World War II. Formerly, a candidate's discussion of economic issues usually included a quasi-philosophical discourse on the elemental question how best to organize the relationship between government and the marketplace. In the postwar rhetorical world, attention focused on outputs – i.e., economic performance – and particularly on the three major indicators of inflation, employment, and growth.[16] The emotionally and religiously charged terms of Populism – *speculation, mammon, usury,* and so forth – were gradually replaced by cooler, more scientific analysis. "It is the national purpose . . . to continue this expansion of the American economy," declared the 1964 platform blandly. "This will require continuation of flexible and innovative fiscal, monetary, and debt management policies, recognizing the importance of low interest rates."[17] Business profits no longer attracted much attention. Consider, for example, the different reactions of the public (and of Democratic party spokespersons) after the two world wars with respect to the profits gained by companies during those wars. "War profiteering" had little or no resonance in the late 1940s and the 1950s. Similarly, the spectacular increase in social inequality from the 1970s to the 1990s occasioned little comment on the part of Democratic orators.[18] It is difficult to imagine Bryan, Wilson, Roosevelt, or Truman remaining silent on such matters.

In the postwar period, the Democrats' traditional praise for the free enterprise system was no longer qualified by a critique of its failings or an attack against its usurpers. Democrats' embrace of "the American capitalistic system" was, for the first time in party history, unalloyed by Jeffersonian suspicions.[19] Monopoly, the Democratic bogeyman of yore,

them to make it the old-fashioned way. No more something for nothing. Make a million dollars . . . investing and putting the rest of America to work, and you can make all the money you want" (speech, 10/28/1992, in Federal News Service 10/28/1992: 5).

16. "Unemployment" and "inflation" were prominently displayed for the first time in the party's 1952 platform (Schlesinger 1971, 4: 3268, 3272). Shades of this new approach can be found in the 1940s, when Roosevelt declared (in marked contrast to his 1936 campaign themes), "The keynote of all that we propose to do in reconversion can be found in the one word, *jobs*" (speech, 9/23/1944, in Roosevelt 1946: 292). The same concern animated all postwar campaigns. "I think this country needs a job creator, not a job destroyer as president," ventured Bill Clinton in 1992 (speech, 10/25/1992, in Federal News Service 10/25/1992: 2).

17. Democratic platform, 1964 (Schlesinger 1971, 4: 3602).

18. For discussion of social equality from the 1970s to the 1990s, see Danziger and Gottschalk (1995).

19. See, e.g., Stevenson, speech, 10/9/1952 (Stevenson 1953: 229).

slipped gradually out of party rhetoric (see figure 12).[20] "Free competitive enterprise," thought the party's platform writers in 1960, "is the most creative and productive form of economic order that the world has seen."[21] The party's platform in the following election declared the American free enterprise system to be "one of the great achievements of the human mind and spirit."[22]

In the halcyon days of postwar expansion, free markets elicited wonder and adoration from Democratic candidates. A psychology of plenitude replaced the previous generation's anxiety over scarcity. "We are finally entering that age of abundance of which we have dreamed so long," thought Stevenson.[23] Speaking on Labor Day at Cadillac Square in Detroit (which replaced Chicago as the unofficial capital of organized labor), Johnson proclaimed, "We no longer struggle among ourselves for a larger share of limited abundance. We labor, instead, to increase the total abundance of us all."[24] Prosperity, said Democrats from Stevenson to Clinton, would conquer poverty and assure equal opportunity.[25] Stevenson envisioned "a new America where poverty is abolished and our abundance is used to enrich the lives of every family," a foreshadowing of Johnson's call, a decade later, to eradicate poverty.[26] An emphasis on growth thus replaced the zero-sum nature of Populist economic theorizing.

Although by no means antistatist, Democratic candidates retreated from

---

20. The 1984 platform observed, almost complacently, that "a recent wave of mergers has been particularly troubling. Any number of large corporations have focused their energies arranging the next merger or defending against the latest takeover bid" (Democratic party 1984: 83B).
21. Democratic platform, 1960 (Schlesinger 1971, 4: 3482).
22. Democratic platform, 1964 (Schlesinger 1971, 4: 3601).
23. Stevenson, speech, 10/24/1956 (Stevenson 1957: 262). The 1956 platform pledged the party to "release the springs of abundance, to bring this abundance to all, and thus to fulfill the full promise of America" (Schlesinger 1971, 4: 3365). Humphrey, echoing the full-dinner-pail approach of the early Republican party, declared that he believed in "fat Democratic paychecks – not lean Republican ones" (speech, 9/25/1968, original text obtained from Minnesota Historical Society).
24. Johnson, speech, 9/7/1964 (Johnson 1965: 1049).
25. It is important to note that themes of boosterism and prosperity mongering could be found in Democratic rhetoric as soon as the Depression lifted – that is to say, by the campaign of 1944. Roosevelt promised, "At the end of this war this country will have the greatest material power of any Nation in the world. It will be a clean, shining America – richer than any other in skilled workers, in engineers, and farmers, and businessmen, and scientists" (speech, 11/4/1944, in Roosevelt 1946: 405).
26. Stevenson, acceptance speech, 8/17/1956 (Schlesinger 1971, 4: 3414). See also speech, 9/13/1956 (Stevenson 1957: 10).

the openly progovernment statements of the Populist era (see figure 3). Of government-sponsored housing policies, Stevenson insisted, "The job has been accomplished in the American way, through private enterprise and local responsibility."[27] Rather than regulating economic behavior, Democrats began to talk hopefully of "freeing" ("unshackling," "liberating," and so on) the private sector.[28] Thus did the hearts and minds of Democratic leaders turn away from the vitriolic economic debates of Free Silver and antimonopoly toward other, presumably loftier affairs.

From Majority Rule to Minority Rights

The rise of black Americans as a regular feature of Democratic rhetoric is one of the notable features of the postwar epoch in party history, and one much remarked upon.[29] The first tentative entry in favor of civil rights (admittedly a very soft plank) appeared in the 1940s, with stronger and more persistent statements beginning in the 1960s. The change was particularly noticeable coming after a century of forthright opposition to such causes as voting rights and antilynching laws and in light of the Republican party's increasingly skeptical stance toward civil rights in the latter twentieth century (see figures 5 and 15). Interestingly, the inimitable Truman tried to frame the racial justice theme from within the Populist idiom. "Racial and religious oppression – big business domination – inflation – these forces must be stopped and driven back while there is yet time," he declared.[30] An attempt was made, in other words, to add racial minorities to that aggrieved category of common people who were suffering at the hands of economic elites. From this angle, the plight of black Americans could be conceived of hand in hand with the oppression of labor.

The Populist approach to the "Negro problem," however, was short-

---

27. Stevenson, speech, 10/3/1952 (Stevenson 1957: 200). "Social progress in our free enterprise economy," Humphrey assured his audiences in the 1968 campaign, "has never been . . . primarily a responsibility of the public sector. . . . Most of the new buildings are designed by private architects, built by private contractors, and paid for by private concerns" (speech, 7/2/1968, in Schlesinger 1973, 4: 2938).
28. The 1960 platform promised to "unshackle American enterprise and to free American labor, industrial leadership, and capital, to create an abundance that will outstrip any other system" (Schlesinger 1971, 4: 3482).
29. See, e.g., Carmines and Stimson (1989).
30. Truman, speech, 10/25/1948 (Truman 1948–49: 22). Truman even linked the Nazi holocaust with the persecution of minorities at home (speech, 10/25/1948, in Truman 1948–49: 21).

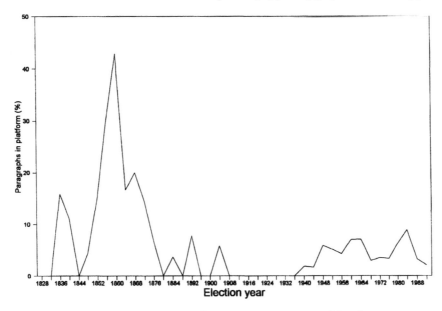

Figure 15. Attention to problems of minorities, as measured by the percentage of paragraphs within Democratic party platforms devoted to African Americans, Asian Americans, Native Americans, Hispanic Americans, recent European immigrants, the Thirteenth, Fourteenth, or Fifteenth Amendments, civil rights, or voting rights. (Does not include references to the foregoing if within the context of immigration, women's issues, states' rights, or "limited government," unless the implication is to disadvantage some minority group.)

lived. The party's 1948 platform framed the issues as questions of "civil rights" or "minority rights."[31]

> The Democratic Party commits itself to continuing its efforts to eradicate all racial, religious and economic discrimination. We again state our belief

31. Prior statements of this sort could be found as early as 1940. "We are a nation," said FDR, "of many nationalities, many races, many religions – bound together by a single unity, the unity of freedom and equality" (speech, 11/1/1940, in Roosevelt 1941: 537). "I see an America of great cultural and educational opportunity for all its people," he added the next day (speech, 11/2/1940, in Schlesinger 1971, 4: 2996). In the following election, Roosevelt portrayed the party as "fighting for a country and a world where men and women of all races, colors and creeds can live and work and speak and worship – in peace, and freedom and security" (speech, 11/4/1944, in Roosevelt 1946: 399). "[O]ur Economic Bill of Rights – like the sacred Bill of Rights of our Constitution itself – must be applied to all our citizens, irrespective of race, or creed or color" (speech, 10/28/1944, in Roosevelt 1946: 374).

that racial and religious minorities must have the right to live, the right to work, the right to vote, the full and equal protection of the laws, on a basis of equality with all citizens as guaranteed by the Constitution. We call upon the Congress to support our President in guaranteeing these basic and fundamental American Principles: (1) the right of full and equal political participation; (2) the right to equal opportunity of employment; (3) the right of security of person; (4) and the right of equal treatment in the service and defense of our nation.[32]

The clear implication was that these issues pertained to special groups of Americans, not the broad masses of common people. "Let me speak first about the issue of freedom which is today causing greatest concern among us – civil rights for our minorities," said Stevenson early in the 1956 campaign.[33] Although Democratic orators attempted to generalize the problems of black Americans utilizing the abstract terminology of "equal rights," "freedom," "liberty," "democracy," or "constitutional rights," it was clear that the affected populations were, in fact, *minorities*. Stevenson put the issue this way: "We have come to see with new clarity the full implications of our Bill of Rights and of our democratic faith, and we are moving forward again to assure the equal rights of man to all Americans, regardless of race or color."[34] The key phrase "regardless of race or color" was a giveaway.

The issue of poverty underwent a parallel transformation at mid-century. During the 1896–1948 period, poverty was seen as a crisis, not a condition. In other words, it had concrete economic sources – panic, depression, stock market speculation, and so forth – and was of temporary duration. Indeed, the term *poverty* did not appear in Democratic rhetoric until mid-century; during the Populist period, candidates typically spoke of problems of jobs and work. When the figure of the poor appeared, it was usually in contrast to the wealthy. "[T]he poor man," said Bryan, "is looking for food for his stomach, while the rich man goes from one watering place to another, looking for a stomach for his food."[35] As the dramatis personae shifted with the elimination of the

---

32. Democratic platform, 1948 (Schlesinger 1971, 4: 3154). In the same platform, the party also put itself on the record in favor of a constitutional amendment guaranteeing equal rights for women, a position that would be repeated on many later occasions.
33. Stevenson, speech, 4/25/1956 (Stevenson 1957: 191).
34. Stevenson, speech, 10/27/1956 (Schlesinger 1971, 4: 3438). Johnson similarly stated, "We have talked long enough in this country about equal rights. . . . It is time now to write . . . it in the books of law, . . . so that we can move forward to eliminate from this Nation every trace of discrimination and oppression that is based upon race or color" (speech, 11/27/1963, in Schlesinger 1971, 4: 3658).
35. Bryan, speech, 1/20/1900 (Bryan 1900: 165).

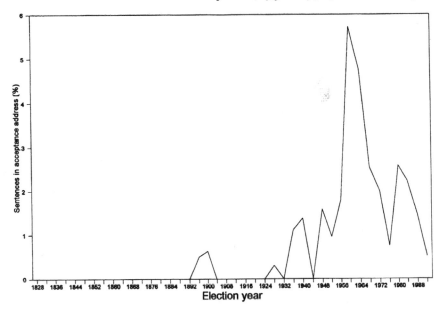

Figure 16. Attention to the problem of poverty, as measured by the percentage of sentences within Democratic nomination acceptance addresses dealing with the poor and underprivileged

stock character "the rich man," the narrative refocused on the abstraction "poverty." Democratic rhetoric came to be *about* poverty in a way that it had not been previously (see figure 16).[36]

The party's analysis of the problem also shifted considerably. By the 1950s, poverty was no longer viewed as the product of unscrupulous dealings and the power of the trusts; rather, poverty became a "social problem," one with many complex sources and many complex public policy solutions. Stevenson declared, "We have done nothing to help the lot of the poor and of our older people," and followed with a long list of intransigent problems associated with the poor (e.g., slum cancer and juvenile delinquency).[37] Johnson, advertising for the Great Society, urged the country to address "the needs of the jobless and the hungry, the poor and the oppressed."[38] There were still victims – the poor – but no

36. The 1956 platform, for example, pledged to work toward "the reduction and elimination of poverty in America" (Schlesinger 1971, 4: 3364).
37. Stevenson, speech, 9/13/1956 (Stevenson 1957: 11).
38. Johnson, speech, 9/7/1964 (Johnson 1965: 1049). Contemporary treatments of the issue of poverty are well illustrated in the following argument for welfare reform during Dukakis's 1988 campaign: "We're going to pass that welfare reform bill that

longer any victimizers. As hard as Democratic orators tried, it was difficult to engender a great deal of indignation toward a war that had no obvious cause and no apparent perpetrators. Indeed, the terms with which the War on Poverty were waged encouraged the public to consider poor people themselves as the opponent (who was "poverty"?). Populist ideology had offered a clear and explicit explanation for all economic woes; Universalist Democrats offered vague economic analyses (e.g., "a lack of opportunities").

The social-class components of Democratic rhetoric shifted substantially around mid-century. Democratic Populism recognized two essential groupings: at the apex of society was a tiny stratum of the rich; forming the base were the vast multitudes of common people. What Bryan and Democrats of his generation meant by the "poor man" was thus the "common man," the ordinary citizen. No special categories of paupers, immigrants, the mentally or physically handicapped, or racial minorities were distinguished. Poor and not-so-poor were united by their common travails. But the meaning of the central trope, the People, depended upon the presence of an elite stratum over and above the common folk. After the bankers, speculators, and trusts were discarded, the meaning of "the people" shifted in subtle but far-reaching ways. Unintentionally, contemporary Democratic rhetoric implied that the poor were a separate class of individuals, with needs and perspectives that were in some way different from the great mass of (middle-class) Americans: "Democratic economic policy must assure fairness for workers, the elderly, women, the poor, minorities and the majority who are middle income Americans," declared the party's platform in 1980.[39] The center was redefined as "middle-income," and the poor, minorities, and other needy populations were excluded. The logic of political identity and political conflict was thus redefined. Denuded of Populist connotations, the figure of the people was no longer able to unite the lower and middle classes, for there was nothing left to unite *against*.

A similar shift could be observed in the party's treatment of "welfare." "[T]he Republican party," charged Bryan, in preparation for the

will make it possible for hundreds of thousands of families on public assistance in this country to get the training they need for real jobs and the child care for their kids so they can lift themselves out of poverty and become a part of this country and a part of the American dream" (speech, 8/24/1988, in Federal News Service 8/24/1988).

39. Democratic platform, 1980 (Johnson 1982: 38). See also Democratic platform, 1984 (Democratic party 1984: 75B).

1900 presidential campaign, "is looking after the interests of wealth and neglecting the welfare of the people."[40] In 1900, welfare meant the well-being of the people at large, not the needs of the poor. By contrast, social spending in the postwar period was usually understood as "targeted to those most in need."[41] In de-emphasizing the confrontational economic themes of the previous period, party leaders paved the way for the party's increasingly minoritarian image.

Early Democratic reforms were based on eradicating the privileges of the few and extending the privileges of the many. "Corruption in government," thought Bryan, "comes from the attempt to substitute the will of a minority for the will of the majority."[42] Roosevelt, speaking of conservation and employment policies and Social Security, made clear that such policies were "for the good of the whole and not for the good of any one privileged group."[43] Of attempted labor legislation, FDR explained, "It has been beset by obstructions and by bitter propaganda from certain minority groups in the community who had been accustomed for too many years to the exploitation of the great mass of people who worked for them."[44] Such terms as *the common man, the common people,* or *the struggling masses* conveyed the sense in which Democratic leaders spoke for the underprivileged – not the chronically poor and the destitute, but those hardworking Americans whose life chances had been impaired by the undemocratic control of industry and government.[45] Privileged elites were identified as "minority groups." This was the basic logic of Democratic Populism.

Beginning in the 1950s and 1960s, Democratic rhetoric moved be-

---

40. Bryan, speech, 1/20/1900 (Bryan 1900: 167).
41. Democratic platform, 1980 (Johnson 1982: 41). Even Social Security, the most universal of all American social welfare programs, was directed at "the elderly" (ibid. 48).
42. Bryan, speech, 9/1908 (Bryan 1913: 365).
43. Roosevelt, speech, 9/2/1940 (Roosevelt 1941: 373).
44. Roosevelt, speech, 9/11/1940 (Roosevelt 1941: 410).
45. "[W]hy is it that the strength of democracy has always been found among the common people?" inquired the Great Commoner. "The great common people believe in a democratic form of government because it is only in the democratic form of government that they are able to protect their rights and defend their interests" (Bryan, speech, 9/7/1896, *New York Times* 9/8/1896). "Always the heart and the soul of our country will be the heart and the soul of the common man," said Roosevelt, by which he meant "the men and the women who never have ceased to believe in democracy, who never have ceased to love their families, their homes and their country" (speech, 11/2/1940, in Roosevelt 1946: 2998). Uppermost in his mind was "to make the forces of democracy work for the benefit of the common people of America" (ibid.: 2997).

yond efforts to benefit the majority to programs like civil rights and antipoverty policies, whose direct benefits would be felt by a small, targeted sector of the general population. Although publicly deploring "interest group politics," Democratic rhetoric, by denying the class appeal of Populism, created a political terrain where interest group politics could not fail to dominate the discursive field. In speaking of technological advances in industry, the 1964 platform declared, "They must not penalize the few while benefiting the many."[46] This sounds rather like a Democratic Populist suffering from dyslexia, for it represented an exact and symmetrical reversal of the party's historic protest. ("They must not penalize the many while benefiting the few," Bryan or Wilson might have phrased it.)

Agenda and rhetoric shifted from majority rule to minority rights. Democratic reforms centered on extending popular control and eliminating institutional boundaries between the people and the servants, and the Democratic political agenda centered on the court system, the Constitution, the bureaucracy, congressional committees, and interest-group intermediation. Having assumed a defensive posture, the party styling itself the party of the people was now, more than ever, open to attacks of "special privilege" – a charge that Republicans had been using since the 1920s but that drew little blood until the late 1940s and the 1950s. "They describe me as a 'captive' candidate. They say I am a 'captive' of the city bosses, and then of the CIO, and then of the Dixiecrats, and then of President Truman, and then of Wall Street, and then of an organization called A.D.A.," began Stevenson – charges he could not effectively repel.[47]

The multifocused Democratic agenda kept spreading outward as the decades progressed, incorporating the demands of an ever wider set of ethnic, racial, sexual, and issue-based groups. Eventually, all sorts of groups were endowed with inalienable rights. The 1972 platform confirmed "the right to be different."[48] "Government," promised the 1984 platform, "has a special responsibility to those whom society has historically prevented from enjoying the benefits of full citizenship for reasons of race, religion, sex, age, national origin and ethnic heritage, sexual orientation, or disability."[49] Environmental concerns, mentioned in party

46. Democratic platform, 1964 (Schlesinger 1971, 4: 3602).
47. Stevenson, speech, fall/1952 (Stevenson 1953: 15–16). Stevenson pledged "to go to Washington only as the servant of all the people, without obligation to any class or interest. I have made no deals or any commitments to any individual, any political clique, or any pressure group" (speech, 10/30/1952, in Stevenson 1953: 295).
48. Democratic platform, 1972 (Johnson 1978: 791).
49. Democratic platform, 1984 (Democratic party 1984: 89B).

platforms on only four occasions prior to 1952, became a standard presence in the postwar era. Economic issues, the mainstay of party rhetoric in the Populist epoch, now shared the limelight with a host of "new politics" issues, from the environment to abortion.[50] The pinnacle of this help-everybody rhetoric was reached in the party's recent embrace of multiculturalism: "As the party of inclusion, we take special pride in our country's emergence as the world's largest and most successful multiethnic, multiracial republic. We condemn anti-Semitism, racism, homophobia, bigotry and negative stereotyping of all kinds. We must help all Americans understand the diversity of our cultural heritage."[51]

Some might argue that the party had returned to its nineteenth-century origins as a protector of the rights and liberties of oppressed groups. In 1868, accepting the nomination of his party, Horatio Seymour singled out his party's central mission to "protect the rights of minorities."[52] In 1952, after a hiatus of five decades, the phrase "minority rights" reentered Democratic rhetoric.[53] In 1984, platform writers warned, "If Mr. Reagan is elected, who would protect women and minorities against discrimination? . . . Justice demands that we keep our commitments and display our compassion to those who most need our help – to veterans and seniors, to disadvantaged minorities, to the disabled and the poor."[54] Evidently, the status of minority had been redefined: whereas the constitutional rights of minorities served to protect the southern states and their antebellum and postbellum systems of racial oppression, by the postwar period a similar rhetorical strategy was being used to energize the federal government's efforts against those very same policies.

Inclusion

Having abandoned the clarion call of Populism, what did Democratic leaders install in its place to justify an increasingly broad range of social, cultural, and economic reforms during the postwar period? It is my contention that an inclusionary rhetoric first articulated in the 1940s and 1950s served as the ideological foundation for this period's efforts at reform. Stevenson, for example, declared, "I want to talk about people – about you and your children and your father and your mother. I want to talk about the family problems of a democracy. . . . We have learned

---

50. The same transition from "material" to "postmaterial" concerns has been noted within the congressional agenda (Berry 1996).
51. Democratic platform, 1992 (Democratic party 1992: 29).
52. Seymour, speech, 8/4/1868 (Schlesinger 1971, 2: 1285).
53. Stevenson, speech, 9/20/1952 (Schlesinger 1971, 4: 3314).
54. Democratic platform, 1984 (Democratic party 1984: 90B).

how important it is to approach the writing of laws, themselves cold things, from clear, warm pictures in our minds: of a family sitting around a supper table; of a rent bill coming due when there has been sickness in the family."[55] Here, in the quotidian details of family life, we find the remnants of a once-strident Populist tradition. Retreating from broad issues of economic and political power, Democrats now inclined toward vague descriptions of peace, prosperity, and harmony. "Yes, the new day is here across America," promised Humphrey apocalyptically. "Throughout the entire world forces of emancipation are at work. We hear freedom's rising course – 'Let me live my own life, let me live in peace, let me be free,' say the people."[56]

"[G]overnment in America," said Stevenson, "*must* identify itself with *people*, have confidence in them, recognize *all* people – and no single group."[57] The theme was people, and Democratic politicians made their appeals in the most personal manner possible. "Let me tell you something, folks," began Clinton in 1992. "I care about you. I came from your roots. I understand what you're going through."[58] "You can trust Bill Clinton and Al Gore, your neighbors and friends."[59] The 1968 platform offered to each individual citizen "a system of government recognizing his inherent dignity and importance as an individual and affording him an opportunity to take a direct hand in the shaping of his own destiny."[60] "The Individual" (the actual title of a plank in the 1964 platform) was at the center of this quest for wholeness.[61]

The driving angle behind all this people talk was that all Americans were pretty much the same: they all shared the same, quintessentially *human* attributes. "I have always believed," Humphrey declared, "that the basic decency within this nation would one day enable us to lift the veil from our eyes and see each other for what we are as people – not black or white, not rich or poor, not attending one church or another . . . but as *people*, standing equally together, free of hate or suspicion."[62] Eschewing a militant call for social justice, Democrats now appealed meekly to "basic decency" and to some presumed togetherness that was

55. Stevenson, speech, 10/3/1952 (Stevenson 1953: 199–200).
56. Humphrey, acceptance speech, 8/29/1968 (Singer 1976: 374).
57. Stevenson, speech, 5/26/1956 (Stevenson 1957: 284).
58. Clinton, speech, 10/27/1992 (Federal News Service 10/27/1992: 4).
59. Clinton, speech, 10/28/1992 (Federal News Service 10/28/1992: 3).
60. Democratic platform, 1968 (Schlesinger 1971, 4: 3823).
61. "Our task is to make the national purpose serve the human purpose: that every person shall have the opportunity to become all that he or she is capable of becoming" (Democratic platform, 1964, in Schlesinger 1971, 4: 3599).
62. Humphrey, speech, 11/3/1968 (text obtained from Minnesota Historical Society, p. 4).

said to characterize the American nation. To all ills, Democratic orators prescribed the curative of inclusion. "We believe with all our hearts in a dream," said the indomitable Dukakis, "a uniquely American dream, a unifying dream, a dream of opportunity for each and every citizen in this land, no matter who they are or where they come from or what the color of their skin. . . . The best America doesn't leave anybody behind; we bring everybody along."[63] "I believe in the spirit of America," he continued two months later. "I believe in the spirit that says, we're all in this together; that regardless of who we are or where we come from or how much money we have or the color of our skin – each of us counts."[64] Democrats would speak no evil.

Democrats took aim at a smorgasbord of spiritual ills. "Free society cannot be content with a goal of mere life without want. It has always had within it a visionary spark, a dream that man, liberated from crushing work, aching hunger and constant insecurity, would discover wider interests and nobler aims. . . . The next frontier is the quality, the moral, intellectual and aesthetic standards of the free way of life," Stevenson said.[65] "Now that physical security has been so very largely achieved, we are reaching out for more spiritual values, for better quality in our living, for a higher purpose and a richer life."[66] Stevenson quotes a certain "gray-haired man" who accosted him on the street one day: " 'Governor, it isn't just social *security* we want. We want a chance to be somebody.' "[67]

Oppression and injustice were out; peace, harmony, and community were in. "We seek a nation where every man can seek knowledge and touch beauty and rejoice in the closeness of family and community," said Johnson in 1964.[68] "What this nation needs today is a spirit of community," cried Humphrey in vain at the end of the long, hot summer of 1968.[69] Postwar Democrats sought "a way out of tension and trouble."[70] It was a far cry from the Populist blame game.

---

63. Dukakis, speech, 8/24/1988 (Federal News Service 8/24/1988).
64. Dukakis, speech, 10/16/1988 (Federal News Service 10/16/1988).
65. Stevenson, speech, 5/31/1956 (Stevenson 1957: 260).
66. Stevenson, speech, 9/27/1956 (Stevenson 1957: 222).
67. Stevenson, speech, 4/24/1956 (Stevenson 1957: 252).
68. Johnson, acceptance speech, 8/27/1964 (Schlesinger 1971, 4: 3677).
69. Humphrey, speech, 9/11/1968 (text obtained from Minnesota Historical Society, p. 10). "Are we going to accept as inevitable the conflict and the hatred which are becoming a part of our every day life or my fellow Americans, are we going to stand up together as one people and say that this can be one America, one family, one community . . . ?" (speech, 9/9/1968, text obtained from Minnesota Historical Society, p. 5).
70. Humphrey, speech, 9/9/1968 (press release: 7). "[T]here is too much talk of conflicting interests," thought Stevenson. "The natural wealth of the United States is our common trust. We must husband and increase it for the future, and our emphasis must be not

Democratic pledges altered "we demand" to "we favor," "we recommend," "we advocate," "we approve," or simply "we will." "I want a future," said Michael Dukakis, "where Americans are investing in America, where American ideas are working for America – where American jobs stay in America, and where American productivity and workmanship are the best in the world. Isn't that the kind of America we all want? Sure, it is; sure, it is."[71] At a loss, apparently, for justificatory ground, Johnson adopted the rhetorical ploy of "Most Americans want . . ." (which he repeated seven times seriatim).[72] Party leaders appealed to "destiny," "leadership," "patriotism," "invention," "challenge," "imagination," "a new frontier," and so on.[73] "Can a nation organized and governed such as ours endure?" Kennedy inquired. "That is the real question. Have we the nerve and the will?"[74] Democratic rhetoric soared into such ethereal questions as the destiny of the nation, the nature of justice, and the difference between good and evil.

The 1950s saw, for the first time in the party's history, a conscious disavowal of ideology. Stevenson hoped and prayed "that we Democrats, win or lose, can campaign not as a crusade to exterminate the opposing party, . . . but as a great opportunity to educate and elevate a people whose destiny is leadership."[75] Stevenson's attack on the opposing party consisted of criticisms of its "negative, defeatist attitude."[76] He defined the contest between the parties in 1956 as "a choice between the party of youth and the party of age, between the party with new

on rivalry or conflict but on co-operation" (speech, 9/8/1952, in Stevenson 1953: 90). The 1964 party platform declared, "The welfare, progress, security and survival of each of us reside in the common good – the sharing of responsibilities as well as benefits by all our people" (Schlesinger 1971, 4: 3595). "[W]e will find in freedom," promised the ebullient 1964 Democrats, "a unity of purpose stronger than all our differences" (ibid.). Johnson tirelessly repeated the same unity theme. "The needs of all cannot be met by a business party, or a labor party, not a war party or a peace party; not by a Southern party or a Northern party. Our deeds will meet our needs only if we are served by a party which serves all our people" (speech, 8/27/1964, in Schlesinger 1971, 4: 3674). Humphrey, in the following election, insisted upon "the necessity . . . for unity in our country, for tolerance and forbearance, for holding together as a family. . . . Are we to be one nation, or are we to be a nation divided . . . ? I take my stand – we . . . must be one nation, united by liberty and justice for all, one nation under God, indivisible with liberty and justice for all. This is our America" (acceptance speech, 8/29/1968, in Schlesinger 1971, 4: 3846).

71. Dukakis, speech, 8/24/1988 (Federal News Service 8/24/1988).
72. Johnson, speech, 8/27/1964 (Schlesinger 1971, 4: 3675).
73. Kennedy, acceptance speech, 7/15/1960 (U.S. Senate 1961a).
74. Kennedy, acceptance speech, 7/15/1960 (Schlesinger 1971, 4: 3545).
75. Stevenson, acceptance speech, 7/26/1952 (Schlesinger 1971, 4: 3295).
76. Stevenson, speech, 9/29/1956 (Schlesinger 1971, 4: 3433).

ideas and the party with old ideas, or no ideas!"[77] "The strange alchemy of time," insisted the self-consciously moderate Stevenson, "has somehow converted the Democrats into the truly conservative party of this country – the party dedicated to conserving all that is best, and building solidly and safely on these foundations. The Republicans, by contrast, are behaving like the radical party – . . . bent on dismantling institutions which have been built solidly into our social fabric."[78]

Gone were the angry, direct attacks on the opposition that had characterized Democratic candidates from Bryan to Truman. (Truman, in his acceptance speech, called his troops into battle saying, "Senator Barkley and I will win this election and make these Republicans like it – don't you forget that! We will do that because they are wrong and we are right, and I will prove it to you in just a few minutes.")[79] In their flight from conflict, Democratic oratory acquired an otherworldly air. Democrats appealed to "dreams," to "ideals," and to "the destiny that history has set for us."[80] "The need is here. The need is now. I ask your help," said Johnson, introducing civil rights reform in the wake of Kennedy's assassination.[81]

Democrats also distanced themselves from the liberal label. Indeed, the term *liberalism* was abandoned by Democratic presidential candidates almost as soon as it was introduced. In 1932, Roosevelt argued

77. Stevenson, speech, 10/19/1956 (Stevenson 1957: 235).
78. Stevenson, speech, 10/3/1952 (Stevenson 1953: 204). Johnson, matching Goldwater's bile with equal quantities of compassion, appealed to "responsible, forward-looking men" to support his party (speech, 9/28/1964, in Johnson 1965: 1154). The present contest was not "between liberals and conservatives, . . . between party and party or platform and platform"; it was, instead, between "courage" and "timidity," between the "forces of common human decency" and the "forces of bigotry and fear" (acceptance speech, 8/27/1964, in Schlesinger 1971, 4: 3677). After the Kennedy assassination, Johnson claimed, "America became a nation of lovers instead of a nation of haters" (speech, 10/7/1964, in Johnson 1965: 1239).
79. Truman, acceptance speech, 7/15/1948 (Schlesinger 1971, 4: 3187).
80. Johnson, speech, 11/27/1963 (Schlesinger 1971, 4: 3657).
81. Johnson, speech, 11/27/1963 (Schlesinger 1971, 4: 3658). Not surprisingly, Democratic rhetoric included a healthy sampling of religious references. "Be strong and of good courage; be not afraid, neither be thou dismayed," counseled Kennedy, advertising the New Frontier (acceptance speech, 7/15/1960, in Schlesinger 1971, 4: 3544). "For who among us dares betray the command: Thou shalt open thy hand unto thy Brother, to thy poor and to thy needy in the Land?" asked Johnson (acceptance speech, 8/27/1964, in Schlesinger 1971, 4: 3675). Dukakis appealed to an unlikely source in John Winthrop, the seventeenth-century American Puritan, to gain support for the modern American welfare state: "We must . . . love one another with a pure heart fervently. We must delight in each other, make each other's condition our own, rejoice together, mourn together, and suffer together. . . . We must . . . be knit together as one" (speech, 9/17/1988, in Federal News Service 9/17/1988).

that the Democratic party, "by tradition and by the continuing logic of history . . . is the bearer of liberalism."[82] Yet in subsequent campaigns the word rarely passed Democratic lips (even Roosevelt's). When *liberalism* did appear, it was usually paired with *communism* or *socialism*, and hence was invoked as an American, rather than a partisan, philosophy. "The New Deal," similarly, was a recurrent figure of speech for Roosevelt and Truman but was virtually abandoned in the postwar period. Even the towering symbol of Franklin Roosevelt tended to disappear from Democratic presidential rhetoric in the Universalist epoch (or was invoked simply as part of a roll call of Democratic leaders of the past). Of course, candidates continued to list the specific programs inaugurated during FDR's administrations (particularly Social Security), but such policy-specific discussions were rarely connected with liberalism, with the New Deal, or with the Democratic party during its hot phase in the 1930s and 1940s. No Democratic candidate from the 1950s to the 1990s would dare to repeat Truman's declaration (in 1948), "I'm proud to be an exponent of the New Deal!"[83]

Conclusions

While campaigning against popular notions of "ideology" – as dogmatic, radical, violent, and (for many) socialist – the Democratic party was in fact articulating an ideology. The party's publicly articulated beliefs were as stable, internally coherent, and externally differentiated during the postwar era as during previous eras. The challenge for modern-day commentators is to understand how the party's nonideological self-presentation fit within a larger ideological framework. An essential part of the postwar party's message, I would argue, was contained in the intertwined concepts of consensus, tolerance, compromise, pragmatism, and mutual understanding. These were the ideals to which Democratic leaders aspired, ideals that were central to the party's Universalist weltanschauung, in which all peoples, all faiths, and all lifestyles were embraced (at least in principle). The political ideal of the 1964 platform was contained in the platform's opening statement: "America is One Nation, One People."[84]

What prompted the fundamental change of perspective from Populism to Universalism? As with other basic-level transformations in party

82. Roosevelt, speech, 7/2/1932 (Schlesinger 1971, 3: 2785). For a history focused on the early years of the liberal label, see Rotunda (1968; 1986).
83. Truman (1948–49: 143).
84. Democratic platform, 1964 (Schlesinger 1971, 4: 3595).

ideology, one must look to a number of interconnected developments. In a sense, the ideology of Populism contained the seeds of its own destruction. Having intervened in the economy during the early twentieth century to combat trusts, speculation, and the Depression, Democrats found themselves enmeshed in an economic reality that was considerably more complex than they had reckoned it to be. Party leaders found themselves moving, almost ineluctably, from a Brandeisian to a Keynesian view of government-market relations. The angry flourishes of Populist rhetoric seemed increasingly at odds with the complexities of modern social and economic management.[85] To this must be added the temporal coincidence of the greatest and most sustained economic boom in the country's history (from the 1940s through the 1960s). War and the resulting prosperity, writes one historian, "helped relegitimize American capitalism among a circle of men and women who had developed serious doubts about its viability in an advanced economy. It robbed the 'regulatory' reform ideas of the late 1930s of their urgency and gave credence instead to Keynesian ideas of indirect management of the economy. . . . No other single factor was as central to the redefinition of liberal goals as the simple reality of abundance and the rebirth of faith in capitalism abundance helped to inspire."[86]

Ironically, the height of labor's organizational power coincided with an increasing reluctance on the part of Democratic presidential candidates to identify themselves publicly with the cause of labor. The reasons for this monumental shift are complex. To begin with, the concepts of labor and worker lost their universal appeal in the latter half of the twentieth century. Labor now increasingly was associated with the concerns of *organized* labor rather than with virtue and American citizenship. An unparalleled spate of strikes in the immediate postwar years, as the country readjusted to a peacetime economy, soured public perceptions of organized labor. The newfound power and visibility of organized labor – as exemplified in the CIO's Political Action Committee (headed by the ultraliberal Sidney Hillman) – made it a credible target for Republican rhetoric. Not surprisingly, Republicans lambasted the CIO as the secret power behind the Democratic throne, a bastion of special privilege.

Second, anticommunist hysteria in Washington put left-identified unions on the defensive. Although anticommunism pertained mostly to foreign affairs (and hence has been treated lightly in the foregoing chapters), the perception of a communist threat, and the party's response to

---

85. On this transition in economic thought, see Brinkley (1995), Hawley (1966), and Lichtenstein (1989).
86. Brinkley (1989: 109).

that threat, was a primary factor in the Democratic party's mid-century transformation. Stevenson's first campaign is suggestive:

> We are engaged in a conflict with forces of darkness which have engulfed seven hundred million human souls. We confront an enemy who is crafty, implacable and far stronger than any foe America has ever known. Like Santa Anna, he is an enemy who offers no quarter. He cannot be appeased . . . his aim is total conquest – not merely of the earth, but of the human mind. He seeks to destroy the very idea of freedom, the concept of God Himself.[87]

Like so many other elements of the Universalist agenda, themes of anticommunism were initiated by Roosevelt and Truman in the 1940s but did not take center stage in Democratic rhetoric until the 1950s.[88]

But the anticommunist agenda was not limited to foreign affairs, as Stevenson made abundantly clear during the 1952 campaign:

> I suggest that we would err . . . if we regarded communism as merely an external threat. Communism is a great international conspiracy and the United States has been for years a major target of that conspiracy. Communist agents have sought to steal our scientific and military secrets, to mislead and corrupt our young men and women, to infiltrate positions of power in our schools and colleges, in business firms and in labor unions and in the Government itself. . . . In the pursuit of their objectives, the communists have been ingenious, disciplined, obedient and ruthless. Along the way, they have gained the help, witting or unwitting, of many Americans. The communist conspiracy within the United States deserves the attention of every American citizen and the sleepless concern of the responsible government agencies. . . . So I would say to any Americans who cling to illusions about communism and its fake utopia: Wake up to the fact that you are in an alliance with the devil.[89]

With state socialism identified as the primary source of evil in the world – and in the United States as well – it became increasingly difficult for Democratic leaders to criticize the private sector. "We are for private, and profitable, business," Stevenson assured audiences. "The Democratic party is against socialism in our life in any form – creeping, crawling or even the imaginary kind which shows up so often in the Republican oratory. I am opposed to socialized medicine, socialized farming, socialized banking, or socialized industry."[90] Although he registered a polite objection to the Republican-led anticommunist drive, there was no question that Stevenson, like other Democratic leaders in

---

87. Stevenson, speech, 10/18/1952 (Stevenson 1953: 262).
88. See, e.g., Democratic platform, 1948 (Schlesinger 1971, 4: 3155). On the influence of anticommunism on American politics generally, see White (1997).
89. Stevenson, speech, 9/12/1952 (Schlesinger 1971, 4: 3309).
90. Stevenson, speech, 10/30/1952 (Stevenson 1953: 293).

the postwar period, accepted the essential premise of the anticommunist crusade. Perhaps the conflictual spirit of Populism was transferred to the fight against the demon of socialism. In any case, it was difficult to sustain a rhetorical war on two fronts, particularly when those fronts were so far apart. The demise of Populism and the rise of Universalism can be explained, in part, as a displacement of the people/elites rhetorical cleavage of 1896–1948 by the capitalist/communist cleavage.

Organizational changes within the party also affected the course of liberalism in the postwar era. During this period, a new brand of party activist joined the party in large numbers. These citizen-activists were middle-class, issue-oriented, hostile to machine-politics, and interested in a broad range of noneconomic policies, from foreign policy to civil rights. (As institutional exemplars of this movement, one might cite the Democratic Advisory Council and the Americans for Democratic Action.)[91] It was this sort of Democratic delegate that went apoplectic at the sound of Adlai Stevenson's cultured, mildly self-deprecating discourse. One must credit the efforts of these reformers for the party's first strong statement of support for civil rights in 1948. Yet even with this influx of "amateurs" into the party organization, very little change would have occurred on the central issue of race were it not for the jettisoning of the party's historic two-thirds rule in 1932 (stipulating that party nominations had to be approved by two-thirds of the party's delegates at the national convention). After 1932, the presidential party could no longer be held hostage by its southern delegations. Thus, changes in personnel and in process combined to open the way for a Universalist agenda.

Finally, there was the reemergence of the race question on the national political agenda. The symbolic power of this issue within a party historically devoted to the cause of white supremacy can hardly be overestimated. Although Truman tried to dress the civil rights issue in Populist garb, this was one issue that would have been difficult to contain within the majoritarian premises of William Jennings Bryan. The party's inclusionary vision in the postwar era was a direct attempt to respond to this new issue and its newly politicized constituencies. The resulting ideology, engineered by candidates from Stevenson to Johnson, was then reinforced by the addition of a passel of new groups seeking to assert their own civil, political, and economic rights. Each took its place within the big tent of Democratic Universalism.[92]

---

91. For descriptions, see Parmet (1976) and Wilson (1962).
92. This analysis mirrors many of the points in Edsall (1984) and Edsall and Edsall (1992).

PART IV

Conclusions:
Sources of Party Ideology

8

What Drives Ideological Change?

The previous chapters have attempted to show that there are plausible grounds for regarding the American parties as ideologically motivated. What, then, might account for the *content* of American party ideology? What mechanisms, pressures, or concerns drive the formation and periodic reformation of ideology within these party organizations?

Work on this question is diverse. Studies employ a wide range of indicators, focus on different periods of American history, and ask different questions of the historical record. Nonetheless, it is possible to distinguish four general theories of party conflict in America: *classical, social-class, ethnocultural,* and *realignment.* This chapter explores these frameworks in light of the empirical findings of this study. I conclude with a few general observations about what "causes" party ideology.[1]

The Classical Theory

Of politics in the Roman republic, Cicero wrote, "Those who have wished their deeds and words to be pleasing to the multitude have been held to be *populares,* and those who have conducted themselves in such a manner that their counsels have met the approval of all the best men have been held to be *optimates.*"[2] Whether we classify these groupings

---

1. This discussion of reigning theories of party conflict – classical, social-class, ethnocultural, and realignment – might seem to contradict the statements of chapter 1, which presented the orthodox view of the American parties as one of "no ideology." However, as chapter 1 also indicated, few historians or political scientists view the American parties as utterly bereft of ideas or as entirely identical to one another. The "no ideology" claim, more accurately portrayed, is that the American parties have been *less* ideological than their brethren in other Western democracies – a difference of degree, rather than of kind. Even Hartz admitted the existence of party disagreements, as we shall shortly observe.
2. Cicero, quoted in Taylor (1968: 11).

as parties or factions, it is clear that for many in the Roman republic, politics was understood as a battle between the rabble-rousers and the better sort, between the democrat (in its older, classical meaning) and the aristocrat.[3] A millennium later, David Hume described political struggle in England in remarkably similar terms. "A Tory," he wrote,

> may be defined . . . to be a lover of monarchy, though without abandoning liberty; and a partizan of the family of Stuart. As, a Whig may be defined to be a lover of liberty though without renouncing monarchy; and a friend to the settlement in the Protestant line. These different views, with regard to the settlement of the crown, were accidental, but natural additions to the principles of the *court* and *country* parties, which are the genuine divisions in the British government. A passionate lover of monarchy is apt to be displeased at any change of the succession; as savouring too much of a commonwealth: A passionate lover of liberty is apt to think that every part of the government ought to be subordinate to the interests of liberty.[4]

In the American colonies, the ancient terms of this civic republican rhetoric were scrupulously maintained, though the preference of the colonists shifted gradually to the "country" side of the equation. Shortly after the ratification of the Constitution, James Madison, its primary drafter, characterized the young republic as torn between

> those who . . . are more partial to the opulent than to the other classes of society . . . [who] having debauched themselves into a persuasion that mankind are incapable of governing themselves, [believe] that government can be carried on only by the pageantry of rank, the influence of money and emoluments, and the tenor of military force . . . [and] those who, believing in the doctrine that mankind are capable of governing themselves and hating hereditary power as an insult to the reason and an outrage to the rights of man, are naturally offended at every public measure that does not appeal to the understanding and to the general interest of the community, or that is not strictly conformable to the principles and conducive to the preservation of republican government.[5]

The opposition of the people to an unrepublican or undemocratically inclined elite was a notion particularly dear to the hearts of Antifederalists, Jeffersonian Republicans, and Jacksonian Democrats.[6] Even for-

---

3. These are, as Taylor (1968: 12) points out, very rough translations of *populares* and *optimates*.
4. Hume, "Of the Parties of Great Britain" (1742), reprinted in Beattie (1970: 25).
5. Madison, "A Candid State of the Parties" (*National Gazette*, 9/26/1792; reprinted in Madison 1973: 247). I am indebted to Howard Reiter for reminding me of this passage.
6. For discussion of this perspective during the Revolutionary era, see Wood (1969). For examples in the early nineteenth century, see John Adams (quoted in Ford 1898/1967: 2); Thomas Jefferson, letter to John Melish, 1/13/1813 (Jefferson 1972: 620–24), letter to John Adams, 6/27/1813 (ibid: 627–28), and letter to Marquis de Lafayette, 11/4/1823 (ibid: 712); Van Buren (1867: 72–73); and selections contained in Blau (1954).

mer Federalist John Adams was moved to declare (in 1825) that "the organization of the state governments gave rise to a great party division upon the principles of government in the collisions between the relative rights of *persons* and *property* – between aristocracy and democracy."[7] A decade later, Tocqueville gave a similar estimation of the origins of party conflict in the United States. Ever since the Revolution, he commented, "the nation was divided between two opinions, . . . the one tending to limit, the other to extend indefinitely, the power of the people." This basic political division was "as old as the world and . . . perpetually to be met with, under different forms and various names, in all free communities."[8]

, True or not, it is certainly the case that this perspective on party conflict has a familiar ring to American ears. Shortly after the turn of the century, Vernon Parrington, one of the most influential voices of the Progressive era, reiterated these same basic themes with respect to party combat in America. One party, wrote Parrington, "has persistently sought to check and limit the popular power, to keep the control of the government in the hands of the few in order to serve special interests, whereas the other has sought to augment the popular power, to make government more responsive to the will of the majority, to further the democratic rather than the republican ideal."[9] Even Louis Hartz, whose work constituted an explicit rebuttal to Progressivism and to conflict-based theories of politics, thought that American politics was riven between an "impulse toward democracy and [an] impulse toward capitalism."[10] This is several steps removed from Cicero, but it does illustrate a persistent and reasonably coherent view of American party politics in which the common people and their representatives face off against an elite (variously described), which I shall label the *classical* view of party conflict.

The Social-Class Theory

Reacting against what he called the "literary theory of politics" – according to which each party derived its essence from God, human na-

---

The same idea of an opposition between "liberty" and "order" can be found in Bryce (1891, 2: ch. 53). For a longer-range view of civic republicanism, see Pocock (1975). It should be noted, however, that what I have called the "classical" theory of party conflict is not by any means identical to civic republicanism, a worldview that explicitly proscribed political parties and that took a dim view of the capacity of "the people" to manage their affairs. Nonetheless, the court/country division that underlies the classical theory has its roots in the republics of Rome and Renaissance Italy.

7. Adams (1825/1941: 4).   8. Tocqueville (1835/1960, 1: 183).
9. Quoted in Hofstadter (1968b: 438).   10. Hartz (1955: 89).

ture, or simply tradition – Charles Beard attempted to bring a more systematic, and explicitly *economic*, perspective to the study of party politics. "The division of voters into parties . . . springs from the possession of different kinds and amounts of property," Beard argued. Accordingly, the party system was divided between a Hamiltonian party – "primarily the working philosophy of business enterprise" – and a Jeffersonian party, based on agrarian principles.[11] "[T]he center of gravity of wealth is on the Republican side while the center of gravity of poverty is on the Democratic side."[12]

Once ensconced in the academy, the Beardian social-class theory of politics exerted an incalculable influence over the study of the parties. Wilfred Binkley's standard text *The Parties: Their Natural History* described national politics as a struggle between "mercantile-financial" interests and "independent farming."[13] Arthur Schlesinger Jr., in his enormously influential *Age of Jackson*, summarized American party politics as an ongoing struggle between the "business community" and "other sections of society."[14]

More than a trace of class analysis remains in recent work on the parties.[15] One of the very few studies devoted explicitly to American partisan ideology takes as its point of departure the Beardian notion that fundamental partisan cleavages arise from economic structures. "In each period in American history," Everett Carll Ladd writes, "a loose collection of social groups can be identified whose political style, interests, values, and policy orientations were controlling for the society."[16] Yeoman farmers, for example, were the dominant group of the early nineteenth century, forming the social base of the majority party from 1790 to 1860. The Jefferson-Jackson Democratic party, representing the interests and perspectives of this constituency base, articulated an essentially agrarian vision of politics, which vied against the mercantile vision of the Whigs. In the wake of the Civil War, as entrepreneurial businessmen displaced agricultural workers in the workforce, they provided the social base, and most of the ideas, for the new Republican party, whereas the Democratic party remained mired in the ideology of the yeoman farmer.[17] The onset of the Great Depression marked the arrival of a fully industrialized economy and a fully mature working class. This class was to compose the backbone of a refashioned Democratic party, which upheld the rights of workers and a redistributive welfare state. The Re-

11. Beard (1929: 6, 135–36).   12. Beard, quoted in Key (1942/1958: 235).
13. Binkley (1943/1945: viii).   14. Schlesinger (1945: 505).
15. See, e.g., Burnham (1970; 1986).   16. Ladd (1970: 4).
17. See Ladd (1970: 5, 151–58).

publican party, following the cues of its business-oriented constituencies, resisted.[18]

A related version of class analysis can be found in the work of Ferguson and Rogers. According to these authors, "What properly defines American party systems is not blocs of voters but patterns of interest-group alignment and coalitions among major investors." Although electoral outcomes, strictly speaking, are the product of getting the most votes, the authors point out that it takes money to get votes. Hence, they conclude, the parties have always been forced to respond to the interest groups that provide the funds essential to carrying on a political campaign. "As a practical matter, then, the fundamental 'market' for political parties in the United States is not individual voters [but rather] major *investors* – groups of business firms, industrial sectors, or in some (rare) cases, groups of voters organized collectively." From 1896 through the 1920s, the dominant bloc of economic elites consisted of manufacturing and mining interests (steel, textiles, coal, and shoes) and supported the Republican party. From the late 1920s through the 1960s or so, the leading sector was multinational, capital-intensive industry and finance; these groups supported the Democratic party. From the 1960s to the present, this group switched its allegiance from the Democrats to the Republicans, causing a right turn in American politics at elite levels.[19]

The Ethnocultural Theory

Beginning in the 1950s and 1960s, historians began to challenge socio-economic views of party conflict. The work of the ethnocultural school focused initially on the nineteenth century, when, these scholars claimed, American political alignments rested more often upon questions of ethnicity and religion than on income, occupation, or, for that matter, slavery. The third party system (1850s–1890s), for example, was composed of two partisan cleavages: "a value-and-interest conflict between Yankee moralist subculture and white southern subculture . . . [and] a religious-value conflict between pietistic and anti-pietistic subcultures."[20] From these ethnic and cultural cleavages the two parties gained their ideological direction. Republicans, sharing a "pietistic" orientation based on

---

18. Ladd predicted the emergence of a fourth party system in the 1970s, the product of a postindustrial society in which conflict would be drawn along lines of perceived status rather than social class or ethnicity.
19. Ferguson and Rogers (1986: 44–45). See also Ferguson (1989; 1995).
20. Kleppner (1979: 58).

the experience of being born again and on the perception of a Christian duty to perform good works, concerned themselves with the regulation of moral behavior, including a wide range of sumptuary laws.[21] The Democrats adopted an antipietistic and libertarian orientation, defending the rights of individuals from the reforming urges of Republican legislators.[22]

An essentially ethnocultural vision of American party politics has been extended by a few writers into the twentieth century.[23] Robert Kelley argues suggestively,

> If Thomas Jefferson were to be brought back to life today, he would have little difficulty seeing where he belonged. The Democratic party is still the party of the outsiders, of the ethnic minorities who are relatively low in cultural and economic status or who in other ways have been made to feel excluded by the host culture. Such outsiders gravitated to Jefferson because [of] his ideology of equality and of personal liberty . . . – an ideology of cultural as well as of economic laissez faire, which in both instances aimed at eliminating privilege. . . . With this voting base, the Democrats continue to conceive of themselves as the party of the poor, as well as of those with middle incomes – that is, of the consuming classes in general as against the merchant, the producer, and the financier. And the outsiders' characteristic paranoia is still Jefferson's: that economic conspiracies among the rich and powerful constantly act to exploit society at large and that business and government ties lead to political corruption.[24]

The ethnocultural "outsiders" in this saga are southerners (whom Kelley considers to embody a separate ethnic identity), westerners (in the Jacksonian period), and those newly arrived from Europe. Later non-European arrivals (along with African Americans) were added to this ethnic base as the twentieth century unfolded. The ethnocultural "insiders" of American politics have been composed, during all periods, of Yankee WASPs, who provided the leadership cadre and the philosophical groundings of the Federalist-Whig-Republican party since the founding of the republic.

The Realignment Theory

The fourth major perspective, realignment, encompasses most work on American political history, including many of the studies discussed ear-

---

21. See Kleppner (1981b: 134).
22. For reviews of the literature, see Argersinger and Jeffries (1986), Kleppner (1972), Lichtman (1983), and McCormick (1986: 29–63). Important works in this paradigm include Benson (1961), Formisano (1971), Holt (1978), Jensen (1971), Kelley (1979), Kleppner (1970; 1979; 1981a; 1981b; 1987), and Silbey (1967b; 1985).
23. See Barone (1990), Kelley (1977), Parenti (1967), Rae (1992), and Wolfinger (1965).
24. Kelley (1977: 558–59).

lier. The core aspects of the theory can be quickly sketched: American electoral history has been rocked by critical elections in or around 1828, 1860, 1896, and 1932. These critical elections marked massive and enduring changes in the party affiliations of the general electorate, creating five "party periods" during which political conflict was minimal and voting alignments relatively stable.[25]

The traditional (nonethnocultural) theory of realignment sketches the history of party ideology as follows. The issues of the first realignment (1828–36) were the existence of the national bank, the prerogatives of the federal government, and the conflict between the western and eastern sections of the country. The second electoral realignment (1860) was largely the product of a single issue, slavery. The third realignment (1896) resolved various problems attendant upon the process of industrialization (particularly the hardships thrust upon agricultural workers during a severe downturn in the business cycle). The last generally acknowledged critical election period (1928–1936) responded to the creation of a sizable urban working class and the crisis posed by the Great Depression.

Analysis

Work on American political history thus contends that the major parties have been divided by (1) attitudes toward popular sovereignty, (2) social-class bases, (3) ethnocultural bases, or (4) periodically redefined social bases. Although evidence can be found to support each of these perspectives – and there is certainly a good deal of overlap between them – I shall argue that none provides a satisfactory synthesis of party ideologies over the course of American history.

The classical framework best explains party differences in the nineteenth and early twentieth centuries. In the nineteenth century (as is documented in chapter 5), the Democrats defended liberty and popular sovereignty against the supposed usurpations of a statist elite. In the early twentieth century, they portrayed themselves as defenders of the people on a broad range of economic and political issues. The shortcomings of the classical framework, however, are equally apparent. Begin-

---

25. Four decades of empirical and conceptual tinkering have produced a remarkable diversity of results, such that realignment has come to mean a great number of things to a great number of people within the disciplines of political science and history. All that can be said with any degree of unanimity is that realignment remains the dominant theoretical perspective orienting research in American political history (McCormick 1986: 64). Important works include Brady (1988), Burnham (1970), Campbell and Trilling (1980), Clubb et al. (1980/1990), Key (1955), Shafer (1991), and Sundquist (1983).

ning in the 1920s and 1930s, for example, the Republican party began to court the American public in terms that were as populist as their Democratic opponents'. The people-versus-power dichotomy describes some periods better than others, and the postwar era hardly at all. Thus, the classical synthesis seems limited in what it can successfully explain.

Social-class analyses of American party politics have been critiqued so many times that it seems churlish to do so yet again.[26] I shall withhold comment on all but two recent formulations. Ladd's narrative, featuring the development of the American economy, seems plausible at first and echoes the general conclusions of many writers. However, it is at odds with the timing and the nature of each party's ideological development as traced in this study. Moreover, given the secular nature of economic change, this macro-level perspective has little to say about when such responses might occur or what form they might take. The Democratic party responded with vehemence to the new industrial order, but why did they do so in 1896 and not earlier (or later), and why did their response take the form that it did? Why populism, for example, instead of socialism?

The "investment" theory of politics outlined by Ferguson and Rogers emphasizes the role of elites but does not go very far toward explaining broad changes in each party's ideology. In fact, the authors do not seem to be explaining changes in ideology so much as changes in the relative success of either party at the polls (due to their access to financial contributions and the institutional support of dominant business interests). Nor have the authors demonstrated empirically that party elites respond to financial interests over and above the views and interests of their constituencies.

The ethnocultural hypothesis deserves more extended discussion. It is certainly true that, upon arrival, immigrant groups tended to form enduring connections with a political party. But did these affiliations create new ideological configurations, or merely affirm existing ones? Perhaps new groups simply latched on to the most congenial host available, leaving that party's views relatively unaffected. The Jacksonian Democratic party, for example, had *already* developed its distinctive issues and values by the mid-1830s, well before the Irish influx of the 1840s.[27] One could make the same argument with respect to German (Protestant) integration into the Whig-Republican party. Clearly, ethnic and religious subcultures contributed to the way party leaders thought about the political questions of the day. Yet, the more impressive fact, perhaps, is the

26. See ethnocultural works listed earlier, as well as Gienapp (1994).
27. See Watson (1990: 194).

resilience of party ideologies in the face of the continual onslaught of European and non-European immigration.

Even in explaining ideological *continuities* within the party system, the ethnocultural explanation must massage the evidence a great deal to reach positive conclusions. The exact demographic characteristics of each party, according to Paul Kleppner, were quite complex. During the Gilded Age, for example, the Republican party was based in religious groups ("native-stock Baptists, Congregationalists, Episcopalians, Free Will Baptists, Methodists, Presbyterians, Quakers, and less confessional Lutherans"), blacks, and English-stock immigrants.[28] The Democratic party, by contrast, was supported by "highly confessional German Lutherans, German Reformed Lutherans, Catholics (except French Canadians), and the Southern wings of the Baptist, Methodist, and Presbyterian faiths."[29] One wonders whether the heterogeneous demographic groups within each party had as much in common as the ethnoculturalist model supposes. Conversely, were there important political differences separating "less confessional" (Democratic) Lutherans and "more confessional" (Republican) Lutherans? Southern English-stock immigrants would seem to differ from northern English-stock immigrants geographically but not ideologically.[30]

Moreover, if ethnocultural divisions underlay the ideology of the major parties, why did it play such a small part in the *rhetoric* of the two parties? The most-discussed issue in the nineteenth and early twentieth centuries, for example, was the tariff. Indeed, one can hardly imagine a more economistic discourse than that purveyed by Republican and Democratic orators in the Gilded Age. In general, party leaders spoke of governmental, economic, and foreign policy matters much more frequently than they did of ethnic or religious matters. Even though ethnocultural concerns were structuring the vote – and the ethnoculturalists offer strong evidence that this was the case – party leaders did not appear to heed these concerns in structuring national party rhetoric.[31]

---

28. See Kleppner (1981b: 132–33).   29. Kleppner, quoted in Silbey (1985: 74).
30. Clearly, religion and ethnicity had something to do with the ideological divisions of the late nineteenth century. But there was a great deal more to it than that. Democrats' persistent opposition to federal control, for example, was *also* fueled by their geographic concentration in the South, with that region's memory of the Civil War and its ongoing concern with Republican interference in elections and civil rights in the South, their belief in the rightness of white supremacy, their agrarian economic philosophy, and their civic republican heritage. Sumptuary laws imposed by moralizing Republicans probably played a minor role in the party's overall attitude toward constitutional matters.
31. See Gerring (1996). For critical commentary on the ethnocultural synthesis, see Argersinger and Jeffries (1986), Lichtman (1982; 1983), and McCormick (1986).

The theory of realignment, similarly, is more effective as an explanation of voting behavior than of elite-level party ideology. The first critical election period, 1828–1836, saw the rise of two party organizations and ideologies (not their "realignment"). The second, during the 1850s, was accompanied by the temporary rise of an issue (slavery) that had been present for some time, and to which one party (the Democrats) had already committed itself well before the Armageddon of 1860 arrived. By the 1870s, with this issue apparently settled, national politics returned to a state of affairs and a state of mind remarkably reminiscent of the antebellum era. Much had changed in the electoral arena, but Gilded Age Democrats and Republicans maintained the same essential public philosophies that their Jacksonian counterparts had inaugurated in the 1830s. The third critical election period, the 1890s, coincided with drastic changes in the agenda of one major party – the Democrats – but not the other, as realignment theory would predict.[32] Even in the case of the Democrats, one may doubt the effect of altered voting patterns in transforming the party's basic philosophy, for the simple reason that, although the party's vote diminished significantly from the "third" to the "fourth" electoral period, it did not change greatly in social composition.[33] The last generally accepted period of realignment, circa 1932, seems merely to have accentuated the established ideological proclivities of the two parties. In sum, the connection between electoral realignments and ideational realignments, as charted in this study, does not seem very close. Secular changes in electoral behavior neither caused nor reflected changes in the ideologies of the major parties. Indeed, two of these critical realignments – those of the 1890s and the 1930s – may have had more to do with economic circumstances than with ideology.[34]

Constituencies versus Elites

Although writers working within the foregoing traditions disagree on the forces behind ideological change, almost all agree that parties can

32. As Burnham comments, "The realignment of 1894–96 *did not* result in a major reversal of dominant public policy or in a drastic change in the 'historic blocs' which lay at the power core of American politics in this period" (1986: 269).

33. "Not only were the upheavals produced by Bryan's candidacies in 1896 and 1900 more modest than historians have suggested, but they produced no lasting rearrangement of earler voting alignments," writes Lichtman (1983: 59). Summing up a number of other studies of this period, Argersinger and Jeffries (1986) conclude that "virtually every group in the electorate shifted toward the Republican party" – meaning, again, that the *composition* of the Democratic vote changed little during this critical election period.

34. For critical commentary on the realignment synthesis, see Shafer (1991).

best be understood as aggregations of constituencies. With a few exceptions, therefore (e.g., Ferguson and Rogers), those who study the American parties have adopted a society-centered view of politics. Paul Kleppner, the leading voice of ethnocultural history, states forthrightly, "Parties and party activities did not create the[ir] antagonistic political cultures. . . . Antagonistic relations between (or among) group political cultures generated party oppositions."[35] Kleppner conceives of parties not as institutions but rather as "broadly based social forces through which 'locally' oriented voters relate themselves to the wider society."[36]

To be sure, in the nineteenth century the Democratic party's longstanding appeal to recent immigrant groups, and in particular to Catholics, reinforced that party's persistent attachment to personal liberty, to constitutional protections, and to freedom of worship. Likewise, the party's laissez-faire economic perspectives were rooted in its largely agricultural voting base. Within the Whig-Republican electorate, Protestants and immigrants from western and northern Europe (except Ireland) were overrepresented.[37] There can be little doubt that their presence contributed to the party's ethos of spiritual uplift and economic progress during the period I have referred to as National. However, the connection between ideology and constituency seems a good deal more attenuated than scholars have traditionally assumed.

To begin with, several decades of research on the nonideological (or at least, *less* ideological) nature of mass publics should lead us immediately to suspect any strong claim of correspondence between the views of masses and elites.[38] Even if parties were constituency machines, they

35. Kleppner (1981b: 136).
36. Kleppner (1970: 4). See also the comments of Richard McCormick (1986: 57). This idea has a long lineage among American academics. The Progressive historians were perhaps the first group of writers to articulate fully the idea that political influence flowed from groups within civil society through the political party and, ultimately, into public policy. Nowadays, the *reciprocal* relationship between elites and masses is more often emphasized (see, e.g., Carmines and Stimson 1989; Clubb, Flanigan, and Zingale 1980/1990; and Macdonald and Rabinowitz 1987: 778). Writers sit differently on the chicken-and-egg question – whether elites lead masses or masses lead elites – but all agree that significant and enduring changes at the top must be reinforced during the same critical election period (i.e., within several years) by changes at the bottom.
37. During the Whig era, for example, the party drew disproportionately from Congregationalists, Unitarians, and "New School" Presbyterians (Howe 1979: 13). For Gilded Age Democratic voting patterns, see Kleppner (1981b: 132). Many of these religious and ethnic voting patterns persisted well into the twentieth century.
38. See, e.g., Converse (1964) and Smith (1989).

were not necessarily conveyor belts for the views of constituents, for the simple reason that rank-and-file voters did not usually articulate clear and logically coherent views on political matters of the day. Voters in the Gilded Age, admits Kleppner, "were more often concerned with matters which impinged on their daily lives directly and which immediately challenged their personally structured value systems than they were with national problems whose direct salience was not clearly perceptible to them."[39]

Second, regardless of how ideological American voters were (and are), their *behavior* seems not to have changed very much over the past century and a half. As summed up by Clubb, Flanigan, and Zingale, "American electoral history has been characterized by stable voting patterns, and the few disruptions that have occurred have been temporary. . . . [H]istorical realignments appear primarily as surges for or against the parties. . . . Only the realignment of the 1930s involved the sharp, massive, pervasive, and lasting electoral change that is often taken as a general characteristic of historical realignments."[40] American voters, then, have been loyal to their parties from generation to generation, and the few moments of flux (with the notable exception of the New Deal) seem to have consisted mostly of "surges for or against the parties," rather than permanent moves by particular constituencies from one party to another. If so, it may make more sense to interpret realignments as shifts in the general popularity of the two parties – as, for example, following the economic downturns of the 1890s and 1930s – rather than as shifts in the ideological predilections of the electorate. In any case, it is difficult to attribute changes in party ideology to shifts in a constituency whose behavior has been so constant.[41]

Third, party constituencies were complex. Constituents divided along religious, ethnic, regional, socioeconomic, and urban/rural lines, and these lines crosscut as often as they reinforced each other. National party leaders could not simply follow local cues in constructing national ideologies, for these cues were diverse and tended to conflict with one another. What played in Peoria might not play in Manhattan. Moreover, from what we can tell, party leaders often did not have a clear idea of who their supporters, or potential supporters, were. It is remarkable, for example, how many times during the latter nineteenth and early twentieth centuries leaders of the Republican party charged into the South

39. Quoted in Silbey (1985: 74).
40. See Clubb, Flanigan, Zingale (1980/1990: 68, 114–15).
41. This leaves the possibility, of course, that party elites respond to general changes in public opinion that do *not* result in changes in party affiliation.

intending to convert the Democratic heathen. It is equally remarkable that Bryan imagined he might capture the votes of urban laborers at the turn of the century (in fact, these constituents turned *away* from the Great Commoner). Clyde Weed, in his study of the Republican party in the 1930s, argues that the party's hard fate was the product, in part, of a massive miscalculation of voter sentiment.[42] Many other examples of political naïveté might be cited from the comfortable armchair provided by hindsight. Given that the proclivities of the general electorate have engendered so much controversy among contemporary pollsters and academics (working with the benefit of national polls and considerably advanced methods of analysis), it is little wonder that politicians in previous eras were regularly deceived as to the views of the general public. These leaders had only hunches, grapevine news, and newspaper reports to go on, and they were compelled to make snap judgments in the heat of battle.

National news reporting, whether analyzed in terms of its sources, its reporters, its ownership, or its actual content, is now an extremely centralized operation. In the nineteenth and early twentieth centuries, however, national news tended to take on considerable local color on its way from Washington, New York, or Chicago to the hinterlands. Thus, although avenues of communication between party leaders and party rank and file were more varied than they are today, they were also more fragmented, ad hoc, and, as a result, unreliable. Even when election results arrived, they were of uncertain import. The absence of survey research and the absence of a journalistic and social-science industry analyzing the vote meant that any one of a large number of interpretations could be conjured up to explain the results. There was no "day of reckoning," for when the masses spoke, they could not always be understood.[43] Without the results of opinion polls staring politicians in the face, and political consultants helping to integrate such information into the campaign's message, party leaders had considerably greater insula-

42. "It is clear," writes Weed (1994: 87), "that party strategists grew increasingly optimistic throughout 1935." In 1936, of course, the party lost in one of the greatest landslides of American history.

43. One need only recall the immense confusion that fell upon Washington in the wake of Reagan's 1980 election victory with respect to his purported "mandate" from the people to appreciate the difficulty of interpreting election results in the nineteenth century. In Reagan's case, both candidates issued clear and sharply differentiated messages and the vote resulted in an electoral college landslide, yet the *meaning* of the election remained hotly contested (at least among political elites). For discussion of the ways in which the development of accurate public opinion polling influenced the conduct of politics, see Geer (1996) and Herbst (1993).

tion from the vox populi than they do today. The very uncertainty of the public's wishes made this the most malleable commodity of nineteenth- and early-twentieth-century politics. It was quite common for two presidential candidates to sit on opposite sides of the same issue, each proclaiming his fealty to "public opinion."[44]

Moreover, even when leaders *could* anticipate the views and opinions of the electorate (or their core constituencies), we have little evidence that they felt compelled to follow those views and opinions. Teddy Roosevelt once commented,

> People always used to say of me that I was an astonishingly good politician and divined what the people were going to think. This really was not an accurate way of stating the case. I did not "divine" what the people were going to think; I simply made up my mind what they *ought* to think; and then did my best to get them to think it. Sometimes I failed and then my critics said that "my ambition had overleaped itself." Sometimes I succeeded; and then they said that I was an uncommonly astute creature to have detected what the people were going to think and to pose as their leader in thinking it.[45]

Quite a number of examples might be cited of presidents and party leaders who refused, despite considerable electoral inducements, to truckle to public opinion. Andrew Jackson did not face down the Bank of the United States because he thought it would earn him points with his constituents; in fact, he worried greatly that the Bank, in his words, would "kill me."[46] Even were this line of action to have proven unpopular, there is little doubt that Old Hickory would have held his ground. When Andrew Johnson faced congressional opposition to his Reconstruction policies – nearly losing the presidency in the process – he did not strain to reach an understanding with Radical Republicans. Grover Cleveland battled to preserve the sanctity of the gold standard and of limited government even in the midst of a major economic downturn in the 1890s. Such policies helped turn the Democrats out of office in the 1894 midterm elections and in the famous 1896 presidential election and had long-term political repercussions, since these elections inaugurated a period of Republican dominance extending through the 1930s.

44. Geer discusses a number of cases, including the 1930s and 1890s, in which inadequate knowledge of public opinion may have led to electoral realignments in the prepolling era. Of the 1896 campaign, Geer (1991: 442–43) notes that the size and general enthusiasm of Bryan's audiences as he toured the country in the fall campaign led many to believe that he would achieve victory in the November vote. The *New York Herald* predicted Democratic victory as late as October in that campaign.
45. Quoted in Merriam (1922: 44).   46. Jackson, quoted in Watson (1990: 143).

More directly, Cleveland's intransigence allowed Bryan and his supporters to capture the Democratic party from Cleveland's goldbugs at the 1896 convention. Herbert Hoover, saddled with a depression of even greater proportions, faced down the multitudes clamoring for change in economic policy with equal tenacity. It was ideology, broadly speaking, that drove these men, not the search for public approval. The list of casualties to public opinion is long and offers little assurance to the traditional assumption that the character of the parties directly reflected constituency demands.[47] I would argue that, on average, nineteenth- and early-twentieth-century politicians had more backbone (or foolhardiness) than do those of today – that is to say, they had a greater willingness to buck the trends of public opinion.

Oddly, although we do not consider political parties to be simple transmission belts for constituency desires in the contemporary period – when, for the first time, such a role is technically feasible – this general view of the prewar parties persists. Consequently, many time-honored questions from the social-class, realignment, and ethnocultural schools must be rethought. Was Democracy the party of farmers, the poor, and the working class? Were Republicans representative of northeastern manufacturing, of the urban classes generally, or of a religiously based Protestant clientele? Empirical questions aside, it is difficult to say with any certainty what it might have meant in policy terms if any of these propositions had been true, since the views of the voting bloc in question might well have been rendered moot by the indifference of the leadership, or mute by the leaders' inability to understand the mumblings of the electorate.

Party constituencies should be thought of as a *constraint*, not a deciding factor, in the creation and re-creation of party ideology. The majority of rank-and-file party voters, largely ignorant of Washington affairs, cared deeply about only a few issues. On these issues party leaders could not trespass. This did not mean that party leaders needed to voice these concerns; it meant simply that they could not openly oppose them. Party constituencies represented obstacles to be negotiated – either placated or persuaded. Their influence was generally negative: anything that offended a voting bloc was studiously avoided by party leaders.[48]

This left party elites with considerable room to maneuver, however.

---

47. For a brief discussion of Republican stalwarts' resistance to Roosevelt in 1912, see Weed (1994: 12).
48. In a more general vein, Sartori (1976: 342) notes that the preoccupation of party leaders was "not to disturb the party's identifiers and, at the same time, to attract new voters (or retain potential defectors)." This, I think, concisely states the role of elites vis-à-vis their supporters in the creation of party ideology.

Within the heterogeneous coalitions that backed each major party, one could be sure to find constituency support somewhere for a wide variety of ideological options. For this reason, one cannot assume that just because a constituency favored a particular ideological shift, this constituency was the decisive force in pushing the party to adopt it. With a set of supporters numbering in the millions, politicians would perforce echo the views of one group or another. But leaders were forced to choose among competing views and competing constituencies. This power of choice meant that, on many issues, leaders would play a decisive role in shaping the party's agenda. It is important to state the obvious: party ideologies were formulated, disseminated, and executed by party leaders. They did not rise spontaneously from *le peuple*. It was party leaders who proposed, and voters who responded, yea or nay. Thus, if voting behavior helps explain the considerable ideological continuity that characterized the parties from decade to decade, it is less helpful in explaining their occasional ideological transformations. Party constituencies were generally conservative forces, whereas party elites were the agents of change.[49]

The Failure of Grand Theory

If mandates for new programmatic commitments are not the lesson to be drawn from electoral realignments, then we are on firm ground in propos-

---

49. Hays concluded on a similar note: "Historians have assumed that national political ideologies represented beliefs which were homogeneous throughout all levels of the political structure. But, in fact, they arose more from cosmopolitan than from local segments of the party structure, reflected leadership strategy more than grass-roots values, and linked together the several levels of party activity. In the decades from 1890 to 1920, for example, highly visible national policies such as tariff and trusts provide an incorrect view of voter preferences. Those preferences rested primarily on ethno-cultural attitudes which rarely appeared in national debate. . . . The party mobilized voters on the community level by stressing ethno-cultural issues which sustained local party loyalties and party differences, and at the same time emphasized altogether different issues, such as tariff and trusts, on the national level of debate" (1967: 161). Richard McCormick reiterated this message two decades later: "The most important message conveyed by ethnocultural analysis is not that voters are ethnically and religiously motivated, but that grass-roots concerns are so irrelevant to public policymaking" (1986: 56).

Recent work seems to be moving closer to an elite-led model of party change. See Aldrich (1995), Carmines and Stimson (1989), Clubb, Flanigan, and Zingale (1980/1990), Crewe and Searing (1988), Gold (1989), Monroe (1983), Page (1978), Weed (1994), and Wilson (1994). Among their predecessors, one might note Schattschneider (1942). Unfortunately, we shall never have the public opinion data necessary to prove these arguments conclusively for periods prior to the 1950s.

ing party elites as the dynamic elements of party change. This is not a trivial point. At the same time, however, any theory placing primary causal weight on party elites runs serious risk of tautology. Party elites of one sort or another are the proximate cause of any party change, for they are the ones, *by definition*, who must implement that change. It is almost always possible to claim, therefore, that a party changed because certain party leaders changed their minds. One could credit Bryan and his followers for the 1890s transformation within the Democratic party, Hoover and his contingent for changes within the Republican party in the 1920s, and Stevenson and the club movement for the second Democratic transformation in the 1950s. But what were the *fundamental* causes? Why did these party leaders decide at a particular moment to alter their political views, and why did these transformations stick?

In the quest for a generalizable theory of party change, scholars have discussed the role of constituents, leaders, party competition, party organization, political culture, regime type, electoral system, and various other "exogenous" factors.[50] Each, it seems, may play a part in inducing a party to break with tradition. Although useful in indicating avenues of investigation, however, this itinerary of causes is not very parsimonious. I would argue that the theoretical insufficiency of work on party change is unlikely to be overcome for the simple reason that the outcome in question – party change – is affected by so many factors. Ideologies are complex, perhaps as complex as political cultures. (Try imagining a causal theory that would explain the rise of the Enlightenment, the Protestant Reformation, civic republicanism, liberalism, *and* postmaterialism.) In most cases, a wide variety of historical events might be cast as precipitating factors in ideological, or political-cultural, change.

In accounting for Bryan's revolution within the Democratic party, for example, one could point to the fusing of the Populist party with the regular Democratic party, the shortage of currency, the rise of monopolies, industrialization and urbanization, the deleterious effects of middlemen on western farmers, the instability of commodity prices, the closing of the frontier, the demise of civil rights, and the "bloody shirt" as organizing themes in the party system. The fact that an extremely severe depression was pinned firmly on the tail of the donkey also made this a propitious moment for ideological reflection.[51] Other contributing

---

50. See Harmel and Janda (1994), Panebianco (1988), Sainsbury (1981), Tingsten (1941/1973), and Wilson (1994). For work on party-*system* change, see Mair (1989) and Mair and Smith (1990).

51. As Burnham (1986: 276) remarks, "The Democrats [were] ousted in 1894–96 in large part because they were the 'ins' when the second-worst depression in American history struck the economy." He adds, "It should be better known than it is that the decade

causes could certainly be appended to this list.[52] Bryan himself offered the following explanation, with particular reference to the income tax (which the party strenuously supported): "Changing conditions make new issues; . . . the principles upon which Democracy rests are as everlasting as the hills, but . . . they must be applied to new conditions as they arise. Conditions have arisen, and we are here to meet those conditions."[53]

The second Democratic *wendung*, in the 1950s, drew upon an equally broad range of historical events, including the longest sustained period of growth in American history; the increasingly middle-class character of American life; the gradual loss of public esteem suffered by the trade union movement; the disappearance of any popular threat to the Democratic party from the left (e.g., the Communist party, Father Coughlin, the Union party, the EPIC campaign, Huey Long and the Share Our Wealth movement, and Henry Wallace's Progressive party); the victory of Keynesianism in academic circles and within Democratic councils, marking a fundamental transformation in the way Democrats viewed the marketplace and economic policy; the shift from "hot" stump speaking to the "cool" medium of television, mandating a softer, more personal, more conciliatory brand of rhetoric; and the belief, among Democratic elites, that political problems were best approached as specific (i.e., isolated) technical problems and that a moderate, compromise-oriented form of leadership would be most successful in addressing those problems. It is difficult to overestimate the effects of the cold war, which helped marginalize the left and legitimate the right; which seemed to vindicate the (Republican) perspective that statism, not individualism, was the primary enemy of the American public; and which granted foreign policy an ascendance over domestic policy that it had rarely enjoyed in the past.[54]

In short, the contributing causes of party change are many and various. (Trying to find the cause of party change is like trying to identify the murderer at a lynching: many were present at the scene of the crime, all had sufficient motive, and all appear to have acted.) Worse yet, there don't seem to be many features that our three cases of ideological transformation shared. There is, in short, no *general* factor at work that might explain the development of American party ideologies. The 1890s, the

1898–1907 was second only to the 1960s in the entire history of American capitalism in its rate of economic growth."

52. See, e.g., the fine account of the 1896 election in Jones (1964).

53. Bryan, speech, 7/8/1896 (Bryan 1896: 203).

54. For discussion of Whig-Republican changes in the 1920s, see chapter 4.

1920s, and the 1940s constituted historical conjunctures – periods when many historical forces impinged on a single party, forcing that party's leaders to reconsider the way they viewed the field of national politics, with effects that would reverberate for many decades.[55] This argument, that "lots of things" drive issue evolution, is critical for an appreciation of the dynamics of American party politics. Sometimes it is important to conclude with what we do not know. We do not know – and, by the nature of the beast, *cannot* know – which particular historical events were critical to the evolution of each party's ideology. The subject is too overdetermined and the number of cases too limited to be able to label any single cause, or set of causes, "necessary and sufficient."

That party ideology is the product of manifold causes does not make it any less important as a topic of historical and political-scientific investigation, however. Although unsatisfying as a dependent variable, ideology seems extremely useful in explaining party behavior during campaigns, the main subject of this book. Ideology exists, therefore – even if its existence cannot easily and parsimoniously be accounted for.

55. The same case can be made for party change in British politics. It is impossible to say very much in general about why British parties changed when they did and in the specific ways they did. But there is a great deal one can say about the nature of specific moments of party change. On the Conservative party, see Cornford (1963) for changes in the late nineteenth century, and Peele (1988) for changes in the later twentieth century.

Epilogue

1996

Since research for this book was completed, another presidential election has transpired. Few would rank 1996 as a landmark in the history of American presidential contests. Nonetheless, readers may wonder how the speeches and platforms of this contest fit into the larger arguments of the book. Did the rhetorical battle between Bob Dole, the Republican nominee, and the incumbent Democrat, Bill Clinton, constitute a departure from established ideological traditions, or more of the same?

My argument will highlight the persistence of an ideological status quo harking back to the 1920s (for the Republicans) and the 1950s (for the Democrats). Dole will be viewed as an exemplar of Republican Neoliberalism, and Clinton of Democratic Universalism, discussed respectively in chapters 4 and 7. Of course, both candidates also adhered to certain partisan convictions that predate these twentieth-century transformations. In this limited sense, Dole and Clinton will be viewed as avatars of more distant ideological legacies stretching back to the nineteenth century.

The Republican Campaign

On the Republican side, the argument for continuity seems inexorable. Even journalistic accounts emphasized the Republican nominee's long career in Congress and his personal ties to the past. Indeed, Dole's age (he turned seventy-three during the campaign) provided a constant source of amusement for late-night comics through the course of an otherwise unamusing and unremarkable contest. Dole was acutely conscious of his weakness on the age/virility issue, choosing for his running mate a former football quarterback from the baby-boomer generation, Jack Kemp. What, then, of the *ideological* content of the Dole-Kemp campaign?

Social values played a fairly prominent role in the 1996 campaign, as they had in every Republican campaign since 1980. This time, drugs and crime were the social blight of choice. In a speech to members of the Associated Press, Dole claimed, "Ultimately our crisis of drugs and crime is a crisis of belief and conviction. . . . , The fate of a generation will depend on the ability of the adult world to communicate values – especially a commitment to embrace life by rejecting drugs."[1] The war against drugs could not be separated from the battle to recover American morality. Unfortunately, "the adult world of politics is not serious about drugs, it is casual, permissive and liberal."[2] (The drug issue, to be sure, was carefully chosen to capitalize on the president's admission that he had smoked marijuana as a youth.) Similarly, one of the main causes of economic poverty was to be found in "moral poverty," which produced crime and other types of dysfunctional behavior.[3]

In dealing with such hot-button items, Dole chose a visceral approach. One speech involved the retelling of a crime that befell the daughter of a couple who were in attendance at the rally. (Dole began by introducing them to the audience.) "Twenty-three years ago, their 12–year-old daughter went around the street selling cookies, Girl Scout cookies. Tragically, a . . . male neighbor two doors down invited the daughter in and proceeded to rape, kill and dump her into the garbage."[4] "It's happening more now, more rapidly – over and over and over again," Dole concluded, chalking up this fact to the "liberal living laboratory of leniency" established by the Clinton administration.[5]

However, the media version of the 1996 campaign vastly overplayed the significance of social issues in the Republican campaign. Indeed, crime and drugs were the *only* social issues featured prominently in the nominee's (postconvention) speeches. Dole opposed late-term abortions on several occasions but refused to dwell on the subject. He went on record as supporting a constitutional amendment to protect the flag but, again, devoted few words to the subject. Immigration figured ambiguously in the campaign. Dole took a hard line against illegal entry into the United States but emphasized the principle of America as an immi-

---

1. Dole, speech, 9/20/1996 (U.S. Newswire 9/20/1996, reprinted on NEXIS).
2. Dole, speech, 9/20/1996 (U.S. Newswire 9/20/1996, reprinted on NEXIS).
3. Dole, speech, 9/16/1996 (Federal News Service 9/16/1996, reprinted on NEXIS).
4. Dole, speech, 9/16/1996 (Federal News Service 9/16/1996, reprinted on NEXIS).
5. Dole, speech, 9/16/1996 (Federal News Service 9/16/1996, reprinted on NEXIS). Elsewhere, Dole proclaimed, "The president has appointed liberal judges who have become notorious nationwide for bending the law in order to let criminals go free" (speech, 9/20/1996, U.S. Newswire 9/20/1996, reprinted on NEXIS).

grant society, open to the world. Affirmative action, which was expected to draw Republican fire, in fact drew only blanks. (Dole stated his support for "nondiscriminatory" policies but refused to be more specific.)[6]

As I have argued, contemporary Republicanism is more properly understood as the product of Herbert Hoover than of Barry Goldwater or Ronald Reagan. Indeed, one does not need to listen very hard or very long to hear the resplendent echo of Neoliberalism in the 1996 election:

> They [the Democrats] have a vision that places government at the center of your lives. If you just send more of your money to Washington and give up more freedom, then the government will take care of us. Now, Jack Kemp and I have a different vision. We say the government has already taken too much of your money and too much of your authority and too much freedom from the American people, and it's time to give it back. That's our vision of America. And sometimes it seems that President Clinton has a million little plans for [how] our government can tell you how to run your life. Well, Jack and I have one big plan: To give you back more of your hard-earned money and more of your freedom, because you can run your own life better than any government bureaucracy ever can or ever will. You have the American spirit, and that's what it's about.[7]

This passage, in which Dole does his best to revive Reagan's fading image, set forth the central direction of the 1996 campaign. Dole, like every Republican candidate since Coolidge, championed the little guy in his (occasionally her) battle with the forces of big government. Though shorn of anticommunism (hardly an effective stance in the post-Soviet world), the antistatist argument still hinged on the contrast between individual liberty and an oppressive state apparatus. "After the virtual devastation of the American family, the rock upon which this country was founded," argued Dole, "we are told that it takes a village, that is the collective, and thus, the state, to raise a child."[8] The Federalist/Antifederalist argument was played out once again. "There is today a great political divide between Washington and our western states," proclaimed the candidate. "Our western states should not be taking orders from faraway potentates on the Potomac. We ought to move it back closer to the states and closer to the people – follow the Tenth Amendment to the Constitution."[9]

It is important to note that Dole's opposition to government intervention in state affairs and in the private sector was not grounded simply

6. Dole's acceptance address offers a good indication of how these topics would be treated in the subsequent campaign (see Dole, 8/15/1996, *New York Times* 8/16/1996).
7. Dole, speech, 9/16/1996 (Federal News Service 9/16/1996, reprinted on NEXIS).
8. Dole, acceptance address, 8/15/1996 (*New York Times* 8/16/1996).
9. Dole, speech, 10/17/1996 (CNN *Special Event*, reprinted on NEXIS).

in pragmatic arguments for more efficient provision of government services and higher rates of economic growth. More important, perhaps, was the *moral* argument. "I do not appreciate the value of economic liberty nearly as much for what it has done in keeping us fed as I do for what it has done in keeping us free," testified Dole. Big government threatened the health of the republic and the liberties of its citizens; individual freedom could survive only in circumstances of market freedom.[10]

What did free-market capitalism and antistatist liberalism mean in policy terms? Like most Republican presidential candidates in the Neoliberal period, Dole put his trust in tax cuts, with an occasional nod to deficit reduction. Searching for the read-my-lips sound bite that would carry his message to the American public, Dole promised "to end the IRS as we know it."[11] Although the rhetoric did not soar, the message was at least consistent: "Remember, it's your money. It's your money. It's your money. It's not his money. And I want to give some of it back to you."[12] More than any other single issue, tax cuts defined the 1996 Republican campaign.

Despite a patently inegalitarian economic agenda, Dole was careful to maintain a grassroots image on the hustings. Indeed, one of the primary successes of Neoliberal Republicanism was its ability to employ populist rhetoric in the service of economic conservatism.

It is demeaning to the nation that within the Clinton Administration a corps of the elite who never grew up, never did anything real, never sacrificed, never suffered, and never learned, should have the power to fund with your earnings their dubious and self-serving schemes. Somewhere, a grandmother couldn't afford to call her granddaughter, or a child went without a book, or a family couldn't buy that first home, because there was just not enough money to make the call, buy the book or pay the mortgage. . . . Why? Because some genius in the Clinton Administration took the money to fund yet another theory, yet another program, yet another bureaucracy. Are they taking care of you, or are they taking care of themselves? I have asked that question, and I say, let the people be free.[13]

10. "The freedom of the market is not merely the best guarantor of our prosperity, it is the chief guarantor of our rights," continued Dole. "A government that seizes control of the economy for the good of the people, ends up seizing control of the people for the good of the economy" (acceptance address, 8/15/1996, *New York Times* 8/16/1996).
11. Dole, speech, 9/20/1996 (U.S. Newswire 9/20/1996, reprinted on NEXIS).
12. Dole, speech, 11/11/1996 (Federal Document Clearing House, reprinted on NEXIS).
13. Dole, acceptance address, 8/15/1996 (*New York Times* 8/16/1996). "Seventy percent of [Clinton's] tax increase is paid by small businessmen and small businesswomen, and senior citizens, and everybody who drives a car. You're paying it – not the rich

Unions, too, were classed with the Washington establishment. Promoting school choice (also known as the voucher plan for educational reform), Dole proposed "to give the schools back to the teachers and the parents, and take them away from the union leaders who sit in Washington, DC, and call themselves the National Education Association."[14] The choice of words is instructive. Dole could have referred simply to the NEA or could have avoided the issue of unions entirely by framing the question in terms of parental choice, improving schools, and so forth. Instead, he singled out "union leaders" as an obstacle to reform, identifying them as a privileged elite.

Finally, one finds the traditional Whig-Republican emphasis on Americanism, in which images of God, country, and strong leadership intermingled:

> When I am President, our men and women [in] our Armed Forces will know the president is [their] commander in chief – not Boutros Boutros Ghali, or any other U.N. Secretary General. This I owe not only to the living but to the dead, to every patriot grave, to the ghosts of Valley Forge, of Flanders Field, of Bataan, the Chosin Reservoir, the Khe Sanh, and the Gulf. This I owe to the men who died on the streets of Mogadishu not three years [ago], to the shadows on the bluffs of Normandy, to the foot soldiers who never came home, to the airmen who fell to earth, and the sailors who rest perpetually at sea. This is not an issue of politics, but far graver than that, like the bond of trust between parent and child, it is the lifeblood of the nation.[15]

"We are placed here, for a purpose, by a higher power," continued Dole in his acceptance address. "Every soldier in uniform, every school child who recites the Pledge of Allegiance, every citizen who places her hand on her heart when the flag goes by, recognizes and responds to our American destiny."[16] America was not simply another place on the map but a "civilization"; and this civilization was charged with a historic mission in the world: "When I look back upon my life, I see less and less of myself and more and more of history, of this civilization that we have made, that is called America. I am content and always will be content to see my own story subsumed in great events, the greatest of which is the simple onward procession of the American people."[17]

The majesty of the moment (crafted, in large part, by speechwriter

he talks about – not the rich" (Dole, speech, 11/2/1996, Federal News Service, reprinted on NEXIS).

14. Dole, speech, 9/11/1996 (*CNN Morning News*, 9/11/1996, reprinted on NEXIS).
15. Dole, acceptance address, 8/15/1996 (*New York Times* 8/16/1996).
16. Dole, acceptance address, 8/15/1996 (*New York Times* 8/16/1996).
17. Dole, acceptance address, 8/15/1996 (*New York Times* 8/16/1996).

Mark Helprin) carried the normally taciturn Dole far above the hum-drum business of cutting taxes and balancing the budget. In the epic sweep of American nationhood, Dole found a memory link to a mythic past and an ideological link to a very concrete Whig-Republican past. Henry Clay and Daniel Webster could not have said it better.[18]

The Democratic Campaign

On the Democratic side, the past was more cleverly hidden from the present. In the fall of 1995, as the Clinton administration began to con-template strategy for the upcoming presidential contest, Christopher Dodd, chair of the Democratic National Committee, convened a group of political consultants to discuss the party's prospects. What did the pollsters prescribe? The debate, according to one report, went as follows:

> On one side was a group of strategists in favor of appealing to middle-class voters by openly taking on corporate America, demanding to know why in a time of rising profits workers were being laid off and wages were flat. Such a message "gets the Democrats back home," said Carter Eskew. . . . Others worried, however, that the appeal of the message was precisely what was wrong with it: it sounded too much like the voice of "old Democrats." It would, they warned, invite charges that the party was inciting class war-fare, and could ultimately end up alienating important constituencies, not to mention some of the party's major contributors.[19]

Here, concisely summarized, was the ideological dilemma of the postwar Democratic party. The left wing – in the Clinton administration, this meant advisers like Eskew, Robert Reich, Harold Ickes, Stanley Green-berg, and James Carville – advocated a return to social-class themes. Only in this fashion, they argued, could the party regain its appeal to middle- and working-class white men.[20] The right wing, populated by such figures as David Gergen, Dick Morris (both sometime Republi-cans), Erskine Bowles, Mark Penn, Bruce Reed, and Robert Rubin, ar-gued (in the words of one correspondent) that "an economic populist appeal is too divisive, and that the Democrats can only forge a majority coalition by emphasizing broad, unifying issues like Medicare and edu-cation."[21]

18. For further elaboration, see chapter 3.   19. Kolbert and Clymer (1996: A1).
20. For a manifesto of the left wing's self-consciously populist positions, see Carville (1996).
21. Ibid., A23. This debate, between what I would call the Populist and Universalist wings of the Democratic party, has been played out many times. See, e.g., Borosage et al. (1997).

It was clear by the end of the 1996 campaign where the president's sympathies lay. Clinton did everything in his power to cast himself as a New Democrat, denouncing ideology ("liberal this – conservative that") at every turn.[22] Eschewing attacks on wealth and privilege, along with most other Democratic candidates in the postwar decades, Clinton expressed his liberalism in an assortment of policy proposals: a $1,500-a-year tax credit for the first two years of college, a tax deduction for families for up to $10,000 per year in college tuition costs, tax-free withdrawals from Individual Retirement Accounts for college education, a $2,600 grant for unemployed and underemployed Americans to get job training, a force of thirty thousand reading specialists and National Service Corps members to mobilize a volunteer army of one million reading tutors for third-graders, expansion of Individual Retirement Accounts to allow young people to save tax-free to buy a first home, an exemption from the capital gains tax for families who profit by up to $500,000 for the sale of a home, and so forth.[23]

Occasional attempts were made to rehabilitate the *instrument* of these well-meaning policies. "Their theory is that the government is always the enemy," began the president. In reality, "the government is you. It belongs to you. It is a reflection of what you want. It is nothing more or less than yours."[24] Popular sovereignty, however, was the only principle to which Clinton could appeal when attempting to counter Republican antistatism. The state could claim no authority except that which derived directly from the people.[25] In 1996, as in 1992, Clinton presented himself as a small-government Democrat. Indeed, there were times when he sounded like the proudest of Republican incumbents. "Our administration," he crowed, "reduced the size of the federal government by 250,000.... As a percentage of our work force it's the smallest it's been since Franklin Roosevelt first took the oath of office in 1933."[26] New Democrats did not expand the scope of government, they "reinvented" it.

Finally, and most emphatically, Clinton emphasized *inclusion*. "My program is simple. Opportunity for all, responsibility from all – an

---

22. Clinton, speech, 10/13/1996 (Federal Document Clearing House, reprinted on NEXIS).
23. Drawn from "Proposals by Clinton" (1996).
24. Clinton, speech, 10/13/1996 (Federal Document Clearing House, reprinted on NEXIS).
25. Here, as elsewhere in American history, the absence of a "state tradition" (Dyson 1980) is notable.
26. Clinton, speech, 9/30/1996 (U.S. Newswire, reprinted on NEXIS).

American community that includes all of us without regard to our race, our gender or when we showed up here."[27] This was the first campaign in which the term *gay* was explicitly used to refer to a group worthy of shelter under the Democratic tent.[28] Appropriately, the central metaphors chosen by the Clinton-Gore campaign in 1996 – the bridge and the village – were both metaphors of inclusion: "That's what this election is all about, a bridge to the future or a bridge to the past; a bridge to the future wide enough that we can all walk across, or everybody trying to build their own little bridge and say, 'We're on our own.' I believe that my wife was right. I think it does take a village. We're better off when we help each other."[29]

Fighting for social justice in the Universalist mode meant justifying welfare-state policies with *compassion*, and not since Jimmy Carter had the Democrats chosen a leader so adept at communicating that he cared:

> The budget I vetoed . . . I vetoed not because I didn't want to balance the budget, but because I thought it was wrong to basically end Medicaid's 30-year guarantee of health care to poor women and little babies, to end the 30-year guarantee of health coverage to middle-class families, who had members with disabilities and they were struggling to take care of those people in their own homes and go to work every day. Wrong to end the guarantee to those who had very limited incomes and needed that help if they had to be in nursing homes. I thought it was wrong to create a two-tier Medicare system, which said to people if you're unfortunate enough to be older, poorer and sicker than most other seniors you could well get second-class care. I thought it was wrong not to keep up with inflation and population growth in Medicare, and instead to have real cuts that were going to force people to make payments out of pocket.[30]

The Democratic plan was the right plan because Democrats like Bill Clinton and Al Gore acted out of fellow feeling, not, like their opponents, out of callous self-interest.

Conclusions

Although it would be rash to consider 1996 simply a repeat performance of previous presidential campaigns, there is a sense in which both can-

27. Clinton, speech, 10/13/1996 (Federal Document Clearing House, reprinted on NEXIS).
28. See Clinton, acceptance address, 8/29/1996 (*New York Times* 8/30/1996).
29. Clinton, speech, 9/6/1996 (Federal News Service, reprinted on NEXIS).
30. Clinton, speech, 9/17/1996 (National Public Radio, reprinted on NEXIS).

didates *were* prisoners of their parties' ideologies. To be sure, Clinton did his best to avoid the subject of his party's past. Yet, as chapter 7 demonstrates, Democratic candidates have been running away from liberalism, the New Deal, the welfare state, and labor unions for a long time. Harry Truman was the last candidate to openly ally himself with these increasingly unpopular verbal symbols, which were henceforth disguised in the all-inclusive, none-offending rhetoric of Democratic Universalism. While maintaining – and indeed greatly expanding – the *policies* of Franklin Roosevelt, Democrats beginning with Adlai Stevenson have steadfastly jettisoned the Populist rhetoric of the New Deal. At the core of postwar Democratic ideology is a public uneasiness about state power and "class warfare" politics. In this respect, Bill Clinton stands in a long line of Democratic prevaricators.

For Dole, party history offered more pleasant grounds for reflection. Indeed, throughout the campaign of 1996, Dole did his utmost to fill Reagan's mythic cowboy boots. The point I have tried to stress (here and in chapter 4) is that the real founder of Neoliberal Republicanism was not Reagan – nor indeed Goldwater – but rather Hoover. It was Hoover who introduced the allied themes of democratic capitalism and antistatism into Republican ideology. "Social values," which entered party rhetoric in full force during the 1980s, scarcely disturbed this idyllic Norman Rockwell–cum–Herbert Spencer scene.

One further point deserves notice. To some, the modest goals embraced by the Clinton campaign in 1996 signified a shift to the right in Democratic ideology. Whereas universal health care dominated Clinton's previous presidential race, 1996 was a "think small" endeavor. Clinton talked about the economy (which was humming along nicely throughout the summer and fall of 1996), balancing the deficit, and education reforms of a minor nature – hardly progressive issues. (Could it be that Harry Truman was *wrong* when he declared that in a fight between a Republican and a Republican, the Republican would win every time?) Yet I would not conclude from this that the party has taken a hard, or irrevocable, turn to the right. Rather, I would interpret Clinton's self-conscious centrism as part of a pattern of Democratic incumbency in the postwar era.

Unfortunately, we have only one other case to compare with Clinton in this respect. Nonetheless, the similarities between the Carter and Clinton presidencies are striking in several ways. Both entered office promising far-reaching change; neither got very far in enacting his agenda (largely because of congressional opposition); both ended up running reelection campaigns that appropriated traditionally Republican themes.

(One can hypothesize that Kennedy or Johnson reelection campaigns would have resulted in similarly middle-of-the-road efforts.) In short, running as an incumbent Democrat in the postwar era means coming to terms with the apparent failure of campaign promises (to end poverty, to conserve energy, to reform health care, and so on). In any case, if economic indicators are optimistic and the United States has not embarrassed itself in ventures abroad, a sitting president can coast to victory without defining a massive policy agenda. If the economy is stumbling and American troops are losing face or experiencing casualties, the president is likely to retreat to safer (i.e., more conservative) ground.[31] Thus, although Clinton's 1996 campaign represents a small move to the center, there is no reason to expect that later Democratic campaigns will follow in his steps. It is difficult to envision a Democratic *challenger* appearing without a substantial – and substantially liberal (Universalist) – policy agenda.

Were there significant differences of policy and principle between the Democratic and Republican candidates in the 1996 election? This would seem a strong case for the consensus argument. Nonetheless, I think it is worth emphasizing the ideological *conflict* embodied in this campaign – a level of conflict that probably outstripped that manifested in recent elections elsewhere in the democratic world. On the eve of this election, one journalist compared Dole and Clinton on sixteen issues – the budget, taxes, funding for the arts, defense, education, foreign affairs, health, abortion, the environment, affirmative action, immigration, term limits, gun control, drug abuse, crime, and welfare – finding significant differences between the candidates on each one.[32] To be sure, there were large areas of agreement between the two parties, particularly on matters basic to American political culture, such as capitalism, democracy, individualism, and equal opportunity. However, it would be difficult to mistake the acceptance addresses tendered by each candidate to his party:

> I am here to say to America, do not abandon the great traditions that stretch to the dawn of our history, do not topple the pillars of those beliefs – God, family, honor, duty, country – that have brought us through time and time again.[33]

31. This centrist dynamic in reelection campaigns probably does not pertain to Republican presidents. Indeed, it may be advantageous for a Republican incumbent to emphasize that he has not joined the Washington establishment – has not accepted the (liberal) status quo – by radicalizing his second campaign (running for government by running against government). This is not an option available to Democrats.
32. See Pear (1996).
33. Dole, acceptance address, 8/15/1996 (*New York Times* 8/16/1996).

Let us build a bridge to help our parents raise their children, to help young people and adults to get the education and training they need, to make our streets safer, to help Americans succeed at home and at work, to break the cycle of poverty and dependence, to protect our environment for generations to come, and to maintain our world leadership for peace and freedom.[34]

34. Clinton, acceptance address, 8/29/1996 (*New York Times* 8/30/1996).

Appendix

The Search for a Method

Because a great many works have already been written on the general subject of ideology, and the specific histories of the American parties have been told many times, readers may be skeptical about the empirical and theoretical yield of the current project. Is there anything new to say about such an established topic? Chapter 1 set forth the substantive claims justifying this enterprise. Here, I shall stake methodological claims. Specifically, I shall argue (1) that ideology needs to be brought to the forefront of the study of the American parties, (2) that these ideologies can be approached through the medium of presidential rhetoric, (3) that 1828 marked the beginning of competitive party politics in America and hence constitutes an appropriate beginning point for this study, and (4) that the textual medium of election rhetoric should be analyzed both quantitatively and nonquantitatively. Since the persuasiveness of the evidence presented in the foregoing chapters rests upon these methodological choices, I shall cover this ground slowly and with considerable care, making clear how my own approach to the subject differs from others'.

Party Ideology in the Academic Mold

Political scientists have studied the American parties within electoral, organizational, and policy-making contexts, but rarely within an ideational context. Leon Epstein's magisterial survey of the field, for example, provides chapters on the congressional parties, the presidency, state and local parties, candidate selection, national organization, party identification, and campaign finance; only in passing does this otherwise splendid book directly address the question of what the parties stand (or stood) for.[1] Even work on American political rhetoric, wherein one

1. See Epstein (1986). For other guides to contemporary work on the parties, see Crotty (1991), Eldersveld (1982), Keefe (1991), and Sorauf and Beck (1988).

might expect some attention to party ideology, has taken a rigorously formal approach to political speech, analyzing its stylistic elements rather than its manifest content.[2] Consequently, as William Riker comments, "we have very little knowledge about the rhetorical content of campaigns, . . . their principal feature."[3]

By the same token, on those occasions where ideas do enter into political scientists' field of vision, the focus is usually on the general function of ideology in political life, rather than on the specific content and history of the ideologies in question. There has been a great deal of work in the spatial-modeling genre, for example, on the question why parties might, or might not, act ideologically.[4] Anthony Downs, from whom much of this literature flows, argues at one point that parties within a two-party system (where the public's preferences are unidimensional and unimodal) tend to avoid clear policy stands and "converge ideologically upon the center."[5] At another point, however, Downs argues that political uncertainty, ideological (rather than issue-based) voting, and factors of party accountability foster ideological differences between parties.[6] The contradictary implications of these various arguments are emblematic of the field. Studies of party ideology within a rational choice framework generally have few empirical referents. Since so many a priori arguments can be made on both sides of the ideology question, little seems to have been proven by such efforts, impressive though they are.[7]

---

2. See Bennett (1977), Chaffee (1975), Devlin (1987), Gronbeck (1978), Hart (1987), Haworth (1929; 1930), Kaid et al. (1974), Kaid and Wadsworth (1986), Kelley (1960), Kessel (1977), McBath and Fisher (1969), O'Keefe (1975), Ragazzini et al. (1985), Riker (1991; 1993), Tulis (1987), and Windt (1986). Among those few studies devoted to the *content* of partisan rhetoric, authors have focused on consensual (nonpartisan) themes of American political culture (Redding 1957; Steele 1957; Steele and Redding 1962) or have maintained such a high level of generality that little can be gleaned about the particular nature of Republican and Democratic ideologies (McDiarmid 1937; Barefield 1966; Namenwirth and Lasswell 1970; Namenwirth and Weber 1987; Smith 1966). Partial exceptions to this general neglect of ideology can be found in Ginsberg (1972), Kelley (1961), Paddock (1982), Page (1978), and Valley (1988).
3. Riker (1991: 225).
4. See, e.g., Alesina and Rosenthal (1995), Budge (1994), Chappell and Keech (1986), Coughlin (1992), Cox (1990), Enelow and Hinich (1990), Hinich and Munger (1994), Ingberman and Villani (1993), Morton (1993), Rabinowitz et al. (1991), and Wittman (1973; 1983), as well as work cited hereafter.
5. Downs (1957: 136, 140).   6. See Downs (1957: ch. 7).
7. Strom's (1990) effort to develop "a unified theory of the organizational and institutional factors that constrain party behavior" demonstrates the immense variety of factors that might (or might not) incline a party to take an ideological approach to electioneering. Such are the limits of grand theory. The difficulties of spatial modeling are discussed in Converse (1966), Page (1978: 18), Sartori (1976: ch. 10), and Green and Shapiro (1994: ch. 7).

Moreover, little is said about what might distinguish the American case from other cases, since the focus of such studies is usually on party behavior *at large*.

In a more empirical vein, political scientists have studied the role of ideology in structuring the vote, in mobilizing political activists, and in creating public policy. They have also studied, ad infinitum, the extent to which the general public is or is not ideological. However, in all these cases the search for generalizable truth has taken precedence over the search for specific, historically contingent truths. Needless to say, empirical work whose purpose is to confirm or disconfirm a general theory tends to examine the historical record in a rather reductionist fashion. Carmines and Stimson state forthrightly, "Our ultimate objective is to develop a general theory of issue evolution, one that is limited neither to the American context nor to any specific political issue."[8] This sort of analysis examines data according to whether they fit or do not fit the theory at hand; further research is irrelevant and actually detracts from the rigorous testing of a hypothesis. The result of this nomothetic genre is description of a rather thin sort. What we learn, for example, from studies of the do-parties-matter variety is that they *do* (or occasionally *don't*); what we don't learn about is the actual content of those ideologies.

The presumed nonideological character of American politics has become something of a self-fulfilling prophecy within the academy. Because it is generally assumed that American politics is driven primarily by organizational and electoral imperatives, little attention has been paid to the content of its ideologies. Lacking such attention from scholars, common wisdom has endured. Here, I will argue that Edmund Burke's notion of party – "a body of men united for promoting by their joint endeavors the national interest upon some particular principle in which they are all agreed" – is in need of resuscitation, if only as a heuristic device.[9] If we do not treat the parties as purposive organizations, we shall never discover what they stand for, or indeed whether they stand for anything at all.

The Importance of Presidential Election Rhetoric

The study of party ideology has also been slighted for the simple reason that American parties are not thought to be terribly ideological, as I discussed in chapter 1. But the source of this long-established predilection is methodologically rooted as well. Many social scientists are con-

8. Carmines and Stimson (1984: 135). See also Ginsberg (1972; 1976), Brady (1988), and other works devoted to testing the theory of realignment (reviewed in chapter 8).
9. Burke (1963: 143).

vinced of the motivating power of values and beliefs in American political life but find these matters difficult to study in a scientifically respectable way. Ideas and ideals are hard to quantify, to explain, or even to classify, and are usually rooted in *particular* times, places, and people. For the theory-building enterprise of social science, ideology has been soggy ground.[10] This brings us to the central preoccupation of this appendix – how to study the content of party ideologies.

Thanks to the work of generations of historians, we now possess an impressive array of studies focused on the major parties. However, general histories of the Republicans and Democrats, although providing extensive chronicles of party life through the decades, do not analyze their respective ideologies.[11] Period-specific studies often explore ideology but do so in disparate ways, rendering their studies incommensurable through time.[12] As illuminating as such studies are, one cannot arrive at a coherent account of each party's ideological development simply by stringing them together. Even within a given period, so much disagreement exists among historians about the ideational character of the parties that "standard" accounts are difficult to construct.

One has only to look at the case of the early-twentieth-century Republicans to appreciate how confusing an issue party ideology can be. Progressive historians, as well as many latter-day commentators, have argued that this was a "party of business," because business leaders were the group that filled the party's coffers, that seemed to account for most

10. See Converse (1964: 206).

11. See Chambers (1964), Goldman (1979; 1986), and Rutland (1979) on the Democrats, and Mayer (1967) and Moos (1956) on the Republicans. Histories covering *both* major parties are slightly more satisfying in this regard. See Bailey (1968), Ladd (1970), Polakoff (1981), Reichley (1992), and Sundquist (1983).

12. For work on the Jeffersonian era, see Banning (1978), Buel (1972), Chambers (1963), Charles (1956), Cunningham (1963; 1957), and Hoadley (1986). On the Jacksonian era, see Ashworth (1983/1987), Brown (1985), Ershkowitz and Shade (1971), Kohl (1989), Latner (1975), McCormick (1966), Meyers (1957/1960), Schlesinger (1945), Shade (1981), Silbey (1985), Watson (1990), Welter (1975), and Wilentz (1982). On the mid-century parties, see Baker (1983), Foner (1970), Gienapp (1987), Holt (1978), and Silbey (1967a; 1967b; 1977; 1991). On the Gilded Age, see De Santis (1963), Dobson (1972), Gould (1970), Jensen (1971), Keller (1977), Kelley (1969), Kleppner (1970; 1979), Morgan (1973), Shade (1981), Silbey (1967a; 1967b; 1977) and Williams (1970). On the Progressive era, see Broesamle (1974), Gould (1974), Harbaugh (1973), Kleppner (1987), and Sarasohn (1989). On the 1920s, see Burner (1967) and Weed (1994). On the New Deal era, see Fraser and Gerstle (1989), Garson (1974), Mayer (1973), and Milkis (1993). On the postwar period, see Fraser and Gerstle (1989), Himmelstein (1990), Huebner (1973), Parmet (1976), Rae (1989), Reinhard (1983), Ross (1973), and Wade (1973). For work on all periods, see Kovler (1992) and bibliographies by ABC-Clio Information Services (1984) and Wynar (1969).

of its legislative agenda, and that benefited from its policies.[13] Others have countered that early twentieth-century Republicans are more aptly characterized as a party of "social harmony," which sought to de-emphasize religious and ethnic issues in favor of a nationalist ideology focused on the holy grail of prosperity.[14] A third interpretation rests upon an evaluation of factional disputes within the party. In this narrative, the progressive west tugs away at the eastern bastions of finance, producing a party with no ideological core at all.[15] Another set of political historians has sought to account for the nature of the party by looking at its leadership – Hanna, McKinley, Theodore Roosevelt, and so forth. Last, some commentators have viewed the turn-of-the-century party as a continuation of the great Republican patronage machine of the previous century. From this perspective, all ideology was bunk, and the party's primary mission was the distribution of the spoils of office.

Evidently, party ideology is a pliable concept, one amenable to a great variety of historical reconstructions. How is one to determine what a party's position is? How is one to measure the *degree* of each party's support? If two parties disagree, how would one measure the distance separating their positions? What constitutes an issue or issue-dimension, and how much weight should one assign to each dimension? I certainly cannot claim to have resolved such problems of definition and opera-tionalization. (Like most definitional problems, they are likely to persist indefinitely.) However, many of the difficulties inherent in the project of analyzing ideology stem from a lack of indicators that are comparable across parties and through time. Presidential election rhetoric is admi-rably suited to overcome these difficulties.

True, electioneering practices have changed considerably since the early nineteenth century. Radio and television have displaced the influ-ence of print journalism; political consultants and the candidates them-selves have displaced party organizations; campaign events are now staged to an extent unimaginable even to the most media-savvy nine-teenth-century party managers; speeches are generally shorter and are delivered by the candidates themselves, rather than by state party lead-ers; campaign advertising, although never absent from presidential cam-paigning, has increased in significance vis-à-vis speeches and public demonstrations.[16] Yet, despite the continual evolution of strategy and

13. See, e.g., Burnham (1981), Josephson (1940), Ladd (1970), and Harbaugh (1973: 2072–73). Burnham's formulation for the Republican party is "the political agent of the new industrial-capitalist dispensation" (1981: 166).
14. See Kleppner (1981a: 102).   15. See, e.g., Gould (1974) and Hays (1957).
16. For histories of campaigning, see Dinkin (1989), Jamieson (1984), Schlesinger (1971), and Troy (1991).

technology, there is no reason to suppose that the campaign speeches and party platforms of today are any less representative of the views of national party elites than they were in the 1830s. Campaign advertising, according to one scholar, "is rarely anything but a digest of the speeches being delivered throughout the country. . . . Contrary to popular belief, the speech remains the staple of paid political broadcasting."[17] Indeed, parties still haggle over their platforms, and party spokespersons are still forced into the same grueling schedule of speech making that has been the centerpiece of the presidential election since the rise of competitive party politics. Consequently, speakers are placed in the same essential rhetorical framework that their forebears encountered, albeit with the aid of teleprompters, cameras, and loudspeakers, and in the presence of a large secondary audience.

Where to Begin

An older view locates the birth of the American parties in the decade of the 1790s, when supporters of Adams and Jefferson jousted over economic policy, foreign policy, constitutional rights, and the purview of the federal government. The campaign of 1800 was not only the first contested election in American history but also one of the most hotly contested. For a moment, lines appeared to be drawn clearly and deeply. It is easy to understand why many historians identified 1800 as the point of origin in American party development.[18]

Recent scholarship has pointed out, however, that partisanship died out rather quickly after this climactic battle. With each passing election, the Federalist grouping looked more anemic and the Jeffersonian-Republicans more hegemonic. Party competition, and with it most signs of party organization, dried up in all but a few states. Thus, from 1804 to 1820, the presidential election served as an occasion for popular ratification of decisions taken earlier by political elites; those nominated by the infamous "congressional caucus" were destined to be chosen in the electoral college. The electoral college itself was still chosen by state legislatures in many states, and rights of suffrage varied a good deal from region to region. Subpresidential elections tended to be based on personal ties rather than abstract ideologies. This was an age of "deferential" politics, according to one scholar, an age in which it was not

17. Jamieson (1984: 450–51).
18. See Bryce (1891), Buel (1972), Chambers (1963), Charles (1956), Cunningham (1957), Ford (1898/1967), Hoadley (1986), and Merriam (1922).

necessary to form cohesive ties either within legislatures or within the general electorate.[19] (Even in 1824, when the outcome remained in question, there was little active campaigning on behalf of the four candidates.)

Most scholars now date the birth of the American parties somewhere in the 1830s. The starting point for this study, 1828, was the first in a series of party-building elections. It was the first election since 1800 to warrant extensive, nationally coordinated campaigning; it marked the victory of Andrew Jackson and the inauguration of a new set of economic policies; it was heralded (and feared) as a turning point in the life of the republic; and subsequent policy programs tended to mirror those put forth by Jackson and Adams enthusiasts. Thus, for reasons of popular acclaim and historical rupture, 1828 seems as good a place as any to begin a history of the American parties.

To be sure, party labels still varied from state to state in this period. Backers of Adams in 1828 and Clay in 1832 were usually known as National Republicans; supporters of Jackson referred to themselves as Democratic-Republicans or simply Jacksonians. By 1836, however, the terms *Whig* and *Democrat* were fairly well established. Given the impressive continuity of persons and programs during this period of party formation, it seemed appopriate to impose these labels upon earlier ventures. Thus, *Whig* refers to the National-Republican campaigns, and *Democrat* to the Democratic-Republican campaigns.

Texts and Sources

Finding texts to represent the ideologies of these parties is a more complicated matter. Prior to 1876, only a few presidential nominees addressed the American public during the course of the general election: William H. Harrison in 1840, Winfield Scott in 1852, Stephen Douglas in 1860, Horatio Seymour in 1868, and Horace Greeley in 1872. All, with the exception of Harrison, were unsuccessful. After 1876, presidential nominees were more voluble but still did not formally "campaign," restricting their remarks to nonpolitical themes and remaining in one location (at home or at the White House). Because presidential candidates themselves held aloof from the hustings, it was necessary to draw on a wide range of partisan rhetoric to represent the parties' views during the nineteenth century. My canvass included all speeches, letters, and government documents authored by the presidential candidate

19. See Formisano (1974), as well as Sharp (1993) and Silbey (1991).

whenever it could be inferred that such texts formed a part of that party's presidential campaign effort.[20] The bulk of each party's campaign activities in this period, however, was assumed by other party notables – typically, the vice presidential nominee, state party leaders, and prominent members of Congress – as well as by anonymous organs of the national party committee, state committees, congressional committees, and affiliated party presses.

In the twentieth century, the candidates themselves became the central spokesmen for each party's campaign. (The 1900 Republican campaign, dominated by the young vice presidential nominee, Theodore Roosevelt, was the last campaign of either party in which the presidential candidate did *not* stand center stage.) In this period, therefore, texts used for this study were restricted to the party platform and speeches given by the presidential nominees themselves (after their official nomination).

Thus, the empirical evidence of this study consists of official party platforms as well as an extensive collection of campaign speeches, letters, and other publications issued by the Whig, Republican, and Democratic parties. A total of roughly two thousand texts were consulted – an average of twenty-four texts per party per election from 1828 to 1992.[21] (As of this printing, a complete list of primary sources can be found

20. Although many of these texts were reprints of earlier communications by the candidate, I have considered not their year of origin but rather their role in a particular election to be of primary importance. The wide circulation of these pamphlets and frequent references made to them attest to their significance as partisan documents, regardless of the time and circumstance of their original publication.

21. Quantitative studies of party ideology have usually relied upon the party platform as their principal source of evidence. However, a quick perusal of party platforms in the nineteenth century ought to engender some skepticism with respect to studies based exclusively on this approach. First, from the 1840s to the 1890s, platforms were extraordinarily brief, comprising fewer than thirty clauses (in all cases but one), and often fewer than ten. Many points relevant to the campaign and to the party's general political philosophy were necessarily excluded from such brief statements of purpose. Second, the rhetorical task of a platform is to set forth the party's position on specific issues, and only secondarily to express its general philosophy of government and politics. If one is looking for the ideas that inform a party's electoral mission – the reasoning that connects its various issue-positions – the platform often turns out to be a rather bland and unrevealing source. Throughout most of American history, party platforms have been written in a highly elevated and remarkably terse prose style. Multiple-clause sentences, coupled with the "resolution" format, lead to a different rhetorical focus than is found in normal speech or in other forms of address. Platforms, in sum, should be considered as only one part of a party's total propagandistic effort in a given campaign. In any case, we have every reason to expect a high level of correspondence between the platform and subsequent campaign statements, a matter researched by Kelly Patterson (1996: 45).

on the World Wide Web at http://www.bu.edu/POLISCI/JGERRING/
PartyIdeol.html.)

These materials were drawn from primary sources of several basic
sorts. Newspapers turned out to be by far the most important source of
documentation through the 1940s, when the tradition of reprinting political speeches was abandoned. During the late nineteenth and early
twentieth centuries, the *New York Times* included campaign speeches
emanating from both parties. For earlier periods, I consulted the *Washington Globe*, the *New York Tribune*, the *New York Evening Post*, and
various newspapers or newsletters published for the duration of a single
campaign (e.g., the *Log Cabin* in 1840).

From the mid-nineteenth century to the mid-twentieth, parties produced lengthy accounts of their national conventions (often called "text
books"), including speeches by party notables and the official letter of
acceptance. Every campaign had its official biography of the standard-
bearer, which was often more in the nature of a scrapbook – including
speeches delivered by the candidate during his political career, testimo-
nials to his virtue from prominent politicians, and various assorted campaign memorabilia. (Not all of these items, of course, were relevant to
the present study.) Occasionally, one finds books that collected the
speeches given by a candidate during his presidential election (more common in the twentieth century than the nineteenth). Incumbent presidents
running for reelection were tailed by official recorders, who, after Hoover, reprinted the president's words in *Public Papers of the Presidents*.
For nonincumbents and incumbents running before Hoover, manuscript
collections devoted to each president (on microfilm) often proved useful.
For the most recent elections (1992 and 1996), virtually all speeches
given by each major-party candidate have been entered into computer
databases run by various news services (CNN, Federal News Service,
and so forth). Finally, there are a few well-known and widely available
compilations of campaign addresses that cover the history of presidential
elections.[22] Wherever possible, I have tried to reference better-known and
more easily accessible sources.

Content Analysis

One way of integrating the prodigious quantity of campaign material
produced by the parties during forty-two elections, without subsiding
entirely into the anecdotal, is through quantitative analysis. This re-

22. See, e.g., Schlesinger (1971) and Bush (1985).

quires, to begin with, the identification of a relatively small group of key texts – texts that can be considered reasonably representative of the themes and issues of the parties' campaign efforts in each presidential election.

Party platforms were an obvious inclusion. Official national platforms, however, were not issued until the 1840s (1840 and 1844 for the Democrats and Whigs, respectively), well after the critical period of party formation. To extend the analysis back to 1828, I reviewed the most widely distributed material issued by the party organizations, selecting the text that seems to have been the most authoritative statement of the party's issue-positions during that campaign.[23]

Campaign acceptance addresses were also subjected to content analysis. In the nineteenth century, these speeches (or letters of acceptance) constituted the main form of communication from the candidate to the general electorate during the general election.[24] Given at the beginning of the formal campaign, acceptance addresses were reprinted in the party's literature and formed the basis of the candidate's (or surrogate campaigner's) stock speech in the subsequent months.[25] It remains today the single most authoritative piece of campaign literature produced by the party, with the exception of the platform itself. Unfortunately, formal acceptance addresses, like party platforms, did not become standard practice until the mid-nineteenth century, and for some time thereafter they consisted simply of terse affirmations of the candidate's fidelity to party principles and to republican values. Hence, prior to 1876, recourse to other texts was often necessary.[26]

23. Preference was given to those open letters or declarations which were most comprehensive (addressing issues of contemporary importance), most representative of that year's campaign efforts, and most authoritative in source (preferably issuing from a national convention or the convention of an influential state, like New York). I also relied on secondary accounts to identify which texts were most significant in the prosecution of each party's campaign. These protoplatforms, in any case, constitute only a small fraction of the total number of platforms analyzed (seven out of eighty-four), so any deviations thereby introduced should not be so great as to prejudice the overall results.

24. In those cases in which candidates produced both a letter and a public speech accepting the nomination, I have used the longer document (hence, the one that took more explicit positions on a wider range of issues).

25. In the nineteenth century, the formal acceptance letter generally did not follow closely on the heels of the convention. Sometimes the party was obliged to wait several months for the arrival of a written confirmation of its candidate's political views.

26. These other texts were selected as follows: (1) If the presidential candidate issued another speech or open letter that set forth his positions on the issues of the day (the functional equivalent, therefore, of the acceptance address), this statement was added to the terse acceptance address or (if no such address existed) substituted for it; (2)

In constructing content analysis categories, I tried to identify those subjects explicitly identified by the parties (in plank headings and textual theme repetition), those revealing interparty differences or intraparty changes over time, and those which would test specific hypotheses about the parties' ideologies in different historical periods. Coding categories were thus developed in interaction with primary material and prior research, for the purpose of developing useful empirical generalizations about party differences and party change.

Nonquantitative Analysis

I should stress that the conclusions reached in this study do not rest solely on that which can conveniently be counted. Despite the care that has been taken in selecting texts and in developing categories of analysis, it would be unrealistic to expect content analysis to bear the entire burden of analysis on a subject as vast and complex as party ideology. To begin with, one would be forced to scale back the quantity of evidence examined in a fairly drastic fashion – from approximately 2,000 texts consulted in this study to 164 platforms and acceptance addresses. Second, and perhaps more significantly, content analysis is somewhat less scientific than it appears. Since the meaning of terms is not static or univocal, words do not fall automatically within content analysis categories. The purpose of antitrust legislation for early Republicans, for example, was to punish violators of the law within the business community. In the contemporary period, by contrast, antitrust has become a policy intended to guarantee the freedom of the small business person from the oppressions of monopoly. The American business class is, in the first case, identified as the opponent, and, in the second case, as the primary beneficiary of antitrust legislation. There is, in short, no such thing as a simple, isolated policy position. Issues are embedded in specific

If no reasonably comprehensive statement from the presidential nominee was forthcoming, the vice presidential candidate's acceptance address or major policy statement was substituted; (3) In several cases, neither of the two ordained representatives of the party made his position known to the electorate, and it was therefore necessary to select an unofficial spokesman for the party during that campaign. Primary attention was given to finding spokespersons who were prominent within the party within that particular election, and whose speech addressed general issues facing the party (rather than being narrowly focused on a single issue or a local set of issues). However, with a few exceptions limited to the 1828–1872 period, the texts labeled "acceptance address" in the appendixes at http://www.bu.edu/POLISCI/JGERRING/PartyIdeol.html (as of this printing) refer to the acceptance speech or letter of each major party's presidential nominee.

political and historical contexts and gain meaning only when properly contextualized.

What did the infamous 1896 battle of Gold versus Silver mean? *All* coding categories are abstractions ("statism," "individualism," etc.), provided by the coder with a particular purpose in mind. Differently constructed, these categories would tell somewhat different stories. Try as one might, one cannot escape the interpretive nature of any study of ideology. Judgments about an ideology's coherence, differentiation, and stability are necessarily judgments of degree. How long, for example, must an ideology remain stable? How stable must it remain? How, precisely, does one tell when an ideology has changed? Such questions are intrinsic to the subject matter. To make claims about party ideologies, one must involve oneself in the meat and gristle of political life, which is to say, in language. Language constitutes the raw data of most studies of how people think about politics, for it is through language that politics is experienced. This does not mean that one must accept the participants' own interpretations of political affairs; it means, rather, that the writer's interpretation must make sense of the text left us by the participants. For present purposes, words speak louder than actions, because they more effectively reveal what those actions *meant* to the participants.

This study takes what might be called a hands-on approach to language. Generalizations are grounded, as much as possible, in copious quotations from the principals. At times, this may seem laborious. However, the inclusion of actual language in a rhetoric-centered study should be seen as equivalent to the inclusion of raw data in a quantitative study; both allow the reader to evaluate the evidence without relying entirely on the author's own authority. It also provides a depth otherwise lacking in discussions of abstract concepts and content-analysis statistics.

Selected Bibliography

ABC-Clio Information Services. 1984. *The Democratic and Republican Parties in America: A Historical Bibliography*. Santa Barbara, CA: ABC-Clio Information Services.

Adams, John Quincy. 1825/1941. *Parties in the United States*. New York: Greenbert.

Address of the National Democratic Party Convention to the People of the United States. 1840. Baltimore, MD: Democratic Party (May 5).

Address of the National Democratic Republican Committee. 1848? Washington, DC: National Democratic Republican Committee.

Address of the Republican General Committee of Young Men of the City and County of New York. 1828. New York: Alexander Ming.

Address of the State Convention. 1828? NJ: Democratic Party, New Jersey.

An Address to the People of the United States, on the Subject of the Presidential Election. 1832. Washington, DC: [National-Republican party].

Aldrich, John H. 1995. *Why Parties? The Origin and Transformation of Party Politics in America*. Chicago: University of Chicago Press.

Alesina, Alberto and Howard Rosenthal. 1995. *Partisan Politics, Divided Government, and the Economy*. Cambridge: Cambridge University Press.

Alexander, Thomas B. 1967. *Sectional Stress and Party Strength: A Study of Roll-Call Voting Patterns in the United States House of Representatives, 1836–1860*. Nashville: Vanderbilt University Press.

Allowances and Extra Pay, a Plain Statement of Facts from the Record. N.d. National and Jackson Democratic Association Committee.

American Political Science Association. 1950. *Toward a More Responsible Two-Party System*. New York: Rinehart.

Anton, Thomas J. 1969. "Policy-making and Political Culture in Sweden." *Scandinavian Political Studies* 4, 88–102.

Appleby, Joyce. 1992. *Liberalism and Republicanism in the Historical Imagination*. Cambridge: Harvard University Press.

Argersinger, Peter H. and John W. Jeffries. 1986. "American Electoral History: Party Systems and Voting Behavior." *Research in Micropolitics* 1.

Arieli, Yehoshua. 1964. *Individualism and Nationalism in American Ideology*. Baltimore: Penguin.

Arnold, R. Douglas. 1990. *The Logic of Congressional Action.* New Haven: Yale University Press.

Arter, David. 1984. *The Nordic Parliaments.* New York: St. Martin's.

Asard, Erik and W. Lance Bennett. 1997. *Democracy and the Marketplace of Ideas: Communication and Government in Sweden and the United States.* Cambridge: Cambridge University Press.

Ashworth, John. 1983/1987. *"Agrarians" and "Aristocrats": Party Political Ideology in the United States, 1837–1846.* Cambridge: Cambridge University Press.

Baer, Denise L. and David A. Bositis. 1988. *Elite Cadres and Party Coalitions: Representing the Public in Party Politics.* New York: Greenwood Press.

Bagehot, Walter. 1867/1963. *The English Constitution.* Ithaca: Cornell University Press.

Bailey, Thomas A. 1968. *Democrats vs. Republicans: The Continuing Clash.* New York: Meredith.

Bailyn, Bernard. 1967. *The Ideological Origins of the American Revolution.* Cambridge: The Belknap Press of Harvard University Press.

   1968. *The Origins of American Politics.* New York: Vintage Books.

Baker, Jean H. 1983. *Affairs of Party: The Political Culture of Northern Democrats in the Mid-Nineteenth Century.* Ithaca: Cornell University Press.

Banning, Lance. 1978. *The Jeffersonian Persuasion: Evolution of a Party Ideology.* Ithaca: Cornell University Press.

Barefield, Paul Acton. 1966. *A Rhetorical Analysis of Keynote Speaking in Republican National Conventions from 1956 to 1964.* Baton Rouge: Louisiana State University Press.

Barnes, John. 1994. "Ideology and Factions." In Anthony Seldon and Stuart Ball (eds), *Conservative Century: The Conservative Party since 1900.* Oxford: Oxford University Press.

Barone, Michael. 1990. *Our Country: The Shaping of America from Roosevelt to Reagan.* New York: The Free Press.

Bartolini, Stefano and Peter Mair. 1990. *Identity, Competition, and Electoral Availability: The Stabilisation of European Electorates, 1885–1985.* Cambridge: Cambridge University Press.

Bauer, Raymond A., Ithiel de Sola Pool, and Lewis Anthony Dexter. 1963/1972. *American Business and Public Policy: The Politics of Foreign Trade.* Chicago: Aldine/Atherton.

Beard, Charles. 1929. *The American Party Battle.* New York: The Macmillan Company.

Beattie, Alan (ed). 1970. *English Party Politics. Volume 1: 1600–1906.* London: Weidenfeld and Nicolson.

Beer, Samuel H. 1965. "Liberalism and the National Idea." In Robert A. Goldwin (ed), *Left, Right and Center: Essays on Liberalism and Conservatism in the U.S.* Chicago: Rand McNally.

   1969. *British Politics in the Collectivist Age.* New York: Vintage Books.

Bell, D. S. and Byron Criddle. 1984. *The French Socialist Party: Resurgence and Victory.* Oxford: Clarendon Press.

Bellah, Robert N. 1967. "Civil Religion in America." *Daedalus* (Winter). Reprinted in Russell E. Richey and Donald G. Jones (eds), *American Civil Religion*. New York: Harper & Row, 1974, 21–45.

Belloni, Frank P. and Dennis C. Beller (eds). 1978. *Faction Politics: Political Parties and Factionalism in Comparative Perspective*. Santa Barbara: ABC-Clio Press.

Bennett, W. Lance. 1977. "The Ritualistic and Pragmatic Bases of Political Campaign Discourse." *Quarterly Journal of Speech* 63 (October).

Bensel, Richard Franklin. 1984. *Sectionalism and American Political Development, 1880–1980*. Madison: University of Wisconsin Press.

   1990. *Yankee Leviathan: The Origins of Central State Authority in America, 1859–1877*. Cambridge: Cambridge University Press.

Benson, Lee. 1961. *The Concept of Jacksonian Democracy: New York as a Test Case*. Princeton: Princeton University Press.

Bentley, Arthur. 1908/1967. *The Process of Government*. Cambridge: Harvard University Press, The Belknap Press.

Berlin, Isaiah. 1967. "Two Concepts of Liberty." In Anthony Quinton (ed), *Political Philosophy*. Oxford: Oxford University Press, 141–52.

Berrington, Hugh. 1967–68. "Partisaniship and Dissidence in the Nineteenth Century House of Commons." *Parliamentary Affairs* 21, 338–74.

Berry, Jeffrey M. 1996. "The Changing Face of American Liberalism." Paper presented to The Politics of Inequality in the Twentieth Century, conference, Kennedy School of Government, Cambridge, MA (September 28).

Best, Gary Dean. 1975. *The Politics of American Individualism: Herbert Hoover in Transition, 1918–1921*. Westport, CT: Greenwood.

Binkley, Wilfred E. 1943/1945. *American Political Parties: Their Natural History*. 2d ed. New York: Alfred A. Knopf.

Blaine, James G. 1887. *Political Discussions: Legislative, Diplomatic, and Popular, 1856–1886*. Norwich, CT: Henry Bill.

Blais, André, Donald Blake, and Stephane Dion. 1996. "Do Parties Make a Difference? A Reappraisal." *American Journal of Political Science* 40:2 (May), 514–20.

Blau, Joseph L. (ed). 1954. *Social Theories of Jacksonian Democracy*. Indianapolis: Bobbs-Merrill.

Bogdanor, Vernon. 1981. *The People and the Party System: The Referendum and Electoral Reform in British Politics*. Cambridge: Cambridge University Press.

Bond, Jon R. and Richard Fleisher. 1990. *The President in the Legislative Arena*. Chicago: University of Chicago Press.

Boorstin, Daniel. 1953. *The Genius of American Politics*. Chicago: University of Chicago Press.

Borosage, Robert L., Stanley B. Greenberg, Will Marshall, and Mark Penn. 1997. "Why Did Clinton Win?" *American Prospect* 31 (March-April), 13–22.

Bourgin, Frank. 1989. *The Great Challenge: The Myth of Laissez-Faire in the Early Republic*. New York: George Braziller.

Boyd, James P. (ed). 1900. *Men and Issues of 1900: The Vital Questions of the Day.* N.p.

Brady, David W. 1988. *Critical Elections and Congressional Policy Making.* Stanford, CA: Stanford University Press.

Brady, David W. and Charles S. Bullock III. 1985. "Party and Factions within Legislatures." In Gerhard Loewenberg, Samuel C. Patterson, and Malcolm E. Jewell (eds), *Handbook of Legislative Research.* Cambridge: Harvard University Press.

Brennan, Mary C. 1995. *Turning Right in the Sixties: The Conservative Capture of the GOP.* Chapel Hill: University of North Carolina Press.

Bridges, Amy. 1984. *A City in the Republic: Antebellum New York and the Origins of Machine Politics.* Ithaca: Cornell University Press.

Brinkley, Alan. 1983. *Voices of Protest: Huey Long, Father Coughlin, and the Great Depression.* New York: Vintage.

1989. "The New Deal and the Idea of the State." In Steve Fraser and Gary Gerstle (eds), *The Rise and Fall of the New Deal Order, 1930–1980.* Princeton: Princeton University Press, 85–121.

1995. *The End of Reform: New Deal Liberalism in Recession and War.* New York: Vintage.

Broesamle, John J. 1974. "The Democrats from Bryan to Wilson." In Lewis L. Gould (ed), *The Progressive Era.* Syracuse: Syracuse University Press.

Brown, Thomas. 1985. *Politics and Statesmanship: Essays on the American Whig Party.* New York: Columbia University Press.

Brownlow, William G. 1844. *A Political Register, Setting Forth the Principles of the Whig and Locofoco Parties in the United States, with the Life and Public Services of Henry Clay.* Jonesborough, TN: Jonesborough Whig.

Bruce, John M., John A. Clark, and John H. Kessel. 1991. "Advocacy Politics in Presidential Parties." *American Political Science Review* 85:4 (December), 1089–1105.

Bryan, William Jennings. 1896. *The First Battle: A Story of the Campaign of 1896.* Chicago: W. B. Conkey Company.

1900. *The Second Battle; or, The New Declaration of Independence, 1776–1900: An Account of the Struggle of 1900.* Chicago: W. B. Conkey Company.

1913. *Speeches of William Jennings Bryan.* Vol. 2. New York: Funk & Wagnalls Company.

Bryce, James. 1891. *The American Commonwealth.* 2 vols. Chicago: Charles H. Sergel.

Buchanan, James. 1908–09. *The Works of James Buchanan, Comprising His Speeches, State Papers, and Private Correspondence.* Vols. 4, 8. Philadelphia: J. B. Lippincott.

Budge, Ian. 1994. "A New Spatial Theory of Party Competition: Uncertainty, Ideology, and Policy Equilibria Viewed Comparatively and Temporally." *British Journal of Political Science* 24, 443–67.

Budge, Ian, David Robertson, and Derek Hearl. 1987. *Ideology, Strategy, and*

Party Change: Spatial Analyses of Post-War Election Programmes in Nineteen Democracies. Cambridge: Cambridge University Press.

Budge, Ian and Richard I. Hofferbert. 1990. "Mandates and Policy Outputs: U.S. Party Platforms and Federal Expenditures." *American Political Science Review* 84:1 (March), 111–31.

Buel, Richard. 1972. *Securing the Revolution: Ideology in American Politics, 1789–1815.* Ithaca: Cornell University Press.

Burke, Edmund. 1963. *Selected Writings and Speeches,* ed. Peter J. Stanlis. Garden City: Anchor Books.

Burner, David. 1967/1968. *The Politics of Provincialism: The Democratic Party in Transition, 1918–32.* New York: Alfred A. Knopf.

Burnham, Walter Dean. 1970. *Critical Elections and the Mainsprings of American Politics.* New York: W.W. Norton.

  1981. "The System of 1896: An Analysis." In Paul Kleppner et al. (eds), *The Evolution of American Electoral Systems.* Westport, CT: Greenwood Press.

  1986. "Periodization Schemes and 'Party Systems': The 'System of 1896' as a Case in Point." *Social Science History* (Fall), 263–314.

Burns, James McGregor. 1956. *Roosevelt: The Lion and the Fox.* New York: Harcourt Brace.

  1963. *The Deadlock of Democracy.* Englewood Cliffs, NJ: Prentice-Hall.

Bush, Gregory (ed). 1985. *Campaign Speeches of American Presidential Candidates, 1948–1984.* New York: Frederick Ungar.

Calhoun, Charles W. 1996. "Political Economy in the Gilded Age: The Republican Party's Industrial Policy." *Journal of Policy History* 8:3, 291–309.

Cameron, David. 1978. "The Expansion of the Public Economy: A Comparative Analysis." *American Political Science Review* 72: 4, 1243–61.

  1984. "Social Democracy, Corporatism, Labour Quiescence, and the Representation of Economic Interest in Advanced Capitalist Society." In John Goldthorpe (ed), *Order and Conflict in Contemporary Capitalism.* Oxford: Clarendon Press.

Campaign Documents Issued by the Union Republican Congressional Executive Committee. 1872. Washington, DC: Union Republican Congressional Executive Committee.

The Campaign Text Book. 1876. New York: Democratic National Committee.

The Campaign Text Book. 1880. New York: Democratic National Committee.

The Campaign Text Book of the Democratic Party for the Presidential Election of 1892. 1892. New York: Democratic National Committee.

The Campaign Text Book of the Democratic Party of the United States. 1904. New York: Democratic National Committee.

Campbell, Angus, Philip E. Converse, Warren P. Miller, and Donald E. Stokes. 1960. *The American Voter.* New York: John Wiley & Sons.

Campbell, Bruce A. and Richard J. Trilling (eds). 1980. *Realignment in American Politics: Toward a Theory.* Austin: University of Texas Press.

Carmines, Edward G. and James A. Stimson. 1984. "The Dynamics of Issue

Evolution: The United States." In Russell J. Dalton, Scott C. Flanagan, and Paul Allen Beck (eds), *Electoral Change in Advanced Industrial Democracies: Realignment or Dealignment?* Princeton: Princeton University Press.

1989. *Issue Evolution: Race and the Transformation of American Politics.* Princeton: Princeton University Press.

Carr, Clark E. 1909. *Stephen A. Douglas: His Life, Public Services, Speeches, and Patriotism.* Chicago: A. C. McClure.

Carter, Jimmy. 1978. *The Presidential Campaign, 1976.* Vol. 1, Jimmy Carter. Washington, DC: United States Government Printing Office.

1982. *Public Papers of the Presidents of the United States: Jimmy Carter, 1980–81.* Washington, DC: United States Government Printing Office.

Carville, James. 1996. *We're Right, They're Wrong: A Handbook for Spirited Progressives.* New York: Random House.

Cass, Lewis. 1847. *Letter from Hon. Lewis Cass, of Michigan, the War, and the Wilmot Proviso.* Washington, DC: Blair and Rives.

Castles, Francis G. (ed). 1982. *The Impact of Parties.* London: Sage.

Castles, Francis G. and Peter Mair. 1984. "Left-Right Political Scales: Some 'Expert' Judgments." *European Journal of Political Research* 12, 73–88.

Chaffee, Steven H. (ed). 1975. *Political Communication: Issues and Strategies for Research.* Beverly Hills: Sage.

Chambers, William Nisbet. 1963. *Political Parties in a New Nation: The American Experience, 1776–1809.* New York: Oxford University Press.

1964. *The Democrats, 1789–1964: A Short History of a Popular Party.* Princeton: Van Nostrand.

Chappell, Henry W. and William R. Keech. 1986. "Policy Motivation and Party Differences in a Dynamic Spatial Model of Party Competition." *American Political Science Review* 80, 881–900.

Charles, Joseph. 1956. *The Origins of the American Party System.* Williamsburg, VA: Institute of Early American History and Culture.

Charmley, John. 1996. *A History of Conservative Politics, 1900–1996.* New York: St. Martin's Press.

Cherny, R. W. 1981. *Populism, Progressivism, and the Transformation of Nebraska Politics, 1885–1915.* Lincoln: University of Nebraska Press.

Christoph, James B. 1967. "Consensus and Cleavage in British Political Ideology." In Roy C. Macridis (ed), *Political Parties: Contemporary Trends and Ideas.* New York: Harper and Row.

Citrin, Jack and Donald Philip Green. 1990. "The Self-Interest Motive in American Public Opinion." *Research in Micropolitics* 3, 1–28.

Clay, Henry. 1828. *An Address of Henry Clay, to the Public, Containing Certain Testimony in Refutation of the Charges Against Him.* New Brunswick, NJ: D. F. Randolph.

1843. *Life and Speeches of Henry Clay,* Vol 2. New York: Greeley & McElrath.

1988. *The Papers of Henry Clay.* Vol 9. Kentucky: University Press of Kentucky.

Cleveland, Grover. 1892. *The Writings and Speeches of Grover Cleveland,* George F. Parker (ed). New York: Cassell Publishing Company.

    1909. *Letters and Addresses of Grover Cleveland,* Albert Ellery Bergh (ed). New York: The Unit Book Publishing Co.

Clubb, Jerome M. 1981. "Party Coalitions in the Early Twentieth Century." In Seymour Martin Lipset (ed), *Party Coalitions in the 1980s.* San Francisco: Institute for Contemporary Studies.

Clubb, Jerome M. and Santa A. Traugott. 1977. "Partisan Cleavage and Cohesion in the House of Representatives, 1861–1974." *Journal of Interdisciplinary History* 7:3, 375–402.

Clubb, Jerome M., William H. Flanigan, and Nancy H. Zingale. 1980/1990. *Partisan Realignment: Voters, Parties, and Government in American History.* Boulder, CO: Westview Press.

Cole, Alistair M. 1989. "Factionalism, the French Socialist Party, and the Fifth Republic: An Explanation of Intra-Party Divisions." *European Journal of Political Research* 17 (January).

Coletta, Paolo E. 1971. "Election of 1908." In Arthur M. Schlesinger Jr. (ed), *History of American Presidential Elections, 1789–1968.* Vol 3. New York: Chelsea House.

Colton, Calvin (ed). 1844. *Junius Tracts.* New York: Greeley & McElrath.

Conkling, Roscoe. 1880. *Honest Payment of the Public Debt: Which Party Favors It?* Chicago: Illinois Republican State Central Committee.

Converse, Philip E. 1964. "The Nature of Belief Systems in Mass Publics." In David Apter (ed), *Ideology and Discontent.* London: The Free Press of Glencoe.

    1966. "The Problem of Party Distances in Models of Voting Change." In M. Kent Jennings and L. Harmon Zeigler (eds), *The Electoral Process.* Englewood Cliffs, NJ: Prentice-Hall.

    1990. "Popular Representation and the Distribution of Information." In J. H. Ferejohn and J. A. Kuklinski (eds), *Information and Democratic Processes.* Urbana: University of Illinois Press.

Coolidge, Calvin. 1924. *Address of Acceptance, August 14, 1924.* Washington, DC: United States Government Printing Office.

    1926. *Foundations of the Republic: Speeches and Addresses by Calvin Coolidge.* New York: Charles Scribner's Sons.

Cooper, John Milton. 1983. *The Warrior and the Priest: Woodrow Wilson and Theodore Roosevelt.* Cambridge: Harvard University Press.

Cornford, James. 1963. "The Transformation of Conservatism in the Late Nineteenth Century." *Victorian Studies* 7:1 (September), 35–66.

Corrado, Anthony. 1996. "The Politics of Cohesion." In John C. Green and Daniel M. Shea (eds), *The State of the Parties: The Changing Role of Contemporary American Parties,* 2d ed. Lanham, MD: Rowman & Littlefield.

Coughlin, Peter J. 1992. *Probabilistic Voting Theory.* Cambridge: Cambridge University Press.

Cox, Gary W. 1987. *The Efficient Secret: The Cabinet and the Development of*

Political Parties in Victorian England. Cambridge: Cambridge University Press.

1990. "Centripetal and Centrifugal Incentives in Electoral Systems." *American Journal of Political Science* 34, 903–35.

Cox, Gary W. and Mathew D. McCubbins. 1991. "On the Decline of Party Voting in Congress." *Legislative Studies Quarterly* 16:4 (November).

1993. *Legislative Leviathan: Party Government in the House*. Berkeley: University of California Press.

Craig, Douglas B. 1992. *After Wilson: The Struggle for the Democratic Party, 1920–1934*. Chapel Hill: University of North Carolina.

Craig, F. W. S. (ed). 1975. *British General Election Manifestos, 1900–1974*. London: Macmillan.

Crawford, Alan. 1980. *Thunder on the Right*. New York: Pantheon.

Cresswell, Stephen. 1995. *Multiparty Politics in Mississippi, 1877–1902*. Jackson: University of Mississippi Press.

Crewe, Ivor and Donald D. Searing. 1988. "Ideological Change in the British Conservative Party." *American Political Science Review* 82:2.

Croly, Herbert. 1909. *The Promise of American Life*. New York: E. P. Dutton.

Crotty, William. 1991. "Political Parties: Issues and Trends." In William Crotty (ed), *Political Science: Looking to the Future*. Vol. 4, *American Institutions*. Evanston, IL: Northwestern University Press.

Crowley, John E. 1993. *The Privileges of Independence: Neomercantilism and the American Revolution*. Baltimore: Johns Hopkins University Press.

Cunningham, Noble E., Jr. 1957. *The Jeffersonian Republicans: The Formation of Party Organization, 1789–1801*. Chapel Hill: University of North Carolina Press.

1963. *The Jeffersonian Persuasion in Power: Party Operations, 1801–1809*. Chapel Hill: University of North Carolina Press.

Curtis, Gerald L. 1988. *The Japanese Way of Politics*. New York: Columbia University Press.

Cyr, Arthur. 1978. "Cleavages in British Politics." In Frank P. Belloni and Dennis C. Beller (eds), *Faction Politics: Political Parties and Factionalism in Comparative Perspective*. Santa Barbara: ABC-Clio Press.

Dahl, Robert (ed). 1966. *Political Oppositions in Western Democracies*. New Haven: Yale University Press.

Dangerfield, George. 1936. *The Strange Death of Liberal England*. London: Constable & Co.

Danziger, Sheldon and Peter Gottschalk. 1995. *American Unequal*. Cambridge: Harvard University Press.

Davidson, Roger (ed). 1992. *The Postreform Congress*. New York: St. Martin's.

The Democratic Campaign Book, 1924. 1924. Washington, DC: Democratic National Committee/Democratic Congressional Committee.

The Democratic Hand-Book. 1856. Washington, DC: Democratic National Committee.

Democratic Party. 1984. "Party Platform, 1984." *Congressional Quarterly Almanac* 40.

1992. "Party Platform, 1992." *Congressional Quarterly Almanac* 50.

The Democratic Policy and Its Fruits. 1848? Washington, DC: National and Jackson Democratic Association Committee.

The Democratic Text Book. 1848. Boston: Redding.

The Democratic Text Book, 1920. 1920. Democratic National Committee/Democratic Congressional Committee.

Derbyshire, J. Denis and Ian Derbyshire. 1996. *Political Systems of the World.* New York: St. Martin's.

De Santis, Vincent. 1963. "The Republican Party Revisited, 1877–1897." In H. Wayne Morgan (ed), *The Gilded Age: A Reappraisal.* Syracuse: Syracuse University Press.

de Swann, Abram. 1973. *Coalition Theories and Cabinet Formation.* Amsterdam: Elsevier.

Devlin, Patrick (ed). 1987. *Political Persuasion in Presidential Campaigns.* New Brunswick, NJ: Transaction.

Dewey, Thomas E. 1946. *Public Papers of Thomas E. Dewey, Fifty-First Governor of the State of New York: 1944.* Albany: Williams Press.

    1950. *Public Papers of Thomas E. Dewey, Fifty-First Governor of the State of New York: 1948.* Albany: Williams Press.

Diamond, Martin. 1981. *The Founding of the Democratic Republic.* Itasca, IL: F. E. Peacock.

Diggins, John Patrick. 1984. *The Lost Soul of American Politics: Virture, Self-Interest, and the Foundations of Liberalism.* Chicago: University of Chicago Press.

Dinkin, Robert J. 1989. *Campaigning in America: A History of Election Practices.* New York: Greenwood.

Dobson, John M. 1972. *Politics in the Gilded Age: A New Perspective on Reform.* New York: Praeger.

Documents Issued by the Union Republican Congressional Committee. 1877. Washington, DC: Union Republican Congressional Committee.

Documents Issued by the Union Republican Congressional Committee. 1880. Washington, DC: Union Republican Congressional Committee.

Dodd, Lawrence C. 1976. *Coalitions in Parliamentary Government.* Princeton: Princeton University Press.

Downs, Anthony. 1957. *An Economic Theory of Democracy.* New York: Harper & Row.

Drucker, H. M. 1979. *Doctrine and Ethos in the Labour Party.* London: Allen & Unwin.

Dunlavy, Colleen A. 1992. "Political Structure, State Policy, and Industrial Change: Early Railroad Policy in the United States and Prussia." In Sven Steinmo, Kathleen Thelen, and Frank Longstreth (eds), *Structuring Politics: Historical Institutionalism in Comparative Analysis.* Cambridge: Cambridge University Press.

Durr, Robert H., John B. Gilmour, and Christina Wolbrecht. 1997. "Explaining Congressional Approval." *American Journal of Political Science* 41:1 (January).

Duverger, Maurice. 1951/1959. *Political Parties*. New York: Wiley.

Dyson, Kenneth. 1980. *The State Tradition in Western Europe*. New York: Oxford University Press.

Edsall, Thomas Byrne. 1984. *The New Politics of Inequality*. New York: W. W. Norton.

Edsall, Thomas Byrne and Mary D. Edsall. 1992. *Chain Reaction: The Impact of Race, Rights, and Taxes on American Politics*. New York: W. W. Norton.

Edwards, George C., III. 1989. *At the Margins: Presidential Leadership of Congress*. New Haven: Yale University Press.

Eisenhower, Dwight David. 1952. *Campaign Speeches*. Obtained from University of Oregon Library.

    1957. *Public Papers of the Presidents of the United States: Dwight D. Eisenhower, 1956*. Washington, DC: United States Government Printing Office.

    1970. *Selected Speeches of Dwight David Eisenhower, Thirty-Fourth President of the United States*. Washington, DC: United States Government Printing Office.

Ekirch, Arthur A., Jr. 1969. *Ideologies and Utopias: The Impact of the New Deal on American Thought*. Chicago: Quadrangle Books.

Elder, Neil, Alastair H. Thomas, and David Arter. 1982. *The Consensual Democracies? The Government and Politics of the Scandinavian States*. Oxford: Martin Robertson.

Eldersveld, Samuel J. 1964. *Political Parties in American Society*. Chicago: Rand McNally.

    1982. *Political Parties in American Society*. New York: Basic Books.

Elkins, Stanley and Eric McKitrick. 1993. *The Age of Federalism*. New York: Oxford University Press.

Ellis, Richard J. 1992. "Radical Lockeanism in American Political Culture." *Western Political Quarterly* 45.

    1993. *American Political Cultures*. New York: Oxford University Press.

Enelow, James M. and Melvin J. Hinich (eds). 1990. *Advances in the Spatial Theory of Voting*. Cambridge: Cambridge University Press.

Epstein, David and Sharyn O'Halloran. 1996. "The Partisan Paradox and the U.S. Tariff, 1877–1934." *International Organization* 50:2 (Spring), 301–24.

Epstein, Leon D. 1986. *Parties in the American Mold*. Madison: University of Wisconsin Press.

Erickson, Paul D. 1985. *Reagan Speaks: The Making of an American Myth*. New York: New York University Press.

Ershkowitz, Herbert and William G. Shade. 1971. "Consensus or Conflict? Political Behavior in the State Legislatures during the Jacksonian Era." *Journal of American History* 108:3 (December).

Evening Post Documents – No. 10, Speeches Delivered at Tammany Hall. 1852. New York: Evening Post.

Ferguson, Thomas. 1989. "Industrial Conflict and the Coming of the New Deal: The Triumph of Multinational Liberalism in America." In Steve Fraser and Gary Gerstle (eds), *The Rise and Fall of the New Deal Order, 1930–1980*. Princeton: Princeton University Press.

1995. *Golden Rule: The Investment Theory of Party Competition and the Logic of Money- Driven Political Systems*. Chicago: University of Chicago Press.

Ferguson, Thomas and Joel Rogers. 1986. *Right Turn: The Decline of the Democrats and the Future of American Politics*. New York: Hill and Wang.

Fine, Sidney. 1956. *Laissez Faire and the General-Welfare State*. Ann Arbor: University of Michigan Press.

Finer, S. E. (ed). 1975. *Adversary Politics and Electoral Reform*. London: Anthony Wigram.

Fischer, David Hackett. 1965. *The Revolution of American Conservatism: The Federalist Party in the Era of Jeffersonian Democracy*. New York: Harper & Row.

Fishel, Jeff. 1985. *Presidents and Promises: From Campaign Pledge to Presidential Performance*. Washington, DC: Congressional Quarterly.

Flint, H. M. 1860. *Life of Stephen A. Douglas. . . .* New York: Derby & Jackson.

Foner, Eric. 1970. *Free Soil, Free Labor, Free Men: The Ideology of the Republican Party before the Civil War*. London: Oxford University Press.

1980. *Politics and Ideology in the Age of the Civil War*. New York: Oxford University Press.

1984. "Why Is There No Socialism in the United States?" *History Workshop* 17 (Spring), 57–80.

Ford, Gerald R. 1979a. *The Presidential Campaign, 1976*. Vol. 2, *Gerald R. Ford*. Washington, DC: United States Government Printing Office.

1979b. *Public Papers of the Presidents of the United States: Gerald R. Ford, 1976–77*. Washington, DC: United States Government Printing Office.

Ford, Henry Jones. 1898/1967. *The Rise and Growth of American Politics*. New York: Da Capo.

Formisano, Ronald P. 1971. *The Birth of Mass Political Parties: Michigan, 1827–1861*. Princeton: Princeton University Press.

1974. "Deferential-Participant Politics: The Early Republic's Political Culture, 1789–1840." *American Journal of Political Science* 68.

1983. *The Transformation of Political Culture: Massachusetts Parties, 1790s–1840s*. New York: Oxford University Press.

Fraser, Steve and Gary Gerstle (eds). 1989. *The Rise and Fall of the New Deal Order, 1930–1980*. Princeton: Princeton University Press.

Gallagher, Michael and Michael Marsh (eds). 1988. *Candidate Selection in Comparative Perspective: The Secret Garden of Politics*. London: Sage.

Garfield, James A. n.d. *The Life and Work of James A. Garfield*, ed. John Clark Ridpath. Cincinnati: Jones Brothers & Company.

Garson, Robert. 1974. *The Democratic Party and the Politics of Sectionalism, 1941–1948*. Baton Rouge: Louisiana State University Press.

Geer, John G. 1991. "Critical Realignments and the Public Opinion Poll." *Journal of Politics* 53, 435–51.

1996. *From Tea Leaves to Opinion Polls: A Theory of Democratic Leadership*. New York: Columbia University Press.

Gerring, John. 1996. "Culture versus Politics: A Split-level View of American Politics." Paper presented at a conference entitled "The Politics of Economic Inequality in the Twentieth Century," Kennedy School of Government, Harvard University, Boston MA (September 28).

1997. "Ideology: A Definitional Analysis." *Political Research Quarterly* 50: 4 (December), 957–94.

Forthcoming. "Does Ideology Matter? A Roll-Call Analysis of Key Congressional Votes, 1834–1992."

Gienapp, William. 1987. *The Origins of the Republican Party, 1852–56*. New York: Oxford University Press.

1994. "The Myth of Class in Jacksonian America." *Journal of Policy History* 6:2.

Gilpin, Robert. 1987. *The Political Economy of International Relations*. Princeton: Princeton University Press.

Ginsberg, Benjamin. 1972. "Critical Elections and the Substance of Party Conflict: 1844–1968." *Midwest Journal of Political Science* 16:4 (November), 603–25.

1976. "Elections and Public Policy." *American Political Science Review* 70 (March), 41–49.

Gitlin, Todd. 1980. *The Whole World Is Watching: Mass Media in the Making and Unmaking of the New Left*. Berkeley: University of California Press.

Glickman, H. 1961. "The Toryness of English Conservatism." *Journal of British Studies* 1, 111–43.

Gold, Howard Jonah. 1989. *Hollow Mandates: American Public Opinion and the Conservative Shift*. Yale University Press.

Goldman, Eric F. 1977. *Rendezvous with Destiny: A History of Modern American Reform*. New York: Vintage Books.

Goldman, Ralph M. 1979. *Search for Consensus: The Story of the Democratic Party*. Philadelphia: Temple University Press.

1986. *Dilemma and Destiny: The Democratic Party in America*. Lanham, MD: Madison Books.

1990. *The National Party Chairmen and Committees: Factionalism at the Top*. Armonk, NY: M. E. Sharpe.

Gould, Lewis L. 1970. "The Republican Search for a National Majority." In H. Wayne Morgan (ed), *The Gilded Age*. Rev. ed. Syracuse: Syracuse University Press.

1974. "The Republicans under Roosevelt and Taft." In Lewis L. Gould (ed), *The Progressive Era*. Syracuse: Syracuse University Press.

1978. *Reform and Regulation: American Politics, 1900–1916*. New York: Wiley.

Granberg, Donald and Soren Holmberg. 1988. *The Political System Matters: Social Psychology and Voting Behavior in Sweden and the United States*. Cambridge: Cambridge University Press.

Grant, Ulysses S. 1880. *General Grant's Speech at Warren, Ohio*. Chicago: Illinois Republican State Central Committee.

Green, Donald P. and Ian Shapiro. 1994. *Pathologies of Rational Choice Theory: A Critique of Applications in Political Science*. New Haven: Yale University Press.

Greene, Julie. 1996. "The Making of Labor's Democracy: William Jennings Bryan, the American Federation of Labor, and Progressive Era Politics." *Nebraska History* 77:3–4 (Fall/Winter), 149–58.

In press. *Pure and Simple Politics: The American Federation of Labor, 1881 to 1917*. Cambridge: Cambridge University Press.

Greenstone, J. David. 1977. *Labor in American Politics*. Chicago: University of Chicago Press.

Grimes, Alan P. 1962. "Contemporary American Liberalism." *Annals of the American Academy of Political and Social Science* 344 (November).

Gronbeck, Bruce E. 1978. "The Functions of Presidential Campaigns." *Communications Monographs* 45.

Hamilton, Alexander, et al. 1961. *The Federalist Papers*. New York: New American Library.

Hand-Book of the Democracy for 1863 and '64. 1864. N.p.: Democratic Party, Democratic National Committee.

Handlin, Oscar and Mary Flug Handlin. 1947. *Commonwealth: A Study of the Role of Government in the American Economy: Massachusetts, 1774–1861*. New York: New York University Press.

Hanson, Russell. 1985. *The Democratic Imagination in America*. Princeton: Princeton University Press.

Harbaugh, William H. 1973. "The Republican Party, 1893–1932." In Arthur M. Schlesinger Jr. (ed), *History of U.S. Political Parties*. Vol. 3. New York: Chelsea House.

Harding, Warren G. 1920a. *Rededicating America: Life and Recent Speeches of Warren G. Harding*, ed. Frederick E. Schortemeier. Indianapolis: Bobbs-Merrill.

1920b. *Speeches of Senator Warren G. Harding of Ohio, Republican Candidate for President, from His Acceptance of the Nomination to October 1, 1920*. N.p.: Republican National Committee.

Harmel, Robert and Kenneth Janda. 1994. "An Integrated Theory of Party Goals and Party Change." *Journal of Theoretical Politics* 6:3, 259–87.

Harrington, Michael. 1972. *Socialism*. New York: Bantam Books.

Harris, Leon. 1966. *The Fine Art of Political Wit*. New York: E. P. Dutton.

Harrison, Benjamin. 1892. *Speeches of Benjamin Harrison*, ed. Charles Hedges. New York: United States Book Company.

Hart, David M. 1998. *Forging the "Postwar Consensus": Science, Technology, and Economic Policy, 1921–1953*. Princeton: Princeton University Press.

Hart, Roderick P. 1987. *The Sound of Leadership: Presidential Communication in the Modern Age*. Chicago: University of Chicago.

Hartz, Louis. 1948. *Economic Policy and Democratic Thought: Pennsylvania, 1776–1860*. Cambridge: Harvard University Press.

1955. *The Liberal Tradition in America*. New York: Harcourt, Brace & World.

Hattam, Victoria. 1990. "Economic Visions and Political Strategies: American

Labor and the State, 1865–1896." *Studies in American Political Development* 4, 82–129.

1993. *Labor Visions and State Power: The Origins of Business Unionism in the United States*. Princeton: Princeton University Press.

Hawley, Ellis W. 1966. *The New Deal and the Problem of Monopoly*. Princeton: Princeton University Press.

(ed) 1981. *Herbert Hoover as Secretary of Commerce: Studies in New Era Thought and Practice*. Iowa City: Iowa University Press.

Haworth, Donald. 1929. *An Analysis of Speeches in Presidential Campaigns from 1884 to 1920*. Madison: University of Wisconsin Press.

1930. "An Analysis of Speeches in the Presidential Campaigns from 1884–1920." *Quarterly Journal of Speech* 16, 35–42.

Hays, Samuel P. 1957. *The Response to Industrialism, 1885–1914*. Chicago: University of Chicago Press.

1967. "Political Parties and the Community-Society Continuum." In William Nisbet Chambers and Walter Dean Burnham (eds), *The American Party Systems: Stages of Political Development*. New York: Oxford University Press.

Heclo, Hugh. 1994. "Poverty Politics." In Sheldon H. Danziger, Gary D. Sandefur, and Daniel H. Weinberg (eds), *Confronting Poverty: Prescriptions for Change*. Cambridge: Harvard University Press.

Heclo, Hugh and Henrik Madsen. 1987. *Policy and Politics in Sweden: Principled Pragmatism*. Philadelphia: Temple University Press.

Heffer, Jean and Jeanine Rovet (eds). 1988. *Why is there no socialism in the United States?/pourquoi n'y a-t-il pas de socialisme aux Etats-Unis?* Paris: Editions de l'Ecole des Hautes Etudes en Science Sociales.

Heidenheimer, Arnold, Michael Johnston, and Victor T. LeVine (eds). 1989. *Political Corruption: A Handbook*. New Brunswick: Transaction.

Henning, Charles. 1989. *The Wit and Wisdom of Politics*. Golden, CO: Fulcrum.

Herbst, Susan. 1993. *Numbered Voices: How Opinion Polling Has Shaped American Politics*. Chicago: University of Chicago Press.

Hermens, F. A. 1941. *Democracy or Anarchy?* Notre Dame, IN: University of Notre Dame Press.

Herring, Pendleton. 1940/1965. *The Politics of Democracy: American Parties in Action*. New York: W. W. Norton & Co.

Herrnson, Paul S. 1988. *Party Campaigning in the 1980s*. Cambridge: Harvard University Press.

Hibbs, Douglas. 1977. "Political Parties and Macroeconomic Policy." *American Political Science Review* 60: 1467–87.

Hicks, Alexander M. and Duane H. Swank. 1992. "Politics, Institutions, and Welfare Spending in Industrialized Democracies, 1960–82." *American Political Science Review* 86:3 (September), 658–74.

Hicks, John D. 1960. *Republican Ascendancy, 1921–1933*. New York: Harper & Row.

Hillard, G. S. 1864. *Life and Campaigns of George B. McClellan*. Philadelphia: Lippincott.

Himmelstein, Jerome L. 1990. *To the Right: The Transformation of American Conservatism.* Berkeley: University of California Press.

Hine, David. 1982. "Factionalism in West European Parties: A Framework for Analysis." *West European Politics* 5 (January), 36–41.

1993. *Governing Italy: The Politics of Bargained Pluralism.* Oxford: Clarendon Press.

Hinich, Melvin J. and Michael C. Munger. 1994. *Ideology and the Theory of Political Choice.* Ann Arbor: University of Michigan Press.

Hirschman, Albert O. 1970. *Exit, Voice, Loyalty: Responses to Decline in Firms, Organizations, and States.* Cambridge: Harvard University Press.

Hoadley, John F. 1986. *Origins of American Political Parties, 1789–1803.* Lexington: University Press of Kentucky.

Hofstadter, Richard. 1948. *The American Political Tradition.* New York: Vintage Books.

1955. *The Age of Reform: From Bryan to FDR.* New York: Alfred A. Knopf.

1968a. "Political Parties." In C. Vann Woodward (ed), *The Comparative Approach to American History.* New York: Basic Books.

1968b. *The Progressive Historians.* New York: Vintage.

Holcombe, Arthur N. 1924. *The Political Parties of To-day.* New York: Harper & Bros.

Holt, James. 1967. *Congressional Insurgents and the Party System, 1909–1916.* Cambridge: Harvard University Press.

1975. "The New Deal and the American Anti-Statist Tradition." In John Braeman et al. (eds), *The New Deal: The National Level.* Columbus: Ohio State University Press.

Holt, Michael F. 1969. *Forging a Majority: The Formation of the Republican Party in Pittsburgh, 1848–1860.* New Haven: Yale University Press.

1978. *The Political Crisis of the 1850s.* New York: John Wiley and Sons.

Hoover, Herbert. 1922/1989. *American Individualism: The Challenge to Liberty.* West Branch, IA: Herbert Hoover Presidential Library Association.

1928. *The New Day: Campaign Speeches of Herbert Hoover.* Stanford, CA: Stanford University Press.

1977. *Public Papers of the Presidents of the United States: Herbert Hoover, 1932–33.* Washington, DC: United States Government Printing Office.

Hosking, Geoffrey and Anthony King. 1977. "Radicals and Whigs in the British Liberal Party, 1906–1914." In William O. Aydelotte (ed), *The History of Parliamentary Behavior.* Princeton: Princeton University Press.

Howe, Daniel Walker. 1979. *The Political Culture of the American Whigs.* Chicago: University of Chicago Press.

(ed). 1973. *The American Whigs: An Anthology.* New York: John Wiley & Sons.

Hubbard, Simeon. 1828. *An Address to the Citizens of Connecticut. . . .* Norwich: L. H. Young.

Huber, John D. 1989. "Values and Partisanship in Left-Right Orientations: Measuring Ideology." *European Journal of Political Research* 17, 599–621.

Huber, John D. and G. Bingham Powell, Jr. 1994. "Congruence between Citizens and Policymakers in Two Visions of Liberal Democracy." *World Politics* 46 (April), 291–326.

Huber, John D. and Ronald Inglehart. 1995. "Expert Interpretations of Party Space and Party Locations in Forty-Two Societies." *Party Politics* 1, 73–111.

Huebner, Lee W. 1973. "The Republican Party, 1952–1972." In Arthur M. Schlesinger Jr. (ed), *History of U.S. Political Parties*. Vol. 4. New York: Chelsea House.

Hughes, Charles Evans. 1908. *Hughes' Reply to Bryan, Youngstown, OH* (September 5).

   1916a. *No Surrender to Force! The Compulsory Railway Wage Law. From the Speeches of Charles E. Hughes at Springfield, IL, September 19, and Dayton, OH, September 25, 1916.* N.p.: Republican Campaign Committee.

   1916b. *Remarks of Hon. Charles Evans Hughes at Republican State Conference, Saratoga Springs, N.Y., September 28, 1916.*

   1916c. *Speeches of Hon. Charles Evans Hughes and Hon. Nathan L. Miller and Platform, Saratoga Springs, New York.* N.p.: Republican State Convention.

Hughes, Christopher. 1962. *The Parliament of Switzerland.* London: Cassell/ The Hansard Society.

Hugins, Walter. 1960. *Jacksonian Democracy and the Working Class: A Study of the New York Workingmen's Movement, 1829–1837.* Stanford: Stanford University Press.

Huntington, Samuel. 1981. *American Politics: The Promise of Disharmony.* Cambridge, MA: Harvard University Press.

Hurley, Patricia A. and Rick K. Wilson. 1989. "Partisan Voting Patterns in the U.S. Senate, 1877–1986." *Legislative Studies Quarterly* 14:2 (May).

Huston, James L. 1983. "A Political Response to Industrialism: The Republican Embrace of Protectionist Labor Doctrines." *Journal of American History* 70:1 (June).

Ingberman, Daniel and John Villani. 1993. "An Institutional Theory of Divided Government and Party Polarization." *American Journal of Political Science* 37:2 (May), 429–71.

Inglehart, Ronald and Hans Klingemann. 1976. "Party Identification, Ideological Preference, and the Left-Right Dimension among Western Mass Publics." In Ian Budge, Ivor Crewe, and Dennis Farlie (eds), *Party Identification and Beyond: Representations of Voting and Party Competition.* Chichester: Wiley.

Jackson, Andrew. 1827. *General Jackson's Letter to Carter Beverley, and Mr. Clay's Reply.* Plymouth: Miller and Brewster.

   1831. *Correspondence between General Andrew Jackson and John C. Calhoun....* Washington, DC: Duff Green.

Jackson, J. S., III, J. C. Brown, and B. L. Brown. 1978. "Recruitment, Representation, and Political Values: The 1976 Democratic National Convention Delegates." *American Politics Quarterly* 6, 187–212.

Jamieson, Kathleen Hall. 1984. *Packaging the Presidency: A History and Crit icism of Presidential Campaign Advertising.* Oxford: Oxford University Press.

Janosik, Edward G. 1976. "Factionalism in the Labour Party." In Richard Rose (ed), *Studies in British Politics.* New York: St. Martin's.

Jefferson, Thomas. 1972. *The Life and Selected Writings of Thomas Jefferson,* ed. Adrienne Koch and William Peden. New York: The Modern Library.

Jenkin, Thomas P. 1945. *Reactions of Major Groups to Positive Government in the United States, 1930–1940: A Study in Contemporary Political Thought.* Berkeley: University of California Press.

Jensen, Richard. 1969. "Armies, Ad Men and Crusaders: Strategies to Win Elections." *History Teacher* 2 (January) 33–50.

1971. *The Winning of the Midwest: Social and Political Conflict, 1888–1896.* Chicago: University of Chicago Press.

Johnson, Andrew. 1866. *Speeches of Andrew Johnson . . .* Boston: Little, Brown.

1970. *The Papers of Andrew Johnson.* Vol. 2. Knoxville: University of Tennessee Press.

1986. *The Papers of Andrew Johnson.* Vol. 7. Knoxville: University of Tennessee Press.

Johnson, Donald Bruce (ed). 1958. *National Party Platforms.* Vol. 1, *1840–1956.* Urbana: University of Illinois Press.

1978. (ed). *National Party Platforms.* Vol. 2, *1960–1976.* Urbana: University of Illinois Press.

1982. (ed). *National Party Platforms of 1980: Supplement to National Party Platforms, 1840–1976.* Urbana: University of Illinois Press.

Johnson, Lyndon B. 1965. *Public Papers of the Presidents of the United States: Lyndon B. Johnson, 1963–64.* Washington, DC: United States Government Printing Office.

Jones, Mark P. 1995. *Electoral Laws and the Survival of Presidential Democracies.* Notre Dame, IN: University of Notre Dame Press.

Jones, Stanley L. 1964. *The Presidential Election of 1896.* Madison: University of Wisconsin Press.

Josephson, Matthew. 1934. *The Robber Barons: The Great American Capitalists, 1861–1901.* New York: Harcourt, Brace & World.

1940. *The Presidential Makers: The Culture of Politics and Leadership in an Age of Enlightenment, 1896–1919.* New York: Harcourt, Brace.

Kaid, Lynda Lee, et al. 1974. *Political Campaign Communication: A Bibliography and Guide to the Literature.* Metuchen, NJ: Scarecrow.

Kaid, Lynda Lee and Anne Johnston Wadsworth. 1986. *Political Campaign Communication: A Bibliography and Guide to the Literature, 1973–1985.* Metuchen, NJ: Scarecrow.

Kammen, Michael. 1972/1980. *People of Paradox: An Inquiry Concerning the Origins of American Civilization.* New York: Oxford University Press.

Karabel, Jerome. 1979. "The Failure of American Socialism Reconsidered." In Ralph Miliband and John Saville (eds), *Socialist Register.* London: Merlin.

Karson, Marc. 1958. *American Labor Unions and Politics, 1900–1918*. Boston: Beacon Press.

Katzenstein, Peter. 1985. *Small States in World Markets: Industrial Policy in Europe*. Ithaca: Cornell University Press.

1987. *Policy and Politics in West Germany: The Growth of a Semisovereign State*. Philadelphia: Temple University Press.

Katznelson, Ira. 1981. *City Trenches: Urban Politics and the Patterning of Class in the United States*. Chicago: University of Chicago Press.

Kayden, Xandra and Eddie Mahe Jr. 1985. *The Party Goes On: The Persistence of the Two-Party System in the United States*. New York: Basic Books.

Keefe, William J. 1991. *Parties, Politics, and Public Policy in America*. 6th ed. Washington, DC: Congressional Quarterly.

Keith, Bruce E., David B. Magleby, Candice J. Nelson, Elizabeth Orr, Mark C. Westlye, and Raymond E. Wolfinger. 1992. *The Myth of the Independent Voter*. Berkeley: University of California Press.

Keller, Morton. 1977. *Affairs of State: Public Life in Late Nineteenth Century America*. Cambridge: Harvard University Press.

1990. *Regulating a New Economy: Public Policy and Economic Change in America, 1900–1933*. Cambridge: Harvard University Press.

Kelley, Anne E. 1961. *Trends in Policy Preferences of American Political Parties, 1840–1960: A Content Analysis*. Tallahassee: Florida State University Press.

Kelley, Robert. 1969. *The Transatlantic Persuasion: The Liberal Democratic Mind in the Age of Gladstone*. New York: Alfred A. Knopf.

1977. "Ideology and Political Culture from Jefferson to Nixon." *American Historical Review* 82:3 (June), 531–62.

1979. *The Cultural Pattern in American Politics: The First Century*. New York: Alfred A. Knopf.

Kelley, Stanley, Jr. 1960. *Political Campaigning: Problems in Creating an Informed Electorate*. Washington, DC: Brookings.

Keman, Hans. 1984. "Parties, Politics, and Consequences: A Cross-National Analysis." *European Journal of Political Research* 12, 147–70.

Kessel, John H. 1977. "The Seasons of Presidential Politics." *Social Science Quarterly* 58:3 (December), 418–35.

1984. *Presidential Parties*. Homewood, IL: Dorsey.

Key, V. O., Jr. 1942/1958. *Politics, Parties, and Pressure Groups*. 4th ed. New York: Thomas Y. Crowell.

1942/1964. *Politics, Parties, and Pressure Groups*. 5th ed. New York: Thomas Y. Crowell.

1949. *Southern Politics in State and Nation*. New York: Vintage.

1955. "A Theory of Critical Elections." *Journal of Politics* 17:1.

Kiewiet, D. Roderick and Matthew D. McCubbins. 1991. *The Logic of Delegation*. Chicago: University of Chicago Press.

King, Anthony. 1981. "What Do Elections Decide?" In David Butler, Howard R. Penniman, and Austin Ranney (eds), *Democracy at the Polls: A Com-*

parative Study of Competitive National Elections. Washington, DC: American Enterprise Institute.

King, David C. and Richard J. Zeckhauser. 1997. "An Options Model of Congressional Voting." Unpublished manuscript, Kennedy School of Government, Cambridge, MA.

Kingdon, John W. 1993. "Politicians, Self-Interest, and Ideas." In George E. Marcus and Russell L. Hanson (eds), *Reconsidering the Democratic Public.* University Park: Pennsylvania State University Press.

Kirkpatrick, Jeane. 1976. *The New Presidential Elite.* New York: Russell Sage.

Kleppner, Paul. 1970. *The Cross of Culture: A Social Analysis of Midwestern Politics, 1850–1900.* New York: Free Press.

1972. "Beyond the 'New Political History': A Review Essay." *Historical Methods Newsletter* 6, 17–26.

1979. *The Third Electoral System, 1853–92: Parties, Voters, and Political Cultures.* Chapel Hill: University of North Carolina Press.

1981a. "Coalitional and Party Transformations in the 1890s." In Seymour Martin Lipset (ed), *Party Coalitions in the 1980s.* San Francisco: Institute for Contemporary Studies.

1981b. "Partisanship and Ethnoreligious Conflict: The Third Electoral System, 1853–1892." In Kleppner et al. (eds), *The Evolution of American Electoral Systems.* Westport, CT: Greenwood Press.

1987. (ed). *Continuity and Change in Electoral Politics, 1893–1928.* New York: Greenwood Press.

Klingemann, Hans-Dieter, Richard I. Hofferbert, and Ian Budge. 1994. *Parties, Policies, and Democracy.* Boulder, CO: Westview Press.

Kloppenberg, James T. 1987. "The Virtues of Liberalism: Christianity, Republicanism, and Ethics in Early American Political Discourse." *Journal of American History* 74:1 (June).

Koenig, Louis W. 1975. *Bryan: A Political Biography of William Jennings Bryan.* New York: G. P. Putnam's Sons.

Kohl, Lawrence. 1989. *The Politics of Individualism: Parties and the American Character in the Jacksonian Era.* New York: Oxford University Press.

Kolbert, Elizabeth and Adam Clymer. 1996. "The Politics of Layoffs: In Search of a Message." *New York Times* (March 8).

Korpi, Walter. 1983. *The Democratic Class Struggle.* London: Routledge & Kegan Paul.

Kousser, J. Morgan. 1974. *The Shaping of Southern Politics: Suffrage Restriction and the Establishment of the One-Party South, 1880–1910.* New Haven: Yale University Press.

Kovler, Peter B. (ed). 1992. *Democrats and the American Idea: A Bicentennial Appraisal.* Washington, DC: Center for National Policy Press.

Krehbiel, Keith. 1993. "Where's the Party?" *British Journal of Political Science* 23, 235–66.

Kristinsson, Gunnar Helgi. 1996. "Parties, States, and Patronage," *West European Politics* 19:3 (July), 433–57.

Krukones, Michael G. 1984. *Promises and Performance: Presidential Campaigns as Policy Predictors*. Lanham, MD: University Press of America.

Ladd, Everett Carll. 1970. *American Political Parties: Social Change and Political Response*. New York: W. W. Norton.

1981. "The Shifting Party Coalitions – from the 1930s to the 1970s." In Seymour Martin Lipset (ed), *Party Coalitions in the 1980s*. San Francisco: Institute for Contemporary Studies.

Ladd, Everett Carll and Charles D. Hadley. 1973. *Political Parties and Political Issues: Patterns in Differentiation since the New Deal*. Beverly Hills: Sage.

1975. *Transformations of the American Party System*. New York: Norton.

Larson, John Lauritz. 1990. "Liberty by Design: Freedom, Planning, and John Quincy Adams's American System." In Mary O. Furner and Barry Supple (eds), *The State and Economic Knowledge: The American and British Experiences*. Cambridge: Cambridge University Press.

Laslett, John H. M. and Seymour Martin Lipset (eds). 1974. *Failure of a Dream? Essays in the History of American Socialism*. Berkeley: University of California Press.

Latner, Richard B. 1975. "A New Look at Jacksonian Politics." *Journal of American History* 111:4 (March).

Laver, Michael and Kenneth A. Shepsle. 1991. "Divided Government: America Is Not 'Exceptional.' " *Governance* 4:3 (July), 250–69.

Laver, Michael and W. Ben Hunt. 1992. *Policy and Party Competition*. New York: Routledge.

Lazare, Daniel. 1996. *The Frozen Republic: How the Constitution Is Paralyzing Democracy*. New York: Harcourt Brace.

Leon, D. G. 1971. "Whatever Happened to an American Socialist Party? A Critical Survey of the Spectrum of Interpretations." *American Quarterly* 23 (May).

Leuchtenberg, William E. 1963. *Franklin D. Roosevelt and the New Deal, 1932–1940*. New York: Harper & Row.

1983. *In the Shadow of FDR: From Harry Truman to Ronald Reagan*. Ithaca: Cornell University Press.

Levinson, Stanford. 1988. *Constitutional Faith*. Princeton: Princeton University Press.

Lewin, Leif. 1988. *Ideology and Strategy: A Century of Swedish Politics*. Cambridge: Cambridge University Press.

Lichtenstein, Nelson. 1989. "From Corporatism to Collective Bargaining: Organized Labor and the Eclipse of Social Democracy in the Postwar Era." In Steve Fraser and Gary Gerstle (eds), *The Rise and Fall of the New Deal Order, 1930–1980*. Princeton: Princeton University Press, 122–52.

Lichtman, Allan J. 1982. "The End of Realignment Theory? Toward a New Research Program for American Political History." *Historical Methods* 15:4 (Fall).

1983. "Political Realignment and 'Ethnocultural' Voting in Late Nineteenth Century America." *Journal of Social History* 16:3 (Spring).

Lijphart, Arend. 1977. *Democracy in Plural Societies*. New Haven: Yale University Press.

1984. *Democracies: Patterns of Majoritarian and Consensus Government in Twenty-One Countries*. New Haven: Yale University Press.

(ed) 1992. *Parliamentary versus Presidential Government*. Oxford: Oxford University Press.

Lincoln, Abraham. 1989a. *Speeches and Writings, 1832–1858*. New York: Library of America.

1989b. *Speeches and Writings, 1859–1865*. New York: Library of America.

Linz, Juan J. and Arturo Valenzuela (eds). 1994. *The Failure of Presidential Democracy*. Baltimore: Johns Hopkins University Press.

Lipset, Seymour Martin. 1977. "Why No Socialism in the United States?" In Seweryn Bialer (ed), *Sources of Contemporary Radicalism*. Vol. 1. Boulder, CO: Westview Press.

1992. "American Exceptionalism Reaffirmed." In Byron Shafer (ed), *Is America Different?* Oxford: Oxford University Press.

Lipset, Seymour Martin and Stein Rokkan. 1967. "Cleavage Structures, Party Systems, and Voter Alignments: An Introduction." In Seymour Martin Lipset and Stein Rokkan (eds), *Party Systems and Voter Alignments: Cross-National Perspectives*. New York: Free Press.

Listhaug, Ola, Stuart Elaine Macdonald, and George Rabinowitz. 1987. "Dynamics of Stuctural Realignment." *American Political Science Review* 81:3 (September), 775–96.

Lowe, Rodney. 1986. *Adjusting to Democracy*. Oxford: Oxford University Press.

Lowell, A. Lawrence. 1909. *The Government of England*. Vols. 1–2. New York: Macmillan.

Lowi, Theodore. 1975. "Party, Policy, and Constitution in America." In William Nisbet Chambers and Walter Dean Burnham (eds), *The American Party Systems*. 2d ed. New York: Oxford University Press, 238–76.

1985. *The Personal President: Power Invested, Promise Unfulfilled*. Ithaca: Cornell University Press.

Loynd, Brian. 1997. "Manufacturing Consensus: Legislative Organization in Post-Industrial Germany and Great Britain." Ph.D. dissertation, Department of Political Science, Duke University.

Macdonald, Stuart Elaine and George Rabinowitz. 1987. "Dynamics of Structural Realignment." *American Political Science Review* 81:3 (September), 775–96.

Macpherson, C. B. 1962. *The Political Theory of Possessive Individualism: Hobbes to Locke*. Oxford: Oxford University Press.

Madison, James. 1973. *The Mind of the Founder: Sources of the Political Thought of James Madison*, ed. Marvin Meyers. Indianapolis: Bobbs-Merrill.

Mair, Peter. 1989. "The Problem of Party System Change." *Journal of Theoretical Politics* 1, 251–76.

Mair, Peter and Gordon Smith (eds). 1990. *Understanding Party System Change in Western Europe.* London: Frank Cass.

Mansbridge, Jane (ed). 1990. *Beyond Self-Interest.* Chicago: University of Chicago Press.

Marshall, T. H. 1964. *Class, Citizenship, and Social Development.* Chicago: University of Chicago Press.

Martin, Cathie Jo. 1995. "Nature or Nurture? Sources of Firm Preference for National Health Reform." *American Political Science Review* 89:4 (December).

Mayer, George H. 1967. *The Republican Party, 1854–1966.* London: Oxford University Press.

　　1973. "The Republican Party, 1932–1952." In Arthur M. Schlesinger Jr. (ed), *History of U.S. Political Parties.* Vol. 3. New York: Chelsea House.

Mayer, William G. 1996. *The Divided Democrats: Ideological Unity, Party Reform, and Presidential Elections.* New York: Westview Press/HarperCollins.

Mayhew, David. 1974. *Congress: The Electoral Connection.* New Haven: Yale University Press.

McBath, James H., and Walter R. Fisher. 1969. "Persuasion in Presidential Campaign Communication." *Quarterly Journal of Speech* 55:1 (February).

McCabe, James Jr. 1868. *The Life and Public Services of Horatio Seymour. . . .* New York: W. E. Turner.

McClellan, George B. 1864? *The Life, Campaigns, and Public Services of General McClellan. . . .* Philadelphia: T. B. Peterson.

McClosky, Herbert. 1964. "Consensus and Ideology in American Politics." *American Political Science Review* 58 (June), 361–83.

McClosky, Herbert and John Zaller. 1984. *The American Ethos.* Cambridge: Harvard University Press.

McClosky, Herbert, Paul J. Hoffmann, and Rosemary O'Hara. 1960. "Issue Conflict and Consensus among Party Leaders and Followers." *American Political Science Review* (June).

McCormick, Richard L. 1981. *From Realignment to Reform: Political Change in New York State, 1893–1910.* Ithaca: Cornell University Press.

　　1986. *The Party Period and Public Policy: American Politics from the Age of Jackson to the Progressive Era.* New York: Oxford University Press.

McCormick, Richard P. 1966. *The Second American Party System: Party Formation in the Jacksonian Era.* Chapel Hill: University of North Carolina Press.

McCoy, Drew R. 1980. *The Elusive Republic: Political Economy in Jeffersonian America.* Chapel Hill: University of North Carolina Press.

McCraw, Thomas K. 1986. "Mercantilism and the Market: Antecedents of American Industrial Policy." In Claude E. Barfield and William A. Schambra (eds), *The Politics of Industrial Policy.* Washington, DC: American Enterprise Institute.

McDiarmid, J. 1937. "Presidential Inaugural Addresses: A Study in Verbal Symbols." *Public Opinion Quarterly* (July), 79–82.

McGerr, Michael. 1986. *The Decline of Popular Politics: The American North, 1865–1928*. New York: Oxford University Press.

McKinley, William. 1896a. *Life and Speeches of William McKinley*. New York: J. S. Ogilvie Publishing.

1896b. *McKinley on Labor: His Public Utterances in Behalf of the Workingmen of the United States*. N.p.

1896c. *Why the Farmers Suffer*. New York: Republican National Committee.

1900. "The National Emergency." In James P. Boyd (ed), *Men and Issues of 1900: The Vital Questions of the Day*.

Merriam, Charles E. 1922. *The American Party System*. New York: Macmillan.

Meyers, Marvin. 1957/1960. *The Jacksonian Persuasion: Politics and Belief*. Stanford: Stanford University Press.

Miliband, Ralph. 1961. *Parliamentary Socialism*. London: Allen & Unwin.

Milkis, Sidney M. 1992. "Programmatic Liberalism and Party Politics." In John Kenneth White and Jerome M. Mileur (eds), *Challenges to Party Government*. Carbondale and Edwardsville: Southern Illinois University Press, 104–32.

1993. *The President and the Parties: The Transformation of the American Party System since the New Deal*. New York: Oxford University Press.

Miller, Warren E. and M. Kent Jennings. 1986. *Parties in Transition*. New York: Russell Sage Foundation.

Mink, Gwendolyn. 1986. *Old Labor and New Immigrants in American Political Development: Union, Party, and State, 1875–1920*. Ithaca: Cornell University Press.

Minkin, Lewis. 1978. *The Labour Party Conference: A Study in the Politics of Intra-party Democracy*. Manchester, England: Manchester University Press.

Monroe, A. D. 1983. "American Party Platforms and Public Opinion." *American Journal of Politial Science* 27, 27–42.

Moos, Malcolm. 1956. *The Republicans: A History of Their Party*. New York: Random House.

Morgan, H. Wayne. 1973. "The Republican Party, 1876–1893." In Arthur M. Schlesinger Jr. (ed), *History of U.S. Political Parties*. Vol. 2. New York: Chelsea House.

Morris, Richard B. (ed). 1953. *Encyclopedia of American History*. New York: Harper & Brothers.

Morton, Rebecca B. 1993. "Incomplete Information and Ideological Explanations of Platform Divergence." *American Political Science Review* 87:2 (June).

Mowry, George E. 1968. "Social Democracy." In C. Vann Woodward (ed), *The Comparative Approach to American History*. New York: Basic Books.

1971. "Election of 1912." In Arthur M. Schlesinger Jr. (ed), *History of American Presidential Elections, 1789–1968*. Vol. 3. New York: Chelsea House.

Namenwirth, J. Zri and Harold D. Lasswell. 1970. *The Changing Language of*

American Values: A Computer Study of Selected Party Platforms. Beverly Hills: Sage Publications.

Namenwirth, J. Zri and Robert Philip Weber. 1987. *Dynamics of Culture.* Boston: Allen & Unwin.

Namier, Lewis. 1965. *The Structure of Politics at the Accession of George III.* 2d ed. London: Macmillan & Co.

Neely, Mark E., Jr. 1993. *The Last Best Hope on Earth: Abraham Lincoln and the Promise of America.* Cambridge: Harvard University Press.

Neumann, Sigmund (ed). 1956. *Modern Political Parties.* Chicago: University of Chicago Press.

Niemi, Richard G. and Anders Westholm. 1984. "Issues, Parties, and Attitudinal Stability: A Comparative Study of Sweden and the United States." *Electoral Studies* 3:1, 65–83.

Nixon, Richard M. 1974. *Public Papers of the Presidents of the United States: Richard Nixon, 1972.* Washington, DC: United States Government Printing Office.

Nordhoff, Charles. 1965. *The Communistic Societies of the United States.* New York: Schocken Books.

Norton, A. B. 1888. *The Great Revolution of 1840: Reminiscences of the Log Cabin and Hard Cider Campaign.* Mount Vernon: A. B. Norton & Co.

Norton, Philip. 1975. *Dissension in the House of Commons, 1945–1974.* London: Macmillan.

Norton, Philip and Arthur Aughey. 1981. *Conservatives and Conservatism.* London: Temple Smith.

Nugent, Walter T. K. 1970. "Money, Politics, and Society: The Currency Question." In H. Wayne Morgan (ed), *The Gilded Age.* Rev. ed. Syracuse: Syracuse University Press.

Odegard, Peter. 1930. *The American Mind.* New York: Columbia University Press.

Official Proceedings of the Democratic National Convention. . . . 1900. Chicago: McLellan Printing.

Official Proceedings of the National Democratic Convention. . . . 1856. Cincinnati, OH: Democratic National Convention.

Official Proceedings of the National Democratic Convention. . . . 1868. Boston: Rockwell & Rollins.

Official Proceedings of the National Democratic Convention. . . . 1884. New York: Douglas Taylor's Democratic Printing House.

Official Proceedings of the Twelfth Republican National Convention. 1900. Philadelphia: Dunlap Printing Company.

Official Report of the Proceedings of the Democratic National Convention. 1904. New York: Publishers' Printing Company.

O'Gorman, Frank. 1986. *British Conservatism: Conservative Thought from Burke to Thatcher.* London: Longman.

O'Keefe, Garrett J. 1975. "Political Campaigns and Mass Communication Research." In Steven H. Chaffee (ed), *Political Communication: Issues and Strategies for Research.* Beverly Hills: Sage.

Orren, Karen. 1991. *Belated Feudalism: Labor, the Law, and Liberal Development in the United States.* Cambridge: Cambridge University Press.

Paddock, Joel W. 1982. *The Changing Substance of Partisan Conflict: Inter- and Intra-Party Variations in Democratic and Republican Platforms, 1956–1980.* Lawrence: University Press of Kansas.

Page, Benjamin. 1978. *Choices and Echoes in Presidential Elections: Rational Man and Electoral Democracy.* Chicago: University of Chicago Press.

Paludan, Phillip S. 1972. "The American Civil War Considered as a Crisis in Law and Order." *American Historical Review* 77.

Panebianco, Angelo. 1988. *Political Parties: Organization and Power.* Cambridge: Cambridge University Press.

Parenti, Michael. 1967. "Ethnic Politics and the Persistence of Ethnic Identification." *American Political Science Review* 61 (September), 717–26.

Parmet, Herbert S. 1976. *The Democrats: The Years after FDR.* New York: Oxford University Press.

Patterson, James T. 1967. *Congressional Conservatism and the New Deal: The Growth of the Conservative Coalition in Congress, 1933–1939.* Lexington: University Press of Kentucky.

Patterson, Kelly D. 1996. *Political Parties and the Maintenance of Liberal Democracy.* New York: Columbia University Press.

Pear, Robert. 1996. "A Guide to Where the Candidates Stand." *New York Times* (November 3).

Peele, Gillian. 1988. "British Conservatism: Ideological Change and Electoral Uncertainty." In Brian Girvin (ed), *The Transformation of Contemporary Conservatism.* London: Sage Publications.

Pelling, Henry. 1968. *A Short History of the Labour Party.* 3d ed. London: Macmillan.

Peters, B. Guy. 1997. "The Separation of Powers in Parliamentary Systems." In Kurt von Mettenheim (ed), *Presidential Institutions and Democratic Politics: Comparing Regional and National Contexts.* Baltimore: Johns Hopkins University Press.

Petrocik, John R. 1981. *Party Coalitions: Realignment and the Decline of the New Deal Party System.* Chicago: University of Chicago Press.

Phillips, Kevin P. 1983. *Post-Conservative America: People, Politics, and Ideology in a Time of Crisis.* New York: Vintage Books.

Pocock, J. G. A. 1972. "Virtue and Commerce in the Eighteenth Century." *Journal of Interdisciplinary History* 3 (Summer), 119–34.

———. 1975. *The Machiavellian Moment: Florentine Political Thought and the Atlantic Republican Tradition.* Princeton: Princeton University Press.

Podell, Janet and Steven Anzovin (eds). 1988. *Speeches of the American Presidents.* New York: H. W. Wilson.

Polakoff, Keith Ian. 1981. *Political Parties in American History.* New York: Wiley.

Polsby, Nelson. 1983. *The Consequences of Party Reform.* New York: Oxford University Press.

Pomper, Gerald. 1967. " 'If Elected, I Promise': American Party Platforms." *Midwest Journal of Political Science* 11:3 (August).

    1980. *Elections in America: Control and Influence in Democratic Politics.* 2d ed. New York: Longman.

    1992. *Passions and Interests: Political Party Concepts of American Democracy.* Lawrence: University Press of Kansas.

Porter, Kirk H. and Donald Bruce Johnson (eds). 1961. *National Party Platforms, 1840–1960.* Urbana: University of Illinois Press.

Proceedings of the Anti-Jackson Convention, Held at the Capitol, in the City of Richmond, with Their Address to the People of Virginia. 1828. Richmond: Samuel Shepherd.

Proceedings of the Eighth Republican National Convention, 1884. 1884. N.p.: Republican National Committee.

Proceedings of the Tenth Republican National Convention. 1892. Minneapolis: Harrison & Smith.

"Proposals by Clinton: Tax Breaks and More." 1996. *New York Times* (August 30).

Pym, Francis. 1985. *The Politics of Consent.* London: Sphere Books.

Rabinowitz, George, Stuart Elaine Macdonald, and Ola Listhaug. 1991. "New Players in an Old Game: Party Strategy in Multiparty Systems." *Comparative Political Studies* 24, 147–85.

Rae, Nicol C. 1989. *The Decline and Fall of the Liberal Republicans from 1952 to the Present.* New York: Oxford University Press.

    1992. "Class and Culture: American Political Cleavages in the Twentieth Century." *Western Political Quarterly* (September).

    1994. *Southern Democrats.* New York: Oxford University Press.

Ragazzini, G., D. R. Miller, P. Bayley. 1985. *Campaign Language: Language, Image, Myth in the U.S. Presidential Election, 1984.* Bologna, Italy: Cooperative Libraria Universitaria Editrice Bologna.

Ranney, Austin. 1962. *The Doctrine of Responsible Party Government: Its Origins and Present State.* Urbana: University of Illinois Press.

Ranney, Austin and Willmoore Kendall. 1956. *Democracy and the American Party System.* New York: Harcourt, Brace.

Reagan, Ronald. 1987. *Public Papers of the Presidents of the United States: Ronald Reagan, 1984.* Bk. 2, *June 30 to December 31, 1984.* Washington, DC: United States Government Printing Office.

Redding, W. Charles. 1957. *A Methodological Study of "Rhetorical Postulates," Applied to a Content Analysis of the 1944 Campaign Speeches of Dewey and Roosevelt.* Los Angeles: University of Southern California Press.

Reichard, Gary W. 1975. *The Reaffirmation of Republicanism: Eisenhower and the Eighty-Third Congress.* Knoxville: University of Tennessee Press.

Reichley, A. James. 1992. *The Life of the Parties: Party Politics and American Democracy.* Washington, DC: Brookings.

Reinhard, David W. 1983. *The Republican Right since 1945.* Lexington: University Press of Kentucky.

Reiter, Howard. 1996a. "Inequalities, Factions, and the American Party System in Historical Perspective." Paper presented at the annual meeting of the American Political Science Association, San Francisco, CA (September).

1996b. "Why Did the Whigs Die (and Why Didn't the Democrats)? Evidence from National Nominating Conventions." *Studies in American Political Development* 19 (Fall), 185–222.

Republican Campaign Textbook, 1904. 1904. Milwaukee: Press of the Evening Wisconsin Company.

Republican Campaign Text-book, 1908. 1908. Washington, DC: Republican National Committee.

Republican Party. 1988. "Party Platform, 1988." *Congressional Quarterly Almanac* 44.

The Republican Platform, 1992. 1992. Washington, DC: Republican National Committee.

Richardson, James D. 1897. *A Compilation of the Messages and Papers of the Presidents.* Washington, DC: Bureau of National Literature.

Ridpath, John Clard. 1880? *The Life and Work of James A. Garfield. . . .* Cincinnati: Jones Brothers.

Riker, William H. 1991. "Why Negative Campaigning Is Rational: The Rhetoric of the Ratification Campaign of 1787–1788." *Studies in American Political Development* 5 (Fall), 224–83.

1993. "Rhetorical Interaction in the Ratification Campaigns." In William Riker (ed), *Agenda Formation* . Ann Arbor: University of Michigan Press.

Roback, Thomas H. 1975. "Amateurs and Professionals: Delegates to the 1972 Republican National Convention." *Journal of Politics* 37, 436–67.

Roback, Thomas H. and Judson L. James. 1978. "Party Factions in the United States." In Frank P. Belloni and Dennis C. Beller (eds), *Faction Politics: Political Parties and Factionalism in Comparative Perspective.* Santa Barbara: ABC-Clio, 329–55.

Rockman, Bert A. 1997. "The Performance of Presidents and Prime Ministers and of Presidential and Parliamentary Systems." In Kurt Von Mettenheim (ed), *Presidential Institutions and Democratic Politics: Comparing Regional and National Contexts.* Baltimore: Johns Hopkins University Press.

Rodgers, Daniel T. 1974. *The Work Ethic in Industrial America, 1850–1920.* Chicago: University of Chicago Press.

1982. "In Search of Progressivism." *Reviews in American History* (December), 113–32.

1992. "Republicanism: The Career of a Concept." *Journal of American History* 79:1 (June), 11–38.

Roemer, John E. 1994. "The Strategic Role of Party Ideology When Voters Are Uncertain about How the Economy Works." *American Political Science Review* 88:2 (June), 327–35.

Rogin, Michael Paul and J. L. Shover. 1970. *Political Change in California: Critical Elections and Social Movements, 1890–1966.* Westport, CT: Greenwood Publishing Corporation.

Rogowski, Ronald. 1989. *Commerce and Coalitions: How Trade Affects Domestic Political Alignments.* Princeton: Princeton University Press.

Rohde, David. 1991. *Parties and Leaders in the Postreform House*. Chicago: University of Chicago Press.

Rokkan, Stein. 1970. *Citizens, Elections, Parties: Approaches to the Comparative Study of the Processes of Development*. New York: David McKay Company.

Roosevelt, Franklin D. 1938a. *The Public Papers and Addresses of Franklin D. Roosevelt*. Vol. 1, The Genesis of the New Deal, 1928–1932. New York: Russell & Russell.

1938b. *The Public Papers and Addresses of Franklin D. Roosevelt*. Vol. 5, *The People Approve, 1936*. New York: Random House.

1941. *The Public Papers and Addresses of Franklin D. Roosevelt, 1940*. Vol. 9: *War – and Aid to Democracies, 1940*. New York: The Macmillan Company.

1946. *The Public Papers and Addresses of Franklin D. Roosevelt*. Vol. 13, *Victory and the Threshold of Peace, 1944–45*. New York: Russell & Russell.

Roosevelt, Theodore. 1910. *Presidential Addresses and State Papers, April 7, 1904, to May 9, 1905*. Vol. 3. New York: The Review of Reviews Company.

1911. *The Strenuous Life: Essays and Addresses*. New York: Century.

1961. *The New Nationalism*. Englewood Cliffs, NJ: Prentice-Hall.

1967. *The Writings of Theodore Roosevelt*. Indianapolis: Bobbs-Merrill.

Rose, Richard. 1967. "Parties, Factions, and Tendencies in Britain." In Roy C. Macridis (ed), *Political Parties: Contemporary Trends and Ideas*. New York: Harper and Row.

1980. *Do Parties Make a Difference?* London: Macmillan.

1986. "British MPs: More Bark than Bite?" In Ezra Suleiman (ed), *Parliaments and Parliamentarians in Democratic Politics*. New York: Holmes & Meier.

1991. *The Postmodern Presidency: George Bush Meets the World*, 2d ed. Chatham: Chatham House.

Roseboom, Eugene H. 1957. *A History of Presidential Elections*. New York: Macmillan.

Rosenstone, Steven J., Roy L. Behr, Edward H. Lazarus. 1984. *Third Parties in America: Citizen Response to Major Party Failure*. Princeton: Princeton University Press.

Ross, Davis R. B. 1973. "The Democratic Party, 1945–1960." In Arthur M. Schlesinger Jr. (ed), *History of U.S. Political Parties*. Vol. 4. New York: Chelsea House.

Rossiter, Clinton. 1960. *Parties and Politics in America*. New York: Cornell University Press, Signet Books.

Rotunda, Ronald. 1968. "The 'Liberal' Label: Roosevelt's Capture of a Symbol." *Public Policy* 17.

1986. *The Politics of Language: Liberalism as Word and Symbol*. Iowa City: University of Iowa Press.

Roubini, Nouriel and Jeffrey Sachs. 1989. "Government Spending and Budget Deficits in the Industrial Countries." *Economic Policy* 8 (April), 100–132.

Rowland, Peter. 1968. *The Last Liberal Governments: The Promised Land, 1905–1910.* London: Barrie & Rockliff/The Cresset Press.

Royed, Terry J. 1996. "Testing the Mandate Model in Britain and the United States: Evidence from the Reagan and Thatcher Eras." *British Journal of Political Science* 26, 45–80.

Rutland, Robert A. 1979. *The Democrats: From Jefferson to Carter.* Baton Rouge: Louisiana State University Press.

Sabato, Larry J. 1988. *The Party's Just Begun: Shaping Political Parties for America's Future.* Glenview, IL: Scott, Foresman.

Sainsbury, Diane. 1981. "Theoretical Perspectives in Analyzing Ideological Change and Persistence: The Case of Swedish Social Democratic Party Ideology." *Scandinavian Political Studies* 4:4.

Sait, Edward McChesney. 1927. *American Parties and Elections.* New York: Century.

Sani, Giacomo and Giovanni Sartori. 1983. "Polarization, Fragmentation and Competition in Western Democracies." In Hans Daalder and Peter Mair (eds), *Western European Party Systems: Continuity and Change.* Beverly Hills: Sage.

Sarasohn, David. 1989. *The Party of Reform: Democrats in the Progressive Era.* Jackson: University Press of Mississippi.

Sartori, Giovanni. 1976. *Parties and Party Systems: A Framework for Analysis.* Cambridge: Cambridge University Press.

Schattschneider, E. E. 1942. *Party Government.* New York: Rinehart.

1956. "United States: The Functional Approach to Party Government." In Sigmund Neumann (ed), *Modern Political Parties.* Chicago: University of Chicago Press.

Schlesinger, Arthur M., Jr. 1945. *The Age of Jackson.* New York: Book Find Club.

1957. *The Crisis of the Old Order.* Boston: Houghton Mifflin.

1959. *The Coming of the New Deal.* Boston: Houghton Mifflin.

1960. *The Politics of Upheaval.* Boston: Houghton Mifflin.

1963. "Ideas and Economic Development." In Schlesinger and Morton White (eds), *Paths of American Thought.* Boston: Houghton Mifflin.

1971. (ed). *History of American Presidential Elections, 1789–1968.* Vols. 1–4. New York: Chelsea House.

1973. (ed). *History of U.S. Political Parties.* Vols. 1–4. New York: Chelsea House.

Schumpeter, Joseph A. 1942/1950. *Capitalism, Socialism, and Democracy.* New York: Harper & Bros.

Schurz, Carl. 1913. *Speeches, Correspondence, and Political Papers of Carl Schurz.* Vols. 1, 3. New York: G. P. Putnam's Sons.

Scott, James C. 1972. *Comparative Political Corruption.* Englewood Cliffs, NJ: Prentice-Hall.

Seward, William H. 1884. *The Works of William H. Seward.* Vol. 4, ed. George E. Baker. Boston: Houghton Mifflin.

Seyd, Patrick. 1987. *The Rise and Fall of the Labour Left.* Basingstoke, England: Macmillan.

Shade, William G. 1981. "Political Pluralism and Party Development." In Paul Kleppner et al. (eds), *The Evolution of American Electoral Systems.* Westport, CT: Greenwood.

Shafer, Byron. 1983. *Quiet Revolution: The Struggle for the Democratic Party and the Shaping of Post-Reform Politics.* New York: Sage Foundation.

——— 1991. (ed). *The End of Realignment? Interpreting American Electoral Eras.* Madison: University of Wisconsin Press.

——— 1992. (ed). *Is America Different?* Oxford: Oxford University Press.

Shalhope, Robert E. 1972. "Toward a Republican Synthesis: The Emergence of an Understanding of Republicanism in American Historiography." *William and Mary Quarterly* 29 (January), 49–80.

Shannon, David. 1968. "Socialism and Labor." In C. Vann Woodward (ed), *The Comparative Approach to American History.* New York: Basic Books.

Sharp, James Roger. 1993. *American Politics in the Early Republic: The New Nation in Crisis.* New Haven: Yale University Press.

Shaw, E. 1988. *Discipline and Discord in the Labour Party.* Manchester, England: Manchester University Press.

Shefter, Martin. 1994. *Political Parties and the State: The American Historical Experience.* Princeton: Princeton University Press.

Silbey, Joel H. 1967a. *The Shrine of Party: Congressional Voting Behavior, 1841–1852.* Pittsburgh: University of Pittsburgh Press.

——— 1967b. *The Transformation of American Politics, 1840–1860.* Englewood Cliffs, NJ: Prentice-Hall.

——— 1977. *A Respectable Minority: The Democratic Party in the Civil War Era, 1860–1868.* New York: Norton & Company.

——— 1985. *The Partisan Imperative: The Dynamics of American Politics before the Civil War.* New York: Oxford University Press.

——— 1991. *The American Political Nation, 1838–1893.* Stanford: Stanford University Press.

Singer, Aaron (ed). 1976. *Campaign Speeches of American Presidential Candidates, 1928–1972.* New York: Frederick Ungar.

Skocpol, Theda. 1980. "Political Response to Capitalist Crisis: Neo-Marxist Theories of the State and the Case of the New Deal." *Politics and Society* 10:2, 155–201.

——— 1983. "The Legacies of New Deal Liberalism." In Douglas MacLean and Claudia Mills (eds), *Liberalism Reconsidered.* Totowa, NJ: Rowman & Allanheld.

——— 1992. *Protecting Soldiers and Mothers: The Political Origins of Social Policy in the United States.* Cambridge: Belknap Press of Harvard University Press.

Skowronek, Stephen. 1993. *The Politics Presidents Make: Leadership from John Adams to George Bush.* Cambridge: Harvard University Press.

Smith, Alfred E. 1929. *Campaign Addresses of Governor Alfred E. Smith.* New York: AMS Press.

Smith, Eric R. A. N. 1989. *The Unchanging American Voter.* Berkeley: University of California Press.

Smith, Marshall S. 1966. "A Content Analysis of Twenty Presidential Nomination Acceptance Speeches." In Philip Stone et al. (eds), *The General Inquirer: A Computer Approach to Content Analysis.* Cambridge: MIT Press.

Smith, Rogers M. 1993. "Beyond Tocqueville, Myrdal, and Hartz: The Multiple Traditions in America." *American Political Science Review* 87:3 (September), 549–66.

Sorauf, Frank and Paul Allen Beck. 1988. *Party Politics in America.* Glenview, IL: Scott, Foresman.

Soule, J. W. and W. E. McGrath. 1975. "A Comparative Study of Presidential Nomination Conventions: The Democrats of 1968 and 1972." *American Journal of Political Science* 19, 501–17.

Steele, Edward D. 1957. *The Rhetorical Use of the "American Value System" in the 1952 Presidential Campaign Addresses.* Stanford: Stanford University Press.

Steele, Edward D. and W. Charles Redding. 1962. "The American Value System: Premises for Persuasion." *Western Speech* 26:2 (Spring).

Steinfels, Peter. 1979. *The Neoconservatives: The Men Who Are Changing America's Politics.* New York: Simon & Schuster.

Steinmo, Sven. 1993. *Taxation and Democracy: Swedish, British, and American Approaches to Financing the Modern State.* New Haven: Yale University Press.

———. 1994. "American Exceptionalism Reconsidered: Culture or Institutions?" In Lawrence C. Dodd and Calvin Jillson (eds), *The Dynamics of American Politics: Approaches and Interpretations.* Boulder, CO: Westview Press.

Stern, Philip Van Doren (ed). 1970. *The Annotated Walden.* New York: Clarkson N. Potter, Inc.

Stevenson, Adlai E. 1953. *Major Campaign Speeches of Adlai E. Stevenson.* New York: Random House.

———. 1957. *The New America,* eds. Seymour E. Harris, John Bartlow Martin, and Arthur Schlesinger Jr. Port Washington, NY: Kennikat Press.

Stewart, Charles. 1991. "Lessons from the Post-Civil War Era." In Gary W. Cox and Samuel Kernell (eds), *The Politics of Divided Government.* Boulder, CO: Westview.

Stone, Walter J. and Alan I. Abramowitz. 1983. "Winning May Not Be Everything, But It's More than We Thought: Presidential Party Activists in 1980." *American Political Science Review* 77:4, 945–56.

Strom, Kaare. 1990. "A Behavioral Theory of Competitive Political Parties." *American Journal of Political Science* 34:2 (May), 565–98.

Sullivan, D. G., J. L. Pressman, B. I. Page, and J. J. Lyons. 1974. *The Politics* of Representation: The Democratic Convention, 1972. New York: St. Martin's.

Sumner, Charles. 1860. *The Speech of the Hon. Charles Sumner, of Massachusetts, on the Barbarism of Slavery. . . .* San Francisco: Towne & Bacon.

Sundquist, James L. 1980. "The Crisis of Competence in Our National Government." *Political Science Quarterly* 95, 183–208.

——— 1983. *Dynamics of the Party System: Alignment and Realignment of Political Parties in the United States.* Washington, DC: Brookings.

Taft, William H. 1908a. *Labor and Capital, Their Common Interest, Their Necessary Controversies, Their Lawful Acts, and the Legal Remedies for Their Abuses* (January 10). N.p.

——— 1908b. *The People Rule: Mr. Taft's Reply to Mr. Bryan, Hot Springs, Virginia, August 21, 1908.* N.p.

——— 1910. *Political Issues and Outlooks: Speeches Delivered between August, 1908, and February, 1909.* New York: Doubleday, Page & Company.

Taylor, Lily Ross. 1968. *Party Politics in the Age of Caesar.* Berkeley: University of California Press.

Taylor, Michael and Michael Laver. 1973. "Government Coalitions in Western Europe." *European Journal of Political Research* 1, 205–48.

Thomas, John Clayton. 1979. "The Changing Nature of Partisan Divisions in the West: Trends in Domestic Policy Orientations in Ten Party Systems." *European Journal of Political Research* 7, 397–413.

Tilden, Samuel J. 1885. *The Writings and Speeches of Samuel J. Tilden.* New York: Harper and Brothers.

Tilton, Tim. 1992. "The Role of Ideology in Social Democratic Politics." In Klaus Misgeld, Karl Molin, and Klas Amark (eds), *Creating Social Democracy: A Century of the Social Democratic Labor Party in Sweden.* University Park: Pennsylvania State University Press.

Tingsten, H. 1941/1973. *The Swedish Social Democrats, Their Ideological Development.* Totowa, NJ: Bedminister Press.

Tocqueville, Alexis de. 1835/1960. *Democracy in America.* Vol 1, ed. Henry Reeves. New York: Vintage.

——— 1840/1945. *Democracy in America.* Vol. 2, ed. Henry Reeves. New York: Vintage.

Troy, Gil. 1991. *See How They Ran: The Changing Role of the Presidential Candidate.* New York: Free Press.

Truman, David B. 1951. *The Governmental Process.* New York: Alfred A. Knopf.

Truman, Harry S. 1948–49. *The Truman Program: Addresses and Messages by President Harry S. Truman,* ed. M. B. Schnapper. Washington, DC: Public Affairs Press.

Tsebelis, George. 1995. "Veto Players and Law Production in Parliamentary Democracies." In Herbert Doring (ed), *Parliaments and Majority Rule in Western Europe.* Frankfurt: Campus Verlag.

Tufte, Edward. 1978. *Political Control of the Economy.* Princeton: Princeton University Press.

Tulis, Jeffrey K. 1987. *The Rhetorical Presidency*. Princeton: Princeton University Press.

Turner, Frederick Jackson. 1932. *Sections in American History*. New York: Henry Holt.

Unger, Irwin. 1964. *The Greenback Era: A Social and Political History of American Finance, 1865–1879*. Princeton: Princeton University Press.

U.S. Senate. 1961a. Committee on Commerce. *Freedom of Communications: Final Report of the Committee on Commerce, United States Senate. . . . Part 1, The Speeches, Remarks, Press Conferences, and Statements of Senator John F. Kennedy, August 1 through November 7, 1960*. 87th Cong., 1st sess. Washington, DC: United States Government Printing Office.

1961b. Committee on Commerce. *Freedom of Communications: Final Report of the Committee on Commerce, United States Senate. . . . Part 2, The Speeches, Remarks, Press Conferences, and Study Papers of Vice President Richard M. Nixon, August 1 through November 7, 1960*. 87th Cong., 1st sess. Washington, DC: United States Government Printing Office.

Valley, David B. 1988. *A History and Analysis of Democratic Presidential Nomination Acceptance Speeches to 1968*. Lanham, MD: University Press of America.

Van Buren, Martin. 1836a. *Letter from the Hon. Martin Van Buren, Vice-President of the United States, relative to the Bank of the United States. . . .* London: John Miller.

1836b. *Opinions of Martin Van Buren, Vice President of the United States upon the Powers and Duties of Congress. . . .* Washington, DC: Blair and Rives.

1840a. *Letter from the President of the United States, in Answer to a Communication on the Subject of a General Bankrupt Law. . . .* New York: Evening Post.

1840b. *Mr. Van Buren's Letter to the Committee of Elizabeth City County, Virginia*. N.p.: New Era Publishers.

1867. *Inquiry into the Origin and Course of Political Parties in the United States*. New York: Hurd and Houghton.

Vaudagna, Maurizio. 1987. "The New Deal and European Social Democracy in Comparative Perspective: The Trend towards Convergence." In Jean Heffer and Jeanine Rovet (eds), *Why Is There No Socialism in the United States?/Pourquoi n'y a-t-il pas de socialisme aux Etats-Unis?* Paris: Editions de l'Ecole des Hautes Etudes en Science Sociales.

Viner, Jacob. 1948. "Power vs. Plenty as Objectives of Foreign Policy in the Seventeenth and Eighteenth Centuries." *World Politics* 1.

1968. "Mercantilist Thought." In David L. Sills (ed), *International Encyclopedia of the Social Sciences*. Vol. 4. New York: Macmillan.

Vogel, David. 1978. "Why Businessmen Distrust Their State: The Political Consciousness of American Corporate Executives." *British Journal of Political Science* 8:1, 45–78.

Wade, Richard C. 1973. "The Democratic Party, 1960–1972." In Arthur M.

Schlesinger Jr. (ed), *History of U.S. Political Parties*. Vol. 4. New York: Chelsea House.

Warwick, Paul, V. 1990. *Culture, Structure, or Choice? Essays in the Interpretation of the British Experience*. New York: Agathon Press.

Watson, Harry L. 1990. *Liberty and Power: The Politics of Jacksonian America*. New York: Farrar, Straus and Giroux.

Wattenberg, Martin P. 1991. "The Republican Presidential Advantage in the Age of Party Disunity." In Gary W. Cox and Samuel Kernell (eds), *The Politics of Divided Government*. Boulder, CO: Westview Press.

Webster, Daniel. 1986. *The Papers of Daniel Webster: Speeches and Formal Writings*. Vol. 1, *1800–1833*. Hanover, NH: University Press of New England.

Webster and Hayne's Celebrated Speeches in the United States Senate, on Mr. Foot's Resolution of January 1830. N.d. Philadelphia: T. B. Peterson and Brothers.

Weed, Clyde P. 1994. *The Nemesis of Reform: The Republican Party during the New Deal*. New York: Columbia University Press.

Welter, Rush. 1975. *The Mind of America, 1820–1860*. New York: Columbia University Press.

White, John Kenneth. 1997. *Seeing Red: How the Cold War Shaped American Politics*. Boulder, CO: Westview Press.

White, John Kenneth and Jerome M. Mileur (eds). 1992. *Challenges to Party Government*. Carbondale and Edwardsville, IL: Southern Illinois University Press.

Wilentz, Sean. 1982. "On Class and Politics in Jacksonian America." *Reviews in American History* 10.

1984. *Chants Democratic*. New York: Oxford University Press.

Williams, Charles Richard. 1928. *The Life of Rutherford Birchard Hayes. . . .* Columbus: Ohio State Archaeological and Historical Society.

Williams, R. Hal. 1970. " 'Dry Bones and Dead Language': The Democratic Party." In H. Wayne Morgan (ed), *The Gilded Age*. Rev. ed. Syracuse: Syracuse University Press.

Williams, T. Harry. 1981. *Huey Long*. New York: Vintage.

Willkie, Wendell. 1940. *This Is Wendell Willkie: A Collection of Speeches and Writings on Present-Day Issues*. New York: Dodd, Mead & Company.

Wilson, Frank L. 1994. "The Sources of Party Change: The Social Democratic Parties of Britain, France, Germany, and Spain." In Kay Lawson (ed), *How Political Parties Work: Perspectives from Within*. Westport, CT: Praeger.

Wilson, James Q. 1962. *The Amateur Democrat*. Chicago: University of Chicago Press.

1973/1995. *Political Organizations*. Princeton: Princeton University Press.

Wilson, Joan Hoff. 1975. *Herbert Hoover: Forgotten Progressive*. Boston: Little, Brown.

Wilson, Woodrow. 1879/1965. "Cabinet Government in the United States." *International Review* 7 (August). Reprinted in *The Political Thought of*

Woodrow Wilson, ed. E. David Cronon. Indianapolis: Bobbs-Merrill, 29–53.

1885/1956. *Congressional Government.* Baltimore: Johns Hopkins University Press.

1913. *The New Freedom.* Englewood Cliffs, NJ: Prentice-Hall.

1956. *A Crossroads of Freedom: The 1912 Campaign Speeches of Woodrow Wilson.* New Haven: Yale University Press.

1982. *The Papers of Woodrow Wilson.* Vol. 38, *August 7–November 19, 1916,* ed. Arthur S. Link. Princeton: Princeton University Press.

Windt, Theodore Otto. 1986. "Presidential Rhetoric: Definition of a Field of Study." *Presidential Studies Quarterly* 16:1 (Winter).

Wittman, Donald A. 1973. "Parties as Utility Maximizers." *American Political Science Review* 67, 490–98.

1983. "Candidate Motivation: A Synthesis of Alternative Theories." *American Political Science Review* 77, 142–57.

Wolfinger, Raymond E. 1965. "The Development and Persistence of Ethnic Voting." *American Political Science Review* 59 (December), 896–908.

Wood, Gordon. 1969. *The Creation of the American Republic, 1776–1787.* Chapel Hill: University of North Carolina Press.

1991. *The Radicalism of the American Revolution.* New York: Vintage.

Woodward, C. Vann. 1951. *The Origins of the New South, 1877–1913.* Baton Rouge: Louisiana State University Press.

Wynar, Lubomyr R. 1969. *American Political Parties: A Selective Guide to Parties and Movements of the Twentieth Century.* Littleton, CO: Libraries Unlimited.

Young, William T. 1852. *Sketch of the Life and Public Services, of General Lewis Cass. . . .* Detroit: Markham & Elwood.

Zieger, Robert H. 1969. *Republicans and Labor, 1919–1929.* Lexington: University of Kentucky Press.

Index

CPSIA information can be obtained at www.ICGtesting.com
Printed in the USA
LVOW06*0855301115

464659LV00007B/72/P